RECONSTRUCTION BEYOND 150

D1565708

A Nation Divided: Studies in the Civil War Era
ORVILLE VERNON BURTON AND ELIZABETH R. VARON, EDITORS

Reconstruction beyond 150

REASSESSING THE NEW BIRTH OF FREEDOM

EDITED BY

Orville Vernon Burton and J. Brent Morris

UNIVERSITY OF VIRGINIA PRESS

Charlottesville and London

UNIVERSITY OF VIRGINIA PRESS

© 2023 by the Rector and Visitors of the University of Virginia

All rights reserved

Printed in the United States of America on acid-free paper

First published 2023

1 3 5 7 9 8 6 4 2

Library of Congress Cataloging-in-Publication Data

Names: Burton, Orville Vernon, editor. | Morris, J. Brent, editor.
Title: Reconstruction beyond 150 : reassessing the new birth of freedom /
edited by Orville Vernon Burton and J. Brent Morris.
Other titles: Reassessing the new birth of freedom | Nation divided.
Description: Charlottesville : University of Virginia Press, 2023. |
Series: A nation divided | Includes bibliographical references and index.
Identifiers: LCCN 2023012263 (print) | LCCN 2023012264 (ebook) | ISBN 9780813949857 (hardcover) |
ISBN 9780813949864 (paperback) | ISBN 9780813949871 (ebook)
Subjects: LCSH: Reconstruction (U.S. history, 1865–1877) | African Americans—Southern States—History—
19th century. | African Americans—Southern States—Social conditions—19th century. |
United States—Race relations—History—19th century.
Classification: LCC E668 .R383 2023 (print) | LCC E668 (ebook) | DDC 973.8—dc23/eng/20230403
LC record available at https://lccn.loc.gov/2023012263
LC ebook record available at https://lccn.loc.gov/2023012264

CONTENTS

FOREWORD

FROM 2011 TO 2015, there were widespread and frequent commemorations of anniversaries of Civil War events and milestones, including the surrender of Confederate General Robert E. Lee at Appomattox Court House, which effectively ended the war. Yet preoccupied with the significant challenges of our own time, Americans have devoted comparatively little attention to the sesquicentennial of Reconstruction, the turbulent era that followed and, many would argue, extended the conflict. This is quite unfortunate, for if any historical period deserves the label "relevant" today, it is the postwar era of Reconstruction.

Issues at the forefront of American politics—questions of citizenship and voting rights, the relative powers of the national and state governments, the relationship between political and economic democracy, the proper response to domestic terrorism—were all Reconstruction questions. Yet despite its contemporary significance, that era has long been misunderstood.

Reconstruction refers to the period, generally dated from 1865 to 1877, during which the nation's laws and Constitution were rewritten to guarantee the basic rights of the former slaves, and biracial governments came to power throughout the defeated Confederacy. For generations, these years were widely viewed as the low point in the story of American democracy. According to this view, Radical Republicans in Congress were determined to punish defeated Confederates, and they established corrupt Southern governments presided over by opportunistic Northern carpetbaggers, traitorous Southern scalawags, and African Americans unprepared for freedom and unfit to exercise democratic rights. The heroes of the story were the self-styled Redeemers, who restored white supremacy to the South.

This interpretation, which received scholarly expression in the early twentieth-century works of William Archibald Dunning and his students at Columbia University, was popularized by the 1915 film *The Birth of a Nation* and by Claude Bowers's best-selling history, *The Tragic Era* (1929). It provided an intellectual foundation for the system of segregation and Black disenfranchisement that followed Reconstruction, as well as for the violence of the Ku Klux Klan and other terrorist organizations bent on restoring and maintaining white supremacy. Any effort to restore the rights of Southern Blacks, it implied, would lead to a repeat of the alleged horrors of Reconstruction.

Historians have long since rejected this old view of Reconstruction, although it retains a stubborn hold on the popular imagination. Today, scholars believe that if the era was indeed "tragic," it was not because Reconstruction was attempted but because it failed.

Some scholars date the beginnings of Reconstruction to December 1863, when Abraham Lincoln announced a plan to establish governments in the South loyal to the Union. Lincoln granted amnesty to most Confederates as long as they accepted the abolition of slavery but said nothing about rights, including voting rights, for freed Blacks. Rather than a blueprint for the postwar South, this was strictly a wartime measure, an effort to detach whites from the Confederacy. Lincoln's ideas on Reconstruction evolved, as they did on so many other questions. Near the end of his life, he eventually called for some degree of Black suffrage in the postwar South, singling out the "very intelligent" (prewar free Blacks) and "those who serve our cause as soldiers" as most worthy.

Lincoln, of course, did not live to preside over Reconstruction. That task fell to his successor, Andrew Johnson of Tennessee. Once praised by historians as a heroic defender of the Constitution against Radical Republicans, Johnson is now viewed overwhelmingly as one of the worst presidents ever to occupy the White House. He was a racist, unwilling to listen even to the most constructive of criticism, and unable to work with Congress. Johnson set up new Southern governments controlled by ex-Confederates. They quickly enacted the Black Codes, laws that severely limited the freed people's rights, and sought to force them back to work on the plantations under conditions resembling enslavement. These measures aroused bitter protests among Blacks, however, and convinced Northerners that the white South was unrepentantly attempting to restore slavery in all but name.

The momentous political clash that followed between Johnson and the Republican majority in Congress ultimately resulted in the enactment, over Johnson's veto, of one of the most important laws in American history; the Civil Rights Act of 1866. It affirmed the citizenship of everyone born in the United States, regardless of race (except Indians, still considered members of tribal sovereignties). This principle of birthright citizenship is increasingly rare in today's world and deeply contested in our own contemporary politics, because it applies to the American-born children of undocumented immigrants. The act also mandated that all citizens enjoy basic civil rights in the same manner "enjoyed by white persons." Johnson's veto message denounced the law for what today is sometimes called reverse discrimination: "The distinction of race and color is by the bill made to operate in favor of the colored and against the white race." In this idea that expanding the rights of nonwhites somehow punishes the white majority, the specter of Andrew Johnson continues to haunt our contemporary discussions of race.

Soon after, Congress enshrined birthright citizenship and legal equality in the Constitution via the Fourteenth Amendment. In recent decades, the courts have used this amendment to expand the legal rights of numerous groups. As the Republican editor George William Curtis wrote, the Fourteenth Amendment changed a Constitution "for white men" to one "for mankind." It also marked a significant change in the federal balance of power, empowering the national government to protect the rights of citizens against violations by the states.

In 1867, Congress passed the Reconstruction Acts, again over Johnson's veto. They set in motion the establishment of new governments in the South, empowered Southern Black men to vote, and temporarily barred several thousand leading Confederates from the ballot. Soon after, the Fifteenth Amendment extended Black male suffrage to the entire nation.

The Reconstruction Acts inaugurated the period of Radical Reconstruction, when a politically mobilized Black community, with its white allies, brought the Republican Party to power throughout the South. For the first time, African Americans voted in large numbers and held public office at every level of government. It was a remarkable, unprecedented effort to build an interracial democracy on the ashes of slavery.

Most offices remained in the hands of white Republicans. But the arrival of African Americans in positions of political power aroused bitter hostility from Reconstruction's opponents. They spread another myth: that the new officials were propertyless, illiterate, and incompetent. As late as 1947, the Southern historian E. Merton Coulter wrote that, of the various aspects of Reconstruction, Black officeholding was "longest to be remembered, shuddered at, and execrated."

There was corruption in the postwar South, although given the scandals of New York's Tweed Ring and President Ulysses S. Grant's administration, Black suffrage could hardly be blamed. In fact, the new governments had a solid record of accomplishment. They established the South's first state-funded public school systems, sought to strengthen the bargaining power of plantation laborers, made taxation more equitable, and outlawed racial discrimination in transportation and public accommodations. They offered aid to railroads and other enterprises in the hope of creating a New South whose economic expansion would benefit Black and white alike.

Reconstruction also made possible the consolidation of Black families, so often divided by sale during slavery, and the establishment of the independent Black church as the core institution of the emerging Black community. But the failure to respond to the former slaves' desire for land left most with no choice but to work for their former owners.

It was not economic dependence, however, but widespread violence, coupled with a Northern retreat from the ideal of equality, that doomed Reconstruction. The Ku Klux Klan and kindred groups began a campaign of murder, assault, and arson that can only be described as homegrown American terrorism. Meanwhile, as the Northern Republican Party became more conservative, Reconstruction came to be seen as a misguided attempt to uplift the lower classes of society.

One by one, the Reconstruction governments fell. As a result of a bargain after the disputed presidential election of 1876, the Republican Rutherford B. Hayes assumed the Oval Office and disavowed further national efforts to enforce the rights of Black citizens, while white Democrats controlled the South.

By the turn of the century, with the acquiescence of the Supreme Court, a comprehensive system of racial, political, and economic inequality, summarized in the phrase "Jim Crow," had come into being across the South. At the same time, the supposed horrors of Reconstruction were invoked as far away as South Africa and Australia to demonstrate the necessity of excluding nonwhite peoples from political rights. This is why W. E. B. Du Bois, in his great work *Black Reconstruction in America* (1935), saw the end of Reconstruction as a tragedy for democracy, not just in the United States but around the globe.

While violated with impunity, however, the Fourteenth and Fifteenth amendments remained on the books. Decades later they would provide the legal basis for the civil rights revolution, sometimes called the Second Reconstruction.

Citizenship, rights, democracy—as long as these remain contested, so will the necessity of an accurate understanding of Reconstruction. More than most historical subjects, how we think about this era truly matters, for it forces us to think about what kind of society we wish America to be.

Eric Foner

RECONSTRUCTION BEYOND 150

Introduction

T HE RECONSTRUCTION ERA WAS in every way a period of rebuilding: it entailed the reshaping of the ideologies of the defeated Old South and the physical reconstruction of the region so desolated by the ravages of war, and, as a nation, developing policies that thoroughly remade and modernized America and laid the foundation for the "Second Reconstruction"—the Civil Rights Movements of the 1950s and '60s. Thus, the post–Civil War end of slavery not only brought freedom to African Americans. It also inaugurated a comprehensive and protracted reshaping of fundamental American institutions and the very definition of American citizenship itself.

Still, sandwiched as it is between the dramas of the Civil War and the Jim Crow era, Reconstruction suffers as one of the most understudied and misunderstood periods in American history. Part of this misunderstanding is due to the history's complexity, and scholars' interpretations of the period have varied widely. The first generation of professional historians at the turn of the twentieth century generally followed the white supremacist arguments of the Dunning School in characterizing the postwar Reconstruction era as one in which formerly enslaved people, urged on by white Northern "carpetbaggers" and turncoat Southern "scalawags," dragged the prostrate South through the darkest and most wretched period of shame and humiliation in its history. Only when Southern whites banded together to (in their misguided terms) "redeem" their region from such "evil" and "corruption" and restore "home rule" and white supremacy did the South's long "nightmare" end. Alternatively, others scholars later interpreted Reconstruction as a bright age of hope that ultimately fell short of expectations, but only insofar as it did not go far enough or achieve its lofty goals. More recently, scholars have agreed with W. E. B. Du Bois's conclusion in his 1935 study *Black Reconstruction in America* that the violent overthrow of Reconstruction was a tragedy, the era ultimately a "splendid failure" whose revolutionary agenda could not overcome the overwhelming forces set against it. Indeed, it is unlikely that any other period of American history has undergone so many and such dramatic reassessments as the post–Civil War years.[1]

The public has largely ignored recent scholarship rather than, often uncomfortably, assess and grapple with conflicting interpretations, and the past five decades of Reconstruction scholarship have had little impact on how most Americans understand the period. For generations, the history of Reconstruction was imprinted on the American popular imagination through books and films such as *The Clansman, The Birth of a Nation,* and *Gone with the Wind.* Epic films and best-selling literature had, for most of the twentieth century, the sanction of the nation's leading (white) intellectuals and was, in many cases, based on their scholarship. Their racist portrayal of Reconstruction was widely adopted and accepted, becoming the prevalent narrative in popular culture and laying the groundwork for segregation and disenfranchisement of African American voters in the South that extended deep into the twentieth century and still resonates today.[2] *Gone with the Wind,* for example, was rereleased in theaters nationwide in 1998 and remains among Americans' favorite movies, including former President Donald Trump, who asserts, "It has stood the test of time. For me, it's a love story combined with a time in our country's history that was pivotal in our evolution."[3] Interpretations that scholars have long discarded endure among the general public because of the persistence of overly simplified and misinformed points of view in popular culture and contemporary political discourse, as well as the many challenges of teaching the period effectively in schools. As we mark the sesquicentennial anniversary of Reconstruction in America, a wide chasm remains between the generally accepted scholarly understanding of the postwar years and the quite different story much of the public continues to embrace.

Yet the story of Reconstruction is a tale of a pivotal period in the nation's history in which a generation of African Americans were active agents in shaping the era's history rather than simply a "problem" confronting white society. The neglected history is one of a period of tremendous and revolutionary accomplishment for formerly enslaved people: dozens of African Americans served in the U.S. Congress and hundreds in state legislatures; men and women once considered property formalized long-standing marriages in church services; once illegal, schools for African Americans proliferated in the South; and, no less important or impressive, African Americans went where they pleased, were paid for their labor, and lived without the once constant fear of arbitrary violence or being sold apart from loved ones.

Moreover, despite falling short of reformers' ambitious initial goals, Reconstruction remains one of the most relevant periods of study for contemporary Americans. A confluence of events—including the massacre of nine churchgoers at

Emanuel AME Church in Charleston, South Carolina, in June 2015 by a white supremacist who unabashedly touted the main tenets of the Lost Cause; the resulting
removal of the Confederate battle flag from the South Carolina Statehouse grounds;
the spotlight social media has shone on continuing racial inequalities through the
#BlackLivesMatter movement and the 150th anniversary of Reconstruction; and
the resurgence of white nationalism in the continuing debate over Confederate
memorialization—has initiated a new thirst for a thorough understanding of the
postwar years where echoes of these thorny issues were first debated.

There are even suggestions by those both within and outside the academy that
a "Third Reconstruction" may be imminent, where the lessons of history offer a vision for the future in which a diverse coalition of citizens fight together for racial,
social, and economic justice for all Americans.[4] Others fear a "second redemption"
intent on rolling back a generation of progressive policies.[5] Indeed, as Eric Foner
points out in the foreword to this volume, the most important (and contentious)
issues at the front of American politics today—citizenship and voting rights, the
relative power of state and federal governments, dealing with racial violence and
terrorism—are all "Reconstruction questions." In the introduction to the most recent edition of his classic book *Reconstruction,* Foner stresses that as long as these
matters remain central to our society, so, too, must an accurate understanding
of the Reconstruction era inform those inquiries. These are not simply esoteric
pursuits for historians or political scientists but moral questions at the heart of
American society. "Whatever the ebb and flow of historical interpretations," Foner
writes to appeal to a new generation of readers, "I hope we never lose sight of the
fact that something very important for the future of our society was taking place
during Reconstruction."[6]

Interestingly, there were some scholars who wondered whether the postbellum
era might diminish as a fertile field of inquiry since Foner's work seemed such a
definitive treatment of the subject.[7] However, Foner's synthesis did not smother
the field. Rather, it provided a foundation for unprecedented further research
into aspects of Reconstruction he could only touch on, each with its own rich
historiography.

Indeed, Reconstruction scholarship of the past two decades has grown steadily.
The essays included in this book represent cutting-edge new work in what the editors believe will be some of the most dynamic new directions in which the next
generation of scholarship will develop.

The work of Eric Foner figures prominently in any historiographic study of the
Reconstruction Era, yet, as already noted (and as Foner himself readily admits),
his tour de force left many questions unanswered and some subtopics only super-
ficially treated and dealt mainly with white elites and African American men. The
first two essays in this volume take up topics and historical actors that may have

been neglected in Foner's work to show the impact Reconstruction's "new birth of freedom" had on the lives of and discourse surrounding even more diverse groups.

Foner's book, for all that it did do, was criticized at its publication in 1988 for its sparse treatment of gender and the concept of the household. More recent scholarship has focused much more closely on gender analyses of freedwomen, often examining the transition from bondage to emancipation and seeking to reject the monolithic views of both enslavement and freedom that had been commonly perpetuated in African American historiography. However, as Arlisha Norwood argues in her essay "'They Loved but Did Not Agree': African American Women Divorcees in Post–Civil War Virginia," while the scholarly literature chronicles the general narratives of Black women after the Civil War, it does not often explore their relationship status and the drastic implications it may have had on their lives. Norwood examines the plight of unattached African American women following the Civil War. Divorced, abandoned, unmarried, and widowed women experienced the upheaval of the postbellum years alone. In this dramatic environment, unattached Black women emerged as major characters in an unfolding narrative. Norwood argues that African American women without partners had a unique postbellum experience. Such women confronted challenges that differed from those experienced by women with mates. In addition, the chapter illuminates the complexities of African American relationships following the Civil War and the interaction between Black women and the state.

Much scholarship that plumbs the intersections of race and gender begins from the assumption that, as activists of the late 1960s pointed out, the personal *is* political, and Norwood is quick to remind her readers of that fact. Of course, more traditionally formal politics, a subfield that has long been at the center of Reconstruction studies, remains important in cutting-edge scholarship as scholars continue to ask new and exciting questions about the period. Mark Elliott bridges the personal and political in his essay "Reconstructing Nationalism: Charles Sumner, Human Rights, and American Exceptionalism." Elliott argues that among the most emphatic postwar nationalists was Massachusetts Senator Charles Sumner, who in many ways was the perfect embodiment of a powerful streak of moral righteousness and messianic nationalism that left its imprint on American politics and culture in the nineteenth century. Although Sumner is often discounted as an "extremist" whose views were unrepresentative of the "mainstream," the chapter demonstrates that he contributed to a "reimagined" nation during Reconstruction that was taken up and echoed in many quarters of the antislavery North. In the 1867 speech "Are We a Nation?" Sumner traced the connection he perceived between human rights and national unity from the colonial era to the present, suggesting that the nation was moving in a historical direction toward a more complete unity among citizens and fuller enjoyment of individual rights for all. Sumner implied that achieving a consciousness of universal rights was a fundamental element in the completion of nationhood. Elliott shows how Sumner's equation of national power with the protection of "human rights" influenced Reconstruction policies for a short time but had a longer impact on ideological constructions of the "nation" in the political discourse of the time. Having claimed the high ground of equal justice and equal liberties, this nationalist vision directly influenced debates over women's rights, workers' rights, treaty rights of American Indians, and American territorial expansion. The equation of America's national mission with the promotion of "human rights" became a favorite means to sharply criticize the government for its failures and shortcomings on these issues. Sumner would exert direct influence over other leading human rights champions such as the women's rights leader Julia Ward Howe, the abolitionist and Indian rights advocate Lydia Maria Child, and the anti-imperialists Moorefield Storey and George F. Hoar. Like Sumner, these figures would express a similar view of progressive political development—the notion that "nation-building" required a long period of historical preparation prior to the establishment of democracy. Debates over the "preparation" of Blacks, women, Indians, and other claimants to equality would hamper arguments based on human rights. Even for radicals, Elliott concludes, their underlying beliefs in progress and national destiny sometimes undermined their discourse of human rights.

A. James Fuller also takes politics as his theme in his chapter, which seeks to restore to historical memory the Indianan Republican politician and Reconstruction leader Oliver P. Morton. In "Oliver P. Morton and the Politics of Reconstruction," Fuller casts Morton as a ruthless, often vindictive, and always opportunistic politician who held fast to the wartime ideology of freedom, Union, power, and party that he and other Republicans forged during the war. Committed to protecting slavery and preserving the Union, Morton thought that it was necessary for his party to wield power to achieve those ends. When the war ended, the Hoosier leader continued to rail against the rebels and the Copperheads in the North, whom he saw as traitorous allies of the rebellion. Throughout the Reconstruction period, Morton resorted to "Waving the Bloody Shirt," reminding voters and fellow Republicans that the war had been a rebellion, an act of treason. Like Abraham Lincoln, Morton slowly came to embrace full equality for African Americans over the course of the war, and by the time he entered the Senate, he had become a leading voice for the Radical Republicans. His 1868 speech on Reconstruction expressed the issues so well that many Republicans hailed it as their party's final word on the matter. A supporter of the Fourteenth and Fifteenth amendments and the civil rights legislation passed during congressional Reconstruction, Morton enjoyed strong support from Southern Blacks who saw him as a champion of their cause. A Stalwart supporter of the Grant administration, Morton was often discussed as an appointee as an ambassador or as a Supreme Court justice. He enjoyed widespread support as a presidential candidate in 1876, but declining health and the changing political climate prevented him from winning the nomination. Instead, he served on the congressional commission that eventually decided the disputed election. Although his role as a Reconstruction senator is largely forgotten, Fuller argues convincingly that Morton helped shape the era and left a long legacy that deserves to be restored to historical memory.

Nicolas Barreyre's chapter, "Building a New Political Order: Reconstruction, Capitalism, and the Contests over the American State," continues the focus on politics while also staking out ground for the Reconstruction Era in the burgeoning body of scholarship plumbing the history of capitalism. Barreyre's chapter approaches Reconstruction in a way that takes seriously what that word meant to its contemporaries, focusing, on the one hand, on the political process of rebuilding a postwar political order and, on the other, the rapid economic transformation that was largely facilitated and abetted by the state, by massive intervention from the central government. He highlights first the central role of the state in reorganizing the political economy of the United States in those postwar years, then demonstrates that building a new political order very much went hand in hand with building a new economic order. Second, Barreyre emphasizes that the process was not preordained or even masterminded but was very much the product of heated political fights and contingent alignments precisely because, unlike in the historiography, in the politics of the time it was difficult to separate issues of citizenship and race, on the one hand, and issues of political economy, on the other. Barreyre argues that if we are to historicize American capitalism, we need to view it not as a system being imposed impersonally from the outside, so to speak, but as the contentious workings of society that are constantly shaped and reshaped by the power of the state, moved not only by ideologies but also the contingencies and the messiness of postwar and Gilded Age politics.

Peter Wallenstein uses an analysis of formal politics to push the boundaries of standard Reconstruction periodization in his chapter "Race, Representation, and Reconstruction: The Origins and Persistence of Black Electoral Power, 1865–1900." He notes that the prevailing periodization of the history of the post–Civil War South assigns the year 1877 (at the latest) as the terminal point of Reconstruction. Yet by extending the era, redefining it in terms of the persistence of Black electoral power, Wallenstein takes an opportunity to reconsider the entire postwar era. Such persistence is well demonstrated by Black candidates' successful state and national campaigns, a metric that Wallenstein uses to push the temporal boundaries of Reconstruction back to a series of markers throughout the 1890s. The chapter reconceives both the origins and the duration of Black electoral power. White Southerners engaged in all manner of resistance to the new political order, yet Black candidates kept running for office and often gaining seats. Thereby they became members of the governing apparatus rather than, as had always previously been the case, objects of lawmaking—thus making governments that, for them, were "by" and "for" the "people" and not merely "of" a huge formerly enslaved and unenfranchised social group. From *Williams v. Mississippi* (1898) to the Wilmington "race riot" of that year and the Virginia Constitution of 1902, the new order came to an end. "Restoration" had been achieved. Reconstruction in the South was over. Then again, the seeds of a "Second Reconstruction," Wallenstein concludes, by then had already been put into place.

Also interested in reconsidering the traditionally accepted "bounds" of the Reconstruction Era is Mari N. Crabtree. She begins her essay "Lynching in the American Imagination: A Historiographical Reexamination" by noting that few scholars quibble with the assertion that lynching was widespread and frequent in the American South by the 1880s, but admits that the origins of lynching are hazier. Typically, historians have held that lynching was a manifestation of heightened social, political, and economic anxieties among white Southerners—anxieties rooted in the idea that, without slavery, African Americans would undermine white supremacy. Accordingly, many scholars argue that lynching emerged after Redemption, the often violent restoration of white Democratic Party home rule, as a ritual reenactment of white supremacy, simultaneously celebrating and justifying the system of racial oppression that became Jim Crow. Though these status anxieties were certainly heightened after the upheaval of the Civil War and the abolition of slavery, such a narrative severs lynching from other forms of racial violence, lifting it from a longer and more expansive history of racial violence in the United States. Crabtree challenges this myopia in two ways. First, she draws connections between the ritual of lynching after emancipation and the ritualistic violence inflicted on enslaved people. Second, she places lynching in relation to other contemporary forms of racial violence—in particular the colonial, genocidal violence against Native Americans. Citing historiography that suggests tethering Civil War memory to the Indian Wars tempers the "redemptive" narrative of 600,000 Civil War dead, leading to a new dawn of freedom, Crabtree demonstrates that emancipation profoundly changed the course of American history; however, the violence directed at Native Americans makes the clean break from the past implicit in that redemptive national narrative less plausible, not just for the memory of the Civil War, but for lynching, too. While recognizing distinctions between various forms of violence and the contexts in which they occurred, Crabtree makes the case for a more fluid periodization of lynching. Rather than reading lynching in isolation, she interprets racial violence to be at the center of the American experience, to be emblematic of the nation's history and identity.

Troy D. Smith maintains this focus on Reconstruction's western theater in his chapter "'Magnificent Resources': Reconstruction in Indian Territory." Smith argues that Reconstruction in Indian Territory involved massive cultural, social, and political restructuring. The tribal governments of all five of the "Civilized Tribes" had allied with the Confederacy, although many tribal members had sided with the Union, leading not only to participation by uniformed Indian troops in the larger conflict but to a series of internal Indian civil wars that were incredibly destructive to both life and property. To gain peace with the United States in the Treaty of 1866, all five tribes had to cede large amounts of their land in what is now western Oklahoma, accede to the building of railroads through their territory, and agree to the abolition of slavery and incorporation of their former slaves as tribal citizens. The last requirement led to a period of racial violence and legal wrangling over the ultimate status of the freedmen that, Smith demonstrates, was never satisfactorily settled and continues to be a point of contention among some of those Oklahoma tribes into the twenty-first century. Meanwhile, Smith also notes the continuing troublesome nature of questions of sovereignty and jurisdiction. The courts of the Five Tribes had no power over non-Indians, which encouraged countless American outlaws to seek refuge in "The Nations," outside the reach of local and state authorities and subject only to the federal court at Fort Smith, Arkansas. "Hanging Judge" Isaac Parker took occupancy of that bench in 1871, the same year as the passage of the Indian Appropriations Act that ended federal recognition of Indians as even semiautonomous and served as the conclusion to the Treaty Era. Smith locates the climax of these concerns in 1872, when the Union Cherokee veteran Zeke Proctor shot and wounded his white former brother-in-law Jim Kesterman and killed Kesterman's new Cherokee wife. The following legal fight over jurisdiction between the Cherokee Nation and federal authorities caused tensions over the interpretation of the treaty to escalate between Cherokee lighthorsemen (police) and federal marshals. A gunfight erupted in the Cherokee courtroom that led to fatalities on both sides and federal indictments for more than twenty Cherokees, significantly slowing the process of Reconstruction in Indian Country.

Don H. Doyle pushes the physical boundaries of Reconstruction scholarship even further in his chapter "A New Birth of Freedom Abroad." Doyle notes that scholarship on the Reconstruction Era has remained almost entirely a self-contained story of domestic policy. Historians of foreign relations, for their part, typically interpret the entire postwar period as part of the "years of preparation," in Walter LaFeber's words, to imperialist aggression in the 1890s, yet few make any important connections between domestic and foreign policy. However, if one isolates the Reconstruction years of 1865 to 1877 and looks for connections between domestic and foreign policy, a very different picture emerges.

After Union victory and against all expectations among European powers, the United States underwent massive and sudden demilitarization. The projection of U.S. power in the world reflected three key themes emerging from the recent trauma of the Civil War when European powers threatened to intervene on behalf of the rebel South. First, the United States, by a combination of peaceful negotiations and the threat of military force, hastened the rapid decolonization of the North American continent: Russia evacuated Alaska and withdrew from the Western Hemisphere; Britain transformed its North American possessions into the Dominion of Canada, a self-governing quasi-republic; U.S. pressure against France forced France's withdrawal from Mexico and helped end the imperial regime under Maximilian; and, finally, the United States tried to negotiate the withdrawal of Spain from its Caribbean colonies after Cuban republicans rose in rebellion in 1868. Second, after 1865 the United States imbued the Monroe Doctrine with a pro-republican ideological meaning that presumed the Americas as the realm of self-governing republics to be protected from aggression by European imperial monarchy. In this connection, Doyle examines the apparent contradiction between U.S. pursuit of expansion of commerce and influence and the simultaneous rejection of territorial conquest and even peaceful acquisition during these years. This was due in part to republican antipathy toward imperialism (meaning colonization), but also to antipathy toward nonwhite, non-Anglo, non-Protestant peoples and aversion toward taking in war-torn slave societies. Third, U.S. foreign policy was adamantly antislavery in its negotiations with Spain and effectively forced Spain and the Cuban rebels to proclaim some plan for emancipation. The U.S. commitment to freedom for Cuba and freedom for Cuban slaves found powerful public support in the United States, but this waned almost simultaneously with the waning of commitment to Black equality at home.

From three essays that touch on regions often forgotten by scholars of Reconstruction, the volume moves to questions of intellectual history and historical memory. David Moltke-Hansen in his chapter "Confederate Reconstructions: Generations of Conflict" situates himself as part of a recent historiographic trend to not limit consideration of Reconstruction to the politics, period, and areas directly shaped specifically by the Reconstruction Acts and argues that the changes attendant on the Civil War and Reconstruction began much earlier, lasted longer, and reached further than conventionally understood. Moltke-Hansen's compelling essay examines the shifting understanding of just what the word and the idea of "reconstruction" meant in the South. Arising out of perennial debates regarding competing visions of the constitutional founding of the United States in 1787, the nation's political economy, and its distinctive cultural values, the antebellum meaning of "reconstruction" emerged in the face of destabilizing and accelerating social, political, and economic dislocation, modernization, and expansion to represent a desire to see the United States conform to a better time, whether in the past or the future. Increasingly in the South, this meant reconstruction of a time when the institution of slavery and its expansion were secured. Support for secession, Moltke-Hansen argues, grew as that "reconstruction" appeared increasingly impossible. In forming the Confederacy, Southerners claimed to be reconstructing and clarifying the original intent of the founders, but once the Civil War ended, the Northern/Republican postwar plan imposed a "reconstruction" whose definition evoked a cognitive dissonance in many Southerners' minds. It now indicated an outright overturning of past government and prior political and social relations—in this case, not only between the former Confederate states and the federal government, but also between Southern African Americans and whites. Moltke-Hansen traces the continuing evolution of just what "reconstruction" meant through the Progressive Era and through the writings of William Gilmore Simms, George Washington Cable, and others to explain the battle over the legacy of the era, as well as white Southerners' special understanding(s) of the term.

Krista Kinslow also delves into the intellectual history of the postwar era in her chapter "Reconstruction at the Centennial Exhibition of 1876." The Centennial Exhibition was the first major World's Fair held in the United States. Although the Centennial Exhibition coincided with Reconstruction, historians have rarely connected the 1876 fair in Philadelphia with the political battles of the time. In fact, Reconstruction debates were intertwined with the exhibition. Government funding for the fair became tied to issues such as civil rights and amnesty for Confederates as Republicans and Democrats debated in the halls of Congress. Both Rutherford B. Hayes and Samuel Tilden, the presidential candidates in the 1876 election, came to the Centennial, using it as a campaign stop. Some political leaders tied the fair to Reconstruction issues such as government overreach and corruption. However, Kinslow points out that Reconstruction pervaded much more than national politics, and the Centennial reflected that, as well. Union veterans went to Philadelphia to celebrate their victory over the South, the reunion of the nation, and the abolition of slavery. To them, the Centennial symbolized Northern triumph, both in crushing the rebellion and in securing the peace during the years that followed. White Southerners, too, linked the fair and Reconstruction, but not nearly so positively. In their minds, the Centennial symbolized a harsh peace complete with a military occupation by their conquering foes. African Americans also recognized the Centennial as something relevant and symbolic. Some saw it as an event to celebrate emancipation and the progress of their race. Others, rather than celebrating the centennial anniversary of the American Revolution, stressed that African Americans did not truly have a place in the nation, denounced the federal government's abandonment of African Americans, and decried the violence against Blacks in the Southern states. Thus, many who attended the Centennial had Reconstruction on their minds. Their many different interpretations of Reconstruction could be found fully displayed at the fair. Some saw it as a successful series of policies being carried out with the expanded powers of the national government. With emancipation secured and the nation reunited, Reconstruction could be hailed as another Union victory and celebrated at the Philadelphia exhibition. Others, however, criticized Reconstruction as going too far or not going far enough. Some saw it as a harsh peace, while others argued that it was letting the rebels off too easy. But Reconstruction continued in 1876, and too many historians have rushed to its conclusion in ways that people at the time did not. Thus, Kinslow suggests that examining Reconstruction through the lens of a cultural event like the 1876 Philadelphia exhibition provides an account that is much different from that of a standard political piece. One can observe the effects Reconstruction had on rhetoric, Civil War memory, and artwork at the Centennial, bringing together social, cultural, and political history. The meaning of the Revolution's centennial was contested by Americans in ways that reflected the conflicts of Reconstruction. The complex layers of meaning found at the Centennial demonstrated how the fairground became a battleground over Reconstruction.

Kinslow's attention to rhetoric, art, politics, literature, and a host of other facets of the Centennial Exhibition offer an appropriate transition to a trio of essays that consider Reconstruction from fresh and exciting interdisciplinary perspectives. By viewing the Reconstruction era from standpoints that are not narrowly historical, scholars are often able to more fully flesh out the complicated interrelations among the era's forces, as well as bring into conversation competing visions of what Reconstruction was and could have been.

J. Mills Thornton's chapter is titled "Mark Twain and the Failure of Radical Reconstruction." In it, Thornton suggests that perhaps no significant American writer of his generation was more deeply conflicted about the events of the Civil War and Reconstruction than Samuel Clemens/Mark Twain. Twain had been an early Confederate volunteer but later deserted, had come from a slave-owning family but later befriended abolitionists, and remembered fondly his youth in the Old South while eventually arriving at a clear understanding of the immorality of slavery. The conflict between Twain's affectionate memories of his childhood and his clarified understanding of the injustice that had given form to his world appears in *Tom Sawyer* and dominates its sequel, *Huckleberry Finn*, which appeared in 1885. But for all its ability to bring the conflict vividly to life, Thornton identifies no solutions to it in *Huckleberry Finn*. We are left, as Twain was also, to recognize and accept the coexistence of both levels of reality as Huck has experienced them. And that, Thornton argues, inevitably led Twain—who had just lived through the failure of Reconstruction—to muse on the possibility of transforming such a society. The result was *A Connecticut Yankee in King Arthur's Court*, published in 1889. Though set in a heavily mythologized sixth century, Thornton shows how *A Connecticut Yankee* is a novel about the capacity of the modernizing democratic faith of a Connecticut Yankee to reform the recalcitrant reality of a world with very different assumptions and ideals. It is, as Thornton convincingly shows in the essay, an allegory about the possibilities of Reconstruction.

Today's scholars who strive toward interdisciplinarity have much to learn from the great W. E. B. Du Bois. Garry Bertholf and Marina Bilbija both situate themselves in the interdisciplinary field of African American studies and take Du Bois as the topic of their chapter "Teaching Du Bois's *Black Reconstruction.*" Though beginning with an acknowledgment of the debt all scholars of Reconstruction owe to Du Bois, Bertholf and Bilbija examine both the benefits and the challenges of teaching *Black Reconstruction* more than eighty years after its initial publication. They argue that this text has much to teach us about interdisciplinarity, not least because it was produced precisely at a moment when so many disciplinary borders seemed already to have been fossilized. Du Bois, they point out, explained that a revisionist history of Reconstruction necessitated an interdisciplinary approach because Black citizenship was thwarted by the coordinated efforts of "Religion, Science, Education, Law, and brute force." Both the book's reception history and the authors' experiences teaching it to undergraduates, however, reveal the difficulty of teaching such an interdisciplinary text to readers who have already been attuned to disciplinary divisions; its status as a "historical text" triggers a particular set of disciplinary expectations that Du Bois necessarily subverts. Bertholf and Bilbija discuss the differences between teaching *Black Reconstruction* and the more familiar (and putatively more "literary") *Souls of Black Folk* in an English classroom to explore both the radical potential of these moments of readerly alienation and the pedagogical impasses that can result from them.

"Three Historians and a Theologian: Howard Thurman and the Writing of African American History," by Peter Eisenstadt, also takes Du Bois's masterwork as a jumping-off point. When in 1936 Howard Thurman became the first African American to meet Mahatma Gandhi, the great leader of the Indian Independence movement, he did have a conservation with him about Du Bois and his interpretation of the post–Reconstruction South. When Thurman is remembered today, it is as a mystic and an inspiration to Martin Luther King Jr., James Farmer, Pauli Murray, and other civil rights leaders. But he was an original and creative historical thinker, and meditations on history had a significant influence on the writing of African American history. The essay examines three historians from the civil rights era with close personal ties and significant intellectual debts to Thurman: Lerone Bennett Jr., Vincent Harding, and Nathan I. Huggins. The three historians and Thurman differ on many issues, especially the question of Black Power. However, central to all of their work was the belief that "the propaganda of history" that Blacks were unfit for equal citizenship could be challenged only by correcting the historical record and demonstrating that Blacks had always had the capacity to make their own history and histories. Thurman's probing analysis of the response of African Americans to their powerlessness in such works as *Jesus and the Disinherited* (1949) provided for the historians profiled in this essay a framework for understanding the complexities of the upsurge in Black activism and Black history writing during the Second Reconstruction. It also provided a model for explaining the connection between personal psychological and spiritual transformation and the impetus for social and political reconstructions past, present, and future.

Many of the themes of preceding chapters are reprised, woven together, and transmuted in the micro-historical analysis Lawrence T. McDonnell offers of the execution of a paroled Confederate veteran by African American troops in postwar South Carolina. That minor incident, reconstructed—and deconstructed—in "Killing Calvin Crozier: Honor, Myth, and Military Occupation after Appomattox," has served as a touchstone of Lost Cause and neo-Confederate "heritage" ever since local whites began spinning tales of martyred white chivalry and barbarous Black perfidy in the 1860s. Monuments, memoirs, and roadside markers have carried the amped-up story to the present day, and music, novels, and film portrayals of the heroic Crozier's death have made this incident iconic. Indeed, the central themes of Reconstruction as a "Tragic Era" were vividly sketched in the retelling of this almost operatic tale—to powerful and persuasive effect. By recontextualizing Crozier's execution and painstakingly reconstructing the events that led to his death by firing squad in September 1865, McDonnell dissolves this potent racist mythology. His chapter argues for the central importance of the local politics of Reconstruction, the remarkably open-ended, contingent direction of events, and the role of violence in establishing—or overturning—an emerging social order. A model of studying "big questions in small places," the chapter asks readers to consider basic questions anew: When is a war truly over? What is the difference between honorable violence and terrorism? Did Reconstruction ultimately fail because Federals failed to use sufficient force to crush out Rebel intransigence? "White lies matter," McDonnell reminds us, urging the importance of building a new history of Reconstruction from the bottom up.

Notes

1. For analyses of early Reconstruction historiography, see John David Smith and J. Vincent Lowry, eds., *The Dunning School: Historians, Race, and the Meaning of Reconstruction* (Lexington: University Press of Kentucky, 2013).

2. See, e.g., Bruce Baker, *What Reconstruction Meant: Historical Memory in the American South* (Charlottesville: University of Virginia Press, 2007); Caroline E. Janney, *Remembering the Civil War: Reunion and the Limits of Reconciliation* (Chapel Hill: University of North Carolina Press, 2017); David Blight, *Race and Reunion: The Civil War in American Memory* (Cambridge, MA: Harvard University Press, 2001).

3. See "Donald Trump's Favorite Movies," CBS News, accessed March 1, 2020, https://www.cbsnews.com/pictures/donald-trumps-favorite-movies/11.

4. "Toward a Third Reconstruction," *The Nation*, March 23, 2015, https://www.thenation.com/article/archive/toward-third-reconstruction; William J. Barber and Jonathan Wilson-Hartgrove, *The Third Reconstruction: Moral Mondays, Fusion Politics, and the Rise of a New Justice Movement* (Boston: Beacon, 2016).

5. Adam Serwer, "Is This the Second Redemption?" *The Atlantic*, November 10, 2016, https://www.theatlantic.com/politics/archive/2016/11/welcome-to-the-second-redemption/507317; Adam Serwer, "John Roberts and the Second Redemption Court," *The Atlantic*, September 4, 2018, https://www.theatlantic.com/ideas/archive/2018/09/redemption-court/566963; Ta-Nahisi Coates, *We Were Eight Years in Power: An American Tragedy* (New York: One World, 2017).

6. Eric Foner, *Reconstruction: America's Unfinished Revolution, 1863–1877*, updated ed. (New York: HarperCollins, 2014), xlii.

7. See Michael Perman, "Eric Foner's *Reconstruction*: A Finished Revolution," *Reviews in American History* 17, no. 1 (March 1989): 73–78.

"They Loved but Did Not Agree"

AFRICAN AMERICAN WOMEN DIVORCEES IN POST–CIVIL WAR VIRGINIA

Arlisha Norwood

O N SEPTEMBER 20, 1862, THE front page of the Richmond, Virginia, newspaper the *Daily Dispatch* covered the Confederate Army's departure from Maryland. The month had been a tumultuous time for the army. As the soldiers trekked back to Virginia feeling defeated but still holding on to "promise," they prepared for another battle. On the second page, couched between this news and the minutes of the Confederate Congress, appeared the local court proceedings. The proceedings covered the affairs of the Mayor's Court, the local authority in Richmond. The edition detailed an appearance by an African American couple, Ben and Lucretia Scott: "Ben Scott, a negro, for threatening to kill his wife, and treating her with great inhumanity, was held on bail, Lucretia, the wife of Ben, convulsed the Court and spectators by applying to his Honor for a divorce."[1]

The short report did not provide a backstory for Lucretia. There was no mention of her enslaved or free status, nor did it give examples of the "great inhumanity" she suffered. Instead, the account covered Scott's plea for a divorce and the reaction of the onlookers. The use of exaggerated words, such as "convulsed," convey the reporter's intent to sensationalize her appearance. Her determined efforts to create a new life seemed to be at odds with those watching from the gallery. However, she gave no consideration to how she would be perceived or the apparent disregard for her suffering. Although Scott was not granted a divorce, Lucretia's experience calls attention to Black women's marital exits during the Civil War and Reconstruction years.

African American women often sought to end marital relationships for several reasons. Conversely, they also were on the receiving end of divorce suits. Women like Scott who filed for divorce illustrate determination to exit violent and undesirable relationships. Their petitions reveal how women endeavored to construct new lives using the judicial system. African American men also petitioned the courts to leave women whom they believed exhibited immoral behavior or engaged in extramarital sexual relations. The women in these cases demonstrate how Black women may have pushed against boundaries of respectability and sexuality in the postwar years. Together, the women boldly entered the uncharted status of divorcees while also exercising agency over their social, political, and sexual lives. These transformations happened against the backdrop of Civil War and Reconstruction Era Virginia.

The existing histography of the Black family includes the work of numerous scholars who have excavated, analyzed and chronicled the institution through the pre–Civil War destruction that occurred during slavery and the subsequent reconstruction that took place during the Civil War and postwar years.[2] In addition, there has been a growing amount of literature on Black marriage.[3] Given the attention to marriage, the absence of information surrounding marital exits in the Black community is apparent.[4] The omission of the Black divorcee's narrative could be attributed to several reasons. In many post–Civil War studies, the Black family is posited as the central familial structure. Historians have focused on African Americans' eagerness to reunite with their families and create new unions; however, they have left out those who chose to exit the normative family unit.[5] The inclusion of Black divorcees in the Reconstruction narrative is imperative to providing a more holistic and inclusive portrayal of Black familial structures in freedom. More important, studying African American women and their interactions with the postwar judicial system articulates how Black women perceived the courts and the protections it could offer.

The history of legal divorce in the United States is a convoluted and varied topic. For most of the nineteenth century, white Virginians, like many other Americans, were unfamiliar with the process of legal separation. Many chose to informally exit undesirable marriages by separating. In the early years of the republic, Virginia offered the divorce process under restrictive terms. Before 1850, divorce suits were granted solely by state legislators. The procedure began when either a man or a woman filed a divorce petition. Petitioners had to inform spouses that the case would be heard during the next legislative meeting. This was usually done by announcing the petition and court date in the local newspaper. This public announcement ensured that both community members and the spouse were aware of the date and time of the proceedings. The petition was drawn up by the divorce seeker or, in some instances, "legal counsel" hired by the petitioner. The context of the petitions proved to be the crux of the entire divorce case. Petitioners laid out their claims with carefully crafted language that was meant to appeal to the legislators.[6]

Irrespective of strategy, getting legislators to grant a separation was difficult. State politicians granted only legal separations, which were commonly known as a divorce of bed and board.[7] Although not a divorce, legislators still were reluctant to issue "bed and board" separations. Petitioners had to prove adultery, cruelty, or insanity. All of these claims could be incendiary; therefore, successful divorce petitions required numerous eyewitness accounts. The testimony worked to corroborate the divorce seekers' accusations. Once the petition was submitted, a legislator from the county laid out the evidence and argument of the divorce petition for the House of Delegates. Afterward, a debate would ensue. Given the legislators' reluctance to grant legal separations, this part of process weeded out several of the petitions. Thomas E. Buckley, a historian of divorce, estimates that, "from the end of the revolution until 1851, Virginia legislators only granted two-thirds of the petitions presented to them."[8]

The earliest instances of African Americans in divorce proceedings can be found in petitions from white Virginians. The institution of slavery was heavily intertwined with the economic and social relations of Southern whites. Enslaved African Americans found themselves forcibly interjected into domestic conflicts. In these early petitions African American men, women, and children were often mentioned as "slave." The absence of names points to the role enslaved property served in divorce proceedings. Based on the laws of coverture, when propertied white women married, their land and assets passed to their spouses.[9] When slaveholding women desired to leave estranged husbands, they had to protect their transferred assets, which included enslaved laborers. In 1826, Mary Birdsong filed for divorce from her estranged husband. Although his abandonment and abuse caused the separation, Birdsong wanted to make sure that, if he returned, he would not stake claim to their "few slaves."[10]

In other cases, African Americans were accused of being participants in adulterous relationships with whites. An accusation of a sexual affair with a Black man or Black woman was viewed as an irreconcilable act. Two of the first "absolute divorce" rulings occurred when white men charged their wives with "committing adultery" with Black men. In 1802, Dabney Pettus filed for divorce after his wife, Elizabeth, delivered a "mulatto child." In addition, Elizabeth openly claimed the child's father was a "negro slave." Legislators unanimously voted to grant Pettus an absolute divorce. White women accused of sexual relationships with enslaved men not only represented the most severe form of infidelity; the intercourse also prodded at the strict lines of racial subjugation and domestic separation that upheld the institution of slavery. It is impossible to determine whether the relationships between white women and Black men and Black women and white men were consensual or nonconsensual. Given the power dynamics that existed between slaveholder and slave, even if the enslaved participant agreed with the intercourse, the relationship still existed in the confines of an antebellum master-slave relationship.[11] When petitioners accused their partners of interracial affairs based on the evidence of a "mulatto" child, they were more than likely granted absolute divorces. In fact, all of the petitions presented to the Virginia state legislature from 1820 to 1840 that mentioned "mulatto" offspring, resulted in divorce. In 1838, Richard Hall accused his wife, Sarah, of delivering a "colored child" six months into their union. His wife must have continued her outside relations, because she had two more children, both of which Hall referred to as "colored." Hall's petition reveals that white women who were accused of sexual relationships with Black men may have been viewed as dishonorable. Hall requested that "the legislature . . . dissolve the union which connects him with one who has thus proven herself so unworthy."[12] When white women bore free mulatto children, the legislature probably saw this as openly antagonistic to attempts to decrease the problematic free Black population in Virginia.

In addition, there were several divorce petitions in which white women accused their husbands of infidelity with Black women. These cases were especially controversial because petitioners often attempted to portray their husbands' relations with Black women as cruelty. In many of the cases, the men lived in separate residences and engaged in "open adultery." Sally Wade Ballinger filed for divorce after her husband poorly managed her inheritance and "took another Negro woman into his house and lived in open adultery with her."[13] The sexual interactions between white men and Black women disrupted plantation households' harmony. The wives of slaveholders were complicit in maintaining the power dynamics of the plantations; therefore, many times they enforced the strict rules that were required to keep the institution intact. An 1837 petition confirms that the affairs between Black women and white men could also lead to open disrespect to white mistresses. Elizabeth Pannell claimed her husband, Edmund Pannell, engaged in "adultery and fornication" with women of all races. He also openly provoked "a slave named Grace with whom he was conducting an adulterous affair, to be insolent toward her."[14]

In the antebellum years, free African Americans filed petitions to end marriages, too. For free African Americans, filing for divorce was a lengthy and cumbersome process. As a result, many may have found it easier to separate informally. The number of divorce petitions from free African Americans in Virginia is very small. In her book *Bound in Wedlock,* the historian Tera Hunter points out that many of the divorce petitions from free African Americans were filed by women.[15] Virginia seems to be the outlier in this claim. The majority of the divorce petitions came from men.[16] Their petitions originated from various locations in the state. Black petitioners still had to abide by restrictive legislative rules, and the petitions were often purposefully combative and malicious. The testimony from members of the community played an integral role in securing a divorce. This was the case for Cornelius Jackson. In 1863, Jackson filed for a divorce from his wife, Sarah Briggs. Three years into their union, Jackson claimed, Briggs began cheating. Her affairs were "flagrant" and notorious. Jackson decided to leave his wife when she bore children from her infidelity. By the time the petition was filed, the couple had been separated for nine years. Briggs did not seek reconciliation and therefore asked for an "absolute annulment of the bond of matrimony." Unfortunately, testimony from neighbors reveal that Jackson had been abusive to Briggs, and, contrary to his claims, he had first been the adulterer. In this rare case, Briggs did not testify against her husband's claims; instead, the community revealed her story. This was an anomaly; in most cases, witnesses supported the accusation of infidelity by the petitioner. In 1859, John Taylor filed a petition to end his marriage with Nancy Taylor. He claimed that the marriage was pleasant until he came home to find Nancy in bed with another man. After the incident, John testified, he "felt compelled to abandon her as his wife." The Taylor divorce petition included six accounts from neighbors and acquaintances who testified that Nancy lived in "open adultery."[17]

When free African Americans entered unions, they had expectations and roles. When those expectations and roles were not met, the parties chose to end the relationship. In 1850, Bryant Day married Mary Jane. The couple lived together for ten years before Day filed for divorce. He accused Mary Jane of being "unkind and devoid of affection." Others testified that Mary was "a drunkard," stating that her alcohol addiction may have been the cause of her distant attitude. These conflicts that centered on marital expectations would also materialize in freedom.

In 1865, when Confederate General Robert Lee surrendered, ideals about reconciliation and reconstruction were unclear. Politicians debated fiercely about the role defeated Southerners would play the new union. Fortunately, formerly enslaved Black men and women appeared ready to handle freedom. By the war's end, they had established successful communities and continued to move towards self-sufficiency. When the federal government created the Bureau of Refugees, Freedmen, and Abandoned Lands (BRFAL) to aid their transition, free African Americans took advantage of the bureau's services. Specifically, Black men and women used the bureau court to legally divorce their partners.

As early as 1865, BRFAL Commissioner Oliver Otis Howard realized that the governing of formerly enslaved African Americans who lived among the "disgruntled" white population required close oversight. Although Union soldiers provided protection, African Americans still faced a prejudice and discriminatory legal system. Black Virginians regularly suffered through unfair sentencing and racist judges who refused to rule in their favor. To solve the issue, Howard proposed the creation of a legal system that would help administer justice for African Americans: the Freedmen's Bureau Court. The court was presided over by a three-person panel, which included a selected representative of the planter class, a representative of the newly freed African American population, and a bureau agent. This system ensured that all interests would be represented and decisions regarding labor, land ownership, and wages would be issued with compromise. Unfortunately, the court was given jurisdiction over "minor cases," so incidents that violated freedpeople's civil rights were referred to federal courts.[18] Black Virginians used the court to resolve domestic issues—namely, separation and divorce.

In 1867, Marie Wallop petitioned the Bureau Court in Drummondtown, Virginia, complaining that Erastus Dennis, her husband, had "abandoned her." Wallop not only claimed "abandonment"; she also stated that all her clothes had been stolen. Wallop requested the court make her estranged husband return her clothes and grant her a divorce. Wallop and other Black women demanded that the BRFAL's court aid them in securing a legal separation and financial support from their estranged spouses. Both would allow Wallop to create a new life that would not include her estranged partner. In some cases, abandoned women who were aware of their husband's locations asked the court to force their partners to return or send money. Ana Marie Brown was aware that her husband, James Brown, was in Maryland and "doing well in the way of work." She complained that he would not send his "wages" back to support her and asked the court to help her.

Some women used the Bureau Court to seek retribution against old partners who they believed had wronged them. Mary Blizzard accused her husband of leaving her for another woman. The court heard testimony from Mary's mother and other witnesses who confirmed her story. Thereafter, her former partner agreed to "pay a set amount and furnish her with rations weekly."[19]

Black mothers also appealed to the court regarding issues concerning childcare. Martha Ann Dudley was married to James Dudley before the war. They "lived together as man and wife" until 1867, when James not only deserted her but also took their oldest child with him. Martha filed a complaint at the local Bureau Court giving her former husband a choice: return the child and support her.[20] These claims show that Black mothers defiantly claimed their maternal rights and the financial support they believed belonged to them.

In addition to their complaints about monetary support for their children, Black women used the BRFAL's court to protect themselves from abusive partners. Domestic abuse in Black marriages and relationships was not new. During enslavement, women and men frequently recalled violent incidents between couples. Katie Johnson of Washington County, Virginia, recalled that "some good masters would punish slaves who mistreated their womenfolk, and some didn't."[21] In freedom, Black women made sure that their abusers received punishment. In 1867, Margaret Davis took her husband to court for assault and battery. Davis's husband pleaded guilty and was sentenced to five days in jail. A few times, women failed or refused to bring charges against their violent partners. Instead, community members interceded on behalf of victims. Although it is unclear whether these women were seeking legal separation or divorce, it is apparent that in freedom Black women looked to the Bureau Court and, eventually, local courts to protect themselves from abuse.

Until 1872, the Freedmen's Bureau Court was used as the only legal authority for Black Virginians. When the bureau was officially dissolved, power was ceded back to local courts. During this time, divorce petitions from African Americans increased.[22]

In 1877, Bettie Jones, a resident of Elizabeth City County, filed for a permanent separation from her husband, Edmund Jones. "She has been to him a constant faithful and dutiful wife," her lawyer wrote. Her husband, on the contrary, had been negligent and "insufferably abusive." In lengthy testimony, witnesses corroborated Jones's story. "I have seen him strike her with a fire iron," recalled one of the neighbors. Harry Petersen, a longtime acquaintance, gave graphic testimony of his failed intervention in one of the couples' domestic disputes: "I witnessed E. J. publicly knock her out in the years and lock her out, I knock there and told him that if he did not stop mistreating his wife I would go down to the court and report him." Unfortunately, Petersen's attempted intervention escalated the situation. During the same heated argument, Peterson recalled, Edmund "seized me in the collar and wanted to beat me for interfering with him." After years of physical abuse, Bettie was granted a divorce, and Edmund was bound "to keep the peace towards her."[23]

From 1872 to 1890, nearly one hundred African American women filed divorce petitions that included some mention of domestic abuse. These petitions not only reveal the severity of their mistreatment. They also illustrate how Black women used the court to protect them and intervene. As in antebellum-era petitions, Black women needed to prove abuse through testimony from those familiar with the alleged abuse. In 1889, Susan Woodson filed for divorce from her husband, George Woodson. From the beginning, George made the "marriage insufferable."[24] He was abusive and violent toward Susan until 1882, when he "willfully deserted her." George's abandonment left Susan single and poor. Community members testified not only to Susan's life in poverty but also to George's abuse. In 1875, Nanny Owens, a Halifax County resident, filed for divorce. Although her husband, Wiley Owens, had long since deserted the family, Nanny filed for permanent dissolution in the hope of preventing Wiley from returning home. Nanny testified that he had "treated her bad and abused her." The abuse became so harsh that Nanny would often seek protection in her neighbor's house. One neighbor testified, "He not only was a cruel husband but beat his children."[25]

Black female divorce seekers also used the court to regain financial self-sufficiency. Even after the Civil War, under Virginia law, women's property and earnings were bound to the husband. Therefore, for landowning women marriage carried a financial compromise and loss. This practice left property-holding Black women vulnerable to men only seeking financial increase. Black women sought separations and financial independence when their ill-intentioned partners left them. Such was the case for Annie E. Robinson when she divorced Edward J. Robinson. Prior to the marriage, Annie owned a small parcel of land in Elizabeth City County, Virginia. In 1887, Edward borrowed $80 against the land and took the money and "left her" to live in New York. In her divorce suit she requested that the court "waive Edward's right to property." Legal divorce in Annie's case was necessary to protect her income and landholdings. Black women also used the local courts to seek monetary compensation from partners. Rachel Morris was abandoned by her husband, William Morris. Together, the couple had seven children, all of whom were supported by Rachel, who was now a "poor colored woman." She filed for separation and summoned her estranged husband to court. Summonses were nailed to the courthouse door and even published in the local newspaper. Essentially, when Rachel Morris filed for divorce, she made her partner's part in the demise of the relationship known to the county and community members. There is a chance that neighbors knew about her husband's abandonment, as they stated, "He only lived across town." Unfortunately, Rachel Morris's husband never responded to the petition, and she was granted a divorce with no compensation.[26]

Regardless of their reasons, African American women looked to the court to aid them in exiting unfavorable relationships. In most cases, the court answered, protecting abused women and granting divorce. Similarly, just as Black women sought legal help to end marriages, so did Black men.

In 1878, Edmund King petitioned for a legal separation from his wife, Betty King. Edmund testified that he had been a "faithful and affectionate husband," but Betty, on the contrary, suffered from a "bad temper" and often engaged in arguments with him. After several years of a seemingly "unhappy marriage," Betty abandoned Edmund and chose to live with her father. One neighbor recalled, "They loved but did not agree." Even after Edmund attempted to seduce Betty back into the relationship, she declined his pleas and openly disowned him and the marriage. In several testimonies, neighbors and acquaintances affirmed Edmund's statement about his partner's behavior. One witness stated, "She was impossible to live with."

Betty's abandonment of Edmund represents an anomaly in the discourse surrounding African American families and marriage. Betty willingly disrupted the family structure and defiantly lived in her community without her husband. Scholars eager to dissect the Black family have drawn attention to the desertion of Black men from the household. However, women who left marriages have been ignored. This makes Betty's story particularly difficult to place into historical context. And Betty's is not the only case. In several postwar divorce suits, African American men requested divorce from Black women who had abandoned their roles as wives and left marriages.[27]

Black women who openly rejected marriage may have been exercising power over their private lives by exiting situations that they found unfavorable, something they could not do if they had been enslaved. In slavery and following the Civil War, Black women lived through regular occurrences of sexual violence and assault. As historians and scholars continue to uncover the ramifications of violence, the activities of Black women in their relationships may communicate how they survived in a sexually and emotionally repressive environment.[28] Women such as Lou Duncombe illustrate how some women decided to live outside communal norms. Duncombe chose to leave her husband and live in a house of "ill repute." Many testified that her husband tried several times to coax her out of "unwifely conduct" but failed. Witnesses could not say for sure that Lou was a prostitute, but they did inform the court that she lived in a house with other women, and they had seen "colored and white men" go in and out.[29]

In 1875, David Jackson filed for divorce from his estranged wife, Ann Jackson. Although he testified to treating Ann well, she left him only three years into the union. David was informed that Ann was living in North Carolina with another man. "I went after her 5 or 6 times, but she wouldn't come home with me," he testified. Many of the community members were aware that Ann lived in an openly adulterous relationship. When David confronted Ann about her infidelity, she vehemently refused to honor their marital bond.

In 1877, Randall Buckner filed for divorce from his wife, Annie. He accused her of deserting him. Randall seemed befuddled about Annie's departure and enlisted the help of his friend to help look for her. Their investigation took them to the home of another man; when they knocked on the door, Annie answered in her "night clothes." The ordeal led one of Randall's witnesses to the conclusion that Annie "was not very good."

Amanda Drummond deserted her husband after he went to work at a fish factory. When she told her next-door neighbor her plans to abandon the marriage, her neighbor warned her that her husband was good. "I could not understand why she wanted to go away," the neighbor testified. A few years after the abandonment, Amanda returned home with a new child. Her old neighbors inquired about the paternity of her child, to which she revealed the father was not her husband. "I asked her why she wasn't ashamed to talk like that when she had a husband," one neighbor recalled.

The Drummond case points to the internal backlash Black women experienced when they openly contested their designated roles as wives. Community members frequently shamed the women and openly reprimanded them. Unfortunately, it is unclear how women responded to these communal accusations. Many times, Black women failed to respond to divorce suits. This could be viewed as an admission of guilt; however, in some cases women may not have been adulterous. Instead, they simply refused to conform to standards that forced the women's social activities to center on the home.

In 1866, Leander Faulkner married Sallie. They lived together until 1877, when he discovered that Sallie had been adulterous with several men. One witness stated, "Sallie has been guilty of adultery, at various times and with various persons, so that in fact she is now a common prostitute." Unfortunately, witnesses were unable to testify to Sallie's behavior. However, they did reveal that she had become "addicted to going out." In the case of Annie Brown, mentioned earlier, witnesses also testified that she had "taken to hanging out." Even when they were unaware of infidelity, witnesses disclosed their attitudes toward women who went out. The community's understanding of a "dutiful wife" was grounded in an image of a woman who sought amusement only in relation to her family and the home, not a woman who looked beyond her household for pleasure or entertainment. Sallie and Annie were probably aware that their actions attracted reproach from neighbors. However, they continued the behavior that eventually led to divorce.[30]

In a few cases, Black men divorced their partners after the birth of a child perceived to be illegitimate. Without DNA testing, it is impossible to know whether these charges against Black women were true. Nonetheless, the cases illustrate the prominent role community members played in divorce suits when giving character testimony. In 1871, Patsy Younger was married to Joe Younger. They had one child, whom Joe "believed to be his." However, after Patsy gave birth to a "very white" baby boy in December 1878, Joe demanded a divorce. "The child is almost white; Joe is very dark, almost black and Patsy is a colored woman, I am therefore certain the child is not Joe's," one witness testified.[31]

Beyond the internal community issues Black women divorcees faced, those who refused to follow normative customs surrounding marriage were confronted with reproach from government officials. As early as 1863, government officials expressed concern about African Americans who refused to comply with the marital contract. John Eaton, superintendent of contraband camps near the Mississippi Valley, implemented strict policies pertaining to marriage. He declared that "all entering our camps who have been living or desire to live together as husband and wife are required to be married in the proper manner."[32] Former slaves were soon informed that the days of informal marriage ceremonies were long gone, and unions in freedom had to be solemnized and documented.

After the war, efforts to legitimize African Americans unions increased. As states debated new constitutions, government officials suggested legislation that addressed African American marital relations. In February 1866, less than a year after the end of the war, Virginia passed an act that legally recognized the marriages of formerly enslaved African Americans and recognized their children as legitimate. Although this helped expedite the legal process for those seeking marriage, it had the converse effect of forcing a binding contract on uninterested parties. Nancy Winder and George Winder were solemnized under the 1866 law. Four years after they were legally united, Nancy left. Her neighbor helped her "carry her stuff." One witness recalled that Nancy stated that "she never wanted to be married anyhow."

Black women and men also communicated differing views on marriage. In enslavement, Black communities created their own customs and indicators for courtship, marriage, and marital exits. In freedom, these standards continued. Although, Black men and women could use the local court to exit marriages, many left informally under the assumption that the departure represented a legal divorce.[33] Such was the case of Staunton and Sophie Jackson. Sophie had been married before the war. She and her former husband lived together, and they were legally married due to the cohabitation law. In 1867, her husband left to live with another woman. After five years of separation, Sophie married Staunton Jackson. He eventually filed for divorce, accusing Sophie of bigamy. Sophie disputed the charge because she believed that a five-year separation legally constituted a divorce. Even Staunton's lawyer believed that Sophie was innocent of ill intent. He stated that she was "acting upon an idea which has persisted among the colored people."[34]

African American women divorcees bring to light what power negotiations looked like in the postwar South. Some women used the courts to escape marriage, while others used the petitions to illustrate autonomy over their lives and bodies. Taken together, the narratives convey a picture of African American women adamant about determining their futures and reconstructing their domestic lives. However, near the end of the nineteenth century, unmarried Black women would contend with a stronger agenda from their own community.

Notes

1. *Daily Dispatch*, September 20, 1862.
2. Important works on the Black family include E. Franklin Frazier, *The Negro Family in the United States* (Chicago: University of Chicago Press, 1939); Herbert Gutman, *The Black Family in Slavery and Freedom, 1750–1925* (New York: Vintage, 1976); Brenda F. Stevenson, *Life in Black and White: Family and Community in the Slave South* (New York: Oxford University Press, 1996).
3. For more information on Black marriages in slavery and freedom, see Laura F. Edwards, "'The Marriage Covenant Is at the Foundation of All Our Rights': The Politics of Slave Marriages in North Carolina after Emancipation," *Law and History Review* 14, no. 1 (1996): 81–124; Noralee Frankel, *Freedom's Women: Black Women and Families in Civil War Era Mississippi* (Bloomington: Indiana University Press, 1999); Tera Hunter, *Bound in Wedlock: Slave and Free Black Marriage in the Nineteenth Century* (Cambridge, MA: Harvard University Press,

2016); Leslie Schwalm, *A Hard Fight for We: Women's Transition from Slavery to Freedom in South Carolina* (Urbana: University of Illinois Press, 1997).

4. In recent years, historians have worked to add Black marital exits to the narrative. See Evam Howard Ashford, "Freedom Courts: An Analysis of Black Women's Divorce in Attala County during Mississippi's Anti-Divorce Campaign, 1890–1940," *Journal of American History and Politics* 4, no. 1 (March 2021): 1–12; Dylan Pennigroth, "African American Divorce in Virginia and Washington, D.C., 1865–1930," *Journal of Family History* 33, no. 1 (January 2008), https://doi.org/10.1177/0363199007308608.

5. See Heather Andrea Williams, *Help Me to Find My People: The African American Search for Family Lost in Slavery* (Chapel Hill: University of North Carolina Press, 2012). With the emergence of digital archives, archivists have created online repositories that exhibit the lengths African Americans went through to find lost family members. See, e.g., *Lost Friends: Advertisements from Southwestern Christian Advocate* (https://www.hnoc.org /research/lost-friends-advertisements-southwestern-christian-advocate), a digital repository that includes 1,200 advertisements from the formerly enslaved "searching for loved ones lost in slavery." *Last Seen: Finding Family after Slavery* (https://informationwanted.org) is a crowdsourcing project that allows the public to transcribe ads from African Americans in search of family and friends. Both sites illustrate the attention that the "reunion" narrative has received.

6. Divorce in the antebellum United States has been the subject of many studies. See, e.g., Thomas E. J. Buckley, *The Great Catastrophe of My Life: Divorce in the Old Dominion* (Chapel Hill: University of North Carolina Press, 2002); Elaine Tyler May, *Great Expectations: Marriage and Divorce in the Post-Victorian America* (Chicago: University of Chicago Press, 1983); William O'Neil, *Divorce in the Progressive Era* (New Haven, CT: Yale University Press, 1967).

7. Glenda Riley, "Legislative Divorce in Early Virginia," *Journal of the Early Republic* 11, no. 1 (Spring 1991): 57.

8. Buckley, *The Great Catastrophe of My Life,* 10–18.

9. See Stephanie Jones Rogers, *They Were Her Property: White Women as Slave Owners in the American South* (New Haven, CT: Yale University Press), 2019.

10. Petition of Mary Birdsong against Charles Gary to the members of the Legislatures of Virginia, 1826, PAR #11682611, *Race and Slavery Petitions Project,* University of North Carolina, Greensboro, https://library.uncg.edu/slavery/petitions.

11. For more information on slavery, sex, violence, and power, see Nikki M. Taylor, *Driven towards Madness: The Fugitive Slave Margaret Garner and Tragedy on the Ohio* (Athens: Ohio University Press, 2016), 92–100; Diane Miller Sommerville, *Rape and Race in the Nineteenth Century South* (Chapel Hill: University of North Carolina Press, 2004).

12. Petition of Richard Hall against Sarah Hall to the members of the Legislatures of Virginia, 1838, PAR #11683835, 13, *Race and Slavery Petitions Project.*

13. Petition of Dabney Pettus against Elizabeth Morris, 1802, PAR #11680206, *Race and Slavery Petitions Project.*

14. Petition of Elizabeth Panell against Edmund Panell to the members of the Legislatures of Virginia, 1837, PAR #11683703, *Race and Slavery Petitions Project.*

15. Hunter, *Bound in Wedlock,* 151.

16. This statistic was taken by counting the cases presented in the *Race and Slavery Petitions Project,* which covers all the petitions presented to the Virginia Legislature.

17. Petition of Cornelius Jackson against Sarah Briggs to the members of the Legislatures of Virginia, 1863, PAR #21686308; petition of John Taylor against Nancy Taylor to the members of the Legislature of Virginia, 1859, PAR #21685907, both in *Race and Slavery Petitions Project.*

18. The structure of the Freedmen's Bureau Court varied from state to state. In addition, in many states the court operated concurrently with the local court system. As a result, the court systems in post–Civil War Virginia were unorganized. Unfortunately, no scholarly work covers the Freedmen's Bureau Court system in depth. However, bureau administrators did leave behind detailed notes on the inner workings of the system: see Freedmen's Bureau Field Office Records, Virginia, M1913, National Archives and Records Administration, microfilm (hereafter, FBFOR), November 1865–August 1866, Proceedings of Freedmen's Court, Albemarle County (Assistant Subassistant Commissioner), roll 67.

19. FBFOR, May 1865–May 1867, Proceedings of Freedmen's Court, Drummondtown (Assistant Subassistant Commissioner), roll 73; FBFOR, Register of Complaints, Albemarle County (Assistant Subassistant Commissioner), roll 67; FBFOR, 1866–67, Fort Proceedings of Cases before Freedmen's Court, Monroe (Assistant Subassistant Commissioner), roll 130.

20. FBFOR, May 1865–May 1867, Proceedings of Freedmen's Court, Drummondtown (Assistant Subassistant Commissioner), roll 73.

21. Charles L. Perdue, Thomas E. Barden, and Robert K. Phillips, *Weevils in the Wheat: Interviews with Virginia Ex-Slaves* (Charlottesville: University Press of Virginia, 1997), 161.

22. For examples of the Virginia Freedmen's Bureau granting divorces, see *Rebecca Woodson v. Henry Woodson,* November 24, 1865, Proceedings of the Freedmen's Court, Richmond, Virginia, and *Mary Blizzard v. James Blizzard,* October 12, 1864, Proceedings of the Freedmen's Court, Elizabeth City, Virginia.

23. *Bettie Jones by Etc. v. E. G. Jones,* 1877–010, Elizabeth City Chancery Causes, 1753–1913, Local Government Records Collection, Elizabeth City Court Records, Library of Virginia, Richmond, 2.

24. *Susan Woodson v. George Woodson,* 1878–028, Halifax County Chancery Causes, 1753–1913, Local Government Records Collection, Halifax Court Records, Library of Virginia, Richmond.

25. *Nanny Owen v. Wiley Owen,* 1875–081, Halifax County Chancery Causes, 25.

26. *Nanny Owen v. Wiley Owen; Annie E. Robinson by Etc. v. Edward J. Robinson,* 1889–015, Halifax County Chancery Causes; *Rachel Morris v. William Morris,* 1879–050, Halifax County Chancery Causes, 2–4.

27. *Edmund King v. Betty King,* 1878–028, Halifax County Chancery Causes, 1–2.

28. See Darlene Clark Hine, "Rape and the Inner Lives of Black Women in the Middle West," *Signs* 14, no. 4 (1989): 912–20; Hannah Rosen, *Terror in the Heart of Freedom: Citizenship, Sexual Violence, and the Meaning of Race in the Postemancipation South* (Chapel Hill: University of North Carolina Press, 2009).

29. *Oliver Duncombe v. Lou Duncombe,* 1878–072, Halifax County Chancery Causes, 5–6.

30. *Randall Buckner v. Annie Brown,* 1885–021, Elizabeth City Chancery Causes; *Samuel Drummond v. Amanda Drummond,* 1886–008, Elizabeth City Chancery Causes; *Leander Faulkner v. Sallie Faulkner,* 1872–048, Halifax County Chancery Causes.

31. *David Jackson v. Annie Jackson,* 1875–078, Halifax Chancery Causes.

32. General Superintendent of Contrabands in the Department of the Tennessee to the Headquarters of the Department, April 29, 1863, Freedmen and Southern Society Project, http://www.freedmen.umd.edu/Eaton.html.

33. See Brandi Clay Brimmer, *Claiming Union Widowhood: Race, Respectability, and Poverty in the Post-Emancipation South* (Durham, NC: Duke University Press, 2020); Anthony E. Kaye, *Joining Places: Slave Neighborhoods in the Old South* (Chapel Hill: University of North Carolina Press, 2007); Michelle A. Krowl, "For Better or for Worse: Black Families and 'the State' in Civil War Virginia," in *Southern Families at War: Loyalty and Conflict in the Civil War South,* ed. Catherine Clinton (New York: Oxford University Press, 2000), 35–57; Beverly Schwartzberg,

"'Lots of Them Did That': Desertion, Bigamy and Martial Fluidity in Late-Nineteenth-Century America," *Journal of Social History* 37, no. 3 (Spring 2004): 573–600.

34. *Staunton Jackson v. Sophie Jackson,* 1882–05, Madison County Chancery Causes, 1882, Local Government Records Collection, Madison County Court Records, Library of Virginia, Richmond.

Reconstructing Nationalism

CHARLES SUMNER, HUMAN RIGHTS, AND AMERICAN EXCEPTIONALISM

Mark Elliott

> Thoughts cannot be confined to our own country. Wherever man exists,
> there must our good wishes travel, with the precious example of our
> Republic, making Liberty everywhere an inspiration.
> —Charles Sumner, "New Year's Day"[1]

MASSACHUSETTS SENATOR CHARLES SUMNER was among the most emphatic nationalists of the Reconstruction Era. He was, at the same time, one of the era's staunchest defenders of human rights. The nationalism at the core of his worldview was overshadowed in his own time by his reputation as an antislavery radical and, especially, his uncommonly fierce commitment to racial equality. Many historians have recognized his importance as an advocate of human rights, and a few have noted his unique brand of nationalism, but none have analyzed how these commitments intersected with each other.[2] A closer look at Sumner's political thought shows his ability to combine a radical commitment to human rights with a messianic American nationalism. This unique combination brought antislavery ideals into the mainstream before the war and provided the ideological basis for a reconstructed nationalism when the war was over. Revitalizing American exceptionalism would be one of the most powerful legacies of the Civil War, and Sumner's contribution to this process was not insignificant.

Sumner's nationalism presents something of a conundrum in light of the recent historiographical debates on the emergence of human rights-based politics. Some scholars argue that the modern concept of "human rights" is inherently incompatible with nationalism. The leading proponent of this view, Samuel Moyn, has cautioned against implicit "Whiggish" presumptions among historians that today's "human rights" movements progressively unfolded from Enlightenment foundations for more than two centuries. Despite the universalistic principles of "natural rights," Moyn suggests, the inherent limitations imposed by the birth of modern nation-states prevented any genuine politics of human rights from emerging prior to the twentieth century. As Stefan Ludwig-Hoffman explained:

> In the revolutions of the late eighteenth and the nineteenth century, human rights were closely tied to the idea of sovereignty or, to put this more generally, to political participation in a democratically constituted polity. Citizenship rights and human rights belonged together, and their location was the nation state.[3]

Revolutionaries of the eighteenth and nineteenth centuries set their sights on the legal framework of the nation-state and sought to implant "natural rights" in the rights of citizens. Thus limiting their horizons to national borders, the rights of those outside the protection of citizenship were largely ignored. Moyn has gone as far as to suggest that the Enlightenment concept of natural rights and modern human rights may be different concepts altogether.[4]

Sumner presents an interesting case study to examine this thesis. While the cautions of Moyn and others are well taken, Sumner was quite emphatic about supporting "human rights," a phrase he often used interchangeably with "natural rights" and "the rights of man." This essay shows that Sumner's own understanding of the phrase "human rights" acknowledged the universality of human rights, including those of American citizens and noncitizens, but that he viewed the political achievement of nationhood as a necessary step toward securing individual rights for peoples around the globe. For Sumner, nationalism and human rights were tied together in his Whiggish view of progress that anticipated the world would become ever more peaceful and democratic, and human rights ever more expansive, through the establishment of more democratic nation-states modeled after the United States. Global in perspective while still nationalist in its emphasis, Sumner's commitment to both human rights *and* nationalism blurred, intersecting and reinforcing each other in some ways while conflicting with and contradicting each other in others. His efforts to reconcile American nationalism with human rights offers an unusually clear case study of the relationship between these commitments in the mid-nineteenth century.

Defining Nationhood

The link between Sumner's nationalism and his championing of human rights is neatly illustrated in a speech he composed in 1867 entitled "Are We a Nation?"[5] He wrote it at a time when the very concept of what constituted a nation was being intensely debated in Europe, with unification movements in Italy and Germany achieving success and other ethnic groups crying out for national independence. At home, secessionism was defeated and Congress had just taken control of Reconstruction, extending the protections of national citizenship to former slaves in the South. In the aftermath of the horrific war to break up the Union, Sumner sought to articulate a new philosophical foundation of national unity. On a brief speaking tour across the North in the fall of 1867, Sumner delivered this speech at least twenty-two times.[6] He sought to define what nationalism should mean for Americans at this crucial moment in American and world history. The speech updated long-held beliefs about American exceptionalism by tracing the historical connection between human rights and national unity from the colonial era to the present and suggesting the nation was moving in a historical direction toward a more complete unity among citizens and fuller enjoyment of individual rights for all.

One element that distinguished "Are We a Nation?" as a meditation on nationhood was its rejection of racial and ethnic qualifications for national belonging.[7] As the historian Dorothy Ross has noted, Sumner joined Frederick Douglass as one of the few nationalists of the time for whom national identity had nothing to do with race, ancestry, or bloodlines. Sumner was unfazed in describing the multiplicity of languages spoken or "great distinction of color we encounter daily" in the United States. He also did not promise that the diversity of citizenry would fade in time or that "unity" meant racial or ethnic "homogeneity."[8] He described nationality as a sense of self-conscious unity among a people developing over a long period of time. While it might have ancient roots, nationalism could reach its fulfillment only in the modern era under democratic forms of government. To be truly united, citizens had to enjoy equal standing with one another—a relationship that was not built on class or caste hierarchies—and share the responsibilities of representative government. Since the French and American revolutions, he wrote, a nation had come to mean a "political unity rather than a unity of blood or language." This was the modern democratic nation-state.

Sumner's definition of a nation is important to quote at length. As he put it:

> In ordinary usage, it implies an aggregation of human beings, who have reached such an advanced stage of political development that they are no longer a tribe of Nomads, like our Indians;—no longer a mere colony, city, principality or State but they are one people throbbing with a common life, occupying a common territory, rejoicing in a common history, sharing common trials, and securing to each the protection of the common power. We have heard also, that a Nation is a people with consciousness of Human Rights.[9]

He placed the achievement of nationhood as a higher stage on a continuum of political development that seemed to build toward a unity of all humanity. To be a community of citizens, not subjects, participating freely in a government by consent, all people within a nation had to enjoy and respect an equality of fundamental rights for all. Sumner most succinctly summarized his definition of a nation as "one people, under one sovereignty, vitalized and elevated by a dedication to Human Rights."[10] That was the whole of it.

While local self-government remained "the pride of our institutions" and essential to a democracy, he believed that fidelity to the nation would come to predominate over local attachments in the minds of Americans as the exertion of national power came to be associated with the protection of "liberty and equality" for all.[11] "No local claim can for a moment interfere with the Supremacy of the Nation in the maintenance of Human Rights," he proclaimed.[12] Slavery had flourished in the South, in Sumner's view, because a narrow-minded and selfish "localism" had allowed slaveholders to wield a tyrannical power over fellow citizens. "In the name of self-government, they have organized local lordships hostile to Human Rights," Sumner explained, "in the name of the States, they have sacrificed the Nation."[13] Sumner believed that the Founders had never intended to establish a federation of separate states, with multiple sovereignties; rather, they had intended to establish a single, sovereign republic. National power, therefore, was essential to progress: it was the force that would unify the nation and safeguard the principles of liberty, democracy, and human rights. It would also encourage individuals to feel a union with others beyond their local communities, to look to a national community and even beyond that, to the unity of mankind as a whole.

No political figure was more central to the political and constitutional revolutions that took place during Reconstruction than Sumner. He was the moral voice of Reconstruction, eloquently demanding the elimination of all vestiges of slavery and racial caste from civic culture. He was also a leading constitutional authority whose legal expertise greatly influenced the Republicans in Washington, DC. To better understand Sumner's influence, one should look beyond his legislative record and reexamine his contribution to the ideology of American exceptionalism that came out of the Civil War. This essay reassesses Sumner's political ideology and argues that it rested on a dual commitment—first, to advancing human rights and uplifting human conditions on a global scale; and second, to the consolidation and use of American national power to achieve his vision of global progress. The apparent contradiction of this dual commitment to global human rights and American national greatness were resolved in his mind by the exceptional nature of America's national mission.

Founding Principles and Human Rights

Speaking to his Senate colleagues in his first major speech as a senator from Massachusetts in 1852, Sumner aptly described himself as a man of conscience who was "by sentiment, education, and conviction, a friend of Human Rights in their utmost expansion."[14] Sumner had been raised to revere the nation's Founders, whom he regarded as the embodiment of enlightened political values. From his education and upbringing, he was taught that the American Revolution had global implications, advancing the cause of human liberty for all peoples; that his generation was responsible for carrying forward and expanding the work of the founders. Sumner continually looked to the previous generation for guidance and inspiration and in many ways viewed himself as revolutionary in their mold. His most radical arguments were usually couched as a return to the original principles of the Founders.

To understand Sumner's unique blend of radicalism and nationalism one must examine his earliest influences. Above all, his father, Charles Pinckney (C. P.) Sumner, instilled a distinct brand of patriotic idealism in his son. That influence remained evident even in his 1867 "Are We a Nation?" speech, which concluded with lines from his father's patriotic poetry.[15] C. P. Sumner was quite literally a child of the American Revolution. Born in 1776 as the illegitimate son of a Revolutionary War officer in Washington's army (Major Job Sumner), he grew up idolizing his mostly absent father, whom he imagined as the embodiment of Revolutionary heroism. Though his father provided sporadic financial support and may have intended to marry his mother, Major Sumner was rarely present and left C. P. facing an uncertain future when he died suddenly in 1789, at thirty-three. With help from his father's friends and family connections, C. P. Sumner managed to overcome poverty and gained admittance to Harvard, from which he graduated with honors.

One suspects C. P. Sumner felt the social stigma his less-than-respectable origins must have generated. He sympathized with the Jeffersonians and the French Revolution during his Harvard years in the 1790s, though he was surrounded by Federalists who supported Washington and Adams. As an aspiring poet, he peppered his verse with allusions to Thomas Paine and the "rights of man." His Speaking Club valedictory poem, "The Compass," predicted a future when war and slavery would cease, and equal rights would be enjoyed by all across the globe. He wrote:

> More true inspir'd, we antedate the time
> When futile war shall cease thro' every clime;
> No sanction'd slavery Afric's sons degrade,
> But equal rights shall equal earth pervade . . .
> No narrow treaty sell the boundless sea,
> Which nature's charter to the world made free;
> When all the compact, which this globe shall bind,
> Shall be the mutual good of all mankind;
> When welcome Cook's earth's union'd round shall sail,
> And view unbounded bliss thro' every land prevail.[16]

These lines anticipate the political principles that would guide his son's career: an aversion to war; opposition to slavery; a belief in equality and human rights; and a progressive understanding of history that anticipated the global perfection of human society.

Perhaps the greatest adventure of C. P. Sumner's life occurred after his graduation from Harvard, when he traveled through the West Indies in 1797–98. Swept up in revolutionary enthusiasm, he seized an opportunity to visit Port-au-Prince, which was then in the midst of the Haitian Revolution. The young man was drawn to General Toussaint Louverture's heroic struggle for national independence, which laid claim to the universal rights laid out in the French *Declaration of the Rights of Men and Citizens.* His sympathies were reinforced by the warm reception he enjoyed from town leaders, who, hailing him as a fellow revolutionary, invited him to a celebration of George Washington's birthday, where C. P. would offer a toast to "Liberty, Equality, and Happiness, to all men."[17] Charles later recalled his father's rapturous accounts of his encounter with liberated slaves in Haiti, which he cited as proof of the equality of all men. Among Senator Charles Sumner's first initiatives as chairman of the Senate Foreign Relations Committee in 1862 would be to attain diplomatic recognition of Haiti—fulfilling the long-cherished dream passed down from his father to see the Haitian Republic take its place as a respected nation among the international community.

Though C. P. Sumner's influence on his oldest son was immense, their relationship was never a close one. Notoriously formal and reserved, the older Sumner kept his family at arm's length, preferring to confide in only a few trusted male friends, some of whom Charles turned to in his place.[18] One in particular became a second father figure to Charles: Joseph Story, a classmate from Harvard, who had remained C. P.'s confidante for many years and encouraged him to pursue a legal career when his financial circumstances became dire. While C. P.'s legal career floundered, however, Story's flourished in spectacular fashion. After attaining a reputation as one of the leading constitutional theorists in the country, Story was appointed to the U.S. Supreme Court by none other than President James Madison (who underestimated the Hamiltonian nationalism lurking within Story's scholarly reverence for the U.S. Constitution).[19] Awed by his friend's success, C. P. encouraged Charles to enroll in Harvard Law School in 1831 after Justice Story became head of the school. Under the great man's mentorship, Charles aspired to become a constitutional scholar of the highest order.[20]

If Charles Sumner's unshakable commitment to human rights began with his father, it was Justice Story who taught him to secure those values to the bedrock of constitutionalism and nationalism. Story viewed the U.S. Constitution as the fulfillment of centuries of legal thought and regarded its separation and balance of governmental powers as a model of republican government for other nations to emulate.[21] Story insisted that his Harvard Law students acquire an exhaustive familiarity with other legal systems, from the ancient world to the present, as a means to appreciate the Constitution's contribution to human progress. No one embraced this vision more fully than Sumner, who credited his mentor with inventing "the science of *Comparative Jurisprudence*" that showed from a world perspective that "admidst diversity there is unity."[22] The bookish Sumner became legendary among his classmates for his mastery of continental and international law. As a consequence of his training, Sumner's speeches would later be overburdened by his compulsion to draw on this vast well of learning, with illustrative examples from throughout world history often excessively cluttering his oratory and exasperating his detractors. Nevertheless, Justice Story was so pleased with his erudition that he groomed Sumner to succeed him as Dane Professor of Law at Harvard.

To this point in his life, there was little that foretold Charles Sumner's future as the political leader of antislavery radicals. Something changed for him in the late 1830s that, perhaps, occurred during his lengthy European tour from 1837 to 1839. Sumner undertook the trip against the advice of both his father and Justice Story, the latter of whom feared that Sumner's patriotism could be undermined by European seductions. Reassuring Story of his national fidelity and high-minded purposes, Sumner spent these years completing his education at European universities and museums, where he conversed with famous scholars and statesmen, including Alexis de Tocqueville, William Wordsworth, Thomas Macaulay, and Richard Cobden. In letters home, Sumner insisted that his familiarity with Europe only confirmed his preference for American institutions, but with one glaring exception. The fierce criticism of American slavery that he encountered abroad convinced Sumner that national honor depended on speedily ridding the nation of the degrading institution. Moreover, when Sumner observed Black students at the Sorbonne being treated as equals by their fellow students without any hint of social discord, he responded (echoing his father's conclusions after observing Blacks enjoying equal citizenship in Haiti) that racial prejudice "does not exist in the nature of things." Though the historian David McCullough depicted this insight as a new revelation, Sumner had in fact long shared his father's views on slavery and racism, and his experiences in Paris only reaffirmed his views.[23]

Even after his return to the United States, Sumner did not rush to become an antislavery crusader. Though his Harvard Law classmate Wendell Phillips joined with the abolitionist William Lloyd Garrison, Sumner balked at the Garrisonian view of the Constitution as irredeemably proslavery and the American political system as utterly corrupt. Sumner found a much more palatable opponent to slavery in the celebrated Unitarian Minister William Ellery Channing, another of his father's friends and former Harvard classmates. C. P. Sumner died while Charles was abroad; upon Charles's return, Channing brought him into the Unitarian church.

Channing had cautiously moved toward immediate abolitionism, to the consterna-
tion of his many conservative followers, which had impressed Sumner as a coura-
geous act of conscience. Channing remained highly critical of the Garrisonians, but
he denounced slave ownership as a violation of Christian ethics, as well as American
political principles. With his health faltering, Channing enlisted Sumner's help to
prepare a pamphlet defending the cause of slaves who revolted on board the slave
ship *Creole*. Sumner had already published multiple articles on the case in the *Boston
Daily Advertiser,* so Channing turned to Sumner for his constitutional expertise. The
resulting pamphlet, which resembled a lawyer's brief on the constitutional status of
slavery, represented the first full expression of the "human rights" constitutionalism that would define Sumner's career hereafter.[24]

Channing's *The Duty of the Free States* (1842) broke from his cautious support for
abolition and embraced a radical antislavery constitutional position.[25] In November
1841, nineteen slaves bound for New Orleans from Virginia seized control of the
Creole by force and piloted it to Jamaica, where they were later declared free by
a British court on the basis that slavery had been prohibited on the island by the
British Parliament. An international crisis unfolded as the Tyler administration,
supported by the Massachusetts Whig Daniel Webster, sided with the American
slaveholders, who demanded compensation by the British for their lost property. In
part, *The Duty of the Free States* anticipated the "higher law" doctrine of the 1850s by
declaring that the "law of nature and of God" sided with the self-liberators because
slavery was incompatible with natural law and the law of nations.[26] Indicative of
Sumner's evolving constitutional thought, *The Duty of the Free States* also offered
an interpretation of the Constitution that reclaimed it as inherently hostile toward
slavery. The authors of the Constitution scrupulously kept the word "slavery" out
of the text because it contradicted its deeper, underlying principles. "They acted
in the spirit of reverence for human rights," the pamphlet argued. "This is eminently
the spirit of the Constitution, and by this it should be construed." In this respect,
Channing argued that slavery was merely tolerated out of necessity as a local institution in a minority of states and that neither Northerners nor the British, or any
other people outside of those states themselves, were required to recognize slaveholding rights. Even the Constitution's detested fugitive slave clause, he insisted,
recognized fugitives not as "slave property" but only as "persons held to service in
other states" and therefore ought to be construed in the most limited way possible
to avoid giving moral sanction to slavery.[27]

Another concern of *The Duty of the Free States* seemed to speak for Sumner, as
well. The pamphlet repeatedly lamented the national shame brought on Americans
by the institution of slavery, especially when traveling abroad. "Our honor as a
people is involved in the construction of the Constitution now pleaded for,"
Channing wrote. "An American, alive to his country's honor, cannot easily bear

this humiliation abroad." To counter this, he suggested that the people of the Free States "should insist that slavery shall be a state interest, not a national concern; that this brand shall not be fixed on our diplomacy, on our foreign policy; that the name of American shall not become everywhere synonymous with oppression."[28] While he wished for a general emancipation such as the British had accomplished, Channing seemed resigned that the best Americans could do in the present was keep slavery a local institution, tolerated by the nation but at odds with the greater principles enshrined in the Constitution. Otherwise, the principles of the American Revolution would lose their influence in the world. "The dishonor it has brought our country," he wrote of the federal efforts to compensate the *Creole*'s slave owners,

> throws in the way of the progress of liberal principles through the earth. The grand distinction of our revolution was, that it not only secured the independence of a single nation, but asserted the rights of mankind. It gave the spirit of freedom an impulse, which, notwithstanding the dishonor cast on the cause by the excesses of France, is still acting deeply and broadly on the civilized world.[29]

American exceptionalism itself was at stake. America alone stood as a beacon of progress, freedom, and human rights to inspire all nations, Channing implied. Slavery was undermining America's chosen place in world history.

The main arguments of Channing's *The Duty of the Free States* would become the core of Sumner's constitutional position on slavery. As the historian James Oakes has shown, Sumner, along with Salmon P. Chase, John Quincy Adams, Joshua Giddings, and a few others, developed an antislavery constitutional position that became crucial to the Republican Party's platform in the 1850s. In his first major address in the Senate in 1851, Sumner offered one of the fullest elaborations of this theory in the speech "Freedom National; Slavery Sectional," a four-hour address that exceeded seventy pages in printed form. The speech attacked the Fugitive Slave Act of 1850 as unconstitutional on the principle that "Freedom" was the "national" condition. "The Constitution must be interpreted openly, actively, and perpetually for Freedom," Sumner insisted.[30] Bolstering the arguments first advanced in *The Duty of the Free States* with historical evidence of the framers' intentions, and an extensive review of legal precedents, he made a strong case that the framers of the Constitution intended to put slavery on the road to extinction by making it a state matter but providing no federal sanction for it in the Constitution.

At the time of the Revolution, gradual emancipation laws were being introduced at the state level, while Congress had banned the extension of slavery into new territories where it had not been established in 1787. That the Founders envisioned the gradual withering and evaporation of slavery would become a central tenet of the Republican Party and the Lincoln administration. Pervading Sumner's constitutional arguments was a belief in national destiny. Sumner reached all the way

back to the famous Somerset Case of 1772, the first great victory for British abolitionists, to show that even British common law traditions, from which American
law was derived, were impossible to reconcile with slavery. The Somerset Case supposedly vindicated the British maxim that "the Air of England is too pure for a slave
to breathe" and instantly emancipated all enslaved men in Britain itself (although
not in its empire). In Sumner's view, this precedent gave further reason to believe
that slavery was a local aberration in American law, and he remarked: "With this
guiding example let us not despair. The time will come yet when the boast of our
Fathers will be made a practical veracity also, and Court or Congress, in the spirit
of this British judgment, [we] will declare that nowhere under the Constitution can
man hold property in man."[31] He perceived a continuum from British common law
through the Somerset Case, and including the founding documents and declara-
tions of the United States, in which freedom and human rights were progressively unfolding.

Channing died in 1842, only a few months after publishing *An Appeal to the Free
States,* and Justice Story died in 1845. Sumner memorialized these two powerful influences on him together in a speech he delivered in 1846 before Harvard's Phi Beta
Kappa society, a society to which they all belonged. He declared them giants of their
age, praising Justice Story for his contributions "not only in the immediate history
of his country, but to the grander history of civilization." If Story infused Sumner
with a global perspective, Channing reinforced his commitment to human rights
and social activism. Channing, he claimed, was entirely free from social prejudice:
"He confessed brotherhood with all God's children, although separated from them
by rivers, mountains and seas—although a torrid sun had left upon them an un-
changeably Ethiopian skin."[32] Finally, Sumner ascribed to Channing the brand of
American exceptionalism that would become familiar in his own writings: "He saw
in our institutions, as established in 1776, the animating idea of Human Rights, distinguishing us from other countries."[33] Having absorbed lofty ambitions from these
two mentors, Sumner now considered how to best make his mark in the advancement of civilization and further the national mission of supporting human rights.

Human Rights and National Destiny

When Charles Sumner finally emerged in the public spotlight as an idealistic
reformer, his unique brand of American exceptionalism was on full display.
Delivered for Boston's Independence Day gathering in 1845, his first major public speech, "The Grandeur of Nations," urged Americans to take leadership in the
spread of peace and democracy throughout the globe. Sumner offended many in

his audience by saying little about the Founders or the patriotic anniversary being celebrated. Rather than praise the nation for the deeds of the past, he lamented that Americans were content to indulge in "illusions of National freedom" instead of working to realize the great principles proclaimed in the Declaration of Independence. Echoing abolitionist rhetoric, this harsh criticism struck many as unpatriotic, such as when he declared it "shameful" for the present generation to base its self-esteem "not on [its] own merits, but on the fame of [its] ancestors."[34] But the sensational rhetoric distracted from his underlying nationalism. Sumner called on Americans to reject cheap patriotism that gloried in expansionism or martial power in favor of a visionary, higher nationalism that aimed at the moral elevation of all nations.

As his title "The Grandeur of Nations" implied, American national greatness—or grandeur—depended on America's moral conduct in the world community of nations. As Sumner spoke, the annexation of Texas was being finalized, and President James K. Polk's expansionist policies in the U.S. West threatened war against Mexico and Britain. Sumner denounced Polk's "ignorant and ignoble passion for new territories" as a violation of the very democratic principles on which the nation was established. He asked his embarrassed listeners: "What just man would sacrifice a single human life to bring under our rule both Texas and Oregon?"[35] Borrowing a favorite point from Justice Story's Harvard class, Sumner repudiated the "false patriotism" that demanded allegiance to "our country, *be she right or wrong.*"[36] A "selfish and exaggerated love of country" that prevented Americans from criticizing their leaders and institutions would only inhibit progress and improvement. Showcasing his training under Joseph Story, Sumner reviewed legal history from antiquity to the present, showing how the "trial of battle" (i.e., settling disputes by duels and violence) had been progressively expunged from the internal laws of civilized nations, giving way to courtrooms and rational procedures that sought to settle conflicts according to truth and justice. Progress pointed toward peace, not war, as a rational solution to international disputes. International law, he believed, would bring about the elimination of warfare in the near-future, replacing it with diplomatic arbitration and international courts of justice.

Sumner repeatedly spoke of "nations," in the plural, in his address, sometimes using the word "Humanity" interchangeably with "nations." One striking passage in the speech made clear that he saw the rights and freedoms of Americans as inseparable from those of all people. "We find that God has not placed us on this earth alone; that there are other nations, equally with us, children of his protecting care," Sumner told his fellow Bostonians. "It is not because I love country less, but Humanity more, that I plead the cause of a higher and truer patriotism."[37] Nations were artificial, created by men, and Americans must remember their obligations to be just extended beyond their borders. Sumner called it a "higher and truer" patriotism because the moral grandeur of the United States depended on its conduct toward all other nations; its part in a greater collective:

> Remember that you are men, by a more sacred bond than you are citizens; that you are children of a common Father more than you are Americans. Viewing, then, the different people on the globe, as all deriving their blood from a common source, and separated only by the accident of mountains, rivers and seas, into those distinctions around which cluster the associations of country, we must regard all the children of the earth as members of the great human family. Discord in this family is treason to God; while all war is nothing else than civil war.[38]

What was true for his own nation was equally true for all others, and in their conduct all nations were obligated to consider the welfare of humanity as a whole.

Like many antislavery leaders, Sumner considered British emancipation a moral example for the United States to follow. In "The Grandeur of Nations," he prophesized a great act, or possibly a court ruling, that would end slavery in the United States peacefully, as had occurred in Britain. Praising Britain for "that great act of Justice" that granted "freedom to eight hundred thousand slaves!" he predicted that American emancipation would be even more influential throughout the world. With three million slaves held in domestic bondage, rather than a smaller number scattered throughout an overseas empire, emancipation in America would be a far more difficult and impressive act of moral righteousness. Sumner declared:

> The day shall come, (may these eyes be gladdened by its beams) that shall witness an act of greater justice still, the peaceful emancipation of three millions of our fellow-men, guilty of a skin not colored as our own, now held in gloomy bondage, under the constitution of our country, then shall there be a victory, in comparison with which that of Bunker Hill shall be as a farthing-candle held up to the sun. That victory shall need no monument of stone. . . . It shall be one of the great land-marks of civilization.

Sumner imagined a *peaceful* emancipation as the great contribution his generation could make to American national greatness. This lofty national goal was inspired by the example of British emancipation, but he believed America was destined to outshine the British and lead the world toward emancipation and world peace.[39]

"Progress"—the belief that human history moved inevitably, though not always linearly, in the direction of moral improvement—enabled Sumner to reconcile many of the contradictions that arose between his dual commitments. One of Sumner's most direct reflections on the subject of "progress" can be found in an oration he delivered in the midst of Europe's tumultuous political revolutions of 1848. Delivered to the students of Union College, "The Law of Human

Progress" ruminated on the blood and carnage that often accompanied political revolutions. Uneasy with the direction of events in Europe, Sumner was nonetheless certain that the rise of liberty and the fall of monarchy were in harmony with human destiny. "Men everywhere [are] breaking away from the Past," he affirmed. "Thrones, where Authority seemed to sit secure, with the sanction of centuries, are shaken, and new-made constitutions come to restrain the aberrations of unlimited power."[40] Nevertheless, he cautioned that "Nature abhors violence and suddenness" and "Nature does everything slowly and by degrees."[41] Remembering perhaps the excesses of the French Revolution, he advised his youthful audience to cultivate a "just moderation" that was not "too impatient to witness the fulfillment of our aspirations." Even reformers would be wise to be "conservative of all that is good." Sumner's passion for classic education and the accumulated wisdom of ages made him recoil against the wholesale rejection of the past. To keep history moving in a progressive direction, Sumner believed, humanity had to eradicate those "earthly wrongs and abuses" that were out of harmony with the progressive improvement of humanity.[42] "Slavery" and "war" were the clearest examples of such "wrongs" that were destined for the dustbin of history, but his faith in the direction of history left Sumner equivocating on what actions were justified by those sought to accelerate the pace of progress.

In "The Law of Human Progress," Sumner acknowledged that technological breakthroughs provided the most obvious evidence of progress, but he was most inspired by the advances he perceived in the moral world. "Wherever we turn is Progress,—in science, in literature, in knowledge of the earth, in knowledge of the skies," Sumner intoned. But his list of human advancements concluded by praising the evidence of progress "in intercourse among men, in the spread of liberty, in works of beneficence, in the recognition of Human Brotherhood."[43] The best examples of moral and political progress were to be found not in the violent revolutions in Europe but, rather, in American charitable efforts in Ireland, where the Potato Famine continued to ravage the population. He also cited an international conference in Frankfurt on prison reform as a sign of a new era emerging. These undertakings signaled a new spirit of international cooperation and humanitarianism, as he explained:

> To me they are of a higher order than any discovery in science, or any success in the acquisition of knowledge, or any political prosperity, inasmuch as they are the tokens of that moral elevation, and of that Human Brotherhood, without distinction of condition, nation, or race, which it is the supreme office of all science, all knowledge, and all politics to serve.[44]

Politics, science, and even the nation itself served the larger purpose of ushering in an age of universal brotherhood and peace.

Sumner's views on progress borrowed heavily from Enlightenment thinkers, drawing on the work of Italian, French, and German philosophers. He was especially taken with the concept of "universal history," associated with Herder, Kant, and Hegel, that sought to illustrate the commonalities within human societies and chart the course of human progress. Karl Marx, drawing on the same thinkers, shared a similar confidence that human history progressed in an observable direction and believed in "universal history," but revolution and violence were essential to his understanding of historical change. Sumner shrank from the political use of violence in 1848, worried that it would not serve the cause of progress if it provoked a counterrevolution, as it had in Revolutionary France. He could afford to be evasive and cautionary about European affairs, but soon he would have to face a similar dilemma closer to home. What if the United States required the use of war to destroy the institution of slavery? Indeed, what if war was required to preserve national existence itself? If the nation was the most powerful progressive force in the world, then its survival was necessary to the advancement of humanity. When war became essential to the abolition of slavery in the United States, Sumner would be forced to make difficult decisions that challenged his allegiance to the nation and to human rights.

The concept of destiny loomed large in Sumner's imagination. In the 1870s, he published the monograph *Prophetic Voices Concerning America,* which collected quotations from philosophers and historical figures from ancient times to the present that seemed to foretell the rise of the United States as a powerful nation (or empire) that would transform world history.[45] When the Civil War broke out in 1861, it was, perhaps, his belief in the inevitability of this glorious future that allowed him to accept the role of military force in fulfilling its destiny. Republicans going back to John Quincy Adams had ventured the possibility of a presidential emancipation proclamation in the event of a slave rebellion or civil war. Yet it was Sumner who first brought to Lincoln's attention this constitutional interpretation of his war powers. As Sumner recalled, he went to Lincoln immediately after his call for troops to put down the rebellion. "I [told him I] was with him now, heart and soul," he wrote, "that under the war power the right had come to him to emancipate the slaves."[46] Lincoln's legal advisers all agreed. There is a deep irony in that Sumner's glorious vision of a national Act of Emancipation could be accomplished only through the prosecution of war and be facilitated by his own expansive constitutional interpretation of executive war powers.

Sumner considered war and slavery relics of barbarism that would progressively fade into oblivion. Temporarily overlooking the fact that European colonization had been achieved through bloodshed and tyranny, Sumner proposed that the expansion of Europe throughout the globe presaged a greater peace among nations and a universal embrace of enlightened truth. "The extending intercourse among the nations of the earth, and all the children of the Human Family," he declared, "gives new promise of the complete diffusion of Truth, penetrating the most distant places, chasing away the darkness of night, and exposing the hideous forms of Slavery, War, and Wrong, which must be hated in proportion as they are seen."[47] According to this vision, the enlightenment of the globe would lead ultimately to world peace and the eradication of human subjection and brutalization. By imagining this future as predestined and inevitable, Sumner elided thorny questions about how to bring about this result.

Reconstructing Exceptionalism

Emancipation transformed nationalism for antislavery radicals such as Sumner. In the aftermath of the war, the national government had approached the moral authority Sumner had so long desired for it. Despite the terrible price paid in lives lost and ruined, Sumner believed that the main obstacle to the realization of universal human rights within American borders had been removed. At the top of Sumner's domestic agenda for Reconstruction was to complete this revolution by extirpating all racial qualifications for citizenship in the United States. The Civil Rights Acts and the Thirteenth, Fourteenth, and Fifteenth amendments anchored individual rights in federal citizenship and asserted the power of the national government to protect those rights against infringement by states.[48]

Sumner's uncompromising advocacy for full and equal citizenship for Blacks took center stage during Reconstruction. His position on Black citizenship remained as unwavering as when he first joined in the legal challenge to school segregation in Boston in the 1840s. Sumner argued tirelessly that all citizens were entitled to enjoyment of rights and inclusion in all areas of public life on an equal basis. Not only did he include public schools in this decree, but he pushed his argument into new realms such as public theaters and streetcars. By defining access to public amusements as a human right, as the historian Amy Dru Stanley has shown, Sumner expanded the definition of "human rights" in an unprecedented way.[49] But Sumner was not only concerned with the rights of American citizens. Looking beyond American borders, he tried to establish a similar relationship between the U.S. government and noncitizens.

In 1867, Sumner set out to reform the federal naturalization laws, which had restricted to "free white persons" the possibility of naturalizing as an American citizen. Sumner opposed this restriction on the basis that it violated the human rights foundation of the republic enshrined in the Declaration of Independence and Constitution. Not only did universal human rights demand equal access to American citizenship; the nation's international prestige demanded it. Sumner argued that removing the word "white" from the naturalization laws would "do more for the character and honor and good name of this republic than any other" reform proposal.[50] But his efforts stirred little enthusiasm, and the issue remained stymied for years by the Judiciary Committee. By chance, in July 1870, a different measure caused the naturalization laws to be brought for discussion to the Senate floor, giving Sumner an opportunity to raise his long-deferred proposal.

With his remarks falling fortuitously on the Fourth of July, Sumner read from the text of the Declaration of Independence and appealed to the founding principles that kept American citizenship open to all peoples. "These are no ideas of mine," he said. "I am speaking nothing from myself; I am only speaking from the history of my country, and from the great Declaration of the Fathers. That is all."[51] The main opposition to this reform came from white Californians who purported to fear that Chinese immigrants would one day outnumber whites and undermine American sovereignty in the state. Sumner scoffed at this concern. "We are told that they are imperialists," he said of the Chinese, "but before they can be citizens they must renounce their imperialism." Naturalization required that they give up all loyalty to foreign nations, but rights and freedoms enjoyed as American citizens would themselves be too great a prize to surrender.[52] Sumner bolstered his points by finding support for them in the words of Abraham Lincoln. He quoted at length from the Lincoln-Douglas debates repudiating the assertion that American citizenship was intended for white men only. He also read four letters from African immigrants living in the American South who desired the full protection of American citizenship and the right to vote. Without these protections, they were no better off than Blacks had been in the South before the Civil War.

While Sumner expressed confidence in the ability of American society to absorb aliens, he did not promise full cultural assimilation. In response to senators who denigrated the Chinese as "Imperialists" and "Pagans," he responded by defending China's cultural heritage. "Senators who have ever looked into those books which have done so much for the Chinese mind will hesitate before they use harsh language in speaking of their belief. Has any Senator read the system of Confucius?" Sumner asked. He praised the teachings of Confucius, which contained "truths marvelously in harmony" with the teachings of Christ, and scoffed at the ignorance that compared the religion of the Chinese to paganism.[53] While Sumner made no promises that Chinese immigrants would assimilate fully to American culture, or convert to Christianity, he did reassure the Senate that they would remain a demographic minority that would have no adverse impact on the dominant culture and would "stand firm" in adherence to American principles and traditions. Underlying Sumner's confidence was his conviction that, as a force for "progress," immigrants would be more transformed by American culture than vice versa. Congress compromised on Sumner's proposal by opening naturalization to Africans but not the Chinese, which denied the promise of American citizenship to a large group of resident aliens at home and millions more abroad.

Another area in which Sumner's nationalism touched on the rights of noncitizens concerned the annexation of Alaska. In what some viewed as a shocking reversal of his anti-imperialist principles, Sumner became the strongest advocate of William Seward's purchase of Alaska from the Russians in 1867. Many expected Sumner, as chairman of the Senate Foreign Relations Committee, to block Seward's controversial scheme. Instead, he argued passionately in favor of it and ensured its passage through the Senate. In his remarkable report to the Senate, Sumner enumerated the many benefits that would come to indigenous Alaskans and suggested that peaceful territorial expansion was unlike Polk's aggressive imperialism. Indeed, he took pains to explain the difference between the acquisition of the territories from Mexico in the 1840s, in which contiguous lands that were more extensively settled by Mexicans were taken by force. Sumner emphasized the spirit of friendship between Russia and the United States and their mutual understanding of each other as "sharers of a common glory in a great act of Emancipation" recently experienced in both nations.[54] Far from an act of imperialism, he described the annexation as anti-imperialism. By the treaty, he argued, "we dismiss one more monarch from this continent. One by one they have retired; first France; then Spain; then France again; and now Russia; all giving way to that absorbing Unity which is declared in the national motto, E pluribus unum."[55] The annexation of Alaska left British Canada as the only territory still subject to a European empire in North America.

The "Guarantee Clause" of the Constitution that required the federal government to see that the states maintained Republican forms of government, which Radical Republicans had relied on to justify the Reconstruction Acts, Sumner interpreted as an imperative to advance Republican principles globally whenever possible.[56] Remarkably, Sumner cited John Adams as a harbinger of an alternative version of Manifest Destiny when he claimed, as Minister to England in 1787, that America would spread liberty to the whole Northern Hemisphere of the New World. Considering that his son John Quincy Adams was an outspoken opponent of the Mexican War, and the author of the Monroe Doctrine, this connection redefined expansionism. Sumner declared:

According to this prophetic minister [Adams] even at that early days was the destiny of the Republic manifest. It was to spread over the northern part of the American quarter of the globe; and it was to be a support to the rights of mankind. By the text of our Constitution the United States are bound to guaranty a "republican form of government" to every State in this Union; but this obligation, which is only applicable at home, is an unquestionable indication of the national aspiration everywhere. The Republic is something more than a local policy; it is a general principle, not to be forgotten at any time, especially when the opportunity is presented of bringing an immense region within its influence.[57]

In other words, the expansion of American sovereignty, far from being imperialistic, would be a triumph for Republican institutions in a global struggle against monarchy and tyranny. He continued:

> More than the extension of dominion is the extension of republican Institutions, which is a traditional aspiration. It was in this spirit that Independence was achieved. In the name of Human Rights our fathers overthrew the kingly power, whose representative was George the Third. They set themselves openly against this form of government.[58]

Not only could nationalism and human rights coexist. So could American territorial annexation and human rights.

All of this begged the question of what benefit indigenous Alaskans stood to gain by American annexation. Would they fare better under "republican institutions" than they had under Russian monarchy? In many ways, Sumner's view of the Alaskans was no different from his view of Chinese immigrants. Both of these groups might well remain distinct minorities, but they would benefit from the protection of American citizenship. Citing all of the reliable sources he consulted, Sumner reported that the Russians ruled with an iron fist, and "is too probable that the melancholy story of our own aborigines has been repeated here."[59] Moreover, slavery and war was rife among the Alaskans themselves, with many Alaskan slaveholders reputed to be "cruel taskmasters," and rumors existed of cannibalism among the remote tribes of the interior. While the population was diffuse and far from the approaching the political unity required for independent nationhood, he believed indigenous Alaskans showed potential for progress, being "quick, intelligent, and in genius, excelling in the chase and in navigation." Furthermore, "there is something in their nature which does not altogether reject the improvements of civilization. Unlike our Indians, they are willing to learn."[60]

Sumner concluded that relations between American settlers and Alaskans were likely to be more peaceful and mutually beneficial than they had been with the Russians. This self-serving optimism rings hollow considering the history of genocide that seemed to characterize American relations with indigenous peoples wherever they met. However brutally they behaved, the small numbers of Russian settlers posed less of a threat to the lives of Alaskans than the potential wave of Americans that U.S. annexation could unleash. Sumner's rosy postwar estimation of American national (and international) beneficence no doubt blinded him to this reality.

In contrast to his support for Alaskan annexation, Sumner famously opposed the annexation of Santo Domingo in 1871, sparking a controversy that ultimately led to his downfall as head of the Foreign Relations Committee and the marginalization of his role within the Republican Party. The fallout with President Ulysses Grant over his opposition to the annexation scheme had serious consequences, not only for Sumner's political influence, but for the program of Reconstruction. What led Sumner to make such a costly stand? No doubt the personal animosity of the dispute, which featured President Grant accusing Sumner of dishonesty and Sumner accusing Grant of corruption and incompetence, deepened their acrimonious split. But Sumner usually acted from fundamental principles, regardless of friend or foe. In this case, the subversion of an independent Black republic was inherently imperialistic because it reversed the "natural law" of progress. "Nationhood" was an achievement that marked the Dominicans' advanced political development along the path to civilization and democracy. Reversing that progress not only went against the law of nature; it set a terrible precedent for the United States, which he hoped would be an international moral example against imperialism and for human rights. Finally, it imperiled the independence of the Republic of Haiti next door.[61]

Throughout the ordeal of his conflict with Grant, Sumner raised the issue of Haiti to the friends and colleagues who attempted to sway him to support the president's annexation plan. In 1862, Sumner had proudly sponsored the bill that recognized the independence of Haiti, which made the United States the first major nation to open diplomatic ties with the first Black republic in the Caribbean. In 1870, Haiti sought to undermine Santo Domingo's President Buenaventura Baez, whose legitimacy Haitians rejected and whose efforts to gain American support they feared. The Haitians strongly opposed Grant's annexation plan, fearing that American military and business interests in Santo Domingo were destined to infiltrate Haiti, as well.

"You must pardon my sympathy with the Haytians which dates to my childhood," Sumner tried to explain to his friend Samuel Gridley Howe. "My father was in Hayti shortly after leaving college, & his stories of the people there are among my earliest memories." He took great offense at the harsh assessments of the Haitians and Dominicans that his Republican allies used to justify annexation. "[My father] did not describe the people as you do," he scolded Howe. "When I heard your harsh words about them—when I heard your indifference to their claims, & [Benjamin] Wade's oaths against even hearing their side, I felt there was not only a shocking violation of the first principles of justice . . . but downright inhumanity." Sumner responded that the people of the island did not desire American annexation—only a small group of corrupt leaders undertook the negotiations—and American annexation would lead to a bloody insurrection and violence. "The Haytians may be as bad as you represent them, they are entitled to justice & the true duty of our country is peace & not war," he concluded.[62]

For Sumner, Alaskans had not developed sufficiently to be ready for political independence, which is why annexation was not imperialism. Absorbing their small, diffuse population into American citizenship would serve their development better. But the Haitians (and to a much lesser extent, the Dominicans themselves) had not only achieved independence on their own; they stood as an example to other politically aspiring nonwhite peoples throughout the world. For the United States to extinguish their independence was abhorrence almost too great for Sumner to contemplate. His opposition was implacable and might have been decisive in sabotaging Grant's plan. When Sumner finally spoke at length against annexation in a speech to the Senate, he depicted it as the epitome of an imperialist power grab—a "Dance of Blood," in his words.[63] One of the points that Sumner made, according to those in attendance, was that Blacks were destined to rule the tropical zones, such as the Caribbean, while Anglo-Saxons thrived in northern climates. Reflecting the scientific theories popular at the time, and promoted particularly by Sumner's close friend Louis Agissiz, this point was used by his opponents in the press to accuse Sumner of hypocritical racism. While overblown, Sumner probably did believe that Agissiz's climate theory had some basis in scientific natural law and that America's destiny was to dominate the entire North American continent.[64] This belief, however, was overwhelmed by his passionate belief in progress and human rights, which told him that Haitians and Dominicans were entitled to their independence. Nor did it lead him to alter his advocacy of open immigration and naturalization from all regions of the globe.

Sumner's belief in human rights infused his politics, intersecting with other beliefs, such as nationalism, cultural imperialism, and even racial climate theory. Sumner's commitment to human rights ran deep, but it did not preclude competing commitments. A belief in national destiny and progress shaped his political actions just as decisively. Just how these various commitments interacted with one another is the task of historians to sort through. In his support for Alaskan annexation, Sumner's faith in American benevolence and the direction of progress led him to discount forces that might well have threatened the indigenous Alaskans with a "Dance of Blood" that would be every bit as destructive as that he warned about in regard to Haiti. Still, even after the end of slavery Sumner was not blindly patriotic or insensible to the possibility of unrighteous acts by his own government. Regarding Santo Domingo, he helped prevent the kind of imperialism that he had warned against in the 1840s. In contrast to his position on Alaska, his understanding of national political development led him to a different conclusion in the Caribbean. In both instances, he prioritized the rights of those beyond

America's borders and envisioned the nation as a mechanism to further universal human rights.

The powerful influence of American exceptionalism after the Civil War has been studied by many historians. How exceptionalism merged with a human rights discourse as a result of emancipation, however, has yet to be fully understood. The moral righteousness that guided American nationalism at least through World War I in its crusade to save democracy for the world can be traced back to anti-slavery nationalists who shaped national reunification after the Civil War. Charles Sumner was foremost among them.

Notes

1. Charles Sumner, "New Year's Day," *The Independent* (New York), January 5, 1871, reprinted in Charles Sumner, *Charles Sumner: His Complete Works, with Introduction by Hon. George Frisbie Hoar,* 20 vols. (Boston: Lee and Shepard, 1900), 18:306.
2. David Donald's two-volume biography of Sumner, published in 1960 and 1970, acknowledges his idealistic commitment to the "rights of man" but highlights his personal and political shortcomings. More positive assessments that counter many of Donald's judgments include Frederick J. Blue, *Charles Sumner and the Conscience of the North* (Arlington Heights, IL: Harlan Davidson, 1994); Anne-Marie Taylor, *Young Charles Sumner and the Legacy of the American Enlightenment, 1811–1851* (Amherst: University of Massachusetts Press, 2001).
3. Stefan-Ludwig Hoffmann, "Human Rights and History," *Past and Present,* no. 232 (August 2016): 285. Hoffmann is describing here the thesis of Samuel Moyn from Samuel Moyn, *The Last Utopia: Human Rights in History* (Cambridge, MA: Harvard University Press, 2010). For a contrasting viewpoint, see Lynn Hunt, *Inventing Human Rights: A History* (New York: W. W. Norton, 2007); Eric D. Weitz, *A World Divided: The Global Struggle for Human Rights in the Age of Nation-States* (Princeton, NJ: Princeton University Press, 2018).
4. Moyn makes this claim in Samuel Moyn, *Human Rights and the Uses of History* (London: Verso, 2014), 69–70. His most recent extension of this critique shows how social and economic rights have been particularly constrained within the nationalist framework of the welfare state: Samuel Moyn, *Not Enough: Human Rights in an Unequal World* (Cambridge, MA: Harvard University Press, 2018).
5. Charles Sumner, *Are We a Nation? The Address of Charles Sumner to the New York Young Men's Republican Union at the Cooper Institute, November 19, 1867* (New York: New York Young Men's Republican Union, 1867).
6. David Donald, *Charles Sumner and the Rights of Man* (New York: Alfred A. Knopf, 1970), 311–12.
7. Dorothy Ross, "'Are We a Nation?': The Conjuncture of Nationhood and Race in the United States, 1850–1876," *Modern Intellectual History* 2, no. 3 (2005): 327–60; Brook Thomas, *Civic Myths: A Law-and-Literature Approach to Citizenship* (Chapel Hill: University of North Carolina Press, 2007): 104–8.
8. Sumner, *Are We a Nation?* 5–6.
9. Ibid., 4.
10. Ibid., 5, 11.

11. Ibid., 32–33.

12. Ibid., 33.

13. Ibid., 32–33.

14. Charles Sumner, *Freedom National; Slavery Sectional: Speech of Hon. Charles Sumner of Massachusetts, on His Motion to Repeal the Fugitive Slave Bill, in the Senate of the United States, August 26, 1852* (Boston: Ticknor, Reed, and Fields, 1853), 9.

15. C.P. Sumner's July 4 poem "The United States, One and Indivisible!" is quoted in Edward L. Pierce, *Memoir and Letters of Charles Sumner*, vol. 1 (London: Sampson Low, Marston, Searle, and Rivington, 1878), 15.

16. Charles P. Sumner, *The Compass: A Poetical Performance at the Literary Exhibition in September, M,DCC,XCV, at Harvard University* (Boston: William Spotswood, 1795), 11–12. For details of C. P. Sumner's life, see Pierce, *Memoir and Letters of Charles Sumner*, chap. 2.

17. Quoted in Taylor, *Young Charles Sumner and the Legacy of the American Enlightenment*, 17.

18. Pierce, *Memoir and Letters of Charles Sumner*, 30.

19. Story's nationalism led him to join forces with Chief Justice John Marshall in many of the far-reaching opinions of the Marshall court on the issue of federal supremacy.

20. R. Kent Newmayer, *Supreme Court Justice Joseph Story: Statesman of the Old Republic* (Chapel Hill: University of North Carolina Press, 1985), 265.

21. Story wrote the most influential guide to American constitutional law of the antebellum era. Though the guide took a tone of clinical objectivity, Story hoped it would spread patriotism and reverence for the Constitution: Joseph Story, *Commentaries on the Constitution of the United States* (Boston: Hilliard, Gray, 1833).

22. Charles Sumner, "Tribute of Friendship: The Late Joseph Story," *Boston Daily Advertiser*, September 16, 1845, 133–48; Charles Sumner, "The Scholar, the Jurist, the Artist, the Philanthropist: An Oration before the Phi Beta Kappa Society of Harvard University, at Their Anniversary, August 27, 1846," in Sumner, *Charles Sumner*, 1:270.

23. Sumner's observation about Black students at the Sorbonne was quoted in David McCullough, *The Greater Journey: Americans in Paris* (New York: Simon and Shuster, 2011), 131.

24. On Sumner's contributions to this pamphlet, see Taylor, *Young Charles Sumner*, 142–46.

25. Edward Bartlett Rugemer, *The Problem of Emancipation: The Caribbean Roots of the American Civil War* (Baton Rouge: Louisiana State University Press, 2008), 175–76.

26. Channing, in fact, used the phrase "higher law" to explain his opposition to the fugitive slave clause as interpreted and enforced by the U.S. Congress in 1842: "A higher law than the Constitution protests against the act of Congress on this point." He defined the "higher law" as "that of nature and God": William E. Channing, *The Duty of the Free States, Second Part*, 2nd ed. (Boston: William Crosby, 1842), 10–11. In a letter to Francis Lieber written while the pamphlet was being prepared, Sumner explained that "slavery is a local institution—unknown to the common law, to the law of nature, & to the law of nations": Charles Sumner to Francis Lieber, February 10, 1842, in Beverly Wilson Palmer, *The Selected Letters of Charles Sumner*, vol. 1 (Boston: Northeastern University Press, 1990), 109.

27. Channing, *The Duty of the Free States*, 15.

28. Ibid., 21.

29. Ibid., 44.

30. Sumner, *Freedom National; Slavery Sectional*, 30. The importance of the constitutional theory advanced in this speech is examined in James Oakes, *Freedom National: The Destruction of Slavery in the United States, 1861–65* (New York: W. W. Norton, 2014).

31. Sumner, *Freedom National; Slavery Sectional*, 33–34.

32. Both quotes are from Sumner, "The Scholar, the Jurist, the Artist, the Philanthropist," 289.

33. Ibid., 268, 288.
34. Charles Sumner, *The True Grandeur of Nations: An Oration Delivered before the Authorities of the City of Boston, July 4, 1845* (Boston: J. H. Eastburn, 1845), 78.
35. Ibid., 7.
36. Ibid.; Sumner, "Tribute of Friendship," 147.
37. Sumner, *The True Grandeur of Nations,* 43.
38. Ibid., 43
39. Ibid., 7.
40. Charles Sumner, "The Law of Human Progress: Oration before the Phi Beta Kappa Society of Union College, Schenectady, July 25, 1848," in Sumner, *Charles Sumner,* 1:244.
41. Ibid., 277.
42. Ibid., 288–89.
43. Ibid., 244.
44. Ibid., 244–45.
45. Charles Sumner, *Prophetic Voices Concerning America: A Monograph* (Boston: Lee and Shepard, 1874).
46. Louis Masur addressed Sumner's instrumental role in guiding Lincoln's emancipation policy: "Ahead on Emancipation," *New York Times,* September 30, 2011. The quote is from Louis Masur, *Lincoln's Hundred Days: Emancipation and the War for the Union* (Cambridge, MA: Harvard University Press, 2012), 28.
47. Sumner, "The Law of Human Progress," 288–89.
48. Eric Foner has been among those who have argued that the constitutional amendments and associated legislation amounted to a "Second Founding" of the nation. Sumner's role in the Second Founding is too complex to address here, but suffice it to say that he advocated stronger versions of each amendment to bolster both individual rights and federal power: see Eric Foner, *The Second Founding: How the Civil War and Reconstruction Remade the Constitution* (New York: W. W. Norton, 2019): 29–30, 62–63.
49. Amy Dru Stanley, "Slave Emancipation and the Revolutionizing of Human Rights," in *The World the Civil War Made,* ed. Gregory P. Downs and Kate Masur (Chapel Hill: University of North Carolina Press, 2014): 269–303.
50. Charles Sumner, "Naturalization Laws: No Discrimination on Account of Color; Remarks in the Senate, July 2 and 4, 1870," in Sumner, *Charles Sumner,* 18:146.
51. Charles Sumner, "Naturalization without the Distinction of Color: Remarks in the Senate on a Bill to Strike Out the Word 'White' in the Naturalization Laws, July 19, 1867," in Sumner, *Charles Sumner,* 15:244; Sumner, "Naturalization Laws," 18:158–59.
52. Sumner, "Naturalization Laws," 153.
53. Ibid., 157.
54. Charles Sumner, "The Cession of Russian America to the United States: Speech in the Senate on the Ratification of the Treaty between the United States and Russia, April 9, 1867," in Sumner, *Charles Sumner,* 15:15.
55. Ibid., 13.
56. On the importance of the "Guarantee Clause" (art. 4, sec. 4) to Radical Republicans, see Joseph Fishkin and William E. Forbath, *The Anti-Oligarchy Constitution: Reconstructing the Economic Foundations of American Democracy* (Cambridge, MA: Harvard University Press, 2022), 109–37.
57. Sumner, "The Cession of Russian America to the United States," 13.
58. Ibid., 25.
59. Ibid., 22.

60. Ibid., 25.
61. Modern historiography has not portrayed Sumner generously in this controversy. See Eric T. Love, *Race over Empire: Racism and U.S. Imperialism* (Chapel Hill: University of North Carolina Press, 2004), 30–54. I thank Brook Thomas for sharing his unpublished manuscript on the Santo Domingo controversy, which corrects common misrepresentations of Sumner's position.
62. Charles Sumner to Samuel Gridley Howe, August 3, 1871 in Palmer, *Letters of Charles Sumner,* 2:565–67.
63. Charles Sumner, "Naboth's Vineyard: Speech in the Senate on the Proposed Annexation of Santo Domingo to the United States," December 21, 1870, in Sumner, *Charles Sumner,* 18:151.
64. Love, *Race over Empire,* 32.

Oliver P. Morton and the
Politics of Reconstruction

A. James Fuller

O
N JANUARY 24, 1868, INDIANA's Republican Senator Oliver P. Morton blamed the Democrats for the rebellion in a powerful speech and defined Reconstruction as a continuation of the Civil War. Paralyzed by a stroke a few years earlier, Morton sat at his desk while speaking, the crutches he needed to move leaning against his chair. But his paralysis did not hinder his oratory as he hammered away with his usual blunt force. He pitched his arguments in light of his nationalist ideology. Morton also employed what had already become his standard style in the postwar years, as he "waved the bloody shirt" to blame the Democrats for the Civil War and the problems of Reconstruction. This rhetorical style, named derisively by Democrats, rallied Northern voters to the Republican standard by reminding them of the sacrifices that had been made to save the Union and emancipate the slaves. His speech that January day catapulted Morton into the national spotlight and made him one of the leading Radical Republicans. He also stood solidly with Ulysses S. Grant, who as president relied heavily on Morton, and the senator served as one of the Stalwart Republicans who supported the administration.

When Morton finished his 1868 *Reconstruction* speech, his colleagues rushed to congratulate him, and Republican newspapers across the country praised his efforts even as the Democrats scrambled to criticize what he had said. His oration was published and widely distributed. When he heard what Morton had said, Grant told one of his aides, "That settles it. . . . That one speech, if not another word is said, insures a Republican victory in the fall." The Indiana senator emerged as a powerful figure in national politics, and he used that position to push for Radical Reconstruction even after others had given up on such policies.[1]

Historians have neglected Morton's role in Reconstruction politics. He is mostly remembered as Indiana's Civil War governor, as scholars rightly point to his reputation as an energetic and ruthless state executive who raised troops, supported

FIGURE 1. "Senator Morton, of Indiana, Receiving the Congratulations of Senators, after His Speech, in the Senate Chamber, Washington, on the 24th of January Last." (*Frank Leslie's Illustrated Newspaper,* February 15, 1868)

Lincoln, and rooted out Copperhead conspiracies, all in the name of saving the Union. Yet Morton served only six years as a governor compared with a decade spent as a U.S. senator during the postwar period. During Reconstruction he became a national leader who helped expand the power of the Republican Party. Often mentioned as a possible nominee for a cabinet post or a place on the U.S. Supreme Court, he also received consideration for diplomatic positions and became a leading contender for the presidency. Because of his personal ambition and skills at political manipulation, many scholars have cynically dismissed him as a mere partisan and an opportunist.[2]

Without denying his opportunism, a closer reading of his career reveals that Morton proved remarkably consistent and principled in his dedication to his core ideology of freedom, Union, power, and party. Although other Republicans shared this nationalist thinking, Morton held to it as strongly as anyone, and longer than most. In his mind, freedom meant an ordered liberty under the law that could be secured only within a republican form of government. That republic, he thought, existed in the form of the federal Union, a political system that represented the American nation. Like Abraham Lincoln, he thought the Union was sacred and indivisible. These two doctrines—freedom and Union, derived from the Founding Fathers—demanded protection from those who would destroy them. That required government power, which might need to be expanded to secure liberty and the nation. Such power, of course, might be subject to abuse, so Morton insisted that it had to be wielded by a political party—his Republican Party—that would use it wisely and judiciously only to defend the higher purposes for which it was intended. These four combined parts of Morton's political thinking served as the primary motivation for his political career.[3]

His ideology drove Morton during Reconstruction. Although many would see his waving the bloody shirt negatively, charging that he did so cynically and only as a partisan ploy, it can actually be seen as an extension of his principled consistency. Yes, the method of blaming the Democrats for the war and reminding voters of the cost of the conflict was a political tool. But Morton saw Reconstruction as the continuation of the rebellion. In his mind, the Democratic Party represented the rebels and the traitorous Copperheads. If they won elections, the Union victory would be squandered. A Democratic government would mean that the cause for which Morton and so many others had fought—freedom and Union—would be lost. White supremacy would overturn the fruits of emancipation. State's rights would be removed from the context of federalism, and state sovereignty would be used to threaten the nation. Democratic policies would diminish the government power needed to secure the victory and waste the great sacrifices that had been made. When Morton waved the bloody shirt, he did so in the name of his party. But this was not merely partisanship. Rather, it served as a means for winning the war, for defeating the rebellion that continued by other means after the Confederacy fell. For Morton, party *was* principle, a part of the nationalist ideology that he held dear and for which he fought throughout his career. His use of the bloody shirt as a means to fight the continuing rebellion could be seen in his leadership in the fight against the Ku Klux Klan, his support for African American politicians in the South, and his refusal to abandon Radical Reconstruction in 1876–77.[4]

Morton served as the Senate floor manager for the Fifteenth Amendment, the last of the three Reconstruction amendments and the one that protected the right to vote regardless of race. He also helped enact other legislation that aimed at securing the Union victory in the postwar era, including laws designed to aid in the government's struggle against the Ku Klux Klan, the secret organization some white Southerners created to resist Reconstruction. Morton, who had helped root out the wartime secret societies of Copperheads in Indiana who opposed the Union efforts, again turned to fighting against underground networks of traitors.

The Indiana senator worried about the terrorism used by the Klan and other such organizations to intimidate African American voters. In debates in the Senate in the spring of 1870, Morton cried out that the "Union men of the south are everywhere falling." He urged the administration and congressional leaders to do something about it: "The time for action has come. There is the smell of blood in the air. . . . When men go to bed at night apprehensive that before morning they will be aroused by the smoke of fire or be summoned to the door by the hoarse voices of the Ku-Klux, all resistance, all endurance gives way; the father trembles for his family; he will abandon his principles, he will surrender his property." Morton lamented that the government had not punished any of the criminals responsible: "No, not one . . . not for treason, not for murder, nor for all the nameless crimes committed by the rebellion." He supported continued military occupation and hoped that the army would root out the secret societies and protect white Unionists and Black Southerners.⁵

In December 1870, Morton called for the creation of a Senate committee to investigate the Klan. Senate Democrats accused him of waving the bloody shirt to whip up fear and hatred to rally voters to the waning Republican standard. They denounced his plan for an investigation as an excuse to establish martial law. They claimed that reports of violence were overblown and that the real cause of any actual incidents was Republican corruption. According to some of his opponents, the Ku Klux Klan did not really exist; it was merely a scare tactic invented by Morton and Grant to whip up fear and push Blacks to vote for the Republicans. Despite the opposition's protests, the Republican majority supported Morton, and the Senate created the committee. They found evidence of terror and violence, which they reported to the full Senate in March. This coincided with President Grant's request for a law to suppress the Night Riders, and Morton joined other Republicans in working to pass the Ku Klux Klan Act of 1871.⁶

The law, called by various titles, including the Third Enforcement Act, the Force Act, and the Civil Rights Act, required a great deal of maneuvering in Congress. In the Senate, Morton joined other Radicals in leading the fight for the new law, although some of his former allies now lined up with others to oppose him. On April 4, 1871, he gave the speech "Protection of Life at the South," in which he argued for African American rights and, once again, waved the bloody shirt against the Democrats. He scoffed at Democrats who said their party did not propose to abolish Black voting rights but wanted to experiment with it in the Southern states, to see if it was possible to do it fairly. Morton snorted that such arguments meant that the Democrats would decide it was not fair and abolish it altogether. He disagreed and charged that the whole Democratic Party was "opposed to granting negroes the right of suffrage. They opposed all constitutional amendments; they opposed the abolition of slavery; they opposed the enfranchisement of negroes at every step."⁷

Republicans had secured what civil rights Africans Americans had managed to obtain. In truth, he said, "Every right they have got, civil and political, has been given to them in spite of the stern resistance of the Democratic party." Morton predicted that if the Democrats took power, the "very first step they would take would be to deprive the colored people of the right of suffrage." He made the case again for the right of blacks to vote before turning to the subject of the Klan. He argued that the organization's oath "excludes every Federal soldier, every Republican, every negro, every member of the Grand Army of the Republic, every member of the Union League, so that no Republican, nobody but a straight-out Democrat, and I may say a secession democrat at that, can belong to that order." For Morton, the Klan was another example of how the rebels and traitors in the Democratic Party continued to fight the rebellion.[8]

He refuted the arguments that the violence in the South was the result of Republican policy and corruption. Although his opponents argued that the Night Riders attacked only to stop corruption, Morton could not find a single case where that was true. Instead, he noted, "The victims have been innocent men." To those who argued that the Klan was simply another example of vigilante justice being carried out against thieves and criminals, the Indiana senator responded by pointing out that "these outrages are committed upon men of certain politics" rather than on horse thieves or other outlaws, as Democrats contended. He also denied that the Republicans were running corrupt governments in the South. Democrats argued that the Reconstruction governments were running up public debt to line the pockets of their cronies, as well as their own. Morton argued that the debt accrued in the Southern states was the result of having to rebuild the infrastructure destroyed in the war, especially to build railroads. Far from being evidence of corruption, the state debts showed that the Republicans were rebuilding

FIGURE 2. Senator Oliver P. Morton, ca. 1870. (Library of Congress)

the South and laying the foundation for economic prosperity. He compared this to Northern states—including Indiana—that accumulated debts in the name of internal improvements. No, the Klan did not ride against corruption. It rode to spread terror to intimidate Blacks and white Unionists.[9]

Morton denounced Democrats' calls for the restoration of self-government in the South because he believed that would mean a return of the traitors who had caused the war. He argued that such arguments meant that the Democrats wanted "to restore the government to the white people, to take it from all the people and give it to part of the people." But Morton said that the Democrats had created the very situation that they wanted to reform: "Southern Democracy resisted Reconstruction, as did the Democracy of the North. They resisted it; they refused to take any part in it. It was thereby thrown into the hands of those whom they call carpet-baggers and scalawags and the colored people." Had they accepted their defeat and joined in Reconstruction, they would have had the self-government that they claimed to want. Instead, they refused to cooperate and "resisted the action of Congress by every means in their power, and the work of reconstruction was thus thrown into the hands of the men who they denounced." Morton criticized the language that Democratic politicians used, saying that their vitriolic verbal attacks on Reconstruction encouraged Klan violence. When Democratic senators said that the Reconstruction laws were unconstitutional, and therefore null and void, it created a state of anarchy within which the secret terrorist society could operate. Morton again blamed the Democrats for inciting rebellious treason. He argued that protecting "the people in their lives, liberty, and property is the highest duty of a government." Facing the widespread terror wrought by the Klan, loyal whites and Blacks were in danger. Morton said, "The colored people, because of the prejudices against their race, because they were formerly slaves and have been released against the will of their masters, and because they, too, are Republicans, have no protection for life and property."[10]

To Democrats' charges that Blacks and Unionists also committed violence, Morton admitted that such acts were justified as self-defense. But he argued that it was "clear beyond all question that the aggressions, as an organized thing, as a systematic thing, is justly chargeable to those who have been the friends of and engaged in the rebellion." To him, the Night Riders continued the rebellion, and the government needed to crush it. The Ku Klux Klan was "a confederacy, existing in a number of States, and binding them together by its secret and murderous ties." The Hoosier politician defended the Union Leagues that sometimes fought the Klan; listed at length the evidence against the secret society; and repeatedly accused the Democrats of creating, fostering, and belonging to the Ku Klux. This was not a heroic fight for freedom against military occupation and corrupt government. Instead, he argued, "The Ku Klux is the result of a general purpose, of a matured plan for the subjugation of the south by a party that is in hostility to the Government of the United States, by the party which organized and conducted the rebellion." Instead of trying to win elections, the Klan "electioneers by murder, and persuades men by the lash and destruction of their property." Morton thought that such tactics would fail in the long term and said that the Democrats could absolve themselves of their crimes by admitting their existence and uniting with the Republicans to suppress the Klan.[11]

He defended the so-called carpetbaggers and scalawags, arguing that the South needed *more* migrants from the North and native Union men. The Union soldiers and businessmen who moved to the South joined with those Southerners who gave up the rebellion to lay the foundation for a stable society and a flourishing economy. The Democrats stirred the same old fears, played to the same old racism, and continued to lead white Southerners down the wrong path. Morton cried out, "Will the people of the South never learn that for thirty years the Democratic party has been their most deadly enemy?" The Democrats had led the South to rebellion and ruin. Now they were leading them in futile resistance to Reconstruction, all so that they could win political power. If they did win power, the Southerners would lead the Democratic Party. That meant that they would overturn the hard-won Union victory. Morton believed that the "southern question will be the great issue in 1872." Economics and reform would matter, but Reconstruction remained the paramount concern of the nation. He promised that his Republican Party would "struggle for life, for the privilege of living in peace and security, while the Democratic party will struggle to regain their former power," using terrorism as their method. Morton called on good Union men to see that "everything is at stake for which we struggled and suffered through ten years of war and storm[. L]et us . . . unite again as a band of brothers, and . . . move forward resolved to conquer for the right."[12]

Throughout the rest of his career, Morton continued to fight against the forces of white supremacy and the night-riding terrorists of the Ku Klux Klan and similar organizations. He also used his position as the powerful chairman of the Committee on Privileges and Elections to help seat African American Republicans elected in the Southern states. But Morton was not always able to overcome the resistance to Black officeholders. An example of how he both championed the cause of African Americans and sometimes failed to win the fight to help Black politicians came in the case of P. B. S. Pinchback.

Morton spent a great deal of time worrying about Louisiana. There, in 1868, the Republicans had elected Henry Clay Warmouth as governor, but he hewed to a more conservative line than they expected. Using his patronage, Warmouth appointed many Democrats to office across the state and lent credence to charges of carpetbagging and corruption. Accused of cronyism and accepting bribes, Warmouth denied the charges generally, avoiding comment about any specific details. But the evidence was overwhelming that the dashing Union veteran from Illinois used his office to get rich. The Radicals took heart when Warmouth sided with the Liberal Republicans in the party divisions of 1872, and they nominated William Pitt Kellogg to oppose him. Having lost his own party's nomination, Warmouth threw his support to the Democrats, officially creating a "Fusionist" campaign uniting the Liberals and Democrats behind John McEnery. Lieutenant Governor P. B. S. Pinchback reported the intimidation of Black voters but thought that the Republicans should have a majority of thirty thousand votes. Louisiana, already infamous for its political corruption, demonstrated how to steal and steal back an election. Knowing that most African American voters were illiterate, Fusionists printed and distributed fake ballots that looked like the official Republican ticket on one side but actually listed Warmouth and the Democrats on the other. Intimidating and defrauding voters at the polls helped, but the Fusionists also packed the electoral boards with Democrats who ensured the results when it came time to count the ballots. They declared victory for McEnery and a majority of Democratic candidates for the legislature.[13]

Republicans fought back with an electoral board of their own that declared Kellogg and a Republican legislative majority the winners. The state legislature began impeachment proceedings against Warmouth. State law required him to step aside during impeachment, so Pinchback became the acting governor. But the Republicans knew that time was short, so they asked the federal government for help. The attorney-general ordered the U.S. marshal for the area to support the federal courts and promised that the administration would send as many troops as were needed to enforce the laws. The Republicans then had a federal judge order the marshal to seize the Louisiana Statehouse and admit only those legislators certified by the pro-Kellogg board. Soon, the state had two legislatures meeting—one dominated by Fusionist/Democrats, and the other led by Republicans. With competing governors and legislatures, violence followed the political chaos. On Easter Sunday of 1873, a force of Black militia faced off against a white posse in Colfax Township in Grant Parish. The African American troops, finding themselves outnumbered and outgunned, took up a defensive position in the courthouse. The white attackers set the building on fire and shot the defenders as they tried to escape. In the end, the Colfax Massacre resulted in one hundred and fifty dead Black men, including sixty-nine buried in a mass grave.

Amid the chaos, President Grant thought about calling for new elections, but his cabinet pressured him not to do it. The federal intervention in the election outraged the Democrats, of course, but it also upset many Republicans. Meddling in elections and setting up puppet governments with armed troops was hardly the way to achieve a successful Reconstruction accepted by everyone.[14]

Morton argued that the federal government should not interfere in Louisiana, saying that, had the Democrats not stolen the election, Kellogg would have won anyway. The Indiana senator called for "masterly inactivity" rather than intervention in Louisiana. Despite the violence that followed, Morton remained steadfast in his position. And the Kellogg government persisted. Because the issue split the Republican leadership, Morton soon became the undisputed leader of the Radical Stalwarts who supported the Grant administration. He helped forge economic policy and advised the president on foreign affairs. His friendship with Grant and influence in the party meant that rumors swirled about his taking a cabinet seat or a diplomatic post, while some talked about Morton running for president or accepting an appointment to the Supreme Court. His consistent ideological commitment to freedom, Union, power, and party combined with his skills as a speaker and political operator to make him a formidable force in the Republican Party. In shaping Reconstruction policy, he repeatedly used his power as an advocate for the rights of African Americans, and Louisiana soon presented another opportunity for him to do so.[15]

The Kellogg government elected Pinchback to the U.S. Senate. The man who had been the first African American elected as a lieutenant-governor sat in the governor's chair for a few weeks after Warmouth was forced out, making him the first Black governor of a state. Elected to Congress in the disputed 1872 contest, Pinchback became the first African American member of the House of Representative elected in Louisiana history. But he wanted the Senate seat left vacant when Kellogg resigned to become governor. Charges of corruption followed Pinchback, and he admitted to using his office for personal gain. While serving on the New Orleans Park Commission, he arranged for the city to buy property that he owned and pay far more than it was worth. Despite this scandal, the pro-Kellogg Republican legislature elected him to the Senate early in 1873. But the competing pro-McEnery Fusionist/Democrat legislature elected the Republican and Union veteran William L. McMillen, and the seating of the next senator became a political issue.[16]

Unsurprisingly, Morton supported Pinchback. When others called for a new election, he argued against it, saying that African Americans needed one of their own to represent them and to protect them. New Orleans businessmen needed stability and order. Only the murderous members of the White League (as commentators called the Klan-like organization in Louisiana) wanted the continuing turmoil. The seating of a new senator was delayed throughout 1873 but came back to the floor in 1874. When it did, Morton delivered the speech "Louisiana Affairs," in which he defended the rights of African Americans in general and Pinchback in particular. But he also repeated his argument that Reconstruction was a continuation of the war. He recounted the history of the election of 1872 in Louisiana, calling the movement to put McEnery in office a fraud.[17]

FIGURE 3. P. B. S. Pinchback. (Library of Congress)

Morton said that the Bayou State was now "covered with blood" because of the Louisiana Democrats, whom he called "the assassins of 1866, 1868, and of 1873." He reminded his listeners about how more than three hundred Blacks were killed or wounded in a New Orleans riot in 1866. In 1868, White League—Morton called it the Ku Klux Klan—members inflicted more than two thousand African American casualties in the two months leading up to the presidential election. And they often did so under the authority of local government. Morton remembered that "Louisiana was a vast slaughter-house; blood was shed in every parish and almost upon every plantation." But not a single person came to trial or received punishment for the crimes.[18]

Then came the nightmarish Colfax Massacre in 1873, in which the white posse trapped Black militiamen in a building. The senator vividly described how the white attackers burned out their victims, detailing how "when the flames had spread throughout the building the colored men in the court-house held out white handkerchiefs" to surrender. But when they came out, some of them on fire, "they were met at the door and murdered, and stabbed, and mutilated." Morton described the gory scene, reading from the grand jury report about how "three or four men would seize a colored man and another man put his pistol in his mouth and blow his brains out; and that they were mutilated and their abdomens ripped open after they were dead." The posse captured some of the Black soldiers and took them to the river. There, they experimented in killing the African Americans, as they "put them breast to back, three or four or five each, and then a man would stand at the end of the line to see through how many bodies he could send a bullet with his rifle." Recounting the awful massacre, Morton argued, "The life of a colored man in Louisiana is considered of no more account than that of a mad dog; and . . . not one of the murderers has been punished."[19]

The senator lamented that, in the context of Louisiana during Reconstruction, murder had become commonplace. Faced with ongoing violence, what could the national government do? Morton worried that a new election would result in additional massacres. He argued strongly for seating Pinchback, appealing to questions of legality and process, as well as to right and wrong. He did not want Congress to step into Louisiana's affairs, and he warned President Grant not to intervene. The Grant administration had certified the Kellogg government, and that meant the Republicans controlled the state. There had not been an insurrection, so the national government could not interfere with Louisiana. He waved the bloody shirt again, blaming the Democrats for the violent situation. Those who had caused the war still refused to accept defeat and resisted Reconstruction. It was time to defeat the rebels and murderers, the Democrats and the Klan, by seating Pinchback. If the Senate did not do that, it would be giving ground to the enemy.[20]

The Democrats continued to contest Pinchback's claim to his seat. Morton refused to give up, pushing for the African American Republican to be seated for the next two years. But despite his efforts, he failed to seat Pinchback. The Republicans were appalled at the boldness with which the Redeemers returned to power and openly rejected the policies of the previous decade. But the party was divided, and few Radicals remained to support the Indiana senator. Thus, the weight of Morton's influence was not enough, and Pinchback never served in the Senate. Constant delays dragged the issue out for years, until the Democrats took control of Congress. They voted to pay Pinchback thousands of dollars in back salary and travel expenses, but they would not let him join the Senate. Instead, the seat remained vacant until the term expired, and a white Democrat won the seat following the end of Reconstruction. The case proved to be a foreshadowing. As other Radical Republicans lost elections, died, or gave up on Reconstruction, Morton increasingly found himself standing alone.[21]

The Hoosier senator did not waver despite the political winds shifting against him. Instead, he forged ahead, even as the so-called Redeemers returned to power across the South. Morton argued that the government needed to continue the military occupation of the former Confederacy and return troops to those states

FIGURE 4. Oliver P. Morton, 1876. (Library of Congress)

from which they had been withdrawn if the rights of African Americans were not protected. This was unrealistic, given that Democrats in Congress had cut funding for the army, virtually guaranteeing that the occupation would end. But Morton knew that the political trends might turn back in his favor. His answer to the weakening public support for Reconstruction that threatened freedom and Union was to turn to power and party. As always, Morton relied on the Republican Party to wield the power of government to save the nation and protect freedom. With the election of 1876 approaching, he decided to seek the presidency. If he could win the White House and help his party secure a majority in Congress, he would be able to revive Radical Reconstruction and salvage the cause for which he had fought so long.

Throughout 1875, the Hoosier senator ranked in the top tier of candidates for the party's nomination. But clear obstacles stood in his path. Many worried about his health, and while Morton enjoyed widespread support among Southern Blacks, Indiana seemed to be the only Northern state firmly committed to him. Other candidates in the crowded field included his fellow senators Matthew Carpenter of Michigan, Simon Cameron of Pennsylvania, James G. Blaine of Maine, and Roscoe Conkling of New York, as well as Secretary of State Hamilton Fish of New York, Secretary of the Treasury Benjamin Bristow of Kentucky, Postmaster

General Marshall Jewell of Connecticut, Minister to France Elihu Washburne of Illinois, and governors such as John Hartranft of Pennsylvania and Rutherford B. Hayes of Ohio. The top tier seemed to be Morton, Conkling, and Blaine, with most of the others strong only in their home states. Some, including Morton's good friend Hayes, were dark-horse candidates who might be nominated as a compromise if the favorites failed to win.[22]

At the national convention in Cincinnati, things did not go well for Morton. The Indiana delegation at the national gathering put forward his name, as expected, but during the balloting, Morton began to lose support, and his supporters quickly realized that they could not secure the nomination. They soon joined others in looking at Hayes as a compromise candidate. Acceptable to all, the Ohio governor had offended almost no one. His political savvy combined with his victory in the 1875 gubernatorial race in Ohio to make him a dark horse in the race. Following

FIGURE 5. "Republican Candidates in Training for the Presidential Race." (*Frank Leslie's Illustrated Newspaper*, July 24, 1875)

the blueprint used by the Lincoln campaign in 1860, the Buckeye Republican became the compromise candidate and, when the front-runners faltered, their supporters turned to Hayes.[23]

Disappointed, Morton threw himself into the campaign for president on behalf of the Republicans, especially Hayes and his vice-presidential running mate, William A. Wheeler of New York. The Democrats nominated New York Governor Samuel J. Tilden and an old enemy of Morton's from Indiana, Senator Thomas A. Hendricks. As if his party loyalty was not enough, Morton was now motivated by the fact that the hated Hendricks was running for vice-president.

In a July speech on internal improvements, Morton waved the bloody shirt and attacked the Tilden-Hendricks ticket. The Democrats, Morton said, were "continually evil" and had the "most damnable record in the history of parties in this or any other country." As always, he blamed his opponents for all of the problems the nation faced. The Democrats were responsible for the increased cost of government and for higher taxes. When a Democratic colleague interrupted him to ask whether or not the party ought to reform the many abuses in government, Morton said that whatever problems there were stemmed from the war. He argued that the Democrats tried to blame others for the problems they had caused. They had started the Civil War, but they tried to say that it was the Republicans who were at fault. Whatever the Republicans did, the Democrats resisted it and then blamed their enemies for the problems caused by their resistance. He pointed to Reconstruction, where his party had tried "to protect the colored people of the South and the white republicans from the numerous slaughters that have fallen upon them," but the Democrats screamed in protest, arguing that such measures were the use of force and a violation of rights, liberties, and the spirit of democracy.

The Republicans pointed to South Carolina, where, just days earlier, a mob of more than a hundred white men had attacked about thirty Black militiamen in an event known as the Hamburg Massacre as part of a plan to disrupt Republican campaign activities. At least six Black soldiers and one white man were killed, and many others were wounded. With white Southerners still using violence and terror to intimidate voters, it was easy to wave the bloody shirt at the Democrats. Morton made the most of it, saying that the Democrats had only two arguments: "The argument has been in the South, violence, intimidation; and the argument in the North is the cry of reform and corruption. The first argument is the shotgun, the revolver, the bowie knife, and it is sharp and murderous; and the second argument is false and hypocritical."[24]

He attacked the Democrats throughout the 1876 campaign. In Indianapolis on August 11, Morton saw, in the Democratic Party of 1876, "assembled the mourners for slavery, the organizers of rebellion, the Ku-Klux and White Liners, the Northern sympathizers and dough-faces, the advocates of state sovereignty, and the representatives of every element that had torn the country with civil war, drenched it with blood, and watered it with the tears of widows and orphans." In another speech, Morton called Tilden and Hendricks "The Confederate Democracy," saying, "I use that name purposely and understandingly," because the Democrats still stood for rebellion. He concluded that the 1876 election was "a struggle between the blue and the gray: between the loyal and the disloyal. . . . They say we wave the bloody shirt; that we keep talking about the war. They would have us forget about the war, but they do not forget about it. Everything, in the South, turns on the war." Only rebels could get elected by the Democrats of the South, which, the senator insisted, was evidence that the war remained the central issue. Even though many Northerners and some in his party wanted to end Reconstruction, Morton refused to give up because he thought the rebellion was still going on.[25]

The senator remained loyal to his party. He liked Hayes and thought that the Buckeye governor would continue Reconstruction while leading the nation forward into economic prosperity. Furthermore, Morton truly believed that the situation was dangerous. If the Democrats won, it would be the end of Reconstruction, and the rebels would return to power. This would destroy what the Radicals had accomplished. African Americans were in jeopardy; their rights and liberties were at risk. The Democrats would encourage the rebels, and the South would try to rise again. It might well result in another civil war. Freedom and Union were again in the balance. As always, Morton believed that only the power of the national government, wielded by his Republican Party, could save the country. Waving the bloody shirt was by now a well-worn tactic, but Morton thought it absolutely necessary as he continued the fight, confident that his methods would again prove effective in bringing out the voters to save the republic from the looming threat of rebellion.

The election attracted the highest turnout in the history of the country, with 81 percent of eligible voters casting ballots. Despite Morton's efforts, the Democrats carried Indiana in both the state elections in October and the presidential contest in November by more than five thousand votes. Nationally, Tilden won by more than a quarter-million votes, and Democrats celebrated their victory. When the Electoral College totals came in, however, Tilden had 184 votes, while Hayes had 165, and twenty votes were disputed. Because 185 electoral votes were needed to win, Tilden was one vote short. Although one Oregon vote was in question, the rest of the disputed votes came in three Southern states: Florida, which had four electoral votes; Louisiana, which had eight; and South Carolina, which had seven. In all three states, it appeared that Tilden and Hendricks had won the popular vote. But the Republicans cried fraud and pointed to deceptive ballots used by the Democrats to trick illiterate voters. The Democrats listed their candidates on a ballot printed with the Republican symbol, including a picture of Abraham Lincoln. Voters unable to read the names of the candidates dutifully cast their ballots for the Democrats while thinking that they had voted for the party of Lincoln. Violence also influenced the results, as terrorists intimidated voters in the disputed states. Both parties claimed to have won all three states, and each declared its candidate the winner. If Hayes received all twenty of the outstanding electoral votes, he would win the election by one vote. With the presidency in the balance, congressional leaders began to argue about how to resolve the dispute.[26]

Morton sincerely believed that Hayes had won the election. The Democrats had stolen it by using violence and voter intimidation. White thugs had intimidated Black voters and in some areas had committed murder to prevent Hayes from winning. For Morton, this was more of the same old story: the rebels refused to accept their defeat and were continuing the Civil War by others means. Already restored to power in most of the South, they had stolen the presidential election to ensure that Reconstruction ended in the last three states where Republicans still held the upper hand.[27]

Of course, the Democrats thought that Tilden had won and wanted to ensure that he did. The turmoil continued, with dual legislatures submitting their returns while Republican-appointed electoral boards presented different results. Some congressional leaders began trying to forge a compromise, and eventually they settled on appointing a fifteen-man commission made up of five senators, five representatives, and five associate justices of the Supreme Court. Morton opposed the plan, insisting that Hayes had won the election and that all of this talk about compromise was just another step toward allowing the rebel Democrats to steal the presidency and end Reconstruction.[28]

Despite his opposition to it—or, perhaps, because of it—Morton was chosen as one of the members of the commission. During its work, the members advocated for their party rather than trying to achieve some sort of actual compromise. This meant the debates were partisan (with the judges joining the party of the presidents who had appointed them). The Republicans supported Hayes, and the Democrats fought for Tilden. The partisan debates brought about a partisan result: the commission voted to award all twenty disputed electoral votes to Hayes, with the eight Republican members carrying the decision over the seven Democrats.[29]

Despite Democratic grumbling and threats about impeaching Grant and possibly taking up arms against Hayes, a group of Southern Democrats soon joined some Republicans in forging what became known as the Compromise of 1877. Rumor held that railroad tycoons such as Jay Gould and Tom Scott wanted to resolve the issue to let them build more tracks across the South, adding to their empires. The negotiations took place between a group of Southern Democrats and Northern Republicans that included a number of newspapermen, as well as congressmen and senators. This would mean that Hayes would have to agree to redemption, removing the last occupying troops from the South and allowing white Southern Democrats to take power over the Black (and the few white) Southern Republicans. The negotiators for the Southern Democrats also wanted one of their own in the Cabinet. The deal would include the president endorsing economic development in the South, including the building of new railroads. Although Hayes avoided making specific promises, the agreement was made, and the Compromise of 1877 was accomplished.[30]

But the Republicans who made the deal worried about the reaction of Morton and the other remaining Radicals. The Indiana senator was an old friend and ally of the new president, and this meant that he remained politically powerful. Morton could not simply be ignored if the party hoped for any kind of unity moving forward. If he or another prominent Radical chose to fight the deal, the whole process might be derailed. Hayes needed to keep Morton on his side to keep the party united at least through the inauguration. To do that, he needed to give Morton and other Radical Republicans political cover. So on February 26, 1877, a group of Ohio Republicans, including future President James Garfield, met with white Southern Democrats at the Wormley House hotel in Washington. At the Wormley Conference, the Democrats pledged to uphold Black rights in exchange for the end of Reconstruction. How many Southerners were swayed by the negotiations remained unclear, but at least a few of them joined Northern Democrats in supporting the Compromise of 1877.[31]

Morton suffered a stroke that summer and did not recover from it. He died on November 1, 1877, his passing a fitting metaphor for the end of the era of Reconstruction. Throughout the decade he served in the U.S. Senate, Morton fought for the Radical policies that planned to rebuild the South and the country in ways that would fulfill the promise of the Founding Fathers. Motivated by his ideology of freedom, Union, power, and party, he hoped to help his Republican Party use the power of government to make the United States a more egalitarian society that truly realized ordered liberty and national unity. He waved the bloody shirt against the Democrats to remind voters that his political opponents continued to fight the rebellion. Only by supporting the Republicans could the American people secure the Union victory and emancipation. Even as other Radical Republicans died, lost elections, or gave up on Reconstruction, the Indiana senator kept up the fight. In the end, he lost the battle and died before he could renew it. Too long forgotten or overlooked, Morton's role illustrated how Reconstruction was a continuation of the Civil War.

Notes

1. Oliver P. Morton, *Reconstruction: Speech of Hon. O. P. Morton, in the U.S. Senate, January 24, 1868, on the Constitutionality of the Reconstruction Acts* (Washington, DC: Chronicle, 1868). For examples of Republican newspapers praising or reprinting the speech, see *Wheeling Daily Intelligencer,* February 6, 1868; *Belmont Chronicle* (St. Clairsville, OH), February 6, 1868; *Gallipolis Journal,* February 13, 1868. For Ulysses S. Grant remarking on the speech, see *Leavenworth Times,* May 16, 1876. For a full account of Morton's life and career, including his work as a senator during Reconstruction, see A. James Fuller, *Oliver P. Morton and the Politics of the Civil War and Reconstruction,* Civil War in the North (Kent, OH: Kent State University Press, 2017).

2. For an example of historians who neglect Morton in their studies of Reconstruction, see Eric Foner, *Reconstruction: America's Unfinished Revolution, 1863–1877* (New York: Harper and Row, 1988). For a recent study that gives Morton at least some of the attention he deserves, see Mark Wahlgren Summers, *The Ordeal of the Reunion: A New History of Reconstruction* (Chapel Hill: University of North Carolina Press, 2014).

3. I draw this interpretation of Morton's ideology mostly from Michael S. Green, *Freedom, Union, and Power: Lincoln and His Party during the Civil War* (New York: Fordham University Press, 2004). I have added the concept of party, which was first suggested (albeit in a cynical and critical way) in Leslie Hamilton Schultz, "Oliver P. Morton and Reconstruction, 1867–1877" (master's thesis, University of Chicago, 1935). Green argues that this nationalist ideology continued during the Reconstruction years: see Michael S. Green, "Reconstructing the Nation, Reconstructing the Party: Postwar Republicans and the Evolution of a Party," in *The Great Task Remaining before Us: Reconstruction as America's Continuing Civil War,* ed. Paul A. Cimbala and Randall M. Miller (New York: Fordham University Press, 2010), 183–203.

4. For essays that argue that Reconstruction should be interpreted as a continuation of the war, see Cimbala and Miller, *The Great Task Remaining before Us.*

5. Morton made his remarks on April 17, 1870: see *Congressional Globe,* 41st Congress, 2ndSession, April 17, 1870, appendix, 274–80. For more on the Ku Klux Klan during Reconstruction, see Allen W. Trelease, *White Terror: The Ku Klux Klan Conspiracy and Southern Reconstruction* (Baton Rouge: Louisiana State University Press, 1971). Another insightful study of the use of terror to resist Reconstruction is George C. Rable, *But There Was No Peace: The Role of Violence in the Politics of Reconstruction* (Athens: University of Georgia Press, 1984). A book that puts the Klan violence of the 1870s into the larger context of the politics of Black voting rights is Xi Wang, *The Trial of Democracy: Black Suffrage and Northern Republicans, 1860–1910* (Athens: University of Georgia Press, 1996).

6. Foner, *Reconstruction,* 454–59; Summers, *The Ordeal of the Reunion,* 267–71.

7. Oliver P. Morton, *Protection of Life, Etc., at the South: Speech of Hon. Oliver P. Morton of Indiana, Delivered in the Senate of the United States, April 4, 1871* (Washington, DC: Rives and Bailey, 1871), 3–4.

8. Ibid.

9. Ibid., 5–8.

10. Ibid., 8–11.

11. Ibid., 11–15.

12. Ibid., 15–16.

13. On Warmouth and the disputed 1872 election, see Summers, *The Ordeal of the Reunion,* 284–85, 330–32.

14. Ibid., 330–32.

15. William Dudley Foulke, *Life of Oliver P. Morton, Including His Important Speeches*, 2 vols. (Indianapolis: Bowen-Merrill, 1899), 2:275–84.

16. For Pinchback's corruption, see Foner, *Reconstruction*, 388. For the disputed Senate seat and Pinchback's life, see James Haskins, *Pinckney Benton Stewart Pinchback* (New York: Macmillan, 1983).

17. Foulke, *Life of Oliver P. Morton*, 2:284–85; Oliver P. Morton, *Louisiana Affairs: Speech of Hon. Oliver P. Morton, of Indiana, in the United States Senate, January 30 and February 2, 1874* (Washington, DC: Chronicle, 1874), 1.

18. Ibid., 2.

19. Ibid.

20. Ibid., 3–16.

21. *Congressional Record*, 45th Cong., 1st sess. (1877), 13–15.

22. For an example of newspapers relating Morton's African American support, see *Chicago Times*, March 20, 1876. There are numerous accounts of the 1876 election, including several published in the wake of the disputed election of 2000, which had many parallels to the nineteenth-century contest. The traditional view holds that the Republicans stole the election and used it to promote the interests of Northern capitalists in the South. The most reliable recent study that challenges the traditional interpretation is Michael F. Holt, *By One Vote: The Disputed Presidential Election of 1876* (Lawrence: University Press of Kansas, 2008). Summers, *The Ordeal of the Reunion*, 372–93, and Foner, *Reconstruction*, 564–87, also provide useful insights. For a recent book that repeats the traditional account of how the Republicans stole the election and mostly ignores the violence and fraud used by Democratic Redeemers, see Roy Morris Jr., *Fraud of the Century: Rutherford B. Hayes, Samuel Tilden, and the Stolen Election of 1876* (New York: Simon and Schuster, 2003).

23. For Hayes becoming the compromise candidate, see Holt, *By One Vote*, 54–66.

24. Oliver P. Morton, John Sherman, and George S. Boutwell, *River and Harbor Bill and the Deadlock: Speeches of Senators Morton, Sherman, and Boutwell, July 18, 19, and 22, 1876* (Washington, DC: Government Printing Office, 1876), 2–4.

25. Oliver P. Morton, "Tilden and Hendricks as Slanderers of Our Good Name," *Cincinnati Gazette*, August 11, 1876; Oliver P. Morton, "The History of Indiana Democracy Ventilated," August 1876, newspaper clipping in Oliver P. Morton Papers, Indiana State Library, Indianapolis.

26. Holt, *By One Vote*, 175–203.

27. For accounts of electoral violence, see ibid., 182, 200.

28. Ibid., 210–13.

29. The report of the Electoral Commission, including Morton's opinions, are in ibid., 184–218. See also Foulke, *Life of Oliver P. Morton*, 2:461–77.

30. Holt, *By One Vote*, 236–40.

31. Ibid., 240–43; Summers, *The Ordeal of the Reunion*, 384. Historians continue to debate whether there really was a Compromise of 1877. C. Vann Woodward famously argued for a compromise in *Reunion and Reaction: The Compromise of 1877 and the End of Reconstruction* (Boston: Little, Brown, 1951). For an opposing view, see Allan Peskin, "Was There a Compromise of 1877?" *Journal of American History* 60 (June 1973): 63–75. For more on the turn away from Reconstruction, see William Gillette, *Retreat from Reconstruction, 1869–1879* (Baton Rouge: Louisiana State University Press, 1979). I thank Mark Summers for sharing his interpretation of the Wormley Conference. See the testimony of E. A. Burke in H.R. Misc. Doc. 31, "Presidential Election Investigation," 45th Cong., 3rd sess., vol. 3: Testimony Relating to Louisiana (Washington, DC: Government Printing Office, 1879).

Building a New Political Order

RECONSTRUCTION, CAPITALISM, AND THE CONTEST OVER THE AMERICAN STATE

Nicolas Barreyre

RECONSTRUCTION SEEMS RIPE FOR reinterpretation. New syntheses have started to emerge again.[1] Historiographical surveys report a vibrant field, both deepening old questions (the use of violence, the transformations of racial relations after abolition, the changes in the lives and the activism of African Americans) and exploring newer issues (the multifaceted role of women, the mutation of gender relations across racial and social groups, the transnational dimensions of post-emancipation politics). Recent scholarship has also taken the history of Reconstruction into previously under-surveyed quarters. Historians of the U.S. West explore the transformations in territorial appropriations and Native American expropriations in the wake of the consolidation of the federal state in what some term the "Greater Reconstruction." Others have broadened the chronological scope and explored changes in ideology, liberalism, or culture that were rooted in the legacy of the Civil War and the path taken during Reconstruction. More locally, new work has also focused on fine-grained descriptions of social relations and the degrees of coercion they could convey in newfound varieties of freedom and unfreedom (a new word) that complicate the older binary between slavery and liberty.[2]

These multidirectional creative endeavors have deepened our knowledge and understanding of American society after the Civil War. But they have also blurred the meaning of "Reconstruction," as its scope has widened increasingly from the previously narrow bounds of the Southern states. So, does Reconstruction stand for the whole postbellum period, made to shoulder the responsibility of accounting for every development in those years lest it be accused of hiding vast swaths of the historical reality? Is it more of a metaphor to designate the large transformations happening in American society after the war, which would account for the large variety of chronological spans now attached to the word? The very richness of the scholarship gave it so many hues that the plural is sometimes in order—Reconstructions—when the word itself is not entirely pushed aside, too polymorphic to be of use anymore.[3]

This essay suggests that more attention to political economy can provide a way to rebuild a definition of "Reconstruction" that can make sense of what contemporaries understood by it, and strove to achieve, while keeping the expansive scope that historiography has given it. The idea is to recover the centrality of Reconstruction as a process, the importance it reached during the period, while making it robust enough that it does not have to account for every single historical development. To do this, it seems that recent debates put forward by the "new history of capitalism" provide useful tools. So far, this particular upswing in historians' interest in political economy appears to have avoided Reconstruction. Indeed, it seems that the history of the South after the Civil War has mostly been disconnected from the story of the spectacular rise of American capitalism (too often told as a Northern story). Now, this essay argues, some of the issues raised by the new historiography provide ways to understand Reconstruction as part of the building of a new political order intimately tied to political economy.

Two points, especially, can be repurposed for this effort. One comes directly from the debates that arose on the issue of slavery and capitalism. The purpose here is not to take sides in the disputes that rage around the contention that slavery was central to U.S. capitalism before the Civil War. This debate is ongoing and not yet satisfactorily answered, mostly because historians and economic historians talk past each other about what the word "capitalism" means, or meant for that period. The discussion has proved fruitful in one insight, however: in the American context, at least, the workings of racial relations and hierarchization were intimately linked to the evolution of the political economy of the country—whether "racial capitalism" as a separate concept ends up being useful to characterize this.[4] The challenge is this: if slavery was central to antebellum capitalism, what happened to capitalism with emancipation? Was the South marginalized, as older takes on U.S. economic history suggested? Or did the revamping of rights and institutions during Reconstruction have an impact on the trajectory of American economic development?

A second trend in the "new history of capitalism" is the growing attention to the financial side of capitalism, in contrast to older emphasis on industrialization, labor relations, and incorporation.[5] With such a focus, what is soon striking is the importance the U.S. government took on in financial matters during the Civil War, a legacy that gave it a prime place in the reshaping of the American economy just as it was undertaking the refashioning of Southern polities. So if we follow the money trail, does it change our understanding of Reconstruction? Does it connect this rebuilding of a political order to the economic order that led the United States on the path to its "Gilded Age," with its extraordinary growth and industrialization, as well as its rising inequalities, accelerating proletarianization, and consumer culture built on social and racial hierarchies and segregation?

Of course, historians have already explored economic dimensions of Reconstruction. A century ago, Progressive historians linked the rise of capitalism and the history of Reconstruction in ways that, if they do not convince us anymore, still yield strong insights.[6] Economic historians have also studied the transformations and dynamics of the economy of the South after the war, especially the emergence of sharecropping and the place of the "New South" in the national economy.[7] This long tradition is insightful and, indeed, should not be pushed out of view.

What this essay defends, however, is different. It argues that attention to political economy—that is, the reshaping of capitalism through the political process—could help us redefine Reconstruction in a focused yet expansive way as the building of a new political order after the collapse, in the Civil War, of the older one. By recovering the state both as a key actor of Reconstruction and as a prime shaper of the economy—as a nexus, therefore—it becomes possible to revisit and intertwine the history of Reconstruction and the concomitant history of U.S. capitalism in a manner that does not depend on any sense of teleology or implacable grand forces. Instead, it insists on choices, contingency, and the political *process*. Confronting both historiographies allows us to rethink the history of Reconstruction as the contest around who could shape and enforce policies and who has a claim on government. In this sense, both the conflicting goals of Reconstruction and the competing visions of the American economy converged, and sometimes clashed, in the newly empowered federal government.

Four years of Civil War had killed and maimed hundreds of thousands, destroyed whole swaths of territory, and ruined the economy of the South. They had also freed four million enslaved people, legally abolished slavery, and left open the future of the United States. The financial consequences were momentous, too: the canceled debt of the Confederacy and the collapse of its currency destroyed even more Southern wealth; the Union had accrued an unprecedented interest-bearing debt of $2.3 billion while issuing paper money that was not convertible into gold or silver; a new national banking system under federal supervision redirected flows of capital across the country; and wide-ranging taxation coupled with a protective tariff both filled the Treasury coffers and reshaped the economy. All of these measures had huge consequences, but since they were aimed at prosecuting the war, and many were dismantled after the conflict, the historiography has tended to see them as a parenthesis, a temporary situation disconnected from Reconstruction—and thus studied separately.[8]

Most contemporaries did not view those financial issues as part of what they called "Reconstruction." Electoral propaganda, for instance, distinguished between the two. Yet they did understand that all those problems—reconstructing the state and political relations in the South, settling the financial legacy of the war—as being born of the conflict and needing a resolution consistent with the goals of the Union and the sacrifices of its soldiers.

This is all the more important as, while informed by clashing ideologies, Reconstruction followed a course that was hard to predict, and Americans' views evolved rapidly. Black suffrage is a well-documented case. In 1865, very few elected officials advocated for it. In 1866, while trying to secure the rights of freedpeople, most Republicans still refused to enact it outright, even in the Fourteenth Amendment. By 1867, however, it had become a bulwark of Reconstruction and the following year made it into the Fifteenth Amendment, winning ratification even in the Northern states that had turned it down just a year before.[9] Political positions were anything but settled, and opinions and coalitions could move extremely rapidly.

In this context, economic views were also in flux. Both parties were uneasy coalitions on these issues, a fact that some historical studies tend to underplay.[10] In the immediate postbellum years, the Republican coalition, for instance, brought together diverse, sometimes contradictory economic views and interests. Moreover, economic conditions evolved rapidly, and so did people. David A. Wells is a telling example: this key expert, overseeing the government's revenues, converted (at first secretly) from protectionism to free trade in the political and financial turmoil of the immediate postwar years.[11]

One small episode of lawmaking can help us shed light on this interplay among pragmatics and ideology, shifting coalitions, evolving conditions, the difficulty of dealing with the multifaceted consequences of the war, and the conflicting demands of Reconstruction and the economy. All are evident in one early episode of postbellum governance. In 1866, Republicans in Congress introduced a bill to regulate bankruptcy nationally—a constitutional prerogative as yet unused. The rationale was the homogenization of rules across the country, which echoed the drive for national unification witnessed throughout the war. It was also an attempt to remedy a specific situation: in the South, many planters owed prewar debts to Northern creditors but had enough influence in state legislatures to get protection from seizure of property. Both economic ideology and Reconstruction motives thus seemed to converge for this new law. And yet this nationalization was stymied by other, *Northern* considerations: within the Republican Party, congressmen from the U.S. West, in support of more settlement in their states and of development of their agriculture, were wary of laws too favorable to (Northeastern) creditors, and moved to protect homesteads from the danger of foreclosure. Their opposition blocked any passage of the bill. It took a Reconstruction measure—the

Military Reconstruction Act of 1867—to ensure that planters' influence in legislatures would diminish and thus facilitate the enactment of a watered-down version of the Bankruptcy Act that same year.[12]

By the scale of postbellum political history, this is only a small example, but it is illuminating: Reconstruction politics and economic policies might have been thought of as separate, but in practice they were inseparably linked. And it is the political process itself, rather than the more substantive content of each issue, that we need to study to understand specific policies and their consequences. Ultimately, this leads us to see the central role of the state, not as an entity separate from society, but as a politically contested arena endowed with the power to regulate—or not—society and the economy.[13]

If we apply this insight to larger questions of the postbellum era, we realize that the economic and financial issues that became prominent in political debates—the tariff, the Union debt, greenbacks—were entangled with Reconstruction in myriad ways. The war debt, for instance, was such a hot issue in 1866 that it made its way into the Fourteenth Amendment, which, with one clause, voided the Confederate debt while making the Union debt inviolable. This idea came directly from the war, when Jay Cooke had drummed up subscriptions to the loans with heavy propaganda that made lending money to the government ("sacrificing your dollars") the equivalent of soldiers shedding their blood for their country. Inevitably, postwar finances were as much a legacy of the Civil War as Reconstruction and could not be separate. For instance, the national banking system, created in 1863, mandated that banks hold Treasury bonds as reserves. This meant that banks received semiannual interest payments on the bonds from the government, a measure that could easily be, and was, construed as a subsidy to bankers. This is how Northern Democrats framed the issue after George Pendleton used it as an electoral weapon in Ohio in 1867, to great effect. Now, cries that Reconstruction was a policy used to subdue proud white Southerners, using the "ignorant" vote of newly enfranchised African Americans to enrich Northern capitalists, could become widespread.[14]

Postbellum debt management also changed the optics and bore on Reconstruction. Efforts to consolidate and fund the debt—that is, to exchange the bonds issued during the war for new bonds bearing lower interest—moved a great part of the debt from the United States to European markets. In four years, as much as $1 billion worth of bonds moved across the Atlantic.[15] This was a momentous shift. It created a concentration of financial resources, as the savings freed by this operation fed a domestic financial market, especially on Wall Street, that became much larger than it had been before the war. It also redistributed capital from small savers to larger financiers. Finally, it channeled money from the South to the North, as very few bonds were held in the South, while the region contributed to the taxes that paid capital and interest—with a special tax on cotton explicitly enacted in 1866 to make the South pay for the financial burden the war had now created for the country.[16] In this sense, postbellum debt management was inextricably linked to Reconstruction. It bound the South to new national circuits of finance that were heavily dependent on the operations of the government in a way similar, and related, to the reworking of the political balance in the federal system.

Thus, economic policies during and after the Civil War could never be safely detached from Reconstruction politics. There are multiple examples of this. In the South, one of the main weapons of fragile Republican governments in the face of racialized hostility was economic development policies and their (putative) access to the national Republican coalition and its backers to give a new life to battered-down local economies.[17] In national economic issues, also, Reconstruction was such a central concern that it helped give political legitimacy to (or withhold legitimacy from) policies and their proponents. Thus, when Pendleton campaigned in Ohio in 1867 on the money question, he did it in part to wield an issue on which, as a former Peace Democrat, he was not at a disadvantage compared with Republicans. He still vocally defended white supremacy, but he thought that only new issues could help Democrats in a Northern constituency where Reconstruction would favor their opponents. He thus denounced Republicans as the party of the fat cats. Why else, he asked, would they insist on paying gold to bondholders (in the form of interest on debt) while paying only greenbacks to everybody else (including veterans)? At a time when government-issued paper money (greenbacks) exchanged at a lower value than government-issued gold coins, this framed the Republicans as the party of the rich.

This worked very well for Pendleton in the short term: Democrats won Ohio that year. But it also associated pro-greenback policies with anti-Reconstruction sentiment. In reality, both parties were divided on the greenback issue, mostly between Midwesterners and Northeasterners. The latter favored a gold currency and the retirement of greenbacks to return to specie, while the former, mindful of the economic dangers of monetary contraction, came to advocate for government-regulated paper money. It was now tempting for hard-money Republicans to tar their soft-money colleagues with the same brush as Pendleton, denouncing their views as antipatriotic. That sword, however, was double-edged. The aggressive retirement of greenbacks from circulation was conducted by Secretary of the Treasury Hugh McCulloch, who had sided with President Andrew Johnson against Congress on Reconstruction. His financial policies would soon come under attack on the ground of his allegiances.[18]

Thus, although financial policies—the management of debt, money, and taxation—were ostensibly distinct from Reconstruction, Reconstruction was explicitly used as a weapon to legitimize or delegitimize economic positions. All seemed to agree that Reconstruction was a separate issue, yet it kept being invoked in debates—in Congress and in newspapers. This had less to do with the substance of those policies that the unstable coalitions that both parties tried to hold together in rapidly shifting circumstances. On Reconstruction alone, as the historiography has amply shown, both parties were deeply divided on the goals to pursue and the means to get there. But Democrats and Republicans were also fragmented on economic issues, along different fault lines—one of the main being sectional, opposing Midwesterners to Northeasterners. This meant that, at particular moments, the balance of power could shift and redirect both Reconstruction and economic policies. So labile was the political terrain that many contemporaries felt the party system could only collapse and be rearranged: with the close of the war, it had but run its usefulness.[19]

This means that disputes on financial issues could destabilize coalitions that fought over Reconstruction, and vice versa. The episode of the veto in 1874 is revealing in that regard. After the Panic of 1873, Congress spent weeks fighting out a solution to the economic crisis. It ended up voting for a moderate increase in greenback circulation, soon termed the "Inflation bill," which President Ulysses Grant then vetoed, to everybody's surprise. This sent the Republican Party into a tailspin, nearly exploding it. It went on to lose the congressional elections that fall. Evidence shows that, if in Southern states the elections played out mostly on Reconstruction issues, in many Northern states economic issues were front and center. The Republican leaders swiftly reacted to repair their coalition during the following lame-duck Congress, where they still had a commanding majority. They pushed through a settlement that brokered peace within the party's ranks on money while tying up Reconstruction before Democrats took over the House. In effect, Republicans used Reconstruction symbolically to force their sectional factions to reach a compromise on financial issues. The result was the passage of the Civil Rights Act without an enforcement bill (in effect, a defanged Reconstruction measure) coupled with the Specie Resumption Act, a financial package that promised the convertibility of greenbacks into gold four years later without, presumably, creating deflation.[20] That compromise was, in a way, very representative of the linkages between Reconstruction and the money question during that period: they were tied together by the shifting balance of power within the party between Moderates and Radicals on Reconstruction, between Midwesterners and Northeasterners on greenbacks. They depended on how voters responded to those different issues; how elections were framed (or not) around them; and what changes on the ground required action and modified perceptions of priorities.

What can we make of those developments? On a larger scale, they plead for the weaving together of two narratives that are too often distinct: Reconstruction and the Gilded Age, or the settlement of the Civil War and the economic transformation of the United States.[21] To the extent that the direction of American capitalism

was changed and shaped by the Civil War and the attendant policies of the federal government, we need to get to an understanding of them that goes beyond
what appeared to be the main strand of economic ideology within the Republican
Party. The policies of debt and money that ended up consolidating a much larger
financial market in New York, a pyramidal banking system that drained capital to
Northeastern cities, and a tax and debt system that redistributed wealth regionally
and socially upward were as much the results of political fights that were shaped
by Reconstruction. Conversely, but crucially, Reconstruction itself was shaped by
those changes in the economy and the policies attending them. The changes were
linked substantively, as some Reconstruction policies were national and preparing for the postwar rebuilding of a new economic order without slavery, but they
were also linked politically, in that financial policies and Reconstruction had their
fate entangled in the unstable balance of power between and within parties, and
between and within sections.

This story goes beyond the rise of liberalism as an ideology.[22] As it became the
dominant framework of the first globalization in the late nineteenth century, pro-
pelled by the imperial endeavors of Britain and France, liberalism nonetheless was
never hegemonic. Within the United States, for instance, the gold standard
was upheld (despite opposition), but protectionism (a decidedly antiliberal policy)
remained firmly in place. If ideological movements were important—and liberalism, being an elite movement to start with, yielded increasing influence—political
cohesion was a primary consideration. It meant that, as parties had to hold together coalitions comprising varying interests in a competitive environment,
they hewed to a political line made up of compromises and trade-offs. It is in this
context that we can understand the trajectory of American capitalism, the fate of
Reconstruction, and the mutual impact they had on each other.

If, indeed, Reconstruction was the rebuilding of a political order after the war,
then its work was limited, even though its consequences were far-reaching. And
as the war had been about slavery and ended in emancipation, that rebuilding revolved mostly around race, as it was fought around the place that freedpeople and,
more largely, African Americans and other minorities would have in the new United
States. This work, as we know, was not finished by the end of Reconstruction,
when the new political order was taken over, largely through violence, by white
Southerners who proceeded to roll back many of the achievements of the process.
Yet Reconstruction did not happen in isolation, and it had a larger impact, just
as other issues shaped its outcome. The main reason is that Reconstruction, ultimately, belonged to the same politics as the economic transformations of the
United States, because the state and, first of all, the federal government was deeply
active in both. As historians start reconsidering the role of the state in the nineteenth century, they find it at the nexus of both Reconstruction and American

capitalism, with its limits as well as its strength. Who it served and how it did so might be a question all the more urgent as today's politics put it at the forefront again. After the Civil War, race and capitalism were intertwined questions, and legitimate claims on the state were where they met.

All of this had consequences, many of them unintended. Reconstruction was central to the reshaping of American capitalism, a centrality that encompasses more than the legal definitions and practical realities of free and coerced labor. Capitalism was then, and still is, part and parcel of the political order. And what was at the heart of Reconstruction was the rebuilding of a political order that had been shattered by secession and the war. This could serve as a robust definition of "Reconstruction" that highlights the centrality, but also the messiness and contingency, of a process that, despite its limits, was far-reaching—and therefore should not be treated as a parenthesis displaced by the rise of the capitalist juggernaut. Such a definition would allow us to historicize the intertwining of the politics of race and capitalism in historically specific ways that avoid essentializing them.

Notes

1. For recent examples, see Michael W. Fitzgerald, *Splendid Failure: Postwar Reconstruction in the American South,* American Ways Series (Chicago: Ivan R. Dee, 2007); Mark W. Summers, *The Ordeal of the Reunion: A New History of Reconstruction* (Chapel Hill: University of North Carolina Press, 2014); Richard White, *The Republic for Which It Stands: The United States during Reconstruction and the Gilded Age, 1865–1896,* Oxford History of the United States (Oxford: Oxford University Press, 2017).

2. See the essays in this anthology.

3. Thomas J. Brown, ed., *Reconstructions: New Perspectives on the Postbellum United States* (Oxford: Oxford University Press, 2006); Gregory P. Downs and Kate Masur, eds., *The World the Civil War Made,* Steven and Janice Brose Lectures in the Civil War Era (Chapel Hill: University of North Carolina Press, 2015).

4. On the argument for the centrality of slavery in U.S. antebellum capitalism, see Sven Beckert and Seth Rockman, eds., *Slavery's Capitalism: A New History of American Economic Development* (Philadelphia: University of Pennsylvania Press, 2016). Stephanie McCurry underlines the limits of the current argument in Stephanie McCurry, "Plunder of Black Life," *Times Literary Supplement,* May 17, 2017. The debate, among noneconomic historians and with economic historians, is ongoing and lively. For a proposition on "racial capitalism," see Destin Jenkins and Justin Leroy, eds., *Histories of Racial Capitalism* (New York: Columbia University Press, 2021).

5. Jeffrey Sklansky, "Labor, Money, and the Financial Turn in the History of Capitalism," *Labor Studies in Working-Class History of the Americas* 11, no. 1 (2014): 23–46.

6. Howard K. Beale, *The Critical Year: A Study of Andrew Johnson and Reconstruction* (New York: Harcourt Brace, 1930); Charles A. Beard and Mary R. Beard, *The Rise of American Civilization,* 2 vols. (New York: Macmillan, 1927). In the same vein, see David Montgomery, *Beyond Equality: Labor and the Radical Republicans, 1862–1872* (New York: Alfred A. Knopf, 1967).

7. Roger L. Ransom and Richard Sutch, *One Kind of Freedom: The Economic Consequences of Emancipation*, 2nd ed. (New York: Cambridge University Press, 2001); Gavin Wright, *Old South, New South: Revolutions in the Southern Economy since the Civil War* (New York: Basic, 1986).

8. Nicolas Barreyre, *Gold and Freedom: The Political Economy of Reconstruction*, trans. Arthur Goldhammer (Charlottesville: University of Virginia Press, 2015), 45–48. On Reconstruction as a parenthesis, see Richard Franklin Bensel, *Yankee Leviathan: The Origins of Central State Authority in America, 1859–1877* (Cambridge: Cambridge University Press, 1990).

9. Eric Foner, *Reconstruction: America's Unfinished Revolution, 1863–1877* (New York: Harper and Row, 1988); William Gillette, *The Right to Vote: Politics and the Passage of the Fifteenth Amendment* (Baltimore: Johns Hopkins University Press, 1965); Kate Masur, *An Example for All the Land: Emancipation and the Struggle over Equality in Washington, D.C.* (Chapel Hill: University of North Carolina Press, 2012).

10. Heather Cox Richardson, *The Greatest Nation of the Earth: Republican Economic Policies during the Civil War* (Cambridge, MA: Harvard University Press, 1997).

11. Marc-William Palen, *The "Conspiracy" of Free Trade: The Anglo-American Struggle Over Empire and Economic Globalization, 1846–1896* (Cambridge: Cambridge University Press, 2016).

12. Barreyre, *Gold and Freedom*, 31–35; Elizabeth Lee Thompson, *The Reconstruction of Southern Debtors: Bankruptcy after the Civil War* (Athens: University of Georgia Press, 2004). Ironically, the law ended up, in practice, favoring Southern planters in court and was repealed only a few years later.

13. Nicolas Barreyre and Claire Lemercier, "The Unexceptional State: Rethinking the State in the Nineteenth Century (United States, France)," *American Historical Review* 126, no. 2 (2021): 481–503.

14. Barreyre, *Gold and Freedom*, 119–29; Thomas S. Mach, *"Gentleman George" Hunt Pendleton: Party Politics and Ideological Identity in Nineteenth-Century America* (Kent, OH: Kent State University Press, 2007).

15. Jay Sexton, *Debtor Diplomacy: Finance and American Foreign Relations in the Civil War Era, 1837–1873* (Oxford: Oxford University Press, 2005), 201. For recent work on the war debt, see David K. Thomson, *Bonds of War: How Civil War Financial Agents Sold the World on the Union* (Chapel Hill: University of North Carolina Press, 2022).

16. Nicolas Barreyre, "Les avatars politiques de la dette américaine. La crise de la sécession et les transformations de l'État fédéral (1861–1913)," in *Les crises de la dette publique, XVIIIᵉ–XXIᵉ siècle*, ed. Gérard Béaur and Laure Quennouëlle-Corre (Paris: Institut de la Gestion Publique et du Développement Économique and Comité pour l'Histoire Économique et Financière de la France, 2019), 475–93.

17. Michael Perman, *The Road to Redemption: Southern Politics, 1869–1879* (Chapel Hill: University of North Carolina Press, 1984); Mark W. Summers, *Railroads, Reconstruction, and the Gospel of Prosperity: Aid under the Radical Republicans, 1865–1877* (Princeton, NJ: Princeton University Press, 1984).

18. Barreyre, *Gold and Freedom*, 127–36.

19. Michael F. Holt, "Change and Continuity in the Party Period: The Substance and Structure of American Politics, 1835–1885," in *Contesting Democracy: Substance and Structure in American Political History, 1775–2000*, ed. Byron E. Shafer and Anthony J. Badger (Lawrence: University Press of Kansas, 2001), 93–115.

20. Nicolas Barreyre, "The Politics of Economic Crises: The Panic of 1873, the End of Reconstruction, and the Realignment of American Politics," *Journal of the Gilded Age and Progressive Era* 10, no. 4 (2011): 403–23; Michael F. Holt, *By One Vote: The Disputed Presidential Election of 1876* (Lawrence: University Press of Kansas, 2008).

21. Richard Schneirov offers a convincing argument to define the Gilded Age by the transformation of the American economy, especially as linked to its social and labor dimensions: see Richard Schneirov, "Thoughts on Periodizing the Gilded Age: Capital Accumulation, Society, and Politics, 1873–1898," *Journal of the Gilded Age and Progressive Era* 5, no. 3 (2006): 189–224. The latest work that analytically links Reconstruction and the Gilded Age is White, *The Republic for Which It Stands*.

22. A number of works have linked the emergence of self-described Liberals, and the ideas they espoused, with Reconstruction, making them the transition between Reconstruction and the Gilded Age: see, e.g., Nancy Cohen, *The Reconstruction of American Liberalism, 1865–1914* (Chapel Hill: University of North Carolina Press, 2002); Heather Cox Richardson, *West from Appomattox: The Reconstruction of America after the Civil War* (New Haven, CT: Yale University Press, 2007); Andrew L. Slap, *The Doom of Reconstruction: The Liberal Republicans in the Civil War Era* (New York: Fordham University Press, 2006).

Race, Representation, and Reconstruction

THE ORIGINS AND PERSISTENCE OF
BLACK ELECTORAL POWER, 1865–1900

Peter Wallenstein

WRITING IN 1901, THE historian William A. Dunning observed that the era of Reconstruction was just then coming to an end. For him, the timing turned on the disappearance of Black electoral power. And the former Confederate states were just then completing the process of amending their constitutions to curtail significant Black voting—thus to put an end, too, to the election of African American candidates to public office.

It seemed then, and it might once again seem now, a highly promising approach to corralling the complexities of the era. Dunning's perspective on race—his casual welcome of the "end"—has of course been cast aside, but his acuity on the unfolding of late nineteenth-century affairs has lost none of its force and deserves its own restoration. Exploring, as he put it, "the undoing of Reconstruction," he tracked three periods; one of them ended at what would become the conventional 1876–77 marker, and the other two broke considerably later, at about 1890 and at the very time he was writing in 1901. Only as the nineteenth century turned into the twentieth, as Dunning had it, did Reconstruction get entirely undone.[1]

Just a few years later, Dunning's volume on Reconstruction in the *American Nation* series placed the end, instead, at 1877.[2] Rather than changing his mind about the appropriate marker, Dunning appears to have been fitting his work into the chronology of the series—and focusing on what, in 1901, he had characterized as the end of the first of three stages of undoing Reconstruction after its launch back in the 1860s.

Regardless, the 1877 date as the terminal point for Reconstruction has been almost universally adopted. In a revisionist synthesis published in 1965, for example, Kenneth M. Stampp employed it to mark a premature demise to an exhilarating experiment—rather than the previous dominant take as a triumphant end to a ghastly interlude.[3] The timing has been brought into some question in recent years but generally remains the fallback date of choice.

Eric Foner, writing in 1988 for the *New American Nation* series—and promoting a very different normative approach from the one Dunning had in the earlier series—moved the starting date up to 1863 but left the 1877 ending in place. Actually, for most of the Rebel states, he moved the terminal point up by as many as seven years, to as early as 1870. Implicitly in 1988, and explicitly a few years later, he characterized the end of Reconstruction as coming when Republicans no longer (if they ever had) controlled both the governorship and the state legislature.[4] Only in Florida, South Carolina, and Louisiana, by that definition, did Reconstruction endure into 1876–77.

Also ripe for reconsideration is the matter of when Black voting began at all—or, rather, the circumstances that made it both necessary and possible. It is easy enough to resist the reflexive sense that surely the Fifteenth Amendment, ratified in 1870, marked the beginning of Black voting. Yet even if it is agreed that, by the hundreds of thousands, Black men in the South began going to the polls in 1867, the best explanation tends to remain obscure.

Two Questions Reconsidered

The conventional view has it that, when Congress adopted Black suffrage in 1867, it was primarily to shore up Black Southerners' ability to fend for themselves. And the conventional date for an end to Reconstruction derives from a viewpoint that focuses on developments in the nation's capital—in particular, the decision to withdraw the remaining federal troops from South Carolina and Louisiana, states that, following the state elections of 1876, had rival governments, dual claimants to state power.

This chapter reverses the two approaches. It emphasizes concerns regarding national power, not any local situation in the South, to explain the advent of Black voting in 1867. And it uses developments on the ground in the South, rather than in national politics in the aftermath of the 1876 presidential election, to measure the persistence of Black electoral power—perhaps a better indication of how long it was before Reconstruction had run its course.

So this chapter reconsiders both the driving force behind Black enfranchisement in 1867 and the "end of Reconstruction"—when it came and how to describe it, what metric best calibrates it. With a focus on Black legislators elected in the eleven states of the former Confederacy, it addresses both the origins of Black voting—the beginnings of an African American share of the electorate—and the continued electability of Black candidates to public office between the 1860s and the 1880s or 1890s.

Extending the era of "Reconstruction," redefining it in terms of the persistence of Black electoral power, offers an opportunity to reconsider the entire postwar era. Such persistence is well demonstrated by Black candidates' successful campaigns for seats in state legislatures, a metric that can push the temporal boundaries of Reconstruction past 1877 to some point in the 1890s.

So this chapter focuses on the Black state legislators who took their seats after 1876 as well as before that date. A similar approach could be taken, and more concisely, with members of Congress. Yet tracking the story of Black electoral power through state legislators covers more states and far more election campaigns. An aggregate of hundreds of victorious Black candidates, from every former Confederate state, permits an even more compelling analysis than can a focus on members of the U.S. Senate and House of Representatives.

In short, this chapter reconceives the origins and duration of Black electoral power in the former Confederate states. Focusing at first on congressional politics in 1865–67, I emphasize the crucial role of section 2 of the Fourteenth Amendment as a basis for restoration of the Union, a basis that Republicans viewed as a nonnegotiable settlement of the implications of the Three-fifths Clause in a world suddenly without anyone to count as three-fifths of a person. Rather than waiting for the Fifteenth Amendment, the Black vote emerged as a means of obtaining ratification of the Fourteenth Amendment—and led immediately to the election in 1867 of Black delegates to constitutional conventions in ten former Confederate states, followed by Black membership in the legislatures elected under those new constitutions. Well after any 1876 cutoff, Black legislators continued to gain election in considerable numbers.

Three-fifths, Emancipation, and the Fourteenth Amendment's Section 2

Scholars tend to focus on section 1 of the Fourteenth Amendment—the language about "equal protection of the laws"—to the exclusion of section 2, which speaks to representation in the U.S. House of Representatives and, through the House, to the Electoral College, and thus on to the federal judiciary. Yet a review of the rhetoric of the time suggests that the emphasis on section 1 has been misplaced.

In a scene from Norfolk in June 1865, a group of Black residents of Virginia's city on the Chesapeake published a manifesto voicing their vision of a post–Civil War world. At that time, Lee's surrender at Appomattox had receded a scant two months into the past, and the Thirteenth Amendment was still making its uncertain way toward ratification. On the one hand, the Norfolk declaration expressed grave concern regarding Black residents' vulnerability as the U.S. Army withdrew after its wartime occupation. On the other hand, the manifesto called on the self-interest of white Northerners to push for the adoption of Black rights, rights that extended into the political sphere:

> You have not unreasonably complained of the operation of that clause of the Constitution which has hitherto permitted the slavocracy of the South to wield the political influence which would be represented by a white population equal to three-fifths of the whole negro population; but slavery is now abolished, and henceforth the representation will be in proportion to the enumeration of the whole population of the South, *including people of color,* and it is worth your consideration if it is desirable or politic that the fomentors of this rebellion against the Union, which has been crushed at the expense of so much blood and treasure, should find themselves, after defeat, more powerful than ever, their political influence enhanced by the additional voting power of the other two fifths of the colored population, by which means four Southern votes will balance in the Congressional and Presidential elections at least seven Northern ones.[5]

At about the same time, Senator John Sherman of Ohio wrote to his brother, General William Tecumseh Sherman, about how he himself perceived the transformed situation:

> As to negro suffrage, I admit the negroes are not intelligent enough to vote, but someone must vote their political representation in the State where they live, and their representation is increased by their being free. Who shall exercise this [additional] political power? Shall the rebels do so?[6]

Often neglected by historians of Reconstruction, despite actually being central to the politics of Congressional Reconstruction, is the devastating implication for white Northern power in general, and Republican control in particular, that the death of slavery brought. No longer enslaved, four million people across the South—including between a quarter-million and a half-million in each of eight states—would henceforth count at full value after each decennial census, not at three-fifths. Unless Black residents voted their own representation—that is, if white Southerners continued to vote it—then secessionists, as a consequence of losing both their bid for political independence and the power to enslave so many of their workers and neighbors, would return to the Union with far more power to commit mischief than they ever had before secession.[7]

Mississippi and South Carolina each had a Black majority; Virginia, Georgia, Florida, Alabama, and Louisiana each had a population more than 40 percent

African American, mostly former slaves. Especially in those seven states, the death of slavery would considerably inflate the congressional representation that, before the war and emancipation, had been based on the old federal ratio of three-fifths. Absent a huge change, white men would continue to vote their state's full representation—and, in each case, that representation would be far greater than it had been under slavery.

So Congress proposed the Fourteenth Amendment, complete with section 2, a compromise provision settled on to address the main question of the day: it promised not a single addition to the electorate of any Southern state, but one way or another it would solve the conundrum of former slaves' representation in post-emancipation national politics. White men would get to decide how, but decide they must. In each state, they could take one of two directions: let Black men vote, and the state's representation in Congress would reflect, in effect, five-fifths rather than the former three-fifths; or continue to deny Black men the vote, and the new formula would be zero-fifths. Black men would vote their own representation. Or nobody would. White Southerners could not be permitted to benefit from the huge boost in power that they would derive from a categorically white electorate with nobody left to count as three-fifths of a person.

When only Tennessee among the eleven former Confederate states approved the proposed amendment, fewer than necessary to obtain ratification, Congress cast about for another way forward and passed the Reconstruction Acts of March 1867 to get the job done. An electorate that included Black men in each of the remaining ten states went to the polls to choose delegates to form new state constitutions.[8] To be acceptable to Congress, the new constitution had to incorporate Black suffrage. The new biracial electorate would choose a new legislature, which had to ratify the Fourteenth Amendment before the state could once again be represented in Congress. Black suffrage came in this manner to ten southern states in 1867; Black delegates served in every convention, and Black representatives were elected to the subsequent state legislatures, all of this well before the Fifteenth Amendment was ratified in March 1870.

What the legal scholar Derrick A. Bell Jr. offered as an explanation for the U.S. Supreme Court's ruling in the 1950s school segregation case *Brown v. Board of Education*—the concept of a temporary convergence of interests, Black and white—can help explain how Congressional Reconstruction gained enactment in the first place.[9] The central objective among congressional Republicans, according to the argument here, was to secure ratification of the Fourteenth Amendment. And the core concern for any number of Republicans in both houses of Congress? Section 2, not section 1—a provision that, while by no means guaranteeing Black political rights, offered a way to address the implications of the three-fifths rule, to prevent the recent secessionists, brought back kicking and screaming into the Union, from endangering the fruits of both abolition and military victory.

Yet finding a means to get section 2 into the Constitution led, in the face of so much opposition in Southern states, to the enactment of Congressional Reconstruction, which very much included voting rights for Black men in the states to be reconstructed before those states could be safely restored. One possible outcome of the Fourteenth Amendment became instead a means to secure its ratification. There followed, from many quarters, a distinction between voting rights and the right to hold the offices that the electorate was empowered to fill—the one provisionally conceded, the other stoutly resisted. But in every former Confederate state, Black men soon held public office, and by no means only in the decade that began in 1867.

A Tour of the States of the Former Confederacy

In 1896, Thomas E. Miller left the South Carolina legislature to become the first president of a new Black land-grant college at Orangeburg, one of the "colleges of 1890." Born in 1849, he served in the South Carolina House of Representatives beginning in 1874 and continuing through the cataclysm that hit Black participation in that state's politics in 1876, often taken as marking the end of Reconstruction there. He subsequently served a term in the State Senate, 1880–82, returned to the House for a term in 1886–87, and was back in the legislature in 1894–96. He also served in the 1895 state constitutional convention, which had been called to put an end to Black electoral power. In addition, Miller ran for Congress in 1888, and was in fact seated after surviving a challenge to his claim of electoral victory, but lost out two years later in another contested election.[10] In short, Miller challenges the customary periodization among historians that seems to say that everywhere, and in particular South Carolina, "Reconstruction" came to an "end" in 1876 or 1877.

The tyranny of the South Carolina paradigm in historical studies of the South in the 1870s does not work particularly well even for that state. What is the story elsewhere?

Postwar Tennessee, alone among the eleven states of the former Confederacy, was exempted from Congressional Reconstruction, because it had already ratified the Fourteenth Amendment. Nonetheless, the broad outlines of politics in the late 1860s proved similar in Tennessee to that in the ten other states, and the Fifteenth Amendment would have brought Black suffrage to Tennessee in 1870 anyway. Tennessee voters did in fact elect a Black legislator in the early 1870s: Sampson Keeble, elected in 1872 from Davidson County (Nashville). But he does not show up for Tennessee in Eric Foner's biographical directory of "black officeholders during

Reconstruction," *Freedom's Lawmakers*. Why? Because Foner did not include men who held office after the "end of Reconstruction," which he defines for each state as "the election that produced simultaneous Democratic control of the governorship and both houses of the state legislature," or 1870 in Tennessee.[11]

More astonishing are the twelve Black legislators elected in Tennessee in the 1880s, even for two or three successive terms, through 1886. The terminal punctuation to this phenomenon came when Jesse Graham, having shown up at the Tennessee House of Representatives following the 1896 election, was denied his seat by his would-have-been fellow legislators. Not until the 1960s would another African American take a seat in the Tennessee legislature. But those who did so in the 1880s make very clear that in no clean way did the year 1876–77, let alone an even earlier date, cleave the postwar era in that state between Black electoral power and its absence, between the ability to gain election to legislative office and a time when such simply could no longer happen.[12]

So Tennessee's postwar history reveals no Black legislators elected before what Foner defines as the end of Reconstruction there and only a single such person before the more conventional 1876–77 cutoff, but many Black legislators in the 1880s and an end point clearly in place by the mid-1890s. Was Tennessee, like South Carolina, an anomaly in this pattern of Black legislators well past 1877?

In North Carolina—like Tennessee, an Upper South state, but one in which Congressional Reconstruction clearly came to bear—Black legislators, the historian Frenise Logan notes, held office all the way from 1868 to 1894. For just the years 1876 to 1894, he counts fifty-two African Americans in the House of Representatives—with fifteen of them elected in 1887, the highest number during that period—and another fifteen in the State Senate. Henry Eppes, a formerly enslaved man who served in the 1868 state constitutional convention, gained election to the Senate later that year, and his legislative career did not end until 1887.[13]

In Virginia, Reconstruction ended in 1873, according to Foner's timeline and the criterion for any Black officeholder's inclusion in his compilation. In fact, however, the greatest Black political power in Virginia came some years later, when a biracial political coalition known as the Readjusters came to power. In the early 1880s, they controlled all three branches of state government.[14]

In 1945, the intrepid Black historian and civil rights activist Luther Porter Jackson published a short book, *Negro Office-Holders in Virginia, 1865–1895*. In it he mourned what had become of the preceding half-century but wanted to show what had once been and might be again, and he tracked down all manner of information about the property accumulation, professional advancement, and policy significance of the men he identified. Work by a team at the Library of Virginia has corrected Jackson's information a bit here or there—modifying an occasional spelling; deleting one man who turned out to be white; and adding five new names, for an adjusted total of ninety-two Black members of the Virginia General Assembly in the late nineteenth century.[15]

In all, then, ninety-two different African Americans, or men of color, served in the Virginia legislature at some point between 1869 and 1890. Most of them do not appear in Foner's compilation. Serving during the 1889–90 session were five Black men: one in the Senate, four in the House of Delegates. As for other officeholders, at least one African American sat on the Richmond City Council for an unbroken quarter-century, every year from 1870 through 1895. For Virginia, the legislative criterion puts the terminal point at 1890, and local officers can push back the boundary a few more years. The 1902 Virginia constitution ended, until the 1960s, even the possibility of any Black legislator in that state.[16]

A study of yet another Upper South state, Arkansas, provides a data set of Black legislators that goes far beyond anything previously available. Blake Wintory has identified eighty-four Black men elected to the Arkansas legislature between 1868 and 1892. In 1873, both numbers reached their highs for the entire era, with twenty in all—sixteen in the House and four in the Senate. But as late as 1891, the total reached twelve, eleven of them in the House. The 1891 legislature set out to put an end to such patterns, enacting various measures to curtail Black political power, as well as a separate coach law to expand the reach of segregation. The 1893 session reverted to five African Americans—four in the House, one in the Senate—and then all such Black representation vanished.[17] By any measure along these electoral lines, Reconstruction was finally over in Arkansas.

Among the seven original Confederate states, Texas, for one, looks a lot like Arkansas in its postwar pattern of Black victories in elections to the state legislature. For Texas, Foner counted seventeen African Americans in the legislature—two in the Senate, fifteen in the House—during what he characterized as "Reconstruction" there—thus, the 1871 and 1873 sessions. By extending the period under review into the 1890s, the historian Merline Pitre found twenty-four more names: two additional state senators and twenty-two additional representatives. In 1897, however, Representative Robert L. Smith had no Black companion in either chamber, and he had no successor until well into the twentieth century.[18] Calibrated in terms of Black legislators, Reconstruction in Texas was over by 1899.

For Florida, Foner identifies forty-eight Black state legislators during "Reconstruction." Canter Brown, after digging deeper and carrying his exploration out farther into the future, developed a list more than twice as long, including additional men from before 1877, as well as dozens from "after Reconstruction." In every session through the 1880s, Florida had Black representation at least in the House. Black legislators in 1887 numbered eleven. As late as the 1889 session (so elected in 1888), there were two.[19]

What about Mississippi? In no state were whites more ruthlessly determined to push Black citizens out of the political process than Mississippi, where whites remained a demographic minority into the 1930s. Even there, every legislative session in the 1880s had at least six Black members. They came from counties such as Adams, Bolivar, and Sharkey, where Blacks vastly outnumbered whites, where whites depended on Black workers for plantation labor, and—in a world in which both groups had political rights—where both found it advantageous to run "fusion" tickets according to which substantive power remained securely in the hands of whites, both in local affairs and in the state at large, but voters in those counties could select biracial delegations for the legislature.[20]

Black Mississippians served in the legislature even after 1890. In both 1892 and 1894, George Washington Gayles represented Bolivar County, and George William Butler represented Sharkey. Together they reflected the tremendous changes that, for a time, transformed Mississippi. Gayles, born into slavery in 1844, served for two terms (1872–75) before the cataclysmic end to Dunning's first phase of Reconstruction in Mississippi, and then—after the commonly held "end" of Reconstruction—served in the State Senate from 1878 to 1886 before gaining election to the lower house in the 1890s, during Dunning's third phase of Reconstruction. Butler, born in 1855, entered the brand-new Black-only Alcorn University at the age of sixteen in 1871, graduated in 1875, and served in the state House of Representatives from 1884 to 1894. Both men were still in their twenties when first elected to the legislature; both saw their ability to help frame the state's laws come to an early end.[21]

Precisely the demonstrated continuing ability in some counties of Black legislative candidates to get elected (as well as the success of the Black candidate John R. Lynch running for Congress in 1880) drove whites to a final showdown, to put an end to the prospect, let alone the accomplishment, of such scattered Black electoral triumphs. To fully close the doors to legislative office for Black Mississippians, white Mississippians had both to contrive a way past the Fifteenth Amendment's ban on a racial screen and to nullify—declare unconstitutional—the act of Congress that had restored Mississippi in 1870 on condition that the state never curtail Black suffrage. Finally, both the Mississippi Supreme Court and the U.S. Supreme Court had to approve the 1890 constitutional convention's nefarious handiwork. The nation's highest court did so in an understudied and underappreciated case from 1898, *Williams v. Mississippi*.[22]

Louisiana's Reconstruction also came crashing to an end in the 1890s. There, as in so many places across the former Confederacy, Black candidates continued to gain election, not only to local offices but also to the legislature, throughout the 1880s and even beyond. Serving in the 1890s were five men of color in the House of Representatives and one in the Senate. Louisiana's constitution of 1898 put an end to the possibility of even such small numbers as that.[23]

Georgia supplies a timeline of its own—extremely thin, occasionally broken, but unusually long. After 1874, Black representation was confined to the overwhelmingly African American counties along the Atlantic Coast south of Savannah, but it persisted in attenuated fashion until 1907. In McIntosh County, voters chose Lectured Crawford for the sessions beginning in 1886, 1890, and 1900, and followed up with William H. Rogers from 1902 through 1907. The trail ended there.[24] From this perspective, Reconstruction was finally over even in Georgia's *coastal* counties.

Alabama is the outlier at the other end of the stretch of time between Black enfranchisement and an end to Black legislators. Even there, no date in the mid-1870s marks an absolute end to Black legislators, but the end did come, and at least a few years earlier than even in Tennessee or Virginia. The usual date given for so-called Redemption in Alabama is 1874. In 1876, however, nine Black candidates won election to the state legislature. Two Black candidates won in 1878, Hugh A. Carson and George English, though the Democratic legislators eventually denied Carson his seat. W. O. Williams, elected in 1882, was the state's last Black legislator of the era. So even Alabama's legislature exhibited some Black presence in the 1880s—and certainly after 1874 or 1877—albeit not much and not for long.[25]

Time, Space, and an "End" to Reconstruction

Foner's distinction as to just when, no later than 1877, Reconstruction came to an end in a given state, because it disaggregates the South, can suggest an alternative approach—one that does not insist on a state-unit analysis but, rather, might distinguish one portion of a state from other portions. Merline Pitre, writing about Texas, points the way, though at the beginning of a chapter titled "The Post-Reconstruction Legislatures": "Although some parts of Texas were redeemed by force as early as 1867, others by the elections of 1872 and 1873, and still others with the drafting of the Constitution of 1875, this was not the case in [all] Black Belt counties." In such electoral units, "by virtue of their numerical strength, blacks exercised [some continuing] political control and were consistently [i.e., from somewhere, at every election] elected to the state legislature [even after 1875] from 1876 to 1896."[26]

In short, the ending of Reconstruction, as measured in terms of the election of Black legislators, came as something of a process in Texas, not a single event or point in time. Even less was it the same moment in every former Confederate state, let alone in the 1870s.

Canter Brown's exploration of Black officeholders in Florida contains a particularly telling observation along these lines. He notes that Foner's compilation "represents the most ambitious attempt to date to focus on [Black] individuals who held [political] office" in the former Confederate states. Brown expresses concern, however, that Foner's approach "adopts a very narrow scope, limiting the meaning of Reconstruction." He nonetheless persists in the very language that concerns him, seeking to extend "Reconstruction" while adopting Foner's rhetoric:

> Some readers doubtlessly will be surprised to learn . . . that Florida's African Americans, in a pattern probably repeated in other southern states, resisted disfranchisement and political exile for a generation or more after the end of Reconstruction. *Perhaps a majority of Florida's black officials served after 1876.*[27]

Thus, the literature cited here offers various observations that can help mark a conceptual and rhetorical journey through this unfamiliar empirical thicket. Carl Moneyhon, who has labored effectively for many years on Black political power in postwar Arkansas, spoke more than three decades ago about how "the end of Reconstruction" did not immediately bring an end to African Americans' "participation in southern politics." Pushing Moneyhon's work further with regard to Black legislators in Arkansas, Wintory characterizes it as "attempting to fill some of the gaps between Reconstruction and disfranchisement."[28]

How best to understand that gap—and proposing a new paradigm—is the burden of the present project. Should historians continue to characterize the gap as coming after "the end of Reconstruction"? Perhaps it would be better to push the end point of "Reconstruction" back to when all of these states converged in the effective end to Black political empowerment, so perhaps no earlier than 1890, yet virtually everywhere by 1898.

The end of slavery led, in a quick succession of stages—that is, not all at once—to a position of non-slavery (somewhere above the status of prewar free persons of color, as well as of enslaved persons), then (under the Civil Right Act of 1866) citizenship without the vote, and then, beginning in 1867, substantial Black political power in every former Confederate state. The initial burst of Black political power ran into tremendous opposition in the late 1860s and the 1870s, yet Black electoral and legislative power persisted to some degree in every state of the former Confederacy, and it even grew to new heights in some places—Tennessee supplies a great example—in the 1880s. Then the prospect of the institutionalization of Black political power elicited a sharply focused effort to complete the overturn of the postwar revolution in politics in the former Confederate states, an overturning that had not yet been completed in the 1870s.

The "big bang" that transformed the possibilities of postwar politics came in March 1867, when Congress enacted Congressional Reconstruction to secure ratification of the Fourteenth Amendment, with its twin concerns regarding "equal protection" and "three fifths." After 1867, we can profitably turn our primary attention away from national politics and toward what was happening on the ground. We can watch *Black Southerners*—who evidently *did not get the memo in 1877 that Reconstruction was over*—continue to vote, and run for office, and hold office, and even shape policy. Their ability to do that would, in time, evaporate—but not yet, by no means everywhere, especially where Black majorities could still work their will in a more or less free election with a more or less fair count, throughout the 1880s, even well into the 1890s.

Historians of the civil rights generation, taking their cue from what white men in the nation's capital did or failed to do, ironically underemphasized Black agency in the southern politics of the post–Civil War generation. Remedying that deficiency projects a very different image from the one that dominates the historiography—and therefore occasions a reconsideration of how best to understand the Reconstruction Era. In *all eleven states* of the recently defeated Confederacy, voters elected one or more—aside from Alabama, many more—Black candidates to the state legislature *as late as the 1880s*. A majority of these states did so into the 1890s, and Georgia persisted in this pattern, a little, even beyond 1900.

If we look at *politics rather than transportation,* enfranchisement rather than integration, *Williams v. Mississippi* (1898) rather than *Plessy v. Ferguson* (1896), we still find a point of departure in the 1890s, but our perspective is a study in contrasts to the currently prevailing view. Rather than dwelling on the *policy* environment associated with *Plessy v. Ferguson,* we might focus on the *political* environment associated with *Williams v. Mississippi.* What legislators might collectively do when in power depended on who those policy makers were going to be. And the electorates of the former Confederate states, sharply diminished in size, became overwhelmingly—even exclusively—white in composition. The Arkansas legislature of 1891 exemplified the connection, with one new law initiating a poll tax requirement for voting and another mandating segregated railway cars.

This chapter urges a centering of section 2 of the Fourteenth Amendment, regarding a struggle between Northern whites and Southern whites as to who would prevail in national politics—a concern with representation and voting, when the great issue was who would vote the Southern states' increased representation after emancipation, in a world in which nobody any longer counted as three-fifths of a person. It urges an emphasis on section 2, regarding voting and representation, even more than section 1, regarding birthright citizenship and "equal protection of the laws." Extending the field of vision from the late 1860s through the late 1890s, moreover, while redirecting the focus to Black Southerners, permits an inquiry into how, even in the presence of furious efforts to push them out of politics and in the absence of effective protection from the national government, they continued into the 1880s or even the 1890s to go to the polls in very substantial numbers and even continued to elect Black legislators.

If historians look for our chief cue to Black Southerners, rather than white Northerners, our assessment of the era cannot stay what it has long been. If we look to Black political empowerment, calibrated in terms of Black candidates' demonstrated electability to legislative office, our sense of Reconstruction—its possibilities and its attenuation—stretches out to 1890 or beyond. Exactly where can depend on which part of a state, as well as which state, we are looking at.

In terms of lawmaking outputs, Black legislators could have a real impact. For example, in the early 1870s, as legislatures grappled with the prospect of federal land-grant funds for higher education, Black legislators sometimes contended successfully for measures designed to benefit their Black constituents. Virginia, for one, divided the funds in 1872: two-thirds for a college for white men, today's Virginia Tech, and one-third for an emerging Black institution, today's Hampton University. In the early 1880s (so after "Reconstruction" had supposedly ended), Virginia's biracial governing majority, the Readjusters, established a new state-supported institution for Black men and Black women, today's Virginia State University (to which the Black land-grant designation was later redirected).[29]

Black Electoral Power beyond the Ten Reconstructed States

The "South" has multiple meanings, frequently uninterrogated, in the history of Reconstruction. Of the eleven former Confederate states, ten were the target of the congressional measures of March 1867 that launched new elections with biracial electorates. Tennessee escaped because that state, having already ratified the Fourteenth Amendment, did not occasion further pressure to do so.

The Border South states went their own way, as did the non-Southern states. The slave states of 1860 that did not secede had no need of political restoration in the aftermath of the Civil War. Not subject to Congressional Reconstruction, they did not hold elections to new constitutional conventions in 1867–68 in which Black men participated as voters and then delegates. The trajectory of Black electoral empowerment in the two clusters of recent slave states therefore diverged in the first postwar years, yet the Fifteenth Amendment brought Black enfranchisement anyway in 1870, though the scale of the Black electorate in Border South states mirrored the relatively small proportions of Black residents in those states.

In at least some of the Border South states—all of which, like those of the former Confederacy, would establish thoroughgoing segregation and long maintain it—this divergence contrasted with the Upper South and Deep South states in ways that also defy conventional understandings. West Virginia's first Black legislator, Charles Payne, gained election in 1896, and others followed: James M. Ellis, elected in 1902, followed by three African Americans in the 1910s. In Missouri, Charles H.

Tandy gained election in 1894; he was not permitted to take his seat, but another African American, Walthall M. Moore, sat in that state's legislature in the 1920s. In Oklahoma—not yet a state during Reconstruction but coming to feature all the trappings of Jim Crow, just like any other Southern state—Albert Comstock Hamlin gained election in 1908 to the new state's first legislature. In Kentucky, after a series of failed efforts, Black voters in 1935 sent Charles W. Anderson Jr. to the legislature, and similar success persisted in that state through most terms from then on. The first Black legislator in Delaware won election in 1948, and the first in Maryland did so in 1954.[30] By then, every Border South state had had at least one Black legislator, all after 1890, though in those states—as in the Upper South and the Deep South—the 1960s at last brought breakthroughs that revived biracial electorates and thus facilitated the more frequent election of Black legislators.

Among states outside the South, Massachusetts proved an outlier in electing its first Black legislators soon after the Civil War—an outlier in how fast those results came in, as well as in the fact that no Reconstruction law passed by Congress forced the possibility. Charles L. Mitchell, a Civil War combat veteran, won a seat in the Massachusetts legislature in 1866, as did Edwin Garrison Walker, son of the fire-brand writer of the 1830s David Walker. Representing largely white constituencies, they took their seats in the 1867 legislative session.[31]

Beginning a decade or so later, so around the "end of Reconstruction," Black candidates also won legislative seats in the Midwest and the Far West. William Jefferson Hardin, for example, gained election to the Wyoming territorial legislature in 1879 and 1881. A Black candidate for a legislative seat first gained election in Illinois in 1876; in Ohio in 1879; and in Indiana in 1880. Many more such election victories followed in those and other states. In the twentieth century, as Black migration out of the South built, the increase in Black voters facilitated the election of California's first Black legislator, Frederick M. Roberts, in 1918, and the first in New Jersey, Dr. Walter Gilbert Alexander, in 1920.[32]

In sum, as Black electoral power receded in all of the former Confederate states—vanished there and then remained nil—it grew elsewhere, whether in the Border South, the Northeast, the Midwest, or the Far West.

Black Representation in Congress

This chapter emphasizes the election of African Americans to state legislatures, but Black representation in Congress echoes the pattern at the state level. Twenty-two Black Southerners served in one branch or the other of Congress during the postwar period. Two served in the U.S. Senate, both of them appointed by the

Mississippi legislature: Hiram R. Revels and Blanche K. Bruce. Both took their seats before 1877, although Bruce's full term took him to 1881.

The twenty African Americans in the U.S. House of Representatives reveal a different pattern. Joseph H. Rainey, of South Carolina, took his seat in December 1870 and went on not only to complete that term, in the 40th Congress, but also to serve from the 41st Congress through the 45th, so until 1879. His last election came in 1876, as he survived the very year of the firestorm that is generally taken to mark the end of Reconstruction in his state and throughout the South.[33] More than that, other Black congressmen represented South Carolina in the 1880s and 1890s.

The average number of Black congressmen per session dropped after the "end" of Reconstruction, but not dramatically, and the final electoral success came many years after 1877. During the 1870s, a total of fourteen Black men represented Alabama, Florida, Georgia, Louisiana, Mississippi, North Carolina, or South Carolina—so all but Arkansas, Tennessee, Texas, and Virginia—for all or part of twenty-four terms. Across the 1880s and 1890s, a total of eight Black congressmen represented Mississippi, North Carolina, South Carolina, or Virginia for all or part of thirteen terms. (Two men—John R. Lynch of Mississippi and Robert Smalls of South Carolina—served both in the 1870s and again after 1880.[34])

Between 1870 and 1898, at least one African American gained election to every Congress except in 1878 and 1886. In view of Blanche K. Bruce's presence in the Senate in the late 1870s, only during the 50th Congress (1887–89) was there no African American in either chamber. Serving in the very next Congress, the 51st, which ended in 1891, were three Black congressmen: Henry P. Cheatham of North Carolina, Thomas E. Miller of South Carolina, and John Mercer Langston of Virginia. One Black congressional candidate gained a seat after each subsequent election, too—through 1898, but not after.

For many years after the conventional "end" to Reconstruction, then, Black candidates continued to gain election to Congress. Two states each reached a new high number after 1880: Virginia, with its sole Black congressman of the era, and North Carolina, with three men each elected to two terms. The horrific white-on-Black violence associated with the so-called Wilmington Riot of 1898 in coastal North Carolina shows what it took to put an emphatic end to such possibilities. Nevertheless, the last Black congressman during the generation after the Civil War, George H. White, left office only at the dawn of the twentieth century, in March 1901, not way back in the 1870s.[35]

The return of Black representation in Congress, decades later, reflected the rise in Black electoral power outside the South. Whether migrants from Virginia beginning in the 1880s or from the Deep South beginning in the 1910s, Black Southerners picked up the right to vote—secured it more permanently this time—as they moved away from the South. In 1928, the Alabama native Oscar DePriest won a seat from Chicago, Illinois, with the support of many thousands of other Alabama natives, and he or some other Black representative from that district continued from then on to sit in Congress. In New York City, Adam Clayton Powell Jr. gained election in 1944, and he or another African American continued thereafter to represent his district. After the 1968 elections, the number of African Americans in Congress finally topped the Reconstruction high of eight, reached in the 1875–77 session.[36] Those developments prefigured, then fostered, and finally reflected what came to be termed the "Second Reconstruction."

The Long Reconstruction

A review of the continuing Black electoral success in campaigns for legislative seats—success during the decade and more after the conventional cutoff for periodizing Reconstruction—offers a revised view of Black power across the hundred years following the Civil War: in the South through the 1880s and 1890s, as well as outside the South not only during those years but through the decades that came after a forced end to Black electoral power everywhere in the former Confederate South.

Congressional Reconstruction launched tremendous new possibilities in the former Confederate South in 1867. The Fifteenth Amendment, three years later, nationalized the right to vote, a right that gained longtime traction in many states that had not occasioned the original impetus in 1867. Reliance, as in this essay, on a metric that explores the continued success of Black candidates to elective office in general, and to their state legislatures in particular, suggests a productive way to understand the possibilities turned loose after Confederate defeat in the War of the Rebellion. In many places, even in the Deep South, those possibilities continued to unfold into the 1880s or even the 1890s.[37]

The historian Carl Becker, in a long-ago study of New York during the era of the American Revolution, spoke of a dual struggle, both for "home-rule" and over who would rule at home.[38] This critical distinction is central to any exploration of political struggles in the South after the Civil War. By 1900—the end of the first post–Civil War generation; the end of the third stage of Dunning's "undoing of Reconstruction"—the counterrevolution had been consolidated. For the next two generations, the results of that white supremacist configuration of "home rule" would leave internal opposition suppressed and federal intervention deflected.

The convergence of interest between Black Southerners and so many white Northerners faded during the 1870s. After the two sets of interests diverged,

Black Southerners forged on alone where necessary and for as long as possible. The struggle over white supremacy and the meaning of Black freedom did not end well for Black Southerners, as of the dawn of the twentieth century. Yet the struggle persisted long after any particular year in the 1870s, the outcome in the balance even in the 1880s and 1890s.[39]

Future president Woodrow Wilson, wearing his academic hat as political scientist and historian, wrote in 1901—in the midst of what he welcomed as the final resolution of the issues of Reconstruction—about how "a host of dusky children untimely put out of school" had dominated Southern politics for a time. "Negro majorities for a little while filled the southern legislatures," he claimed, but "at last the whites who were real citizens got control again."[40]

By the 1950s, though, soon after *Brown v. Board of Education,* commentators were deploying the term "New Reconstruction" or "Second Reconstruction," though the emphasis was generally placed on the Fourteenth Amendment's section 1 and "equal protection of the laws."[41] Adoption of the term came not so much because African Americans were proving restive over the manifold restrictions on their freedom—the continuing chasm, that is, between white liberty and Black liberty—since resistance had long continued, in many forms and venues. But there was growing evidence of what Derrick Bell would later call a convergence of interests, as the federal government was once again stepping in and stepping up. This time around, in the 1950s, the Supreme Court did so far more than Congress—a reversal from the post–Civil War years—but Congress would return to a civil rights stance in the 1960s, when the term "Second Reconstruction" became more widely used, with a return to federal intervention in Southern racial affairs.

In the years after World War II, elderly members of both teams could remember—from personal experience, not just community memory—a time in the 1880s and 1890s when things had seemed uncertain and the final resolution had not yet been determined. William H. Rogers, for one, lived into the 1950s, a half-century after the early years of the twentieth century, when he had represented McIntosh County as the sole African American in the Georgia legislature.[42] Whether to comprehend the struggles of the First Reconstruction or the fervor on both sides in the emergence of the Second Reconstruction, it is well to remember how long the post–Civil War outcome had remained unsettled, and not just how long it took for a great deal of the promise of Reconstruction to come back into place and then press—often uncertainly—beyond.

Reconstructing the Historiography of Reconstruction

The dominant chronological paradigm currently in use can stand some renovation. The end of Reconstruction, whenever it came, is now generally seen by scholars not as a welcome relief to an unfortunate era but, rather, as an unfortunate conclusion to a welcome interlude. Extending the observed era through the 1890s offers promising new ways to comprehend what was at stake, on both sides, and how it played out. This chapter has urged larger spatial, temporal, and conceptual contexts for the study of Reconstruction and Black electoral power.

Eric Foner's collection of biographical sketches of Black officeholders during "Reconstruction" has, for decades now, provided an extraordinary new tool for understanding the late 1860s and early 1870s in the former Confederate states. In terms of both space and time, however, its prodigious strengths also limit its reach. Because the period it covers extends no further than his definition of Reconstruction in any given state, it does not include the very many Black officeholders who gained their positions after some date between 1870 and 1877. Therefore, much of the post–Civil War era—the longer Reconstruction—never comes into view. And because it focuses only on the states of the former Confederacy, people elected to office elsewhere never appear.

Continued Black agency in the political sphere—well beyond any point in the 1870s—provides a path to revisit the last third of the nineteenth century. In exploring post–Civil War political developments in Texas, Pitre argued for redirecting the study of Reconstruction by "placing more emphasis on what blacks were doing for themselves as opposed to what was done [by whites] to and for them"— that is, "focus upon the active and determined roles of these black politicians [and the Black voters who sent them to the legislature] in reconstructing their lives, their communities, and their state."[43] That would include all the mothers, daughters, sisters, and wives who—despite grave danger and in the face of frequent futility—encouraged their sons, fathers, brothers, and husbands to keep up the struggle for political power.

And of course Texas was not alone in its pattern of continuing successful election campaigns, well past 1876, by Black candidates for legislative seats. In Florida, Brown found "a pattern" that, he suggested, was "probably repeated in other southern states."[44] Brown was thus musing in broader terms than his counterparts in other states tended to. Each of the other scholars discovered that the particular state under his or her investigation turned out to be an anomaly. A survey of the entire former Confederate South reveals, instead, that every state was an anomaly—or, rather, that none was. If any state was an outlier, it was Alabama, where the last successful Black candidate for a seat in the state legislature, while coming after 1877, did not break past that conventional marker by very much.

A struggle between white Southerners and white Northerners led to secession, and the war that followed led to abolition. A subsequent struggle between
white Northerners and white Southerners made space for Black electoral power. The
struggle of white versus white gave rise to Reconstruction, brought such promise to
so many people—and generated such a perceived threat to so many others—and
then led down a path in which the combined impulses propelling Reconstruction
subsided, not gently in the former seceded states but, rather, through immense
upheaval and bloodshed. The temporary convergence of interests, noted by Derrick
Bell in the context of the origins and long aftermath of the Supreme Court's ruling
in *Brown v. Board of Education,* can help guide scholars through the thicket of politics
during the long Reconstruction.

The crucial significance of Black agency in prolonging Black electoral power must
become and remain a central feature as scholars seek to take the measure of what
was wrought by the War of the Rebellion. In the end, Dunning got it wrong, too,
for the final resolution of Reconstruction had far from run its course at the time he
wrote his essay. He did not anticipate a Second Reconstruction (including *Brown v.
Board of Education,* as well as the return of Black electoral power) building on the
First Reconstruction (certainly including Black enfranchisement and officeholding)
and looking to fulfill its promises. He did not anticipate the undoing of the *end* of
Reconstruction.

Notes

1. William A. Dunning, "The Undoing of Reconstruction," *Atlantic Monthly,* vol. 87, October
   1901, reprinted in William A. Dunning, *Essays on the Civil War and Reconstruction* (New
   York: Harper and Row, [1904] 1965), 353–85.
2. William Archibald Dunning, *Reconstruction: Political and Economic, 1865–1877* (New York:
   Harper and Brothers, 1907).
3. Kenneth M. Stampp, *The Era of Reconstruction, 1865–1877* (New York: Alfred A. Knopf, 1965).
4. Eric Foner, *Reconstruction: America's Unfinished Revolution, 1863–1877* (New York: Harper
   and Row, 1988), a magisterial volume that, though chipped away at on various fronts, has
   provided the standard ever since its appearance. Foner expressly introduces the tighter
   timeline in *Freedom's Lawmakers: A Directory of Black Officeholders during Reconstruction*
   (Baton Rouge: Louisiana State University Press, [1993] 1996), xiii.
5. *Equal Suffrage: Address from the Colored Citizens of Norfolk, Va., to the People of the United
   States,* reprint ed. (Wilmington, DE: Scholarly Resources, [1865] 1969), 4–5.
6. John Sherman to William T. Sherman, May 16, 1865, in Rachel Sherman Thorndike, ed., *The
   Sherman Letters: Correspondence between General and Senator Sherman from 1837 to 1891* (New
   York: Charles Scribner's Sons, 1894), 251.
7. For an extended analysis, see Peter Wallenstein, "Historicizing the Politics of Reconstruction: Congress and the Fourteenth Amendment, Section 2," in *Ending the Civil War and Consequences for Congress,* ed. Paul Finkelman and Donald R. Kennon (Athens: Ohio University

Press, 2019), 103–34. Two books published subsequent to the writing of that essay bear comment. Foner introduces the subject in his chapter on the Fourteenth Amendment, but then passes it by in favor of an emphasis on section 1, in *The Second Founding: How the Civil War and Reconstruction Remade the Constitution* (New York: W. W. Norton, 2019), 61. See also ibid., xix ("key issues"), xxv ("historical circumstances"). Michael A. Belleisles does much the same in *Inventing Equality: Reconstructing the Constitution in the Aftermath of the Civil War* (New York: St. Martin's, 2020), 9–14, 165. Such an approach has not gone unchallenged. Previous writers also emphasizing section 2 are Garrett Epps, *Democracy Reborn: The Fourteenth Amendment and the Fight for Equal Rights in Post–Civil War America* (New York: Henry Holt, 2006); Mark Wahlgren Summers, *The Ordeal of the Reunion: A New History of Reconstruction* (Chapel Hill: University of North Carolina Press, 2014), 3–4, 90–104; Xi Wang, *The Trial of Democracy: Black Suffrage and Northern Republicans, 1860–1910* (Athens: University of Georgia Press, 1997), 14–28.

8. Richard L. Hume and Jerry B. Gough, *Blacks, Carpetbaggers, and Scalawags: The Constitutional Conventions of Radical Reconstruction* (Baton Rouge: Louisiana State University Press, 2008).

9. Derrick A. Bell Jr., "*Brown v. Board of Education* and the Interest–Convergence Dilemma," *Harvard Law Review* 93 (1980): 518–33. In an earlier formulation of the concept, Bell briefly surveyed pre-1950s contexts, but regarding the Fourteenth Amendment he focused on section 1: "Racial Remediation: An Historical Perspective on Current Conditions," *Notre Dame Law Review* 52 (1976): 9–11.

10. George Brown Tindall, *South Carolina Negroes, 1877–1900* (Baton Rouge: Louisiana State University Press, [1952] 1966), 48–49, 55–56, 229–30; Maurine Christopher, *America's Black Congressmen* (New York: Thomas Y. Crowell, 1971), 113–19. For the first dozen years after the Civil War, see Thomas Holt, *Black over White: Negro Political Leadership in South Carolina during Reconstruction* (Urbana: University of Illinois Press, 1977). Extending the story into a later period is Lawrence C. Bryant, ed., *Negro Lawmakers in the South Carolina Legislature, 1868–1902* (Orangeburg: South Carolina State College, 1968).

11. Thomas B. Alexander, "Political Reconstruction in Tennessee, 1865–1870," in *Radicalism, Racism, and Party Realignment: The Border States during Reconstruction,* ed. Richard O. Curry (Baltimore: Johns Hopkins University Press, 1969), 37–79; Foner, *Freedom's Lawmakers,* xiii; Linda T. Wynn, "Sampson W. Keeble," *Tennessee Encyclopedia,* http://tennesseeencyclopedia .net/entry.php?rec=732. Foner, *Reconstruction,* 356–59, references some Black officeholders from Tennessee in the early post–Civil War years. He identifies twenty in his encyclopedic *Freedom's Lawmakers,* 257, yet he gives the figure zero as the number of Black legislators elected in Tennessee during "Reconstruction" (xvi)—though his sketch of Thomas A. Sykes as a member of the North Carolina legislature mentions that Sykes later served as a Tennessee legislator, in 1881–83 (208).

12. Joseph H. Cartwright, *The Triumph of Jim Crow: Tennessee Race Relations in the 1880s* (Knoxville: University of Tennessee Press, 1976).

13. Frenise A. Logan, *The Negro in North Carolina, 1876–1894* (Chapel Hill: University of North Carolina Press, 1964), 26–29, 217; Deborah Beckel, *Radical Reform: Interracial Politics in Post-Emancipation North Carolina* (Charlottesville: University of Virginia Press, 2011), 198–211.

14. Foner, *Freedom's Lawmakers,* xiii; Brent Tarter, *The Grandees of Government: The Origins and Persistence of Undemocratic Politics in Virginia* (Charlottesville: University of Virginia Press, 2013), 238–52.

15. Luther Porter Jackson, *Negro Office-Holders in Virginia, 1865–1895* (Norfolk: *Guide* Quality Press, 1945); email from Brent Tarter, April 2012, attaching a memorandum by Sara Bearss of the Library of Virginia from October 2011.

16. Michael B. Chesson, "Richmond's Black Councilmen," in *Southern Black Leaders of the Reconstruction Era*, ed. Howard N. Rabinowitz (Urbana: University of Illinois Press, 1982), 191–222; Tarter, *The Grandees of Government*, 255–75.

17. Blake J. Wintory, "African-American Legislators in the Arkansas General Assembly, 1868–1893," *Arkansas Historical Quarterly* 64 (Winter 2006): 385–434.

18. Foner, *Freedom's Lawmakers*, xvi; Merline Pitre, *Through Many Dangers, Toils and Snares: The Black Leadership of Texas, 1868–1900* (Austin: Eakin, 1985), 205–8. Pitre included one additional legislator from 1871, Benjamin F. Williams.

19. Canter Brown Jr., *Florida's Black Public Officials, 1867–1924* (Tuscaloosa: University of Alabama Press, 1998).

20. Vernon Lane Wharton, *The Negro in Mississippi, 1865–1890* (Chapel Hill: University of North Carolina Press, 1947), 199–215.

21. Mississippi State University Libraries, "Against All Odds: The First Black Legislators in Mississippi," online exhibition, http://msstate-exhibits.libraryhost.com/exhibits/show /legislators.

22. R. Volney Riser, *Defying Disfranchisement: Black Voting Rights Activism in the Jim Crow South, 1890–1908* (Baton Rouge: Louisiana State University Press, 2010); *Sproule v. Fredericks*, 698 Miss. 898 (1892); *Williams v. Mississippi*, 170 U.S. 213 (1898).

23. A. E. Perkins, "Some Negro Officers and Legislators in Louisiana," *Journal of Negro History* 14, no. 4 (October 1929): 523–28; William Ivy Hair, *Bourbonism and Agrarian Protest: Louisiana Politics, 1877–1900* (Baton Rouge: Louisiana State University Press, 1969), 234–79. In his book *Black Legislators in Louisiana during Reconstruction* (Baton Rouge: Louisiana State University Press, 1977), 220, without giving names or dates or any citation whatever, Charles Vincent says, regarding the years that followed the ninety-nine Black representatives and twenty-five state senators he had identified and discussed for the years 1868–77: "In the post-Reconstruction years, nine blacks served as senators and twenty-one as [r]epresentatives. The last senator left office in 1890 and the last representatives in 1900."

24. Edmund L. Drago, *Black Politicians and Reconstruction in Georgia: A Splendid Failure* (Baton Rouge: Louisiana State University Press, 1982).

25. Richard Bailey, *Neither Carpetbaggers nor Scalawags: Black Officeholders during the Reconstruction of Alabama, 1867–1878*, rev. 5th ed. (Montgomery, AL: NewSouth, [1991] 2010), 263, 277, 281.

26. Pitre, *Through Many Dangers, Toils and Snares*, 53.

27. Brown, *Florida's Black Public Officials*, ix, emphasis added.

28. Carl H. Moneyhon, "Black Politics in the Gilded Age, 1876–1900," *Arkansas Historical Quarterly* 44, no. 3 (Autumn 1985): 221; Wintory, "African-American Legislators in the Arkansas General Assembly," 387–88.

29. Peter Wallenstein, *Cradle of America: A History of Virginia*, rev. 2d ed. (Lawrence: University Press of Kansas, [2007] 2014), 233–36, 243–44.

30. Peter Wallenstein, "Pioneer Black Legislators from Kentucky, 1860s–1960s," *Register of the Kentucky Historical Society* 110, nos. 3–4 (Summer–Autumn 2012): 543–53, reprinted in John David Smith, ed., *New Perspectives on Civil War–Era Kentucky* (Lexington: University Press of Kentucky, 2023).

31. Stephen Kantrowitz, *More than Freedom: Fighting for Black Citizenship in a White Republic, 1829–1889* (New York: Penguin, 2012), 312–20. Regarding an even earlier Black legislator, in 1836, see Michael T. Hahn, *Alexander Twilight, Vermont's African-American Pioneer* (Shelburne, VT: New England Press, 1998).

32. Wallenstein, "Pioneer Black Legislators from Kentucky," 537–43, 554–55.

33. Christopher, *America's Black Congressmen*, 25–37.

34. Three Black congressmen gained election in 1876, none in 1878. For a full list, see ibid., 267–68. See also Philip Dray, *Capitol Men: The Epic Story of Reconstruction through the Lives of the First Black Congressmen* (Boston: Houghton Mifflin, 2008); Stephen Middleton, ed., *Black Congressmen during Reconstruction: A Documentary Sourcebook* (Westport, CT: Greenwood, 2002). Biographies include Andrew Billingsley, *Yearning to Breathe Free: Robert Smalls of South Carolina and His Families* (Columbia: University of South Carolina Press, 2007), and John F. Marszalek, *A Black Congressman in the Age of Jim Crow: South Carolina's George Washington Murray* (Gainesville: University Press of Florida, 2006).

35. Benjamin R. Justesen, *George Henry White: An Even Chance in the Race of Life* (Baton Rouge: Louisiana State University Press, 2001); David S. Cecelski and Timothy B. Tyson, eds., *Democracy Betrayed: The Wilmington Race Riot of 1898 and Its Legacy* (Chapel Hill: University of North Carolina Press, 1998); David Zucchino, *Wilmington's Lie: The Murderous Coup of 1898 and the Rise of White Supremacy* (New York: Atlantic Monthly, 2020).

36. Christopher, *America's Black Congressmen*, 168–208; Wil Haygood, *King of the Cats: The Life and Times of Adam Clayton Powell Jr.* (Boston: Houghton Mifflin, 1993).

37. Analyses of the end of Black political power in the former Confederate states around the end of the nineteenth century include Paul E. Herron, *Framing the Solid South: The State Constitutional Conventions of Secession, Reconstruction, and Redemption, 1860–1902* (Lawrence: University Press of Kansas, 2017), 210–25; Tarter, *The Grandees of Government*, 255–75; Xi Wang, *The Trial of Democracy: Black Suffrage and Northern Republicans, 1860–1910* (Athens: University of Georgia Press, 1997); Joel Williamson, *The Crucible of Race: Black-White Relations in the American South since Emancipation* (New York: Oxford University Press, 1984), 224–47.

38. Carl Lotus Becker, *The History of Political Parties in the Province of New York, 1760–1776*, in *Bulletin of the University of Wisconsin, History Series*, vol. 2 (Madison, 1909), 5.

39. For a striking account of continued Black resistance, including a heroic resurgence in the 1920 federal elections, capped with a horrific suppression of it, see Paul Ortiz, *Emancipation Betrayed: The Hidden History of Black Organizing and White Violence in Florida from Reconstruction to the Bloody Election of 1920* (Berkeley: University of California Press, 2005).

40. Woodrow Wilson, "The Reconstruction of the Southern States," *Atlantic Monthly*, vol. 87, January 1901, 6, 11. Wilson was writing propagandistic fiction, of course, when he claimed that Black "majorities for a little while filled the southern legislatures."

41. Bruce E. Baker, *What Reconstruction Meant: Historical Memory in the American South* (Charlottesville: University of Virginia Press, 2007), 145–60; Carol Polsgrove, *Divided Minds: Intellectuals and the Civil Rights Movement* (New York: W. W. Norton, 2001), 28–37; C. Vann Woodward, "The 'New Reconstruction' in the South: Desegregation in Historical Perspective," *Commentary*, June 1956, 501–6.

42. For examples from South Carolina, see Baker, *What Reconstruction Meant*, 89–109.

43. Pitre, *Through Many Dangers, Toils and Snares*, xi.

44. Brown, *Florida's Black Public Officials*, ix.

Lynching in the American Imagination

A HISTORIOGRAPHICAL REEXAMINATION

Mari N. Crabtree

THE CONVENIENCES OF WHISKING up historical actors into the grand sweeps of history, of neatly fitting the past into eras and compartmentalizing historical processes by region or nation, are at the very core of the historian's craft. After all, finding meaning in the past, even when done by the most cautious and nuanced of scholars, necessarily imposes on the past. The boundaries between eras may be more or less blurred, and the connections across regions may be drawn with a heavier or lighter touch, but choices as seemingly large as the emplotment of narratives and as seemingly small as the turn of a phrase leave traces of historians in their narratives. Precisely because historical narratives are what Hayden White called "an essentially *poetic* act"—that is, a reflection of a historian's vision of the past, a reconstruction of the past, and a construction of the present—these choices regarding how to divide and how to interpret must be scrutinized, even when the grand sweeps of history and regional divisions have become so entrenched in the historiography that they become naturalized, gates rusted in place after countless historians left them undisturbed.[1] Such scrutiny is healthy, just as jostling a rusty hinge will either prolong its utility or cause it to crumble and require it to be replaced.

This tendency to avoid meddling with received definitions is no less true of lynching historiography. Few scholars quibble with the assertion that lynching was widespread in the South by the 1880s, and peaked in the 1890s, with a slow decline in frequency until its eventual evolution into new forms of racial violence in the 1940s and beyond. Vigilante lynchings of cattle rustlers and murderers in the West preceded these Southern lynchings by a few decades, but because the victims are assumed to be white and the violence itself is disconnected from the various colonial projects the U.S. government was undertaking, the very nature of that violence has been deemed categorically different from lynching in the South. Typically, historians of lynching have followed the lead of Ida B. Wells, the fiery antilynching activist, who, at the turn of the twentieth century, contended that lynching was a manifestation of heightened social, political, and economic anxieties among white Southerners and a direct consequence of emancipation. These anxieties were rooted in the idea that, without enslavement, African American "progress" would undermine white supremacy.[2] Lynching, she argued, ritually reinscribed white supremacy, simultaneously enacting and justifying the system of racial oppression that became Jim Crow.

Though white status anxieties were certainly heightened after the Confederacy's defeat in the Civil War and emancipation, such a narrative severs post-emancipation Southern lynchings from lynchings elsewhere, isolating it from a longer and more expansive history of white supremacist violence in the United States. This essay challenges this myopia—tests the rusty hinges of lynching historiography, if you will—both temporally and geographically by making three historiographical claims. First, Southern lynching after emancipation and the ritualistic violence inflicted on enslaved people before emancipation bear obvious similarities. Although context matters in deciphering and distinguishing forms of anti-Black violence, post-emancipation Southern lynching grew out of centuries of violence against Black bodies deployed to protect white power: whipping and torture, rape and murder, dismembering families and imposing alien identities on enslaved people, and, yes, even pre-emancipation lynchings in the South. The monetary value of enslaved bodies never provided complete protection from lethal white violence, nor did emancipation bring an end to anti-Black violence. I do not say this to diminish the meaning of legal freedom and a long overdue constitutional guarantee of citizenship, but the tendency to envision a clean break between enslavement and freedom ignores the tiny flakes of rust released by some jostling at these temporal borders.[3]

I give another firm shake to these historiographical gates, this time looking westward from the vantage point of southeastern lynching historiography. Throughout the nineteenth century, Anglo settlers violently displaced ethnic Mexicans and Native Americans in the West, through war and other colonialist violence that included lynching, and yet, until recently, most lynching historiography has tabled lynching in the West as a prehistory of white "frontier justice" only loosely connected to post-emancipation lynching in the South.[4] Similarities between the lynching of enslaved and free Black people in the South and the lynching of Black people, ethnic Mexicans, and Native Americans in the U.S. West, however, come down to more than a matter of form in the ritual enactment of racial violence on nonwhite bodies—mutilation, torture, spectacle, an attempt to terrorize nonwhites into submission, and the like. These patterns of racialized, colonialist violence also served a common goal across regions: they enforced an essential American code wedded to white supremacist logics of U.S. citizenship that protected and reinforced white political and economic dominance. The race of the lynching victim and whether the lynching was connected to Jim Crow or U.S. colonial expansion certainly matters a great deal, for erasing these distinctions is hardly an improvement over erasing ethnic Mexicans and Native Americans wholesale from historical accounts of lynching in the U.S. West.[5] However, in identifying convergences, the very definition of lynching and existing accounts of its historical emergence come into question.

And so I offer one final, gentle gate rattling to send flakes of rust not flying off the hinges so much as floating down to historians. I echo Ari Kelman's argument in A Misplaced Massacre that tethering Civil War memory to wars of colonialist expansion often referred to as the Indian Wars tempers the redemptive narrative of 600,000 Civil War dead leading to the new dawn of freedom that Abraham Lincoln's "Second Inaugural Address" and W. E. B. Du Bois's Black Reconstruction in America (1935) imagine.[6] Emancipation profoundly changed the course of U.S. history, despite the almost immediate reinstatement of racial caste in most of the nation, but the violent dispossession of Native Americans and the mutilation of Native bodies in massacres and battles—acts perpetrated by the very Union Army fighting for national unity and emancipation—makes the clean break from the past implicit in that redemptive national narrative less tenable, not just for the memory of the Civil War but for lynching, too. Placing lynching in relation to other contemporary forms of racial violence—namely, the colonialist genocide of Native Americans and the colonialist expansion of the United States into Mexico and, later, Cuba and the Philippines—potentially changes the trajectory that many U.S. historical narratives map across the nineteenth century. My point is not to flatten any gains in freedom after the Civil War but, rather, to layer and give depth to these processes that overlap and fade into one another far more than historians typically acknowledge. This might mean reconceiving the periodization of U.S. history survey courses such that the Civil War is displaced as the primary pivot point. This might mean placing white supremacist violence at the center of U.S. history. This might mean recognizing these overlapping layers of white supremacist, colonialist violence as emblematic of the nation's creed.

Most lynching scholarship adopts a narrative in which lynching emerged in the 1870s alongside Redemption—a terrorist campaign to intimidate African Americans and white Republicans, effectively ending Reconstruction. This narrative contends that, in reaction to growing economic and political power among African American Southerners, white lynch mobs used lethal violence to police the boundaries of a destabilized racial hierarchy, and violence took on a distinctly ritualistic and public form. While these scholars recognize that, well before the Civil War, bands of vigilantes in Western states used extralegal "justice" to punish (mostly white) cattle rustlers, murderers, and others who transgressed social norms, they place the racialization of lynching in the South and in the decades following the Civil War.[7] Then as now, this understanding of lynching as Black, Southern, and post-emancipation has persisted. The lynching statistics tabulated by the National Association for the Advancement of Colored People (NAACP) and Tuskegee Institute certainly cemented the association between lynching and Black Southerners, as did the visibility of antilynching activists who were largely African American or Southern. Contemporary news coverage of lynchings similarly reinforced that regional and racial connection. In the early twentieth century, public debates in print and on the floors of legislatures typically weighed whether the victim "deserved" to die at the hands of a mob and whether lynching as a tool for asserting social control was a social good. That the victim was Black and the purpose of lynching was to reinforce white supremacy, however, simply went without saying.

Despite the seeming consensus over the racial and geographic boundaries of lynching, the definition was far from settled in the nineteenth and twentieth centuries and remains so to this day. Underlying these disagreements is a series of competing political agendas and, as Ashraf Rushdy put it, that "'lynching' is a term more evocative than descriptive."[8] In 1940, several anti-lynching organizations met to settle on a common definition after discrepancies over whether particular lynchings in the late 1930s "counted." By focusing on *form*, the Association of Southern Women for the Prevention of Lynching wanted to define lynching out of existence to rehabilitate the white South's image, whereas the NAACP recognized that the form of lynching was in the process of evolving so they emphasized the *motive* of lynchers to terrorize specific groups. The definition they settled on required that a group had illegally killed the victim "under the pretext of service to justice, race, or tradition."[9] However, even this consensus definition places greater emphasis on the legality of the act rather the intent of the lynchers to reify white supremacy and U.S. Empire.

Scholars have taken cues from antilynching activists, the press, and public debates as they construct and shape lynching historiography, but to understand the dominance of this narrative, we must return to Wells, a journalist and well-known antilynching crusader. In *A Red Record*, a pamphlet she published in 1895, she argued that lynching arose once white interests in preserving the monetary value of Black bodies disappeared with emancipation:

> During the slave regime, the Southern white man owned the Negro body and soul. It was to his interest to dwarf the soul and preserve the body. . . . While slaves were scourged mercilessly, and in countless cases inhumanly treated in other respects, still the white owner rarely permitted his anger to go so far as to take a life, which would entail upon him a loss of several hundred dollars. The

slave was rarely killed, he was too valuable; it was easier and quite as effective, for discipline or revenge, to sell him "Down South."

But Emancipation came and the vested interests of the white man in the Negro's body were lost. . . . In slave times the Negro was kept subservient and submissive by the frequency and severity of the scourging, but, with freedom, a new system of intimidation came into vogue; the Negro was not only whipped and scourged; he was killed.[10]

Wells was unsparing in her indictment of cruel enslavers whose punishments she described as "merciless" and "inhumane," but her contention that "the white owner rarely permitted his anger to go so far as to take a life" gave too much credit to the rationality and restraint of enslavers and discounted the calculated "benefits" of lethal punishments for particularly "difficult" enslaved people. In some cases, selling someone "Down South" as punishment was not an option because finding a willing buyer for an enslaved person who repeatedly ran away or had attempted to murder a white person or had a reputation for being "unruly" could carry disastrous consequences (for enslavers, at least)—an insurrection, for instance.[11]

Historical records, though spotty, bear out the regularity with which enslavers killed the people they enslaved, despite forfeiting the monetary value of each pound of flesh. Slave narratives describe several instances of such killings, and the offenses that led to these deaths run the gamut from murdering an overseer and running away to mistakenly fishing on a neighboring plantation and refusing to submit to a whipping. For instance, an enslaved man named Augustus, an acquaintance of Solomon Northup's from an adjoining plantation, fled after an overseer severely whipped him, and when a pack of fifteen hounds tracked him down, they attacked him, tearing into his flesh and bones. Augustus died the following day from his wounds, and his suffering and death served as a cautionary tale to other enslaved people in the area.[12] Augustus's killing was a calculated attempt to demonstrate to enslaved people the sheer enormity of white power, an explicit decision to terrorize and to compel submission from enslaved people.

Punishments, lethal or not, were used to threaten enslaved people as a collective, just as post-emancipation lynching made an example of an individual Black person to terrorize the entire community. Enslavers subjected enslaved people to iron collars, forced iron bits into their mouths, and mutilated their bodies as punishments, and this violence played the double role of terrorizing Black people into their "place" and reassuring whites of their status.[13] Everyday punishments tended to be public by design—stripping people of their clothing before shredding their backs to ribbons with a whip inflicted excruciating pain *and* public humiliation—and bodies, scarred and maimed through various tortures, were themselves permanent physical reminders of the price enslaved people paid for transgressing the white suprema-cist racial hierarchy. These scars functioned much the way that "souvenirs" severed from lynched bodies and displayed in shop windows did in the Jim Crow era, as physical reminders of white power. An enslaver's eyes might survey each scarred ridge of an enslaved person's mangled back to feel powerful, and the reassurance that white eyes searched for in a lynching photograph after emancipation was much the same, though the terrain, flattened into a postcard, lost some of the im-mediacy that flesh-and-blood bodies possessed.

Enslaved bodies held more than just monetary value to enslavers—more than the prices paid, the labor extracted, the skills and knowledge exploited. They held symbolic value, too. Death could prove valuable to enslavers. Death could result from calculations made with actuarial precision about the long-term impacts of "unruly property." An overseer who worked for Frederick Douglass's enslaver, Mr. Gore, for instance, shot and killed an enslaved man named Demby for flee-ing into a creek to avoid a whipping. Gore convinced Demby's enslaver that the enslaved man's death was well worth the financial loss because failing to make an example of Demby "would finally lead to the total subversion of all rule and order upon the plantation."[14] Douglass hardly needed further evidence that his life could be taken on a white person's whim—the daily brutality of enslavement made that possibility perfectly clear—but Demby's death had a chilling effect nonetheless. As with post-emancipation lynchings, Gore avoided legal consequences for murder, and Gore's reputation as an effective and terrifying overseer, in fact, grew as a result of shooting and killing Demby.[15]

Both lethal and nonlethal punishments, then, turned enslaved bodies into sites for enacting, in well-rehearsed rituals of violence, the power of white supremacy. Like post-emancipation lynchings, such violence during enslavement was both a tool for controlling Black people *and* a means to solidify a collective white identity that underpinned white supremacy, thereby discouraging white dissent against the status quo. Nonelite whites such as the overseer Gore could use anti-Black vio-lence to enhance their social status without owning property, just as lynchings after emancipation served as a means to quell white status anxieties, especially among whites whose economic precarity put them on the brink of slipping to or below the class of their Black neighbors. Therefore, although the monetary value of enslaved people might appear to have protected African Americans from lethal violence, some enslavers (and whites too poor to be enslavers) rationalized these killings as a means to protect their financial interests, social status, and physical safety. Emancipation removed some of the financial incentives to preserve Black life, even if punishment just short of death was a matter of routine during slavery, but the underlying meaning of violence against Black people—its social value as a means to assert and maintain white control—remained generally consistent before and after emancipation.[16]

These examples from Douglass and Northup may strike some as cases of murder rather than lynching because Gore alone fired the bullet that killed Demby, and the bloodhounds, presumably accompanied by a posse of white men, inflicted the wounds that led to Augustus's death. However, some killings of free and enslaved Black people before 1865 even more closely resembled the form of post-emancipation lynchings. In 1851, a Black man was burned to death by a lynch mob in Paudling, Mississippi, for allegedly raping a white woman and murdering her son.[17] Soon after rumors of a Mississippi slave insurrection surfaced in 1835, a lynch mob in Clinton, Mississippi, hanged an enslaved boy suspected of planning another rebellion, and a judge who had attempted to save the boy's life counseled the boy's enslaver to not press charges out of concern that her own life might be in danger.[18] Perhaps the most obvious pre–Civil War equivalents are the executions of free and enslaved Black people for planning insurrections or revolting—most often by hanging and usually carried out by the state, but sometimes by private citizens. Much like the "legal lynchings" of the post-emancipation era, the execution of free and enslaved Black people for transgressing the white power structure sometimes were preceded by something approximating a legal trial, and in certain cases enslavers were compensated by the state for the value of executed enslaved people.[19] These trials and executions were, in essence, performances, rituals of raw brutality designed to reassert white dominance and ease white paranoia of subsequent, even more deadly attacks on white supremacy.

The public execution of African Americans involved in insurrections carried the same symbolic weight as post-emancipation lynchings. Northup recalled a story about enslaved people in central Louisiana who gathered supplies and planned an escape to Mexico in the 1840s. The leader betrayed the plot, and his enslaved coconspirators (and others suspected of complicity) faced summary execution by hanging without the benefit of legitimate legal trials. Only when planters eventually protested the enormous financial losses from so many executions carried out by "the populace"—by which Northup presumably meant local white civilians acting outside of the legal system—did the state, with the help of a Texas regiment, halt the remaining executions.[20] Although the high property value of these enslaved people ultimately put an end to the killing spree, the will of the white community, acting out of fear for their lives and their way of life, was to resort to summary execution outside of the law. The difference between the actions of "the populace" in central Louisiana in the 1840s and that of white lynch mobs in the 1890s seems largely to be a matter of time period. In both cases, white citizens subverted the legal process—killing African Americans and terrorizing African

American communities—to assert control and reassure themselves of their place in the South.

The Louisiana slave conspiracy that Northup described was far from an isolated incident. Herbert Aptheker's classic study, *American Negro Slave Revolts* (1944), painstakingly catalogued hundreds of insurrections, several of which ended with extreme violence used to punish insurrectionists.[21] Quite often, the level of violence and the ritualistic nature of the violence in these executions far exceeded that prescribed for other executions. Death itself was not punishment enough. Excess could be measured in the ghastly desecration of bodies. Insurrectionists suffered through torture and mutilation, their corpses often left to rot for weeks as a warning to Black passersby. Excess could also be measured in numbers. To apprehend those involved in insurrections, armed militias or bands of local white civilians often engaged in deadly skirmishes with armed groups of enslaved and free Black people, and the executions that followed, often by the dozen, were as much a show of draconian force to deter future insurrections as a reflection of white fear.[22]

In most of the revolts Aptheker describes, the state, not private citizens, carried out these executions, but white public hysteria surrounding these insurrections distinguishes these legal proceedings from other cases that resulted in executions. In case after case, wild conjecture about slave conspiracies reflected white fears and guilt more than reality, and as rumors spread, the number of conspirators ballooned and the freedom dreams of enslaved people, distorted by white anxieties and guilt, were transformed into a vengeful wrath aimed at indiscriminately massacring white people. The same gross exaggeration and distortion of reality appeared in sensationalist narratives of the ghastly crimes attributed to lynching victims. Moreover, the popular image of lynching is that of an extralegal execution by an unruly mob, but in light of "legal lynchings" and state officials actively participating in post-emancipation "extralegal lynchings," the line between state and non-state actors was blurry, at best, even after emancipation. More to the point, because executions of insurrectionists were public, and bodies (or severed body parts) were often gibbeted, the *performative* element of these pre-emancipation executions bear clear similarities to post-emancipation lynchings in the South.[23]

The Civil War and the emancipation of more than four million enslaved people serves as a convenient pivot point, not just in conventional definitions of lynching, but in U.S. historical narratives more generally. On the cusp of the war, however, the smoothness of that pivot comes into question when scrutinized more closely. Amid the chaos of John Brown's raid at Harpers Ferry in 1859, the local Virginia militia not only shot and killed one of the Black men who had joined Brown, a former enslaved man named Dangerfield Newby, but castrated him and sliced off his ears as souvenirs.[24] The sexual mutilation of Newby and the taking of souvenirs from his dead body bear an eerie resemblance to the rituals of post-emancipation lynching in the South, but under the conventional periodization of lynching, the nature of Newby's death seems to have happened a decade too soon. However, this kind of excessive violence—this performance of hypermasculinity and white supremacy—was no anachronism in 1859. The mutilation of Newby's body, the mass executions of insurrectionists in Louisiana, and other examples of anti-Black spectacle violence that preceded emancipation force us to reconsider the post–Civil War starting point that historians impose on the definition of lynching.

Reaching back into the pre–Civil War South to unearth examples of lynching is but one part of the temporal and geographical expansion I envision in redefining lynching. To take in the full scope of lynching requires us to look westward from the southeastern United States and see among the faces of victims and survivors Native Americans, Latinx people (especially ethnic Mexicans), and Asian Americans (especially Chinese immigrants). Shifting our gaze westward also compels us, again, to wade back in time before emancipation and to expand the scope of white supremacy bolstered by lynching to also include genocide, wars for territorial expansion, and colonialism. I bring lynching in the U.S. West into the same frame as lynching in the South not only to counteract the tendency to erase victims who were neither white nor Black but also to provide a more complete and therefore less distorted image of U.S. lynching.[25]

The relative invisibility of ethnic Mexican and Native American victims, especially in popular and scholarly notions of lynching, started early, and the scholarship on Native American and ethnic Mexican lynching in the American West remains small relative to the literature on Southern lynching.[26] Scholars have relied heavily on the lynching records compiled by the Tuskegee Institute, the NAACP, and the Association of Southern Women for the Prevention of Lynching as sources, all of which focused on the South after 1880. However, many, if not most, Western lynchings occurred before 1865, and, with a largely Southern regional focus, these records often grossly underestimate the number of lynchings in the West and distort the racial demographics of Western lynching. Some records further erased Native American, Latinx, and Asian American victims by ignoring them or lumping them in with white victims. For instance, one of the more complete sources identified forty-eight white victims and two African American victims in California, but Ken Gonzales-Day's research uncovered a total of 352 California cases, of which eight victims were African American; forty-one, Native American; twenty-nine, Chinese; 120, Anglo-American or persons of European descent; 132, Latin American or Mexican; and twenty-two, race unknown.[27] Numbers alone do not fundamentally challenge the dominant definition of lynching, but these numbers—precisely because they demonstrate the erasure of lynchings in the Western United States and disrupt the Black-white racial binary—should compel a reconsideration of lynching narratives.

I want to be clear, though, that my point in expanding the definition of lynching is not to deflect attention from Southern lynchings of African Americans, which is so often the true intent behind the refrain "But whites were lynched, too." Yes, whites were lynched, too, but those deflections, at their heart, are motivated by a desire to dismiss the centrality of white supremacy and the race of the victims and perpetrators in understanding the broader social significance of lynching. The emphasis on African Americans as the targets of lynching, both as victims and survivors, brings into sharp focus the underlying racial politics of the practice. To expand the scope of lynching to include violence against Native Americans, Latinx people, and Asian Americans is not to deny African American victimhood or displace white supremacy, as in the "But whites were lynched, too'" deflection. This more comprehensive vision of lynching also does not intend to crowd white victims out of the frame. Rather, it seeks to draw connections among several forms of white supremacy that interlock across time and space through the ritual of lynching.

The lynching of African Americans in the South and the lynching of Native Americans, ethnic Mexicans, and Asian Americans in the West bear many clear similarities, but the explanatory power of Southern lynching has its limits in these other historical and geographical contexts. When, for instance, Anglo vigilantes lynched seven ethnic Mexican shepherds who worked on a Mexican-owned ranch near Corpus Christi, Texas, in 1873, their deaths (and the subsequent "inconclusive" investigation) not only precipitated significant economic losses for the ranch owner but also sent a message to other ethnic Mexicans about their precarious position in an Anglo-dominated U.S. territory. Nearly three decades after the Treaty of Guadalupe Hidalgo granted full U.S. citizenship rights to ethnic Mexicans who remained in Texas, Anglo vigilantes intended to intimidate the Mexican rancher who employed the seven lynching victims into abandoning or selling his ranch, much as white mobs in the South often targeted successful Black farmers to seize their land.[28] As was the case with so many post-emancipation Southern lynchings, the investigation conducted by local law enforcement concluded that the seven lynching victims "were found hung to trees by parties unknown."[29] The courts and law enforcement refused to pursue or punish the perpetrators, in essence giving official state sanction to these lynchings and the violent transfer of property to Anglos. Whereas Southern lynchings gave legitimacy to Jim Crow and slavery, this mass lynching near Corpus Christi and others in the U.S.-Mexico borderlands furthered the U.S. government's colonialist agenda to assert control over a region, recently seized in a war, with a large, well-established non-Anglo population. These lynchings were part of a broader pattern of racialized violence sponsored—or, at least, condoned—by the U.S. state in its colonialist project to wrest territory and political control from nonwhites and impose a white supremacist social order in the region.

In an article about state-sponsored anti-Mexican violence, Monica Muñoz Martinez writes that such violence must be "located at the nexus of histories of vigilantism in the United States against domestic racial groups, practices of genocidal colonialism against indigenous nations in the Americas, and histories of U.S. Empire."[30] These borderlands had long been sites of contestation as the United States, over the course of the nineteenth century, forcibly seized larger and larger expanses of Native American and Mexican land. Colonial relationships between Anglos and ethnic Mexicans were still very much in flux during the second half of the nineteenth century—they were still being negotiated on the ground long after diplomatic negotiations had been formally settled in 1836 with Texas independence, in 1848 with the Treaty of Guadalupe Hidalgo, and in 1854 with the Gadsden Purchase. Even with these diplomatic agreements in place, state agents, whether the military or pseudo-vigilante groups such as the Texas Rangers, used violence against ethnic Mexicans as a tool of empire.[31] In light of continued struggles over power and influence in the West, these lynchings, which continued into the 1930s, cannot be disentangled from negotiations over political power, economic control, and access to citizenship.

The same could be said about Native Americans lynched by white mobs during the nineteenth and early twentieth centuries. The lynching of Native Americans generally took the same form as Southern lynchings and served a similar general purpose—policing racial boundaries and maintaining racial hierarchies—but these deaths also contributed to the colonial project that European nations and the United States had been engaged in since at least the sixteenth century.[32] Lynching was but one form of racialized violence among many, including massacres, wars, cultural genocide, military executions, and displacement onto reservations, used to remove and, in some cases, exterminate Native Americans.[33] That lynching was one of the methods used to enable colonial expansion into Native American territories is hardly surprising. Lynchings and massacres not only shared the same political ends but also inflicted gratuitous violence on their victims and desecrated their bodies. The U.S. regiments that massacred an encampment of Cheyenne and Arapaho near Sand Creek, Colorado, in 1864, for instance, not only killed hundreds of Native Americans but also mutilated their bodies, cutting off the ears and genitals of men, scalping an unborn baby cut out of its mother, and taking as souvenirs the genitals of women. The Native Americans killed in what became known as the Sand Creek Massacre had settled near Fort Lyon to be protected by U.S. troops, but instead they became casualties of the ongoing wars for colonialist expansion. Their violent deaths harked back to the mutilation and gibbeting of enslaved Black people and the systematic killing of ethnic Mexicans in the U.S. government's pursuit of more territory, and their frozen corpses littering the creek bed foreshadowed the thousands of lynchings that followed the Civil War, which ended only a few months later.[34]

The Sand Creek Massacre and the Indian Wars, then, bring us back to the South, the site of so many Civil War battles. Such a return seems particularly fitting since the war itself erupted over the question of whether the enslavement of Black people, which by 1861 was largely contained to the South, would leach into the West.[35] Racialized violence already had a long history out west, which led Ned Blackhawk, writing about the expansion of the U.S. Empire into the region, to the grim conclusion that every facet of national expansion was steeped in bloodshed:

> From the use of the U.S. Army to combat and confine Indian peoples, to the state-sanctioned theft of Indian lands and resources, violence both predated and became intrinsic to American expansion. Violence enabled the rapid accumulation of new resources, territories, and subject peoples. It legitimated the power of migrants, structured new social and racial orders, and provided the preconditions for political formation. From the initial moments of American exploration and conquest, through statehood, and into the stages of territorial formation, violence organized the region's nascent economies, settlements, and polities. Violence and American nationhood, in short, progressed hand in hand.[36]

Blackhawk writes about colonial expansion specifically, but given the deep connections between enslavement and that expansion—that is, the ways in which various forms of racial hegemony were mutually reinforcing—his words ring true for the nation as a whole. Enslaved people and their descendants certainly understood that, as Blackhawk puts it, "Violence and American nationhood . . . progressed hand in hand." Ethnic Mexicans in the U.S.-Mexico borderlands and Chinese immigrants in the West did, too. Rather than thinking about the distinctions among slavery, Jim Crow, U.S. colonialism, and genocide—as real as these differences are—as reasons to separate the lynching of African Americans from the lynching of other nonwhites, we should understand lynching to be a ritual performance of white supremacy that binds together these various systems of racial oppression. The deeper significance of lynching comes into sharper focus when we consider just how geographically dispersed it was, how long the practice took place, and how, despite similarities in form and function, lynching could enforce and reinforce a range of racially oppressive systems. Despite the tendency to erase Native American, ethnic Mexican, and Asian American lynching in the West and the twin tendency to separate post-emancipation lynching of African Americans from African American lynching during slavery, a comprehensive understanding of lynching exposes how the United States has drawn in blood the boundaries of race and place, not only for African Americans, but for all nonwhites.[37]

Stretching and reshaping the lens for viewing lynching to capture all the dimensions of the practice requires other adjustments not only to the definition of lynching itself but to the historical narrative of the United States. In the limited space I have here, I offer an impressionistic sketch of what these adjustments might look like and what is at stake in reimagining both lynching and the historical narrative of the United States. Reading Southern and Western lynching in concert with each other reveals how significant lynching was to state-building and constructing citizenship as white in both the South and the West. Furthermore, these insights that bind together lynching across time and place disrupt received historical narratives about the very arc of the nineteenth-century United States.

So often, scholars have described lynching as a form of "extralegal violence," as executions performed by non-state actors to carry out the will of the (white) community. In fact, when I first started writing about lynching, I often slipped into this very language, using "lynching" and "extralegal violence" interchangeably. When examined more closely, however, the distinctions drawn between "legal" and "extralegal," as well as between "state" and "non-state," though never terribly clear anyway, become increasingly hazy in light of Southern lynchings before the Civil War and Western lynchings during colonialist expansion.[38] Even post-emancipation lynchings of African Americans in the South blurred these categories. Sheriffs charged with protecting prisoners often handed them over to lynch mobs. Senators joined or led lynch mobs. In 1899, law enforcement officials in Georgia, for instance, not only refused to save Sam Hose from a lynch mob, but the governor failed to prevent the lynching, even after newspapers widely publicized both the location and time of the lynching, which had been delayed in order to set up a special excursion train to bring more spectators to watch Hose tortured to death.[39] In fact, a former U.S. senator from Mississippi, W. V. Sullivan, personally led the lynch mob in Oxford, Mississippi, that killed Nelse Patton in 1908. Afterward, he proudly proclaimed, "Of course I wanted him lynched. . . . I saw his body dangling from a tree this morning, and I'm glad of it."[40] "Legal lynchings" and lynchings that followed hastily prosecuted cases (where the mob seizes the defendant from the courtroom immediately following a verdict) also raise serious questions about how to disentangle the will of the white community from the actions of the state. But even when state institutions or state officials did not personally participate in mobs as Sullivan had, that most lynchings went uninvestigated and unprosecuted; that most investigations concluded that the victim died "at the hands of persons unknown"; that most communities remained tight-lipped about naming lynchers; that sheriffs who investigated lynchings risked being voted out of office; and that elected officials were cheered by their constituents for defending lynching makes the line between legal and extralegal and the line between state and non-state largely disappear.[41]

Western lynchings make these distinctions even hazier. Most lynchings in the West that targeted Native Americans and ethnic Mexicans directly served the U.S. government's colonial agenda. In the U.S.-Mexico borderlands, Anglo vigilantes lynched ethnic Mexicans while state agents, law enforcement officers, and Texas Rangers who wielded legal authority acted as pseudo-vigilante groups, carrying out summary executions into the 1920s. In both cases, the goal was to seize land from ethnic Mexicans and remove them from the region. For instance, in 1915 a plot to overthrow U.S. rule in south Texas, allegedly written by Mexican insurrectionists, came to light. State lawmakers and courts in Texas gave the Texas Rangers and local law enforcement nearly free rein to kill ethnic Mexicans, including those who were U.S. citizens, simply for being in physical proximity to the alleged crime. Not only were the Rangers immune from prosecution for killing ethnic Mexicans; so were vigilantes with little or no official connection to the state. Some scholars describe this systematic murder of hundreds of ethnic Mexicans as "ethnic cleansing" and "state-sanctioned racial terror," and I would argue that, in the lived experience of ethnic Mexicans and in the memories they passed on to their descendants, pseudo-vigilantes with legal authority advancing the state's colonialist goals and vigilantes without legal authority (but who suffer no legal repercussions for committing murder) advancing those same colonialist goals are functionally the same.[42]

In light of the direct connection between lynching and other U.S. empire-building practices in the West, scholars of Southern lynching may want to reconsider whether similar connections exist in the South. After all, state-sponsored and state-sanctioned racial terror during slavery also underpinned the social order and shaped the meaning of citizenship. After emancipation, state-sanctioned racial terror uprooted Reconstruction governments and brought about the era of white supremacist Redemption in the 1870s and 1880s. Rather than thinking about Southern lynching primarily in terms of social policing enacted by lynch mobs, Southern lynching should be framed as a means to consolidate state power and define citizenship around a white supremacist racial order. Since members of lynch mobs rarely faced indictments, the state clearly sanctioned these racially motivated killings. Like ethnic Mexicans living in U.S. territory who were granted citizenship rights under the terms of the Treaty of Guadalupe Hidalgo, African Americans gained legal protections as citizens with the ratification of the Fourteenth Amendment. But for both groups, lynching, in conjunction with other state practices, systematically gutted U.S. citizenship of its meaning while encoding citizenship as racially white. The state not only tolerated these restrictive notions of citizenship and the consolidation of state power in the hands of whites but actively sought to protect this racial hegemony for its own legitimacy.

Recognizing how lynching consolidated state power in a variety of temporal and geographic contexts has broader implications for the historical trajectories historians cast, especially over the nineteenth century. Western and Southern stories of lynching are tightly enmeshed and bound together by a national narrative, yet despite this tightly wound tangle, these regional stories often appear deeply conflicted because of the ways in which the national narrative has been told. That the moment of emancipation—a moment of triumph and hope after centuries of oppression—arrives as colonialist wars in the U.S. West continue to escalate challenges any linear or neat notion of justice and history. National redemption, however, is what so many Americans sought in the abolition of slavery and the promise of Reconstruction. Du Bois described Reconstruction as a "splendid failure" because this culminating moment of national redemption after centuries of enslavement failed, not because African Americans were ill-suited to becoming citizens, but because racial terrorism and an abandonment of democratic principles eroded that promise of freedom.[43] Du Bois described emancipation as a celebration marked by unimaginable jubilation, and it certainly was for the more than four million African Americans freed by the Emancipation Proclamation and the Thirteenth Amendment. For the nation as a whole, and for African Americans during and after Reconstruction, this redemptive narrative rings hollow.[44] Perhaps the nation's failure to live up to the promise of the Reconstruction amendments and the promise of its creed should be unsurprising, since the same federal government that reconstructed the South through state building was engaged in wars of territorial expansion that killed and displaced hundreds of thousands of nonwhite people.

Viewing lynching in the South and lynching in the West in the same frame decenters the gaze of the East in U.S. historical narratives; a wider frame also allows us to see continuities in the deployment of racialized violence and ongoing liberation struggles throughout U.S. history. My point is not to replace one frame with another—it is not to displace 1865 as a pivotal moment with 1836—but to consider how the march of the U.S. Empire across both the nineteenth century and the North American continent tempers the redemptive narrative of the Civil War (and the promise of Reconstruction) and provides significant points of convergence across time and space that otherwise would be missed. These narratives often do not converge, as one would expect, but even so, I prefer a thoughtful layering of narratives to the near-dominance of one at the exclusion of others. What unifies lynching across the United States is not simply the ways in which racial violence has both served to oppress various nonwhite people and given shape to the national narrative. Unity also rests in the potential for solidarity among people of color built on these shared experiences with violence that resonate across racial, temporal, and geographical boundaries. In fact, these shared experiences of violence have already galvanized multiracial social justice movements, and historians have a critical role to play in the freedom dreams of these movements. Lynching has had a long afterlife that still seeps into the present. Only if historians reconfigure our national narrative such that we recognize that white supremacist violence is *intrinsic* to the United States will the promise of those liberatory movements come to fruition.

Notes

A conversation with Edward Baptist about the seemingly anachronistic "lynching scene" in the film 12 Years a Slave *(2014) planted the seed for the historiographical interventions at the core of this essay. I thank him for that initial spark of inspiration and for subsequent suggestions regarding sources to track down and ideas to critically unpack. I also benefited immensely from insights into the history of U.S.-Mexico borderlands, colonialist violence against Native Americans and ethnic Mexicans, and the punishment of enslaved people from Lisa Covert, Maeve Kane, Nicole Maskiell, and especially Nicole Guidotti-Hernández, who provided extensive comments on the essay manuscript for the School of Languages, Cultures, and World Affairs Junior Faculty Colloquium at the College of Charleston.*

1. Hayden White, *Metahistory: The Historical Imagination in Nineteenth-Century Europe* (Baltimore: Johns Hopkins University Press, 1973), x.

2. The historical record largely bears out these fears, but for reasons that greatly differ from those that white supremacists imagined to be true. During slavery, African Americans actively undermined their enslavement by running away, slowing down their work, cultivating distinct cultural institutions, and even maiming themselves to make them less "valuable." After the Civil War they attempted to reconstruct the South into a truer, more just, more racially egalitarian democracy that included not only the extension of voting rights but also public schools. Many white Southerners, however, convinced themselves that a desire for revenge after centuries of enslavement would lead African Americans to turn the tables on the white supremacist social order, which reflected more about white guilt and anxieties than reality: Ida B. Wells, *A Red Record*, in *Southern Horrors and Other Writings: The Anti-Lynching Campaign of Ida B. Wells, 1892–1900*, ed. Jacqueline Jones Royster (Boston: Bedford/St. Martin's, 1997), 75.

3. For insights into ongoing debates over when lynching ended, see Ashraf Rushdy, *The End of American Lynching* (New Brunswick, NJ: Rutgers University Press, 2012).

4. I use the term "ethnic Mexicans" to refer to Mexicans, Mexican Americans, and Mexicans whose citizenship changed after the U.S. seizure of Mexican territory following the Mexican-American War.

5. Here my usage of "Western lynching" (i.e., lynching in the U.S. West) is analogous to my usage of "Southern lynching" (i.e., lynching in the South).

6. Ari Kelman, *A Misplaced Massacre: Struggling over the Memory of Sand Creek* (Cambridge, MA: Harvard University Press, 2013), 31, 278–79.

7. See, as an example, W. Fitzhugh Brundage, *Lynching in the New South: Georgia and Virginia, 1880–1930* (Urbana: University of Illinois Press, 1993), 3–8.

8. Ashraf Rushdy, *American Lynching* (New Haven, CT: Yale University Press, 2012), 6.

9. Rushdy, *The End of American Lynching*, 97–98.

10. Wells, *A Red Record*, 75.

11. Walter Johnson points out that, as enslavers studied the bodies of enslaved people at auction blocks and in slave markets, they looked for scars from whippings that might indicate

that the person had run away, was particularly "unruly," or might encourage other enslaved people to revolt, and those scars alone often dissuaded a prospective buyer from making a purchase. In 1828, Louisiana went as far as to require traders to prove the "good character" of enslaved people older than twelve with a certificate signed by three witnesses, if the trader brought them across state lines, but even then a back crisscrossed with scars might make selling an enslaved person "down South" all but impossible: Walter Johnson, *Soul by Soul: Life inside the Antebellum Slave Market* (Cambridge, MA: Harvard University Press, 2001), 145–47.

12. Solomon Northup, *Twelve Years a Slave* (Auburn, NY: Derby and Miller, 1853), 243–44.

13. Edward E. Baptist, *The Half Has Never Been Told: Slavery and the Making of American Capitalism* (New York: Basic, 2014), 140–42.

14. Frederick Douglass, *Narrative of the Life of Frederick Douglass, an American Slave, Written by Himself* (Boston: Anti-Slavery Office, 1845), 23.

15. Ibid., 22–24.

16. Daina Ramey Berry and Walter Johnson both illuminate a variety of (often) competing understandings of Black value held *by* and imposed *on* enslaved people, and they recount instances in which killing enslaved people could be strategic and even profitable for enslavers: Daina Ramey Berry, *The Price for Their Pound of Flesh: The Value of the Enslaved, from Womb to Grave, in the Building of a Nation* (Boston: Beacon, 2017); Johnson, *Soul by Soul*.

17. Ken Gonzales-Day, *Lynching in the West, 1850–1935* (Durham, NC: Duke University Press, 2006), 67. Philip Dray also points to pre-emancipation lynchings in the South that targeted Black people: Philip Dray, *At the Hands of Persons Unknown: The Lynching of Black America* (New York: Modern Library, 2002), 22–29.

18. Bertram Wyatt-Brown and Herbert Aptheker identify several cases of pre–Civil War lynchings in the South, including the case from Mississippi described here. Several of the specific cases Brown cites involved white victims, but he makes passing reference to "politically motivated lynchings" such as those "to prevent slaves from developing leadership for rebellions": Bertram Wyatt-Brown, *Honor and Violence in the South* (New York: Oxford University Press, 1986), 188. See also Herbert Aptheker, *American Negro Slave Revolts* (New York: International Publishers, [1943] 1969), 52–53.

19. With "legal lynchings," I refer to cases in which a perfunctory trial leads to a foreordained guilty verdict that is followed swiftly by a state execution, often to preempt a lynch mob. "Legal lynchings" provided local law enforcement and politicians (rather weak) cover to deflect accusations that the state tolerated or even encouraged extralegal violence and denied justice to Black defendants. Local African American communities often did not distinguish between "lynching" and "legal lynching" because the miscarriage of justice and the outcomes were virtually identical.

20. Northup, *Twelve Years a Slave*, 224, 246–48.

21. The first documented American revolt Aptheker identified, which involved white indentured servants and enslaved Black people in Virginia conspiring together in 1663, ended with "the display of several bloody heads from local chimney tops": Aptheker, *American Negro Slave Revolts*, 164–65. In another case, this time in Louisiana in 1732, a woman was hanged and four men were "broken on the wheel" for plotting an insurrection, and their severed heads were posted on poles at the city limits of New Orleans: ibid., 182. More than a century later in 1856, an enslaved man in Alabama swore he would sooner die than reveal an insurrection plot spurred on by rumors that the Republican presidential candidate, John Frémont, would abolish slavery. He received an incredible seven-hundred-fifty lashes and took his secrets to the grave: ibid., 58, 164–65, 182.

22. To provide some perspective on the numbers, a sampling of major slave revolts reveals how many Black lives were lost in these mass executions: Stono Rebellion, Charleston, SC, 1740, about thirty-four shot in skirmishes and forty shot, hanged, or gibbeted alive after being apprehended; New York Conspiracy, New York City, 1741, thirteen burned alive and eighteen hanged (two in chains); Gabriel's Rebellion, Henrico County, VA, 1800, at least thirty-five executed; Vesey Conspiracy, Charleston, SC, 1822, thirty-seven hanged; Nat Turner's Insurrection, Southampton County, VA, 1831, twenty hanged; unnamed rebellion, New Orleans, 1856, twenty hanged: ibid., 188, 195, 222, 271, 302, 348.

23. Gibbeting and other public displays of punishment—whether public whipping, hanging, breaking on the wheel, and so on—were not exclusively used to punish nonwhites. Not only were African American, Native American, or mixed-race people the vast majority of those subjected to excessive, public displays of violence, but practices such as gibbeting and castration ended for white people earlier than for nonwhites. Also, into the twentieth century punishments for the same crime differed based on the race, gender, and free status of the accused: Stuart Banner, "Traces of Slavery: Race and the Death Penalty in Historical Perspective," in From Lynch Mobs to the Killing State: Race and the Death Penalty in America, ed. Charles Ogletree and Austin Sarat (New York: New York University Press, 2006), 98–101; Winthrop Jordan, White over Black: American Attitudes toward the Negro, 1550–1812 (Chapel Hill: University of North Carolina Press, 1968), 154–56.

24. Baptist, The Half Has Never Been Told, 385.

25. This erasure is also produced by the myth that "frontier justice" brought law and order to the U.S. West, making lynching seem disconnected from white supremacist or colonialist histories: Gonzales-Day, Lynching in the West, 35.

26. Although the scholarship on Western lynching is relatively new, several scholars not only have done the difficult and tedious work of uncovering and compiling hundreds of Western lynchings, but have demonstrated how this racialized violence served the ends of U.S. state building and solidified the racial regime of white supremacy in the region: ibid.; William D. Carrigan and Clive Webb, Forgotten Dead: Mob Violence against Mexicans in the United States, 1848–1928 (New York: Oxford University Press, 2014); Nicole M. Guidotti-Hernández, Unspeakable Violence: Remapping U.S. and Mexican National Imaginaries (Durham, NC: Duke University Press, 2011); Monica Muñoz Martinez, The Injustice Never Leaves You: Anti-Mexican Violence in Texas (Cambridge, MA: Harvard University Press, 2018); Monica Muñoz Martinez, "Recuperating Histories of Violence in the Americas: Vernacular History-Making on the U.S.-Mexico Border," American Quarterly 66, no. 3 (September 2014): 661–89.

27. Ken Gonzales-Day also found that, of 103 cases of legal and military executions in California after September 9, 1850, one was African American, ten were Native American, nine were Chinese, eighteen were ethnic Mexican, fifty-nine were Anglo-American or people of European descent, and six were of unknown race: Gonzales-Day, Lynching in the West, 9, 47, 207–35.

28. Carrigan and Webb, Forgotten Dead, 17–18.

29. Ibid., 18.

30. Martinez, "Recuperating Histories of Violence in the Americas," 663. Martinez explicitly ties the lynching of ethnic Mexicans (and Native Americans) to genocide and colonialism, but Carrigan and Webb's book has some troubling deficiencies, the most glaring of which is the near-absence of U.S. colonialism as the primary subtext for understanding most lynchings of ethnic Mexicans in the West. Carrigan and Webb frame these lynchings as interpersonal conflicts tinged with racial animosity. Although they recognize that these lynchings were part of a concerted effort by Anglos to wrest land (and therefore economic and political

power) from ethnic Mexicans, they do not tie these land grabs to the colonial project of "clearing" the West for white American settlers.

31. As Martinez points out, the Texas Rangers effectively functioned as vigilantes with legal authority, and many began their careers in the Spanish-American War and the Philippine-American War, both of which expanded the U.S. Empire into majority-nonwhite territories. She argues that, given the transfer of military tactics from wars of empire to the U.S.-Mexico borderlands, the systematic killing of ethnic Mexicans, whether through executions, lynchings, or something in between, should be read as part of the U.S. project of empire building: ibid., 666–71.

32. The research on Native American lynchings is particularly sparse, even in studies of lynching in the West. Gonzales-Day identifies forty-one Native American victims of lynching or summary execution and ten legal and military executions of Native Americans in California between 1850 and 1925: Gonzales-Day, *Lynching in the West*, 27, 83, 203–35. See also Carrigan and Webb, *Forgotten Dead*, 68.

33. For more on the application of the term "genocide" to describe U.S. colonialist violence against Native Americans, see Andrew Woolford, Jeff Benvenuto, and Alexander Laban Hinton, ed., *Colonial Genocide in Indigenous North America* (Durham, NC: Duke University Press, 2014); Benjamin Madley, *An American Genocide: The United States and the California Indian Catastrophe, 1846–1873* (New Haven, CT: Yale University Press, 2016).

34. Kelman, *A Misplaced Massacre*, 24. Southern lynch mobs not only desecrated the bodies of African American men—through castration, dismemberment, cutting off "souvenirs" from bodies, and so on—but they also desecrated the bodies of African American women. When a Georgia mob lynched Mary Turner in 1918, a man cut open her belly and killed her unborn child. Then the mob riddled her body with bullets. In Oklahoma seven years earlier, several white men raped Laura Nelson before a mob lynched her. Similarly, lynch mobs and state officials in Texas often left the corpses of ethnic Mexicans out to rot to terrorize other members of the Mexican community and further desecrate these nonwhite bodies: Leon Litwack, *Trouble in Mind: Black Southerners in the Age of Jim Crow* (New York: Vintage, 1998), 288–90. See also Martinez, "Recuperating Histories of Violence," 661, 669.

35. Kelman, *A Misplaced Massacre*, 8–9. By "contained to the South," I mean that the enslavement of African Americans was legal in the South, though, as Baptist, Johnson, Sven Beckert, and others have argued, the economic and political ties between the development of capitalism in the North and investments paid for in enslaved bodies and enslaved labor were significant. Furthermore, Andrés Reséndez has argued that the West, though nominally made up of "free states," had a long history of enslaving Native Americans rooted in Spanish rule, and that enslavement continued beyond the ratification of the Thirteenth Amendment: Baptist, *The Half Has Never Been Told;* Sven Beckert, *Empire of Cotton: A Global History* (New York: Alfred A. Knopf, 2014); Walter Johnson, *River of Dark Dreams* (Cambridge, MA: Harvard University Press, 2013); Andrés Reséndez, *The Other Slavery: The Uncovered Story of Indian Enslavement in America* (Boston: Houghton Mifflin Harcourt, 2016).

36. Ned Blackhawk, *Violence over the Land: Indians and Empires in the Early American West* (Cambridge, MA: Harvard University Press, 2006), 9.

37. Lynching contributes to the drawing up and signing of what Charles Mills calls the "racial contract" in which "the purpose of this state . . . is . . . specifically to maintain and reproduce this racial order, securing privileges and advantages to the full white citizens and maintaining the subordination of nonwhites": Charles Mills, *The Racial Contract* (Ithaca, NY: Cornell University Press, 1997), 14.

38. Parsing the distinctions drawn between legal and extralegal, public and private, state and non-state often obscures the broader issue that, regardless of whether lynchings were "more legal" or "state-sanctioned," they were a strategy to uphold white racial domination. To deem certain acts of racial violence "legitimate" due to their proximity to the law or the state ignores the ways in which both the law and the state are implicated in protecting and reinforcing white supremacy: Timothy V. Kaufman-Osborn, "Capital Punishment as Legal Lynching?" in *From Lynch Mobs to the Killing State: Race and the Death Penalty in America*, ed. Charles Ogletree and Austin Sarat (New York: New York University Press, 2006), 31–36.

39. Litwack, *Trouble in Mind*, 280–83.

40. "Glad He Led Lynchers: Ex-Senator Sullivan Will Stand Consequences for Directing Shooting," *New York Times*, September 10, 1908.

41. Jacqueline Goldsby makes a related argument against the usage of "extralegal" to describe lynching. She argues that "the citizenship rights of African Americans were actively nullified by the state, making lynchings not as 'extralegal' as the word encourages us to suppose": Jacqueline Goldsby, *A Spectacular Secret: Lynching in American Life and Literature* (Chicago: University of Chicago Press, 2006), 283. Goldsby also argues, as do I, that lynching had become such an unremarkable part of U.S. culture and that "violence directed against African American people had become so entrenched a practice that it was a normal routine in national life": ibid., 284. Goldsby focuses on African American lynching victims and antilynching activists, but by expanding the scope of lynching to recognize other nonwhite victims and systems of racial oppression other than Jim Crow, violence directed against nonwhites in the United States becomes even more, to borrow a word from Blackhawk, *intrinsic:* ibid., 283–84; Blackhawk, *Violence over the Land*, 9.

42. Martinez uses the phrase "state-sanctioned racial terror," citing work by Benjamin Johnson, who describes this killing spree as "ethnic cleansing" in *Revolution in Texas:* Martinez, "Recuperating Histories of Violence in the Americas," 668.

43. W. E. B. Du Bois, *Black Reconstruction in America, 1860–1880* (New York: Free Press, [1935] 1992), 708.

44. Christina Sharpe has challenged the temporal boundaries of enslavement itself with her theorization of contemporary Black life as being lived in the wake of enslavement amid a pervasive anti-Blackness that reproduces the precarity experienced by the enslaved: Christina Sharpe, *In the Wake: On Blackness and Being* (Durham, NC: Duke University Press, 2016), 7, 13–14, 21.

"Magnificent Resources"

RECONSTRUCTION IN INDIAN TERRITORY

Troy D. Smith

WHEN THE AMERICAN CIVIL War erupted, Indian country was caught in the middle. More specifically, Indian Territory—the area now known as Oklahoma, to which multiple tribes from east of the Mississippi were removed in the 1830s and 1840s—was caught in the middle, both literally and figuratively. It was bordered by Texas to the south, Arkansas to the east, and Kansas to the north and touched the corner of Missouri to the northeast. There were also cultural borders. Many of the financial and political elites of the so-called Five Civilized Tribes (Cherokees, Creeks, Choctaws, Chickasaws, and Seminoles) were heavily invested in cotton agriculture and the institution of slavery and identified closely with their former neighbors in the southern regions from which they had been removed. They were also invested in a sense of individual national identity framed by citizenship and a system of laws and by a racial hierarchy that those laws defined. Many individual tribal members, however, were opposed to slavery and the "modern" concepts of race and citizenship, especially the more traditional among them. Many of those Indians believed that honoring their treaty commitments to the United States were more important than getting enmeshed in the goals of the Confederacy.

The area was strategically important to both sides. Possession of it meant control of access to the U.S. West. There were also abundant resources, particularly the salt and lead mines in the northern section of the territory. Confederate officials estimated that the lead mines alone would provide enough to supply bullets to the entire Confederate Army.[1] The Confederacy, in particular, was willing to negotiate with the leadership of the Five Tribes to have that access and those resources. It also meant denying the region to the Union as a base for invading Texas or Arkansas. The United States, by contrast, was in a vulnerable position in Indian Territory when open hostilities began. The handful of forts it had previously established in the region, in part to protect the Five Tribes from the nomadic tribes indigenous to the area (as stipulated in the removal treaties), were far from Union supply lines and close to enemy territory. Federal troops withdrew, abandoning the forts, in April 1861, after having already ceased sending annuities for the tribes due to security concerns about transporting them.

The leaders of the Five Tribes were left with serious concerns. Without the annuities due them, their treasuries were stretched thin. Many Indians viewed the withdrawal of troops as a reneging on treaty obligations on the part of the United States. Confederate diplomats took advantage of the opportunity to seek alliances with the Five Tribes, making them several appealing offers. The tribes' sovereignty would be guaranteed, including their right to determine who their citizens were (or were not) and jurisdiction over anyone committing crimes within their borders, and they would be treated as independent nations. Each tribe would have representation in the Confederate Congress. Annuities owed by the United States would be assumed by the Confederacy. Slavery, and therefore the property rights of slave owners, would be guaranteed. In return, the tribes would raise troops; the Confederacy would help equip them and promised they would not be sent outside Indian Territory without the tribes' permission.

The leaders of four of the Five Tribes quickly signed alliance treaties with the Confederate diplomats, who were led by a lawyer and poet named Albert Pike, but one tribe demurred. The Cherokee leader John Ross strongly wished for his nation to remain neutral in the coming conflict. This was, in part, out of a desire not to break treaty agreements with the United States, but geography played a part, as well. The Cherokee Nation is located in the northeastern corner of Oklahoma, bordering the Union state of Kansas, and Ross knew that if the Cherokees were drawn into the war they would be the first to suffer any Union invasions. Further, Ross, who was one-eighth Cherokee by blood (although blood quantum was at that time not a factor for the matrilineal Cherokees), received his strongest support from the traditionalist faction who were, at best, ambivalent about supporting slavery or the Confederacy. This was so despite the fact that Ross himself was a slave owner.

The Confederates put pressure on Ross by making overtures to his political rival, Stand Watie. Ross feared this would lead to division among his people—a realistic fear, considering events of the previous quarter-century. Ross had been principal chief since 1828, during the years leading up to Removal, and had resisted Andrew Jackson's Indian policies with vigor. Most of this resistance had taken place in the courts, as Ross and his supporters tried to use the tools of the United States—education and the law—to maintain and protect their sovereignty. Although initially stymied in the Supreme Court by the ruling, in *Cherokee Nation v. Georgia* (1831), that Indian tribes could not bring suit in court, they had more success before the bench in *Worcester v. Georgia* (1832), as the focal point of the case was a missionary to the tribe, Samuel Worcester, who had been imprisoned for violating a Georgia law against whites living among Indians without state approval. The Marshall Court ruled in favor of the Cherokees and their allies, as only the federal government has constitutional approval to treat with Indian tribes. President Jackson famously refused to enforce the court's decision, however, and a few years later Cherokee political dissension would help lead to removal by force.

While Principal Chief John Ross, and a majority of his people, remained adamantly determined to continue resistance in the courts, other prominent Cherokees viewed further resistance as futile. This contingent was led by Major Ridge, his son John Ridge, and his nephews Elias Boudinot and Stand Watie. The Ridges signed the Treaty of New Echota, ceding the Cherokees' eastern lands to the United States in return for lands west of the Mississippi—even though they did not have the authority to do so. It was official in the eyes of the U.S. government, however. The Ridges and their followers made the move to Indian Territory voluntarily, while Ross and the majority of the Cherokee Nation were rounded up and sent by force. Once there, bitter anger over what traditionalists perceived as a gross betrayal erupted into several years of unofficial Cherokee civil war, beginning with the assassinations of the Ridges and Elias Boudinot and the attempted assassination of Stand Watie, who still stood in 1861 as the chief rival of John Ross.

Ross did not want to see a new eruption of violence among his people, so in the interests of national unity he reluctantly agreed to side with the Confederacy. It was a vain hope, for many of his people chose to fight for the Union, including three of Ross's sons. Stand Watie, meanwhile, became a Confederate brigadier-general. Thousands of Indians from the various tribes, as well as many free Blacks, joined the camp of the pro-Union Creek leader Opothleyahola and embarked on an exodus for Kansas, pursued by Confederate forces (Indian and non-Indian). Three bloody battles were fought along the way, in late November and December 1861. The American Civil War had become an Indian civil war. Indian Territory became a battleground. In many cases, especially among the Cherokees and Creeks, sides were chosen along the fault lines of Removal-era politics, with factions who had been amenable to removal supporting the Confederacy and those who had resisted supporting the Union.

As Ross feared, it was those nations in the northern section of Indian Territory— that is, Cherokees and Creeks—who suffered most. No one, however, was immune. The number of people killed, both military and civilian, was high, as was the number of missing, which included many people who left and never came back, as well as those who died but whose deaths were never officially verified. A Cherokee named Mrs. Tom Rattling Gourd said, "My father was killed in the Civil War and was never buried. Mother looked for his bones for a long time but never could find them."[2] A Cherokee census taken halfway through the war revealed that one-quarter of the children were orphans and one-third of the women were widows. By the end of the war, the Choctaws, Creeks, Seminoles, and Cherokees had each lost between one-fifth and one-sixth of their population; one out of nine Chickasaws were completely unaccounted for. Indian Territory suffered as much death or devastation as any Southern state, and probably more.[3]

A Creek woman named Lizzie Wynn, who was about twelve when the war started, told an interviewer about her experiences in 1937. Wynn's account was not an uncommon one.

> Opuithli Yahola [Opothleyahola] didn't own negroes so he took the ones that didn't own negroes North. Daddy had two families, besides three others, that worked at the house. I don't know just how many but there were quite a few.
>
> The war started by some wanting to free the negroes so daddy said he guessed that he would be safe if he just turned them loose. But he took a notion to do like the rest were doing. He had freed all but the old woman, and for some reason she was going with us. We got close to Wetumka when he got very sick and had to be put to bed. We had stopped at an Indian house. The Northern soldiers came to the door and I was standing at the head of his bed. They told us to move but I thought if I stayed there they surely wouldn't shoot him. They shot him and blood and brains spattered all over me. I wasn't scared but I was mad. After they had killed him, they left and the old negro woman said that they would go after some wagons and come back after us. We covered daddy up and shut the doors and left him laying in the bed. There was a hill at the back of the house so we ran to it so that we could get away without being seen.[4]

The son of the old slave woman, who had previously been "turned loose" by Lizzie's father, hid the family in a wagon, and together they escaped to the Chickasaw Nation, near the Texas border, where they stayed for the remainder of the war.[5]

The citizens of each indigenous nation were divided, some more than others, but the tribal governments of all of the Five Tribes had officially allied with the Confederacy. John Ross and his supporters switched sides during the war, and for a while there were two competing Cherokee governments: one pro-Union (which emancipated all slaves in the Cherokee Nation) and one pro-Confederate. The latter was led by Stand Watie, who on June 23, 1865, had the distinction of being the last Confederate general to surrender. At the end of summer, representatives from all of the tribes in Indian Territory were assembled at Fort Smith, Arkansas, at the command of the U.S. government for a "peace council." They included the tribes from the western part of Indian Territory, beyond the Five Tribes (in fact, they were usually referred to as "wild" in contrast with the Five "Civilized" Tribes)—the Comanches, Osages, Wichitas, and Quapaws—as well as other groups that had been removed from the east, such as Shawnees, Senecas, and Delawares. The western tribes, unlike the Five Tribes, had not entered into alliance and fought beside the Confederate states, but they had signed nonaggression treaties with them.

On September 11, 1865, Commissioner of Indian Affairs Dennis N. Cooley delivered a speech to the assembled Indians that outlined their situation:

> By these nations having entered into treaties with the so-called Confederate States, and the rebellion being now ended, they are left without any treaty whatever, or treaty obligation for protection by the United States . . . all these nations and tribes forfeited and lost all their rights to annuities and lands. . . . We, as representatives of the President, are empowered to enter into new treaties with the proper delegates of the tribes located within the so-called Indian Territory.[6]

This was followed by seven stipulations that these new treaties would all require, with the first being that each nation and tribe would enter into said treaties independently of one another. Perhaps the most significant stipulations, though, were numbers three and four:

3. The institution of slavery which has existed among several of the tribes must be forthwith abolished, and measures taken for the unconditional emancipation of all persons held in bondage, and for their incorporation in the tribes on an equal footing with the original members, or suitably provided for.

4. A stipulation in the treaties that slavery, or involuntary servitude, shall never exist in the tribe or nation, except in punishment of crime.[7]

In fact, each tribe's peace agreement with the United States (collectively and individually known as the Treaty of 1866) as ultimately signed did include these provisions. Several elements of the treaties were unique to Indian Territory, such as the loss of lands by some of the Five Tribes to accommodate the placement of previously removed tribes that had been in Kansas and for future tribes who might be brought into the region. The parts about emancipation and the citizenship status of freed slaves, however, tied these treaties into the broader project of Reconstruction. There was not going to be a return to the status quo. Property held in slaves was to be property no more. Further, slaves were not only to be freed; they were to be "incorporated on an equal footing with the original members," whether they had any Indian blood or not. Many of them did, of course, and had grown up speaking the native languages and thinking of themselves culturally as Cherokee, Creek, and so on, but many others had been bought as adults from neighboring Southern states. There were some variations. The treaties signed by Cherokees, Creeks, and Seminoles required the tribes to grant citizenship (or the rights of citizens) to their freedmen, while those signed by the Choctaws and Chickasaws did not. Although reluctant at first, the Choctaws eventually granted citizenship to their former slaves in 1883, but the Chickasaws—whose freedmen potentially outnumbered them and could have been a potent political force—never did.[8]

These changes called for a major restructuring of the cultural and legal systems of the Five Tribes, which had already been restructured once to fit the prevailing early nineteenth-century notions of "civilization"—to wit, slavery-driven capitalism and slavery-defined citizenship.

If the federal government's requirements regarding slavery and Black citizenship were similar in the former Confederate states and in Indian Territory, so, too, in many cases, were the defeated people's reactions to it. As in most southern states, there had been a strong pro-Union or "loyal" component in the Nations; many of these unionists resented being lumped in with their disloyal fellow tribesmen and suffering the same repercussions as them. While support for the Confederacy shrank as the war continued, bitterness and frustration directed at Blacks increased, even among some of the traditionalists who had opposed slavery. This was exacerbated after the Treaty of 1866, with many feeling that tribal sovereignty was being trampled by the United States in its determination to dictate to the tribes who was to be considered their citizens. Just as in Southern states, anger about their postwar status was manifested by increasingly violent attacks against Blacks.[9]

In 1865, the missionary Cyrus Kingsbury, who had been serving the Choctaws since 1818, noted: "I fear there are many who will no more hesitate to take the life of a negroe, than of a dog. It is sickening to contemplate the prospect that is (I hope but for a little season) with us."[10]

Another observer, a federal soldier, spoke with a group of Blacks who had been attacked by Chickasaws after the war ended:

> They state that these tribes have the bitterest feeling toward the blacks, and are determined that they shall not pass through their country; nor leave it, and that they hold on to their slaves with the greatest tenacity, swearing in their enmity to the blacks that if it had not been for them (the blacks) the federals could never have whipped the south—that they (the Indians) are not whipped and that they are going to manage and control things in their country to suit themselves. I am satisfied that many of them [the Indians] are as disloyal as ever; and that the blacks are suffering a reign of terror.[11]

Despite these conditions, not only did most freedmen not leave Indian Territory, but many of those who had been slaves there but were dispersed during the war were determined to return because, to them, Indian Territory was home. The Cherokee freedwoman Chaney McNair explained, "The Indians' slaves didn't like it in Kansas, and most of them returned to the Indian Territory after the war. They found many empty buildings here, belonging to people who had left the country during the war, seeking a place of safety." Indian Territory was where she belonged, she said, and kept calling her back.[12]

Politics, like race, would also be a challenge during Reconstruction in Indian Territory, with comparative unity during the war influencing the peace that came after. The populations of the Choctaws and Chickasaws had been largely pro-Confederacy, with the Union factions in each tribe relatively small. They were able to gather consensus not only within their own boundaries but with one another, as well, signing a joint Reconstruction treaty with the United States in 1866 rather than individual treaties. Their biggest point of internal contention remained the status of their freed slaves. The Seminoles also reached internal accord quickly, with the pro-Union leaders in charge after the war extending amnesty to their pro-Confederate tribesmen and signing the treaty extending citizenship to their freedmen with less controversy that the other tribes.

The Cherokees and Creeks had been the mostly sharply divided during the war; they had also had the most violent divisions a quarter-century earlier during Removal. Not surprisingly, they had more difficulties than the other tribes in reunifying when the war was finished. The factions of each tribe that had supported the Confederacy initially expressed the desire for the United States to recognize them as separate nations from their pro-Union tribesmen. Those requests were not granted, but Commissioner Cooley followed Albert Pike's prewar example by playing Stand Watie against John Ross, with the threat of Watie's faction gaining independence pressuring Ross to make more concessions, including the sale of the Cherokee Strip to the United States.[13]

Beyond unification of the Indian Nations, the status of their freedmen, and the resumption of U.S. relations with the tribes, two other points that would affect the sovereignty of all Five Tribes appeared in the 1866 Reconstruction treaties: consolidation of the tribes into a single territorial government and the construction of railroads. These two points would be revisited by the U.S. government within a few years after the treaties were signed.

Commissioners had presented seven stipulations to the tribes at the Fort Smith peace council in 1865, with the declared intent of having them all included in any resulting treaty. In addition to abolishing slavery, tribes would have to submit to all being consolidated into one territorial government. This was not a new idea. The amalgamation of all Five Tribes into a single entity had been discussed in Congress in the 1840s, with the possible intent of statehood for Indian Territory. Opponents of the measure at that time had suspected it was being proposed as a means to bring in a new slave state and increase the South's political power. The leaders of the Five Tribes, however, had also not been amenable to the idea. Being fused into a single Indian entity would endanger each tribe's sovereignty and sense of self. The Choctaw diplomat Peter Pitchlynn, who would serve as principal chief during the Civil War, had testified in Congress in 1849. "My country, my people, my home and my children," he said, "all that can stimulate a man, are at stake in this matter."[14]

Postwar efforts at consolidation by the United States did not involve statehood, and the protection of slavery obviously was no longer a factor. Washington's goal was a single territorial government, no doubt in the belief that dealing with a single Indian entity would be more effective than convincing several disparate nations to accede to their wishes. In September 1870, the federal government called the various tribes living in Indian Territory to Ocmulgee, in the Creek Nation, for a constitutional convention to put this new government together. Most of the smaller tribes, and the Plains tribes from the western end of the territory, did not show up. Neither did the Choctaws. Delegates from the Cherokee, Creek, Chickasaw, and Seminole nations did attend, and a federal constitution was drawn up but failed to be ratified by the tribes' citizens. The U.S. government made similar efforts annually for several years, eventually getting the participation of the other tribes, with no success. The majority of tribal members, and many of the Indian delegates to these meetings, were opposed to a single territorial government and the loss of their own sovereignty.[15]

The U.S. government had started laying plans for the restructuring of Indian Territory immediately after the end of the war, and those plans would not be facilitated by the existence of several different tribal governments. Only a month or so after the peace council at Fort Smith in 1865, Commissioner Cooley had outlined those plans in his annual report to Secretary of the Interior James Harlan:

> Whenever, in the progress towards a final settlement of the questions remaining open in regard to the reorganization of the Indian country, the proper time shall come, it will be advisable to provide for the construction of internal improvements in that region calculated to develop its magnificent resources. With a territorial government organized and in operation, its feuds healed, the scars of war gone from view . . . , and the industry of the country in full process of development, will have come a time when railroads must traverse the country, binding its several parts together, and all to one common Union, and giving a choice of markets and depots for exchange and shipment of produce, either on the Gulf of Mexico, say at Galveston, or northward, to connect with the great central converging points of railroads in Kansas. Whatever can properly be done by the government of the United States in paving the way for these improvements should, in my judgment, be done now, and thus avoid difficulties which may arise in the future.[16]

Indian Territory, in other words, was a veritable gold mine due to both its central location and its "magnificent resources," which must not go undeveloped. This had been true before the war, and was the reason the Confederacy had been so eager to gain alliances with the Five Tribes. Now the United States was going to be able to gain access to those advantages due, in large part, to the fact the tribes had allied with the Confederacy and lost and were therefore now vulnerable to a reframing of their treaties.

The U.S. government was not alone in desiring to see the development of infrastructure that would make Indian Territory's resources accessible. Private individuals and corporations, especially railroad companies, lobbied Congress regularly to make Indian lands public. The 1866 Reconstruction treaties with all of the Five Tribes included requirements to allow the building of railroads, though the tribes were able to negotiate the amount of land on each side of the rail line that would be ceded as right of way, and tracks were being laid by the early 1870s. Non-Indians poured into the region, establishing new towns on the lands surrendered to the railroads and investing in businesses and industry. Non-Indian cattlemen came to the area, as well, sometimes leasing land from the tribes to graze their herds. The racial and cultural makeup of Indian Territory was in flux. With each passing year, the newcomers, and those who might potentially join them, gazed enviously at the lands and "magnificent resources" as yet unavailable to them.

The flood of non-Indians also presented thorny issues for the Five Tribes' legal systems and resulted in further encroachments on tribal sovereignty. The United States had long maintained that Indian courts and law enforcement had no jurisdiction over U.S. citizens within their boundaries and that tribal authority extended only to Indians. The Confederate offer to recognize Indian sovereignty, even over Confederate citizens within the borders of the Nations, was one of the facets that had made a Confederate alliance attractive to the tribes in 1861. This meant that, for example, a criminal fleeing authorities in Texas could enter the Choctaw Nation and commit further crimes, and neither the Texas state authorities nor the Choctaw sheriffs or lighthorse (the name given to Indian tribal police) could touch him. He would be under the authority only of the federal government, in the form of federal marshals operating out of one of the federal courts located in nearby states. This situation was exacerbated by the Major Crimes Act of 1885, when Congress declared that seven major crimes (murder, rape, burglary, arson, manslaughter, assault with intent to kill, and larceny) would no longer be under the jurisdiction of Indian tribes, even if everyone involved were members of that tribe. Not surprisingly, many bandits operating in surrounding states used Indian Territory as their base of operations and sanctuary, "lighting out for the Nations" when things became too hot for them elsewhere.[17]

U.S. deputy marshals, most of them attached to the court in Fort Smith, Arkansas, frequently led posses into Indian Territory to capture non-Indian criminals (and, after 1885, Indian murderers, rapists, and robbers). When Fort Smith District Judge William Story was impeached for corruption in 1875, he was replaced by the Ohio native Isaac Parker, who would become known by the sobriquet "the Hanging Judge" for the frequent executions over which he presided, a good many of them Indians from the Five Tribes. Parker's jurisdiction over Indian Territory was final; there was no provision for appeal of his decisions until an 1889 act of Congress. Judge Parker's deputies often hired Indians from the Nations to be their guides and posse members, and some Indians served as deputy U.S. marshals themselves. Many of Parker's deputies were African American. Some, such as the legendary Bass Reeves, may have been former slaves from Confederate states who had served in Indian Territory and become familiar with its inhabitants during the Civil War. Quite a few, though, were freedmen: men who had been enslaved by Indian masters in the Nations. These men spoke the local languages, knew the area, and were familiar with native culture, giving them an advantage when trailing outlaws in Indian Territory. The historian Art Burton has asserted that, since most Indians were distrustful of white peace officers, Black deputies who spoke their language were more likely to meet with cooperation.

Whether that was the case or not, white and Black deputies operating within the Five Tribes served as reminders of U.S. Reconstruction goals in the region. Issues of race and sovereignty intertwined in very physical ways, resulting in heightened tensions among the Indians. Freed slaves were returning to the Nations, wearing the badges of the federal government, and they and their white colleagues (and some Indian allies, as well) were imposing the sovereignty of that government over the Five Tribes.

Strain over issues of sovereignty and jurisdiction was clearly demonstrated in an event that occurred in the Goingsnake District of the Cherokee Nation in 1872. The incident took place during the murder trial of a Cherokee Union veteran named Ezekiel "Zeke" Proctor. He was a member of the Keetowah Society, also known as "Pin Indians" for the crossed pins they wore on their lapels for identification. Taking their name from the village considered the "mother town" of the Cherokee people, the Keetowahs were hard-line traditionalists who had long opposed the modernization of the Cherokees, including the adoption of slavery.

Proctor had traveled the Trail of Tears to Indian Territory as a child. His father was white, and his mother was Cherokee. Since Cherokees are matrilineal, Proctor was considered a full member of the tribe. He had a reputation for being "resourceful, self-reliant, bold . . . a strong man with a strong man's vices." It was said that "he always carried a gun buckled to his hip and would never sit with his back to any man."[18]

On the morning of February 27, 1872, Proctor was involved in an altercation with a white man named Jim Kesterman (also spelled Chesterman) and his Cherokee wife, Polly Beck, at the mill she had inherited from her deceased previous husband. There are several conflicting versions of the reason for the confrontation. Kesterman had previously been married to Proctor's sister Susan, and one popular story was that Proctor was enraged when she and her children were abandoned by Kesterman and came to confront his brother-in-law about it. Another version holds that Proctor had also been involved with Polly Beck and that the fight was sparked by jealousy. In some accounts, the staunch Keetowah traditionalist Proctor was angry that a Cherokee woman was involved with a white man (although his sister had, in fact, been married to him). Finally, some maintained that it was a dispute over cattle. Perhaps it was some combination of two or more of these factors.

Whatever the cause, a fight erupted, and Proctor shot first Kesterman and then Polly Beck. Kesterman received a minor head wound, but Beck was killed. Kesterman claimed Proctor had coldly shot them both, while Proctor maintained that his shooting of the woman was an accident due to her jumping into his line of fire. Proctor surrendered to Cherokee authorities in the Goingsnake District, and a trial date was set, with Judge Blackhawk Sixkiller to preside.

Kesterman and Beck's Cherokee relatives wanted Polly's killer to be tried in federal court, believing he would not be convicted in a Cherokee venue because of his political connections. As the assault had been made on a white man, and the deceased had been the wife of a white man, they asked that an arrest warrant be issued for Proctor and that he be brought to Fort Smith for trial. Their request was granted, with the understanding that no action would be taken if Proctor was convicted of murder in the Cherokee court. If he was acquitted, however, he would be taken into federal custody and face another trial in Fort Smith. The Cherokee tribal government, and many Cherokee people, viewed this as a violation of their sovereignty. The death of a Cherokee woman in the Cherokee Nation was a Cherokee matter.

Fearful of an attack by the Beck family or interference from the U.S. government, Cherokee authorities moved the trial from the courthouse to the more defensible school building and went forward with the proceeding on April 15. Most of the men present were heavily armed. Two deputy U.S. marshals, Jacob Owens and Joseph Peavey, were dispatched to the trial to take custody of Proctor in the event he was acquitted, accompanied by a posse of ten men. Five of the ten were members of the Beck family. The posse ordered away, at gunpoint, the Cherokee lighthorsemen assigned to guard the front door of the schoolhouse. Despite efforts of the marshals to restrain them, the Becks charged into the improvised courtroom and started shooting. The heavily armed trial participants returned fire, with the beleaguered Zeke Proctor procuring a gun and taking cover behind the stone chimney. The resulting melee would become known as "the Goingsnake Massacre." (Testimony from the posse members differed somewhat, stating that the trial officers barged out the front door with guns blazing and the fight took place outside, where the marshals had no cover.)

Six posse members were killed outright, and a seventh, as well as Deputy Owens, died of their wounds the following day. Marshal Peavey and three other posse members were wounded less seriously, with only one member of the twelve-man party escaping injury. Three Cherokees were killed on the other side: Zeke Proctor's brother, his attorney, and a bystander, with six others wounded, including Proctor and Judge Sixkiller. The trial was quickly moved to the home of the jury foreman, Arch Scaper, wounded judge and defendant notwithstanding, and Proctor was promptly acquitted. Proctor, Judge Sixkiller, and several others went into hiding, sheltered by members of the Keetowah Society. A second, larger posse arrived from Fort Smith and arrested several participants in the battle at the schoolhouse, though charges against them were later dropped. In October of the following year, the district court dropped its case against Zeke Proctor, and he came out of hiding, celebrated among many of his tribesman as a hero who had successfully resisted the U.S. government. He later served as a senator in the Cherokee Nation and was elected sheriff of the Flint District. In the 1890s, he worked as a deputy U.S. marshal for the Fort Smith court.[19]

The Goingsnake Massacre was a dramatic, physical representation of Cherokee--U.S. jurisdictional and racial issues. A second such representation occurred twenty years later, when a Cherokee man named Ned Christie was falsely accused of murdering a deputy U.S. marshal. Christie, who had served on the tribal council and been an adviser to the principal chief, believed it was impossible for him to have a fair trial at Fort Smith. He and several followers fortified themselves in a rocky area and withstood a long siege by federal marshals, finally dying on November 3, 1892, when a posse procured a cannon and breached their defenses. Years later, a witness's testimony posthumously cleared him of the murder charge. Like Proctor, he became a symbol of Cherokee resistance.[20]

To those non-Indians living in the Nations, however, violent confrontations such as the one at the Goingsnake schoolhouse were evidence that the tribal governments were unable to maintain order. As a popular saying of the time put it, "There's no Sunday west of St. Louis—no God west of Fort Smith." Almost a quarter of all federal marshals killed in the line of duty died in a two-decade span in Indian Territory, and the Goingsnake incident had the highest number of deputized casualties in the history of the marshal's service until the attack on the World Trade Center on September 11, 2001.[21] It is unfair to blame the tribal governments for an environment created by federal policy, but many of those making complaints had an ulterior motive. Lawlessness invites federal control, and federal control would create public lands that would be accessible to private citizens and businesses.

Not all methods of creating inroads into Indian Territory, and of curtailing native sovereignty, were so dramatic. The beginning of the end of tribal government in Indian Territory was initiated by a dispute over excise taxes. The 1866 Reconstruction Treaty with the Cherokees had, among other things, guaranteed that anything manufactured or produced in the Cherokee Nation could then be sold in other states without paying federal excise taxes. In 1868, however, Congress passed the Internal Revenue Act, which gave it the right to tax anyone within the nation's boundaries. Stand Watie and his nephew Elias Boudinot Jr. refused to pay taxes on the tobacco they grew and sold on the grounds that the treaty gave Cherokees immunity, and their case made its way to the Supreme Court. Former Confederate General Albert Pike, who had negotiated the alliances with the Five Tribes at the beginning of the Civil War, was one of their lawyers. In the *Cherokee Tobacco* case (1870), the court ruled against the claims of Watie and Boudinot:

> Treaties with Indian nations within the jurisdiction of the United States, whatever considerations of humanity and good faith may be involved and require their faithful and good faith may be inobligatory. They have no higher sanctity, and no greater inviolability or immunity from legislative invasion can be claimed for them. The consequences in all such cases give rise to questions which must be met by the political department of the government. They are beyond the sphere of judicial cognizance. In the case under consideration, the act of Congress must prevail as if the treaty were not an element to be considered. If a wrong has been done, the power of redress is with Congress, not with the judiciary, and that body, upon being applied to, it is to be presumed, will promptly give the proper relief.[22]

In essence, the court, relying on precedents set in the Marshall Court during the lead-up to removal, ruled that treaties with Indian tribes are not binding on Congress because those tribes are not foreign nations. Congress did not "give the proper relief" to tribes; on the contrary, the following year (1871) it added an amendment to an appropriations act that ended the practice of signing treaties with Indians, and no further treaty was ever signed. While promising that no previously signed treaty was invalidated, the act specified that "no Indian nation or tribe within the territory of the United States shall be acknowledged or recognized as an independent nation, tribe, or power with whom the United States may contract by treaty."

William Boudinot, brother of Elias Boudinot Jr., realized the ramifications of the court's decision: "Congress can take away our lands, while we hold them in common, and give them to others." Chief Justice John Marshall, in the 1831 ruling in *Cherokee v. Georgia*, had described tribes as "dependent nations" whose relationship to the United States was like that of a ward to a guardian: not entirely independent, in other words, but still having sovereignty of a sort over their own territory. It had now been established, however, that Congress did not have to treat tribes as nations, dependent or otherwise; rather, it would treat them as individuals.[23]

Politicians were already beginning to discuss the idea of allotment. Tribal lands were controlled by the tribes, not by their individual members. Among the Five Tribes in Indian Territory, a citizen could settle on tribal land and make improvements on it, such as buildings and fences, as long as they were not impinging on someone else's claim. (They could not come closer than a quarter-mile to their neighbor's improvements.) The settler would own the improvements, but not the land itself, and therefore could not sell it. Abandoned claims reverted to the tribe, and any unfenced, unclaimed area was considered communal property.[24] If lands were taken away from tribes and redistributed equally to the tribes' members, those areas left over would be public lands that the government could sell or offer to homesteaders.

The *Cherokee Tobacco* case of 1870 and subsequent end of the treaty era in 1871 were among the first links in the chain that would achieve the goal of allotment. The next link was crafted as a result of something that transpired outside Indian Territory: a murder on the Great Sioux Reservation in South Dakota in 1881. One Lakota, Crow Dog, shot and killed another, Spotted Tail, with whom he had a long-standing feud. Crow Dog offered restitution to the dead man's family: $600, eight horses, and a blanket. Spotted Tail's family accepted the offer, satisfied, and the matter was concluded as far as the Lakotas were concerned. The reservation agent, however, had Crow Dog arrested and charged with murder. He was tried in a Nebraska court, convicted, and sentenced to hang, but his lawyers appealed, and his case made it to the U.S. Supreme Court in *Ex Parte: Crow Dog* (1884). Albert Pike was on Crow Dog's legal team, as well. The Supreme Court ruled that the federal government had no jurisdiction over crimes committed on Indian land with only Indians involved. It was the public outcry about this ruling, and the perceived lack of "law and order" in Indian country, that led Congress to pass the Major Crimes Act of 1885. The following year, in the case of *United States v. Kagama* (also a murder case involving two Indians, this time in California), the Supreme Court ruled the Major Crimes Act constitutional. The ruling rested on the Indians' status as dependent nations, as well as on the plenary power Congress held over them, and allowed the federal government to assume jurisdiction over a specified list of crimes because the tribes were considered unqualified to look after their own interests.

All this would provide a basis for Congress to pass the Dawes Act in 1887, which led to the end of tribal governments and to allotment. The Five Tribes were exempt at first, due to their perceived "civilized" status, but the original act was amended by the Curtis Act of 1898, which specifically extended the law to the Five Tribes. The governments they had established after removal, including the constitutions and legal systems they had set up, were abolished, not to rise again for almost a century.

The process begun with the Reconstruction treaties of 1866 was complete. Native sovereignty was shredded; native lands were open to settlement; and the emigration boom that began in the 1880s led to the formation of Oklahoma, which was admitted to the Union as a state in 1907. Race relations between the Indians and their former slaves—and those slaves' descendants—remained complicated, and the racial repercussions of the Civil War echo into the twenty-first century, with the controversy over sovereignty versus racial equity unabated.

Notes

1. Arrell Morgan Gibson, "Native Americans and the Civil War." *American Indian Quarterly* 9, no. 4 (Autumn 1985): 386–87

2. "Interview with Mrs. Tom Rattling Gourd," oral history, Indian Pioneer Histories, Oklahoma Historical Society (hereafter, IPHOHS), vol. 52, 216.

3. Mary Jane Warde, *When the Wolf Came: The Civil War and the Indian Territory* (Fayetteville: University of Arkansas Press, 2013), 264.

4. "Interview with Lizzie Wynn," IPHOHS, vol. 101, 50.

5. Ibid.

6. Annie Heloise Abel, *The American Indian and the End of the Confederacy, 1863–1866* (Lincoln: University of Nebraska Press, 1993), 186–88.

7. Ibid., 189.

8. Warde, *When the Wolf Came,* 274–75.

9. For broader discussions about American Indians, emancipation, and citizenship, see Steven Hahn, "Slave Emancipation, Indian Peoples, and the Projects of a New American Nation-State," *Journal of the Civil War Era* 3, no. 3 (January 2013): 307–30; Stephen Kantrowitz, "'Not Quite Constitutionalized': The Meaning of 'Civilization' and the Limits of Native American Citizenship" in *The World the Civil War Made,* ed. Gregory P. Downs and Kate Masur (Chapel Hill: University of North Carolina Press), 2015.

10. Reverend Cyrus Kingsbury to Reverend S. B. Treat, December 4, 1865, Cyrus Kingsbury Collection, Western History Collection, University of Oklahoma, Norman folder 5, file 4.

11. Ibid., fn. 519.

12. "Interview with Chaney McNair," IPHOHS, vol. 59, 270–71; Celia Naylor, *African Cherokees in Indian Territory: From Chattel to Citizens* (Chapel Hill: University of North Carolina Press, 2008), 156.

13. Warde, *When the Wolf Came,* 274–77.

14. *House Miscellaneous Documents,* 30th Cong., 2nd sess., no. 35. See also Angie Debo, *The Rise and Fall of the Choctaw Republic* (Norman: University of Oklahoma Press, 1934), 67.

15. Warde, *When the Wolf Came,* 300–301.

16. U.S. Office of Indian Affairs, *Annual Report of the Commissioner of Indian Affairs, for the Year 1865* (Washington, DC: Government Printing Office, 1865), 42.

17. Michael Wallis, *Way Down Yonder in the Indian Nation: Writings from America's Heartland* (Norman: University of Oklahoma Press, 1993), 163.

18. "Interview with Eli H. Whitmire," IPHOHS, vol. 97, 374.

19. "Newspaper Clipping Tells Story of Early History," *Stillwell Democrat-Journal*, February 14, 1963, 2; "Interview with Eli H. Whitmire," 375–78; "Interview with Zeke Proctor," IPHOHS, vol. 73, 178–82; "Interview with Henry Downing," IPHOHS, vol. 25, 346–49.

20. "Interview with R. Y. Nance," IPHOHS, vol. 66, 77–78.

21. Wallis, *Way Down Yonder in the Indian Nation*, 163; "Line of Duty Deaths Prevalent in Old West," U.S. Marshals Service website, December 5, 2016, https://www.usmarshals.gov/history/line-of-duty-old-west.htm.

22. *The Cherokee Tobacco*, 78 U.S. 616 (1870), December 5, 2016, https://supreme.justia.com/cases/federal/us/78/616/case.html.

23. Warde, *When the Wolf Came*, 301.

24. David A. Chang, *The Color of the Land: Race, Nation, and the Politics of Land Ownership in Oklahoma, 1832–1829* (Chapel Hill: University of North Carolina Press, 2010), 29.

A New Birth of Freedom Abroad

Don H. Doyle

The working men of Europe feel sure that, as the American War of
Independence initiated a new era of ascendancy for the middle class, so
the American Anti-Slavery War will do for the working classes. They consider it an earnest of the epoch to come that it fell to the lot of Abraham
Lincoln, the single-minded son of the working class, to lead his country
through the matchless struggle for the rescue of an enchained race and
the reconstruction of a social world.

—Karl Marx, "Address of the International Working
Men's Association to Abraham Lincoln"[1]

L INCOLN'S PROPHECY OF A "new birth of freedom" is commonly thought to
refer to the Emancipation Proclamation and the end of slavery within the
United States. Whether he intended to or not, Lincoln also made a broader
meaning available, one with implications for the world beyond the United States.
A close reading of the address reveals how he deftly elevated his subject from
the nation founded "four score and seven years ago" to "*any nation* so conceived
and so dedicated." He then placed the American struggle within a global framework, noting, "The world will little note, nor long remember what we say here,
but it can never forget what they did here." He asked his audience to resolve that
"*this nation* . . . shall have a new birth of freedom," then once again globalized the
Union's cause as one of ensuring "that government of the people, by the people, for
the people, shall not perish from the earth."[2]

Lincoln was not a worldly man by the usual connotations of that term. He never
traveled abroad and was not conversant in foreign languages; nor did he routinely
read the foreign press. Nonetheless, from early in his career his speeches and writings showed an impressive understanding of how America's experiment in government by the people related to the sweep of modern history. He was familiar
with the British antislavery movement. The Revolutions of 1848 made a strong
impression on him. He understood that events in the United States mattered to

the wider world and that world opinion mattered to America. "I hate [slavery]," he said in a speech at Peoria in 1854, "because of the monstrous injustice of slavery itself. I hate it because it deprives our republican example of its just influence in the world—enables the enemies of free institutions, with plausibility, to taunt us as hypocrites."[3]

Though as president he left most foreign policy matters to William Seward, Lincoln grasped how important diplomacy and world opinion was to the Union's success. He and Seward worked in tandem to advance the notion that the conflict was something more than America's war with itself over national sovereignty and the right of states to secede. It was more even than a conflict over systems of labor, slave or free. Early in the war, Lincoln saw it as a trial of the republican experiment in popular government: "On the side of the Union it is a struggle for maintaining in the world that form and substance of government whose leading object is to elevate the condition of men; to lift artificial weights from all shoulders; to clear the paths of laudable pursuit for all; to afford all an unfettered start and a fair chance in the race of life." This contest, he went on, "presents to the whole family of man, the question, whether a constitutional republic, or a democracy—a government of the people, by the same people—can, or cannot, maintain its territorial integrity, against its own domestic foes."[4] His phrasing anticipated the Gettysburg Address and, in this instance, with the broadest international implications.

Whether Lincoln's universalizing language at Gettysburg was intended to apply his "new birth of freedom" to the wider world, events in the years that followed seemed to ratify that possibility. The American republic demonstrated an unexpected strength by the end of the Civil War that astonished foreign observers, and this emboldened a whole host of revolutionaries, reformers, and abolitionists to act. Instead of the feeble and irresolute democracy skeptics had portrayed, the Union presented a powerful nation at arms boasting a citizen army of more than two million men who had sustained four grueling years of war. Equally impressive was America's national will, inscribed in three momentous amendments to the Constitution: first, to emancipate four million slaves (two-thirds of the entire enslaved population of the American hemisphere), immediately and without compensation to owners; second, to declare former slaves citizens with equal rights before the law; and third, to enfranchise them by granting the right to vote. From outside the nation, at least among progressive, reform-minded people, America's Reconstruction was frequently praised as an experiment in radical social reform. "The eyes of Europe and of the world are fixed upon your efforts at re-construction," Karl Marx wrote in an open letter to America, "and enemies are ever ready to sound the knell of the downfall of republican institutions when the slightest chance is given. We warn you then, as brothers in the common cause, to remove every shackle from freedom's limb, and your victory will be complete."[5] Marx and many other Europeans were disgusted with Andrew Johnson's reactionary betrayal of Reconstruction, but they continued to view the war as a revolutionary blow in favor of the emancipation of labor in America and Europe.[6]

Between the spring of 1865 and the summer of 1871, a burst of revolutions, reforms, and emancipations spread across the Americas and Europe. Not all were *caused* by Lincoln's actions or the American Civil War, but were all in some way interconnected parts of a contagious new birth of freedom abroad. To put this another way, had the Southern slaveholders' rebellion succeeded, it would have meant a new birth of slavery in the American hemisphere, a major setback to the experiment in government by the people, and a demoralizing blow to reform-minded people everywhere.

Lincoln's Gettysburg speech went to the heart of a transatlantic debate about what many called the republican or democratic "experiment" that went back to the American and French revolutions. Many Europeans, including liberals who believed fervently in individual liberty and freedom of speech and religion, believed that dynastic monarchies, properly checked by constitutional restraints and balanced by popularly elected parliaments, had proved the most stable, workable system of government. Democracies, they believed, were inclined toward what Tocqueville called the "tyranny of the majority" and "mob rule" by the lowest common denominator of the citizenry. The lesson of history, skeptics advised, was that from the time of the ancient Greeks and Romans, self-governing republics had proved inherently fragile. They were suited only to small, homogeneous city-states where people knew and trusted their leaders. By that logic, republicanism seemed bound to fail, given the vast territory and polyglot immigrant population of the United States. Eventually, common wisdom had it, all republics were doomed to descend into anarchy or despotism. In the 1860s it appeared to many that what had been the most successful and durable model of self-government, the American Great Republic, was about to give spectacular proof of the truth of this theory.[7]

When he wrote earlier that the United States represented the "last best hope of earth," Lincoln was not boasting, as so many do when invoking this phrase. It was more a plaintive lament from a lonely and gravely imperiled bastion of popular government. Across the Atlantic world, the Age of Revolution had suffered more defeats than victories since the French Revolution. In Europe, the last gasp of revolutionary fervor is commonly thought to have been extinguished in 1849 when, one by one, the flurry of revolutions that erupted in the "springtime of nations" the previous year failed.[8]

Several dynasties of the old regime answered the Age of Revolution by following the British model—that is, granting constitutional concessions that included the creation of parliaments and extending civil rights to freedom of speech and assembly. Britain was among the freest of European nations in the 1860s. It enjoyed a strong Parliament and a proud tradition of free speech and political expression that made London an asylum for dozens of revolutionary exiles, among whom were Karl Marx and Giuseppe Mazzini. The country had taken some small steps toward democratization—notably, in the Great Reform Act of 1832, which curbed the monopoly of the aristocratic governing classes on officeholding by reducing the number of "rotten boroughs," those sparsely populated districts whose wealthy members of Parliament (MP) usually bought their seats. The right to vote in Britain, however, was based on restrictive property qualifications that allowed only one in six adult males to vote. The Liberal Party was a coalition of former Whigs and Radicals, the latter led in the 1860s by John Bright, who wanted to take reform further and democratize suffrage along the American model. The American question in Britain became a proxy war between those favoring and opposing the democratization of the British government.[9]

Foreign observers on both sides of the political spectrum began to interpret the American Civil War as an epic battle over systems of government, labor, and society, a contest that would have consequences far beyond the borders of the United States. In Britain especially, where people were free to express themselves, the heightened concern about the fate of slavery and democracy in America was joined to a remarkable surge in popular interest in foreign affairs. This cosmopolitanism was something revolutionaries like Marx actively nourished by insisting that the interests of workers transcended any national boundaries.

A letter sent to Lincoln in April 1862 illustrates how much the hopes of European revolutionaries depended on the outcome of the distant war in America. The authors were Karl Blind, a German Forty-Eighter expelled from France; Mazzini, the international leader of the Italian Risorgimento; and Alexander Auguste Ledru-Rollins, a French refugee from the Revolution of 1848. All three were living in exile in London, the international center of Europe's many revolutionary movements.

They were writing to ask Lincoln to fund their clandestine revolutionary activities in Europe, and they laid out the reasons that Lincoln's struggle and theirs were the same: "As republicans, we have felt too well that the rending asunder of your great Republic would furnish arms to all the despotisms of Europe (i.e., the enemies of the principles we represent) not to have aided you morally with all our sympathy and with all our efforts, especially as regards the movement of public opinion in Europe. . . . In serving the cause of liberty, *your* cause—we are serving our own."

Europe's "monarchical governments on their part have done their worst to lead the judgment of Europe astray" against the Union and to take advantage of America's difficulties to carry out their nefarious program to tyrannize Mexico. "*Fresh* attempts," they warned, "will sooner or later be made."

European peoples were ready to challenge their monarchical rulers and make it difficult for them to carry out further wars of aggression against American republics. "Everything is ready for action in Europe," they told Lincoln; all that was needed was money. "Would it not be a page worthy of American history if, in future years, men were to read that . . . President Lincoln had, while establishing the liberty of the New World on an ever-lasting foundation, aided at the same time the cause of independence and freedom in Europe?"[10]

Lincoln let this invitation to ignite revolutions in Europe go unanswered, but the idea took hold on both sides of the Atlantic that the cause of popular government and emancipation—broadly conceived to include slaves, women, workers, Jews, and all humanity—was a transatlantic endeavor. The American Civil War gave reformers a model and vocabulary by which to cast the privileged aristocracy of Europe with the Southern slaveholders in opposition to downtrodden workers and Black slaves. "If the upper classes could have their way without hindrance," Edward Beesly, a history professor and working-class reformer, told a large audience assembled to honor Lincoln and his emancipation edict, "at length you would differ from negro slaves in nothing except the colour of your skin."[11] Truth may have suffered by these habits of conflation, but they worked as powerful rhetorical devices to arouse popular indignation at once against distant slaveholders and the nearby ruling class.

British opinion on the American question was divided early in the war, but, among the liberal middle class and a growing cadre of politically educated workers, that began to change once Lincoln's Emancipation Proclamation transformed the Union's purpose in January 1863. What occurred in Britain was an unusual coalition of middle-class reformers and workers who created new political action organizations. They not only borrowed from Chartist traditions of public demonstrations and processions but also developed new methods of staging massive public demonstrations with tens and sometimes hundreds of thousands of people, and they used these shows of strength to exert pressure on the government to enact specific legislation.

This awakening of political activism was most evident in the political mass meetings and grassroots organization during the American war. John Bright, a Quaker cotton mill owner and MP from northern England, took a leading role in supporting the Union during the *Trent* crisis in December 1861. He spoke out boldly against what appeared to be a mindless stampede toward war with the United States led by the British upper classes. He spoke eloquently about the common bonds between Anglo-American peoples and denounced the privileged classes of England for wanting to make war on "their children" in America. Since 1858, Bright had advocated extending voting rights to the middle class and workers. Now he linked the Union cause to that of American-style democracy for Britain.

As Bright and the Radicals embraced the cause of enfranchising workers, Marx and his band of socialist revolutionaries found common cause in promoting parliamentary reform. Marx had grown despondent with the sorry state of working-class political organization in Europe. The Communist League that he and Friederich Engels helped organize in 1847 had disbanded shortly after the failed Revolutions of 1848. After coming to London in 1850, he devoted most of his time to the British Library working on his magnum opus, *Das Kapital* (1867). But he paid his rent (with help from his friend, Engels) by publishing newspaper articles on the American Civil War for journals in the United States and Europe. Marx and Engels became obsessed with events in America, and their public and private writings about the war reveal a growing enthusiasm for the idea that the plight of slaves in America and workers in Europe were connected. What Marx saw unfolding in Lincoln's skillful hands was revolutionary democratic social change—the "reconstruction of a social world," as he referred to it in his letter to Lincoln. This revolution was taking place within the violent maelstrom of war, but what impressed him about Lincoln was that he carried out revolutionary change by constitutional methods. Writing to his uncle late in 1864, Marx marveled at the radical turn Lincoln had taken. "When you reflect, my dear Uncle, how at the time of Lincoln's election 3 ½ years ago it was only a matter of making no further concessions to the slave-owners, whereas now the avowed aim, which has in part already been realised, is the abolition of slavery, one has to admit that never has such a gigantic revolution occurred with such rapidity. It will have a highly beneficial influence on the whole world."[12]

In September 1864, at a large meeting in St. Martin's Hall, London, Marx played the leading role in forming the International Workingmen's Association (IWA), a coalition of workers from industrial nations in Europe and the United States. In his inaugural address, he reviewed the miserable condition of the working class in Europe since the Revolutions of 1848 had been "crushed by force" and "the most advanced sons of labour fled in despair to the Transatlantic Republic [United States], and the short-lived dreams of emancipation vanished before an epoch of industrial fever, moral marasme, and political reaction." Going forward, Marx said, the "great duty of the working classes" is to "conquer political power." The workers had numbers on their side, "but numbers weigh only in the balance, if united by combination and led by knowledge." He pointed to the movement of Britain and France to war against the beleaguered United States. "It was not the wisdom of the ruling classes, but the heroic resistance to their criminal folly by the working classes of England that saved the West of Europe from plunging headlong into an infamous crusade for the perpetuation and propagation of slavery on the other side of the Atlantic." America, along with the example of Poland, he explained, "have taught the working classes the duty to master themselves the mysteries of international politics. Proletarians of all countries, Unite!"[13]

Marx's call to the international proletariat was the "first polemical work for mass consumption he had written" since the Communist Manifesto in 1848. He still saw clearly the need for radical remedies to the oppression of the working class in modern society, but on this occasion he carefully avoided any appeal to socialist revolutionary change and presented the path forward as one through the ballot box, not the barricade.[14] Marx and the IWA also joined with bourgeois reformers who supported expanding the suffrage. One of its first moves toward conquering political power was the formation of the Reform League in February 1865. It would become Britain's leading force for universal manhood suffrage. Though it enjoyed backing from wealthy reform-minded men, its leadership was dominated by working-class men, including some old Chartists from the 1840s, most of them involved in the IWA council and many supporters of the Union cause in America. Borrowing from the Chartist tradition of public demonstrations and processions to show popular support, the Reform League wanted monster meetings and street demonstrations in support of suffrage. "Without the trade unions, no mass meeting is possible," Marx understood, "and without us, the trade unions are not to be had." That was why reformers had come to the IWA, Marx understood, and he used his leverage to make the league something like a popular front for the IWA.[15]

Marx was enormously pleased with the rapid success of the Reform League. While the IWA drew a few dozen delegates to its offices on Greek Street, the league was drawing thousands to large public meeting halls. "Without us this Reform League would never have come into existence, or else it would have fallen into the hands of the middleclass," Marx boasted to Engels in May 1865. "If we succeed in re-electrifying the political movement of the English working class, our Association will already have done more for the European working class, without making any fuss, than was possible in any other way. And there is every prospect of success."[16]

The launch of Britain's movement for universal manhood suffrage in the spring of 1865 coincided with the huge wave of demonstrations responding to Lincoln's assassination. The mass meetings and other expressions of sympathy for Lincoln and the American republic, along with the forced contrition of America's and Lincoln's conservative critics, seemed to flow together as part of the same pro-democratic spirit sweeping across the British Isles and the European continent that spring.

In large cities and small villages across the British Isles, thousands of men and women crowded into public meeting halls, shire council halls, and churches to eulogize Lincoln and sometimes remonstrate against those political leaders who had refused to stand by him and the Union. Three huge meetings took place in St. James's Hall in London on April 28 and 29 and May 1, 1865. The Emancipation Society convened the April 29 meeting; the hall was draped in black, an American flag at one end of the gallery, and filled with women dressed in mourning while on the platform was "an array of Parliamentary gentlemen, and many leading citizens, of the metropolis." MP William E. Forester, a stalwart friend of America throughout the war, spoke of this as a "time when the tie of blood binding English-men to Americans was indeed truly felt. A thrill of grief, horror and indignation, which had passed through the length and breadth of Europe, and especially pos-sesses the heart of every Englishman as though some painful calamity had fallen on himself. [Cheers.]"[17] Thomas Bayley Potter, a Radical MP, linked the crisis in America to Britain: "Lincoln destroyed slavery in America. It should be their wish to destroy serfdom at home. And he trusted the result of the conflict in America would be to give an impetus to the cause of reform in Europe."[18]

A mass meeting of London workers gathered in St. Martin's Hall on May 4 to commemorate the slain American leader. George Potter, a labor leader, honored Lincoln as a martyr to universal emancipation: "Let us not forget that he was a work-ing man. . . . It was to emancipate slavery and to elevate labour, Abraham Lincoln lived and died. We lament his loss, and we hope and trust that his martyrdom will be the death knell of slavery and oppression throughout the world."[19] Mr. Leicester, a glassmaker, rose to move approval of the workers' letter to Mrs. Lincoln, taking the occasion to roundly denounce the British ruling class for siding with the South, "a kingdom founded on human blood," while the workers stood by the Union and Lincoln and against slavery.[20]

"Under a strain such as no aristocracy, no monarchy, no empire could have sup-ported," Edward Beesly noted, "Republican institutions have stood firm. It is we, now, who call upon the privileged classes to mark the result."[21]

Mark the result they did. Radicals saw the Union victory as ratification of American democracy and of their goal to democratize Britain. As the American war ended, a class war in Britain began to take form.

Most historians have viewed the Reform Act of 1867 as a story of high politics involving Benjamin Disraeli and the Tories outflanking Gladstone and the Liberals. They pay less attention to the origins of the Reform League, a coalition of middle-class reformers and working-class socialist elements who carried out massive public demonstrations and forced the British political establishment to enact suffrage reform. The league had its origins in September 1864 when the "Universal League for the Material Elevation of the Industrious Classes" first met in the offices of the IWA on Greek Street in London's Soho district. By February 1865, it had been reconstituted as a coalition with working-class groups and called itself the Reform League. The leadership, Marx boasted to Engels, was fully in the hands of the IWA.[22] "Without us this Reform League would never have come into existence, or else it would have fallen into the hands of the Middleclass." "If we succeed in re-electrifying the political movement of the English working class," Marx enthused, "our association will already have done more for the European working class, with-out making any fuss, than was possible in any other way. And there is every pros-pect of success."[23]

Marx was a socialist revolutionary who instinctively rejected piecemeal reform in favor of radical transformation of the class system that was immiserating workers in all modern societies. It was in part due to his growing regard for Lincoln's achievements that he came to understand that in America, Britain, and other nations based on representative government and the rule of law, the "reconstruction of a social world" might come about by enfranchising and educating the masses. In the United States he witnessed a revolutionary democracy supported by workers who, he insisted, pushed Lincoln and the Republican Party to the left. To enfranchise workers in Britain, Marx and the IWA joined forces with bourgeois reformers and the labor aristocracy in the trade union organizations. In the Reform League they had created an organization devoted exclusively to expanding the right to vote.[24] Because workers could not vote, they would exert pressure on the government by staging "monster meetings" in the public square and fill the newspapers with accounts of their speeches and resolutions. This show of popular strength would force Parliament to act. The Reform League drew support from old Chartists; veterans of 1848; trade unionists; middle-class Radicals led by Bright; some Liberals, including John Stuart Mill; and an array of other reformers, from abolitionists to woman suffrage advocates. Marx saw to it that much of the leadership of the league was in the hands of the IWA.

Many of the Reform League leaders had been schooled in mass politics in connection with protests involving the American Civil War, along with a number of other foreign causes. Giuseppe Garibaldi's march on Rome in the fall of 1862 aroused enormous interest among workers and immigrants in Britain. Mass meetings drawing tens of thousands took place in Hyde Park, and violence broke out when Irish supporters of Pope Pius IX assaulted the Garibaldi supporters. In May 1864, Garibaldi's visit to London set off the largest public demonstration the city had ever seen. It took hours for the Italian hero to make his way from the train station through the city surrounded by massive throngs of admiring people.[25] The Polish uprising in January 1863 also became a cause célèbre among workers inspired by the IWA's emphasis on working-class solidarity across national boundaries.[26]

Above all, the American Civil War served as a galvanizing force in arousing and educating members of the working and middle class in Britain. "All agree that no question of English politics since the Reform Bill [1832] has called out such warm, even passionate, feeling as the American," one American observer wrote from London. "As we all saw, the great European struggle of popular rights against privilege, of Democracy against Aristocracy, was fought over our shoulders. Nothing could exceed the intensity with which every feature of the great contest was discussed in almost every household of the kingdom." No event in recent English history, he added, "has aroused such a deep and universal emotion" as "the murder of President Lincoln."[27]

The antislavery sympathies of British and European peoples had engendered great sympathy toward Lincoln as the Great Emancipator, but his appeal went well beyond his role in ending slavery. Lincoln's role as the personification of the common man and champion of democracy garnered even wider popular admiration. "The sense of identification with the democratic cause," one historian of British suffrage reform wrote, "grew into a self-sacrificing devotion to Lincoln and the future of the Union."[28] Looking back on the multiple origins of the movement, George Howell, secretary of the Reform League and ally of Marx, recalled: "The one event which knit us together more than any other was the American Civil War. For years one test of a man's Liberalism was—What was he on the American question?"[29] George McCauley Trevelyan, Bright's biographer, agreed that the American question was certainly a litmus test for British sentiment on democracy at home, but he preferred to think of it the other way around: it was British concerns with voting rights that "largely determined" people's stance on the Civil War. In either case, "The victory of the North accelerated the more peaceable victory of democracy in England."[30]

The Union's victory came as something of a surprise to many government leaders in Europe. From the beginning of the war, many believed that even if the Union held great advantages of military manpower and industrial capacity, a democracy would never be able to carry on protracted warfare without the government losing popular support. The South, engaged in an existential struggle to win independence and protect its slave-based economy, would sustain the fight until the Union finally exhausted itself or was undermined within by protests from war-weary citizens and those opposed to freeing the slaves and elevating Blacks as equals.

When reports that Robert E. Lee had surrendered his army to Union forces arrived in Europe, they stunned many Confederate sympathizers. The news of Lincoln's death gave some to hope that the war would resume and the rebellion might yet prevail. But the popular response to the assassination took a very different turn in Europe.

Within hours after reaching Europe on April 26, news of the assassination flashed across the British Isles and the European continent, reaching every major city and soon dispersing to every small village in the land. Within a few days, governments and newspapers were responding to the news from Eastern Europe and Russia across northern Africa and India. In the Western Hemisphere, the news moved southward by steamship, reaching Cuba and Mexico within a matter of days but not arriving in Chile and Peru until the end of May. Everywhere, people received the news with a mix of horror and disbelief. Rumors and news flowed through the streets and in taverns, in print, and across a vast telegraph network for weeks.

At first, some thought it was just another ruse orchestrated by Confederate sympathizers, or perhaps some ploy by stock-jobbers to profit off the market's turbulence. Even at the stock exchange in Liverpool, a stronghold of Confederate sympathizers, a man at the front desk read the news out loud, causing "the most profound and painful sensation [and] brought tears to the eyes of many present, while others turned pale and faint." One Southern sympathizer issued a "faint 'hur-rah,'" and other members of the exchange promptly ushered him out of the room. Six hundred employees put their names to a petition imploring Liverpool's mayor to hold a meeting that evening to give vent to public sympathy for America.[31]

At the London exchange, American stocks and bonds plunged 7–8 percent in value while cotton prices soared on rumors the war would resume. Even the mori-bund Confederate Cotton Bond revived slightly. Rumors continued to roil the mar-kets and public emotions: Seward was dead, Edwin Stanton had been shot; the war was resuming; Northerners would reject Andrew Johnson as president.[32] The uncertainty and confusion was everything John Wilkes Booth and his cocon-spirators had hoped.

The governments of all the Great Powers of Europe issued formal messages of condolence, as did the international press, all with predictable obsequies, ex-pressions of admiration for the fallen leader, and retroactive affirmations of their abiding faith that Lincoln would lead the "Great American Republic" to victory. Most of this was exaggerated or outright falsehood. Ever since Lincoln was elected, European conservatives had ridiculed him for his coarse breeding and lack of quali-fication for office, the deplorable result of universal suffrage and "extreme democ-racy" they warned their followers. They had blamed Lincoln for bringing on the war and excoriated him for issuing his emancipation edict, which they characterized as an invitation to servile insurrection and racial holocaust.

In the face of America's victory and resentment, it was time for contrition. No journal had been crueler than the British satirical magazine *Punch,* court jester to the Tory press, as Karl Marx characterized it. *Punch* and its cartoonist John Tenniel had spent four years portraying Lincoln as a rustic, violent tyrant. Now Tenniel published a moving image of Britannia laying a wreath on Lincoln's bier, flanked by a weeping Black man and an angel. The drawing accompanied a poignant apology composed by the editor Tom Taylor: "Yes, he had lived to shame me from my sneer, To lame my pencil and confute my pen—To make me own this hind of princes peer, This rail-splitter a true-born king of men." The British press, one historian summarized the mood that spring, "poured out . . . a great stream of laudation for Lincoln almost amounting to a national recantation."[33]

Marx, on behalf of the International Working Men's Association (known as the First International), relished the unctuous displays of sympathy from political lead-ers who had heaped abuse on Lincoln and America the previous four years and now were forced by public outrage to pay homage to the fallen leader. In an open letter to President Andrew Johnson, Marx, on behalf of the IWA, wrote, "It is not our part to cull words of sorrow and horror, while the heart of two worlds heaves with emotion. Even the sycophants who year after year, and day by day, stuck to their Sisyphus work of morally assassinating Abraham Lincoln and the great republic he headed, stand now aghast at this universal outburst of popular feeling, and rival with each other to strew rhetorical flowers on his open grave."[34]

The popular demonstrations of sympathy and solidarity startled even the most seasoned among the U.S. diplomatic corps abroad. Across Europe, in Latin America, within days of the news arriving, people of all ranks felt moved to express their own sentiments of sympathy, outrage, and solidarity with America and Lincoln's legacy. U.S. legations and consulates reported people gathering in the streets outside their doors, at first to confirm the truth of the news, later to deliver messages of sympathy or stand vigil as a mark of respect before American flags, lowered to half-mast and draped in black crepe.[35]

Men and women, workers and students, Masons, abolitionists, intellectuals, socialists, and reformers, in great cities and small villages, came together, listened to speeches and eulogies, issued group resolutions of sympathy and solidarity, and assigned committees to draw up letters of condolence. By early May and well into the summer of 1865, hundreds of these condolence messages poured into American diplomatic posts around the world.

At the end of 1865, the U.S. State Department gathered more than one thousand condolence messages, signed by tens of thousands of citizens, carefully translated those not in English, and published them as an appendix to the annual diplomatic correspondence. The volume of condolence messages went out to all governments around the world. It was an ingenious exercise in the new art of public diplomacy, for it told those government leaders, many of whom had been indifferent if not hostile toward the Union cause: this is what your people think of Lincoln, America, and its republican government. The sharp edges on some of the condolence messages must have added to the anxiety European governments felt. Having expected the Union to be dismembered and weakened, they now beheld one of the most powerful military forces in the world, about to turn, they feared, against their aggression in the Americas.

After British Prime Minister Palmerston, the stodgy leader of the Liberal Party, died in October 1865, John Russell and William Gladstone formed a new government. With Palmerston no longer obstructing matters, Gladstone put a moderate reform bill before Parliament in March 1866. The bill was intended not to enact universal manhood suffrage but to selectively extend voting rights to "respectable artisans" by applying property requirements. Nonetheless, it brought forth a vitriolic reaction from aristocratic MPs who feared any odor of democracy and caused a rupture in the Liberal Party when a faction of reactionaries voiced disdain for the unwashed masses.

The leading voice for what came to be called the "Adullamites" (a biblical refer-ence to those who sought refuge from King Solomon in the cave of Adullam) was Liberal MP Robert Lowe, a pugnacious man who despised democracy because of his firsthand exposure to it while living in Australia and America. One biographer speculated the cause might also have been "the accident of having been hit over the head during an election riot in 1860."[36]

During the tedious debates in Parliament, Lowe rose to speak: "Look at *America*. A section of the American democracy revolted and broke up the Union, the rest fought to preserve it; the war was fought out to the bitter end, and now that the war is concluded they are almost ready to go to war again to prevent the doing of that which they took up arms to accomplish." There, he went on, "where the people have undisputed power, that they do not send honest, hardworking men to rep-resent them in Congress, but traffickers in office, bankrupts, men who have lost their character and been driven from every respectable way of life, and who take up politics as a last resource." As the debate dragged on over the next several weeks, Lowe became fed up with the cloying adulation of the common man and proposed to "say exactly what I think" of the unwashed multitude: "If you want venality, if you want ignorance, if you want drunkenness, and facility for being intimidated; or if, on the other hand, you want impulsive, unreflecting, and violent people, where do you look for them in the constituencies?" The question, to the minds of Lowe and the Adullamites, required no answer.[37] The debate on reform in Britain had, in the process, become a referendum on American-style democracy.

Conservative opposition to democratic reform coalesced predictably around a defense of ancient English traditions and fears of social leveling and mob rule. If the Reform Bill passed, Benjamin Disraeli, the Tory opposition leader, lamented, the House of Commons would be left with "no charm of tradition; no families of historic lineage; none of those great estates around which men rally when liberty is assailed. . . . Instead of these, you will have a horde of selfish and obscure mediocri-ties incapable of anything but mischief."[38]

In Britain, it was the Liberal Adullamites who defeated the movement for genu-ine democratization of the electorate. The Liberal Party grew out of the old Whig Party, which believed in increasing the powers of Parliament at the expense of the Crown. The Whigs' great achievement, the Reform Act of 1832, ironically had led to their demise. A new coalition of old Whigs and Radicals, styling themselves Liberals, rallied around free trade and laissez-faire capitalism. Liberals such as John Stuart Mill believed in representative government and freedom of expression, but he and other Liberals distrusted democracy precisely because they feared that the "tyranny of the majority," as Tocqueville called it, threatened individual liberty. Members from both parties might agree that democracy was well enough suited to America, lacking as it did a traditional aristocracy and filled with immigrants, but it was not for Britain. That America had been tearing itself apart during four bloody years of Civil War, as Lowe testified, served as proof enough of the dangers democracy held in store for Britain.[39]

To upper-class fears of democracy, Britain's workers and suffrage reformers answered by praising American democracy and its fortitude in the recent civil war. For them, Lincoln was an icon of honesty and republican virtue, a firm reproach to the notion that democracy could not produce capable leaders. Instead of a frightful vision of anarchy and mob rule, for British reformers America was a land of opportunity and respect for the common man.[40]

When Gladstone's reform bill failed in June 1866, so did his Liberal government. The Tories formed a new government led by Lord Derby as prime minister and Disraeli as chancellor of the Exchequer. Whatever else Gladstone's weak reform bill failed to do for democracy in Britain, its failure aroused the Reform League to take democracy to the streets of London and other cities across the British Isles. In the summer of 1866, the Reform League staged a series of spectacular demonstrations. In late June 1866, twenty thousand gathered for speeches in Trafalgar Square; five days later, fifty thousand men and women filled the square. Their rallies combined processions of men and women with signs and banners, brass bands, speeches, chants, and cheers. Some brandished bright red flags with red caps of liberty atop the staff, symbols of revolution borrowed from the Chartists and the French Revolution. At rallies and during processions they often sang the French revolutionary anthem, *La Marseillaise,* all frightening gestures to British Conservatives and many Liberals who feared democracy because it might lead to mob rule. The French Revolution and the Revolutions of 1848 left a lasting anxiety among the British upper class who were willing to concede just enough to reform as necessary to avoid revolution.[41]

Several demonstrations took place in London and other industrial cities in the summer and fall of 1866. When the Reform League next announced plans for an even larger demonstration in Hyde Park, the London police banned public meetings in the park. It played into the Reform League's hand, for suddenly the right to vote was joined to the venerable rights of free-born Englishmen to meet and speak as was their right.

The July 23 demonstration was said to involve some 200,000 demonstrators and thousands of police and soldiers. It began with a large procession marching from league headquarters in Adelphi Terrace toward Marble Arch, where the constables and military guarded entry to the park on foot and horseback and blockaded the perimeter with rows of carriages and omnibuses. The main body of demonstrators turned away and worked their way toward Trafalgar Square through St. James and Pall Mall streets, jeering in front of the Carlton Club, a Conservative gentlemen's club, cheering before the Liberal Reform Club, and smashing windows in the homes of prominent opponents along the way. At Trafalgar Square, they were treated to speeches, resolutions, and more cheering.[42]

Back at the Marble Arch, the Clerkenwell Branch of the Reform League challenged the police, pulled down the railings erected to keep them out, burst onto the park grounds, and proceeded to make speeches. They were there, one speaker told the crowd, "to assert their rights as Englishmen." Their defiance of Police Commissioner Richard Mayne's ban proved "they had not yet given up that right. ('Hear, hear.') . . . 'Englishmen' were not to be ruled by their own servants, the police and the soldiery." When an imposing force of Foot Guards and mounted soldiers approached them, the crowd welcomed "the people's Guards" and shouted "hurrah for our brother in the red coats." When the police arrived, however, the crowd hissed, and some boys hurled stones. Then the crowd formed a procession and marched away, singing an adapted version of the famous American Civil War song "John Brown's Body": "We'll hang Sir Richard [Mayne, commissioner of police] on a sour apple tree. As we go marching on. Glory! Glory! Hallelujah! As we go marching on."[43]

Marx wrote to Engels from London after the Hyde Park "riot": "The government has almost caused a mutiny here. Your Englishman first needs a revolutionary education, of course, for which two weeks would suffice if Sir Richard Mayne had absolute powers of command." Marx went on to imagine London going to the barricades: "If the railings had been used—and it almost came to that—for offence and defence against the police, and some score of the latter killed, the military would have had to 'step in', instead of merely parading. And then things would have got quite jolly."[44] Small demonstrations and violent clashes between reformers and police continued over the next three days. The Times reported with unrestrained disgust dozens of attacks on property and police by "the lowest scum" of London. On July 25, a group of protestors entered Hyde Park and set fire to a large tree near the Marble Arch. The "roughs" later marched away, once again singing "to the tune of 'John Brown'" a jingle calling for the "suspension" of Police Chief Mayne.[45]

More mass meetings and public demonstrations continued in London and other British cities while Parliament went into recess that summer. The demands of the Reform League, meanwhile, were shifting to the left. At a league meeting in December 1866, Bright, the Radical leader, answered a taunting cartoon in Punch that had depicted him cowering before a burly worker and stammering, "I have no fe-fear of ma-manhood suffrage." Now, he announced in a bold voice before the enthusiastic crowd: "I have no fear of manhood suffrage."[46]

More extraordinary, women began agitating for their right to vote. During the parliamentary debates over the qualifications for voting, Liberal MP John Stuart Mill intervened with a proposition to substitute the word "persons" for "men" with the well-wrought argument that all the qualifications for men to vote could equally apply to women. Though Mill's amendment failed amid the "braying and brainless hilarity" of the MPs, it "fired the starting gun for a campaign" that a half-century later Emmeline Pankhurst's generation would bring to fruition.[47] Less well-known were the many women who took action, speaking, writing, and organizing to advance the cause of women's political rights in the 1860s. They joined rallies and processions, brandishing banners and placards proclaiming "Rights for Women," and took to the podium at Reform League rallies. They also began petitioning the government and organizing to advance their cause. Local woman suffrage societies took form in Manchester and London, and reformers founded the Manchester Society for Woman Suffrage. Later the same year, Lydia Becker founded the National Society for Women's Suffrage.[48]

Young Emmeline Pankhurst, the future leader of the suffragist movement, experienced her political awakening as a young girl in Manchester. Sometime during the war, her mother helped organize a "great bazaar" to "relieve the poverty of the newly emancipated negro slaves in the United States." "From infancy," she recounted, "I had been accustomed to hear pro and con discussions of slavery and the American Civil War." Her father was an "ardent abolitionist," and her mother read to her the story of *Uncle Tom's Cabin.* "These stories, with the bazaars and the relief funds and subscriptions of which I heard so much talk, I am sure made a permanent impression on my brain and my character."[49]

Many in the reform movement noted that the inhabitants of Britain's former and present colonies in America and Australia enjoyed more voting rights than British subjects. The American debate over enfranchising former slaves lent itself to more invidious comparisons with the voting rights of British men and women. Speaking before the Edinburgh branch of the National Society for Women's Suffrage, Jacob Bright (brother of the Radical MP) said he knew of "no parallel in Christendom . . . to the legal position of married women in this country. . . . If I wanted a parallel— the nearest I could find—I could go to the Southern States of America, amongst the negro population before the presidency of Abraham Lincoln."[50]

The Reform League continued to apply pressure on Parliament in the spring of 1867 as it struggled to fashion a bill that would concede political power to "qualified" artisans and calm the public demonstrations but not give in to demands for universal suffrage. In the end, one million men were added to the voting roles, doubling the electorate and moving Britain, slowly and, for many in the governing class, reluctantly toward mass politics. Men of both parties viewed the 1867 Reform Act as a necessary bulwark against the advance of democracy as much as a breach in the thick walls of privilege. Disraeli explained after putting the final touches on the bill, "We do not live—and I trust it will never be the fate of this country to live—under a democracy." Reform would acknowledge the vast changes in British society since 1832 but "with a due deference to the traditions of an ancient State."[51]

Further expansion of voting rights did not come until 1884, when a Third Reform Act again doubled the number of voters. Votes for women also came in slow, measured installments beginning in 1918, when married female householders older than thirty and holding degrees from British universities were permitted to vote. It was all done in classic British fashion, but in a series of small reluctant steps, the country moved toward democracy, the skeptics congratulating themselves for avoiding the excesses of the American prototype and the reformers holding up the United States as their model.[52] Marx's vision of emancipated workers empowered by enfranchisement to effect real social and economic change by democratic means was far from realized in Europe at this time. In Europe and the United States, the "reconstruction of a social world" that he hoped Abraham Lincoln would make possible still awaited the future.

Notes

1. Karl Marx, "Address of the International Working Men's Association to Abraham Lincoln, President of the United States of America" (1865), in Karl Marx and Friedrich Engels, *The Collected Works of Karl Marx and Friedrich Engels*, ed. E. J. Hobsbawm et al., trans. Peter and Betty Ross, digital ed. (hereafter, *MECW*), vol. 20: Marx and Engels 1864–68 (London: Lawrence Wishart, 2010), 20.

2. Don H. Doyle, *The Cause of All Nations: An International History of the American Civil War* (New York: Basic, 2015), 281–83; Don H. Doyle, "Widely Noted and Long Remembered: The Gettysburg Address around the World," in *The Gettysburg Address: Perspectives on Lincoln's Greatest Speech,* ed. Sean Conant (New York: Oxford University Press, 2015), 274–99.

3. Sidney Blumenthal, *Wrestling with His Angel: 1849–1856* (New York: Simon and Schuster, 2018), 151–66, 372–73; Roy P. Basler, ed., *The Collected Works of Abraham Lincoln* (New Brunswick, NJ: Rutgers University, 1953), 9 vols., 2:255.

4. Basler, *The Collected Works of Abraham Lincoln,* 4:426, 438.

5. Karl Marx, "To the People of the United States of America," in *Minutes of the General Council of the International Workingmen's Association, 1864–1886* (Moscow: Progress, 1964), 310, https://www.marxists.org/history/international/iwma/documents/1865/to-americans .htm.

6. Herbert M. Morais, "Marx and Engels on America," *Science and Society* 12, (Winter 1948): 9–13.

7. Robert Saunders, *Democracy and the Vote in British Politics, 1848–1867: The Making of the Second Reform Act* (Burlington, VT: Ashgate, 2011), chap. 5; Doyle, *The Cause of All Nations,* 95–96.

8. R. R. Palmer and David Armitage, *The Age of the Democratic Revolution: A Political History of Europe and America, 1760–1800* (Princeton, NJ: Princeton University Press, 2014); E. J. Hobsbawm, *The Age of Revolution, 1789–1848* (New York: Vintage, 1996).

9. Hugh Dubrulle, "'We Are Threatened with . . . Anarchy and Ruin': Fear of Americanization and the Emergence of an Anglo-Saxon Confederacy in England during the American Civil War," *Albion* 33, no. 4 (December 1, 2001): 583–613.

10. Karl Blind, "Karl Blind, Joseph Mazzini, and Alexandre A. Ledru-Rollin to Abraham Lincoln, Thursday, April 24, 1862," Abraham Lincoln Papers, Library of Congress, http://memory.loc .gov.

11. Paul Foot, *The Vote: How It Was Won and How It Was Undermined* (London: Bookmarks, [2005] 2012), 126.

12. *MECW*, 42:48.

13. Ibid., 20:5–13.

14. Foot, *The Vote*, 129.

15. *MECW*, 42:74.

16. Ibid., 42:150, 158.

17. "The Assassination of the President," *New York Times*, May 11, 1865.

18. Ibid.

19. Gustav Mayer, *The Era of the Reform League: English Labour and Radical Politics 1857–1872* (Mannheim, Germany: Palatium, 1995), 91.

20. Ibid., 91.

21. H. C. Allen, "Civil War, Reconstruction, and Great Britain," in *Heard round the World: The Impact Abroad of the Civil War*, ed. Harold Hyman (New York: Alfred A. Knopf, 1969), 73, quoting Edward Beesly.

22. Mayer, *The Era of the Reform League*, 115, quoting Marx to Engels, September 25, 1865, in *MECW*, 42:108.

23. *MECW*, 42:150, 158, capitalization altered for readability.

24. On Marx's interest in democratizing Britain, see ibid., 42:604nn116–17.

25. Sheridan Gilley, "The Garibaldi Riots of 1862," *Historical Journal* 16, no. 4 (December 1973): 697–732; Marcella Pellegrino Sutcliffe, "Garibaldi in London," *History Today* 64, no. 4 (April 2014): 42.

26. Mayer, *The Era of the Reform League*.

27. C. L. B., "European Social Reforms; Change in English Opinion Union of America and England," *New York Times*, July 9, 1865.

28. F. M. Leventhal, *Respectable Radical: George Howell and Victorian Working Class Politics* (London: Weidenfeld and Nicolson, 1971), 47.

29. George Howell, "Working Class Movements of the Century, XV," *Reynolds's Newspaper*, November 29, 1896, 4. Howell admitted to divisions among workers on the American question early in the war. For more on the connections between the American Civil War and the mobilization of working-class reform, see Mayer, *The Era of the Reform League*, chap. 2; Eugenio F. Biagini, *Liberty, Retrenchment and Reform: Popular Liberalism in the Age of Gladstone, 1860–1880* (Cambridge: Cambridge University Press, 2004), 257–75.

30. Saunders, *Democracy and the Vote in British Politics*, 132.

31. *Shields Daily Gazette* (Tyne and Wear, UK), April 27, 1865, 2; *London Evening Standard*, April 27, 1865, 2.

32. *Morning Advertiser* (London), April 27, 1865, 4; *Morning Post* (London), April 27, 1865, 3.

33. Ephraim Douglass Adams, *Great Britain and the American Civil War* (New York: Russell and Russell, [1924] 1958), 2 vols., 2:259. "Britannia Sympathises with Columbia," *Punch*, May 6, 1865, http://www.historygallery.com/prints/PunchLincoln/1865death/1865death.htm.

34. U.S. Department of State, *The Assassination of Abraham Lincoln, Late President of the United States of America: And the Attempted Assassination of William H. Seward, Secretary of State, and Frederick W. Seward, Assistant Secretary, on the Evening of the 14th of April, 1865: Expressions of Condolence and Sympathy Inspired by These Events* (Washington, DC: Government Printing Office, 1867), 349–50.

35. The condolence messages describe the meetings and events of this occasion: see ibid. Images of the original letters can be viewed at "Foreign Messages on the Death of Abraham Lincoln," U.S. National Archives, accessed October 8, 2018, https://catalog.archives.gov/id/1079739.
36. Robert Blake, *Disraeli* (London: Faber and Faber, 2012), 440–41.
37. *Hansard Parliamentary Debates,* vol. 182, Adjourned Debate Seventh Sight, HC, April 26, 1866; Adjourned Debate Second Night, March 13, 1866, https://hansard.parliament.uk/Commons.
38. Foot, *The Vote,* 146.
39. Saunders, *Democracy and the Vote in British Politics,* esp. chap. 5.
40. See the account of the London workers meeting on May 5, 1865 in Mayer, *The Era of the Reform League,* 90–93; Adam I. P. Smith, "Land of Opportunity?" in *America Imagined,* ed. Axel Körner and Nicola Miller (New York: Palgrave Macmillan, 2012), 34–37; Adam I. P. Smith, "The 'Cult' of Abraham Lincoln and the Strange Survival of Liberal England in the Era of the World Wars," *Twentieth Century British History* 21, no. 4 (December 2010): 486.
41. Mayer, *The Era of the Reform League,* 241; Saunders, *Democracy and the Vote in British Politics,* chap. 1. Newspaper accounts of demonstrations frequently describe revolutionary symbols of the reformers.
42. "The Reform Demonstration in Hyde Park," *The Times* (London), July 24, 1866, Times Digital Archive, https://www.gale.com/c/the-times-digital-archive.
43. Mayer, *The Era of the Reform League,* 178–84.
44. *MECW,* 42:300.
45. "The Gathering in Hyde Park Yesterday," *The Times,* July 26, 1866; "The Hyde Park Rioters," *The Times,* July 27, 1866; "The Reform League Assembles Once More in Force," *The Times,* July 30, 1866; "Last Evening at 8 O'clock a Meeting of Large Dimensions," *The Times,* July 31, 1866, all in Times Digital Archive.
46. Mayer, *The Era of the Reform League,* 194–95, 195n53.
47. Saunders, *Democracy and the Vote in British Politics,* 258; Mills's motion is in *Hansard Parliamentary Debates,* vol. 187, HC, May 20, 1867.
48. Dozens of pamphlets and newspaper articles give evidence of a lively debate over women's right to vote. For a few examples, see Lydia Becker, *The Franchise for Women* (Manchester, UK: A. Ireland, 1867); Barbara Leigh Smith Bodichon, *Reasons for and against the Enfranchisement of Women* (London: London National Society for Women's Suffrage, 1869); Helen Taylor, *The Claim of Englishwomen to the Suffrage Constitutionally Considered* (London: Trubener, 1867).
49. Emmeline Pankhurst, *My Own Story* (London: Vintage, 2015), 3–4.
50. London and National Society for Women's Service Edinburgh Branch, *Women's Suffrage: Public Meeting in Edinburgh in Queen Street Hall, on 17th January 1870* (Edinburgh: John Greig and Son, 1870), 12.
51. Saunders, *Democracy and the Vote in British Politics,* 1.
52. Foot, *The Vote;* Saunders, *Democracy and the Vote in British Politics.*

Confederate Reconstructions

GENERATIONS OF CONFLICT

David Moltke-Hansen

T HE WORD "RECONSTRUCTION" DID not mean before the American Civil War what it did after. It mattered when and where in their life courses former Confederates experienced the stunning changes in denotations and connotations. Those who lived most of their lives before the war necessarily had different takes, both personally and collectively, from those who entered adulthood later. By following reactions and thoughts of a dozen-plus cultural and political leaders, this essay seeks to delineate this process. Selected here because of their preeminent roles, these men sought to shape contemporaries' views on Reconstruction, not just in the South, but also in the North.

Many older former Confederates resisted at every turn the unprecedented Reconstruction program that emerged after slavery's end. Born in 1806, the generation's best-known Southern man of letters, William Gilmore Simms, did. Most of the younger men who had fought for the Confederacy did so as well. Some, however, not only came to terms with Reconstruction, but even embraced the principles underlying Reconstruction's constitutional and civil rights agendas. No white Southern writer did so more vigorously than George Washington Cable. Thirty-eight years Simms's junior, he had by the mid-1880s become perhaps the region's best-known fictionist.

Despite his acclaim, the children and younger siblings of Confederate soldiers almost universally rejected Cable's arguments for racial equality. Young Southern progressives would, too, although critical of slavery and the Old South. Born in the Civil War's second year, William Peterfield Trent did. Friend of Teddy Roosevelt and a leading literary scholar through the 1930s, Trent agreed that the South should handle its racial issues as whites there saw fit. He even contemplated the division of citizens into two classes: an elite subset with the franchise and the rest with personal legal rights and protections but without the vote. Most of his contemporaries did not see the need to go so far. Their campaign to suppress the Black vote and promulgate laws segregating every aspect of Southern society achieved its purposes.

Historical Concepts of Reconstruction

Over three-quarters of a century, Simms, Cable, and Trent highlighted their respective political generations' evolving and conflicted relationship with the concept of Reconstruction. Additional men included here flesh out that story through their postbellum work and interactions. First, however, to understand aspects of the background to and unfolding of these shifting attitudes and decisions, one must consider earlier uses of the reconstruction concept. On the eve of America's so-called second war of independence, the War of 1812, the immediate past president of the United States, Thomas Jefferson, fostered translation of French Count Antoine Destutt de Tracy's *A Commentary and Review of Montesquieu's Spirit of Laws*. First published in Paris in 1806, *Spirit of the Laws* distinguished between degrees and kinds of political upheavals in the shift from an old to a new regime. The count recognized, on the one hand, "revolution and destruction," and on the other, "all the rest," which "is only organization and reconstruction" of the body politic. He had in mind most immediately the American and French experiences of their revolutions and the aftermaths in the last quarter of the eighteenth century. What constituted "all the rest" became the open question.[1]

The use of the term "reconstruction" to describe political, as well as social and cultural, adjustment or recovery, rather than upheaval and dramatic change, had some currency in the 1810s. Only very occasionally earlier, back in the mid-sixteenth century, had the word appeared in print in either French or English. The few times it did, it generally referred to the built environment, language, or memories. The emphasis on restoration of what had fallen into disrepair or been destroyed, forgotten, or lost had predominated. One was not building or creating anew but, to the extent possible, rebuilding, recovering, or re-creating what had existed, albeit often in more-or-less different circumstances.[2]

Clearly, however, no one employing the word "reconstruction" in the last third of the eighteenth century could have understood it the way white Southerners came to a hundred years later. Then, after four years of bloody war and two more of continuing, often violent resistance by former Confederates, the U.S. Congress passed the first of the Reconstruction Acts. These laws prescribed the means by and conditions under which former Confederate states could gain readmittance to the Union and full political representation in Congress. The acts also spelled out the U.S. Army's role in supervising compliance with them. In time, those laws, along with the Thirteenth, Fourteenth, and Fifteenth amendments to the U.S.

Constitution and federal courts' judicial decisions, legally defined Reconstruction. Military supervision at the outset ensured some enforcement of the acts, amendments, and judgments in limited areas. Recognizing the fact, commentators extended the Reconstruction era back to include federal occupation of Confederate locales during the war. The withdrawal of the military from oversight ended it politically in 1877. Yet it took decades of judicial, legislative, and executive actions to conclude the unwinding.[3]

For former Confederates who had grown to maturity before the Civil War, the understanding undergirding the development of the Reconstruction regime perverted the concept's historical denotations. After all, the radical nature of the Reconstruction amendments and acts legitimated the overthrow of an existing order, not its restoration and preservation or (re)organization and adjustment. Therefore, it constituted an example of Destutt de Tracy's "revolution and destruction." Older Confederates' younger siblings and children, who fought in and survived the war, all experienced these connotative shifts. The militarily enforced demands embodied in this emergent Reconstruction concept confronted veterans with contested realities and potentialities that they needed to resist and negotiate. Ultimately, they could not restore the ruins of the old order. In many senses, the end of slavery meant the end of the Old South.[4]

Yet federal Reconstruction did not continue. In the course of the estimated extrajudicial killing of thousands, even tens of thousands, of African Americans, white Southerners successfully overturned many hallmarks of the program. Soon after U.S. troops ended their "occupation" of portions of the last of the defeated Confederate states, the "redemption," recovery, and reconstruction of white power in the region became cause for celebration by whites. A ruling fiction emerged. It bracketed the Reconstruction era between two periods of racial hierarchy and peace. For former Confederates, elimination of African Americans from the public sphere meant the return at last of key elements of the old order. This white reclamation of government and other, once racially integrated Reconstruction Era functions, activities, and spaces occurred in myth and memory in the literature of the Lost Cause. The subsequent imposition of segregationist, or Jim Crow, laws and state constitutions ensured the perpetuation of that order and cause. Thus, former Confederates ended one kind of Reconstruction with another—a restoration à la Destutt de Tracy.[5]

Successful imposition of a narrative of redemption—as opposed to radical, revolutionary "reconstruction"—resulted in a growing consensus among historians about the failures of federal Reconstruction. The Columbia University professor who, in the eyes of many, headed this informal "school" of analysis, William Archibald Dunning, came from New Jersey, but the majority of those among his students and colleagues who joined in elaborating this interpretation had Southern roots and, often, careers. They saw Reconstruction undermined not only in the states where its federal enforcement occurred over more or less a decade but also in national politics. Corruption and inexperience, as well as the realities of race, many scholars argued, foredoomed the Reconstruction project. Effective governments, some also insisted, returned only when Southern whites reestablished what they considered necessary racial and hierarchical social and political order.[6]

Reconstructing Old Southerners

The possibilities of reconstruction looked more-or-less different in the decades immediately before the Civil War. According to David Prior, Americans then "reflected their engagement with Western European sources" when using the term to mean either "the resurrection of politics" or "the transformation of society." At the time, many Americans of a variety of political opinions sought either to restore or to remake their country, its politics, and its culture. Vehement abolitionists did, as did staunch defenders of slavery. Free trade advocates did, as did supporters of protective tariffs for manufactures. All hoped to see the United States conform to a better time, whether in the past or in the future. They did so in the face of destabilizing and accelerating social, political, and economic dislocation, modernization, and imperialistic expansion by Western powers.[7]

Other developments more immediately anticipated elements of federal Reconstruction. The Mexican American War, following as it did the military-supervised Native American removal from east of the Mississippi River in the 1830s, gave the U.S. Army added experience with the coercive establishment or (re)construction of government, law, and order in the wake of conflict and upheaval. These dynamics profoundly influenced those who became adults in the decades before the Civil War.[8] In the eyes of many of the future Confederates among them, only the protection and expansion of the American slavery regime would preserve Southern political rights, social order, and economic viability. Therefore, to avoid a revolution in social and political relations, the nation needed to reconstruct its politics and culture. If the path of reform failed, revolution—that is, civil war to destroy the Union—must ensue, breaking up the compact of free and slave states.[9]

Only a few Southern opinion makers, however, had reached these conclusions by the early 1830s. Two in particular have claimed attention. After several years of escalating his rhetoric, Robert Barnwell Smith (later known as Robert Barnwell Rhett after a notable ancestor) insisted that slave owners would be insane not to "hold their destinies in their own hands." He was speaking to the South Carolina Convention of March 1833, called in November 1832 to support the Palmetto State's right to nullify inimical federal laws—in this case, high federal tariffs on the state's imports. Later, this longtime member of Congress and future publisher of the *Charleston Mercury* ratcheted up his campaign for eventual secession.[10]

Nathaniel Beverley Tucker, lawyer, judge, and (from 1834 onward) law professor at the College of William and Mary, made a different case. He argued that states did not have the right to nullify laws, but they could secede or withdraw from the Union. The federal compact embodied in the U.S. Constitution served as a revocable contract among the states. Any party to the contract could terminate its involvement upon due notice. In an 1836 novel, *The Partisan Leader: A Tale of the Future,* Tucker imagined patriotic Virginians in some dozen-plus years fighting a guerrilla war against U.S. forces in the Commonwealth. As he described them, they wanted to leave the Union and join states farther south in their newly independent confederacy. Those Deep South states, according to the story, had exercised their contractual rights by seceding. Yet the despotic federal government sought to keep the Old Dominion from doing the same.[11]

By 1849, when Tucker forecast Virginia's partisan resistance to Union control, more men were joining the secessionist ranks. Although a Unionist earlier, the writer and editor William Gilmore Simms did so in 1847. Like later joiners in the secession movement, Simms in part came to his position reactively; he also did so over time. In a Fourth of July address in Aiken, South Carolina, in 1844, he said that he thought the breakup of the United States was not just possible, but likely. Notwithstanding this judgment, however, he did not yet advocate the idea. Indeed, that fall he and his family again took an enslaved nurse with them when visiting in the North. At the time, Simms still vigorously supported the nationalist cultural program of those who became known as Young America. Members of this informal, New York–centered, mostly Democratic and pro-slavery group shared the ambition to evoke and propagate "Americanism," not only in literature, but also in other domains. They also promoted westward expansion, the United States' Manifest Destiny, and the political assertion of ethnic nationalisms.

By the time of the liberal nationalist revolutions in Europe in 1848, however, Simms no longer considered himself a Young American. In the previous summer he had decided that the South had to claim independence on behalf of an emerging Southern people. He had come to this conclusion after determining that he could no longer have his wife and children accompany him on his annual summer visit to friends and publishers in the North. As he told a close Young America colleague in New York, "Your vexatious abolitionists forbid that we should cross the Potomac [with] a coloured nurse."

Concluding that secession certainly would and should come, Simms became a vociferous advocate. He did so while still writing books for a largely Northern audience, producing many of what are now his best regarded works. His columns and reviews in Southern cultural journals and newspapers proved more influential in the South. In them, he argued, inter alia, that the South should do what the British American colonies had done three-quarters of a century before in their revolution from Great Britain: claim the right to self-determination and independent people-hood while following largely native leadership. Via revolution, the South would become a nation. Having grown hugely in both territorial extent and population, as well as in economic strength, and having developed a society and a culture that increasingly distinguished its people from those in the North, the region needed to take the next step and declare itself a nation among the nations. By doing so, the South would not just fulfill, by reconstructing, its revolutionary mandate from 1776; it would also advance and protect its interests.[12]

When the Civil War erupted, Simms found himself at once optimistic and gal-vanized, then frustrated. The work of organizing for war and administering a new nation proved much more difficult than he or many others had anticipated. The military ardor he saw buoyed him, but he became impatient with the slow progress toward effective governance and military defense. He gave advice that did not get heeded. After all, he did not represent his state in the Provisional Confederate Congress, as did Robert Barnwell Rhett. Meeting in Montgomery, Alabama, the representatives adapted the Confederate Constitution from that of the United States to clarify and correct what they deemed deficiencies and lacunae in the historical document's protection of slavery and states' rights. They claimed to be reconstructing and clarifying the original intent of the founders. At the same time, these latter-day framers were also designing and establishing a central govern-ment, thereby correcting (or reconstructing) the old.[13]

Members soon concluded that the circumstances they faced compelled not only temporary modification and, sometimes, disregard of normal, peacetime govern-ment restraints, but also extraordinary extension of centralized government au-thority and power. In the North, too, the war justified extraconstitutional actions in the minds of leaders. Whether there or in the Confederacy, suspension of *ha-beas corpus*, the military requisitioning of goods and services, the imposition of expanded press censorship, and other, often informal community-driven limita-tions of free speech—none of these things reflected business as usual. Yet these and many other changes initially did not alter fundamental understanding of govern-ment, law, and politics. However abridged or abrogated in practice early in the war, the rights of property and citizens remained basically unaltered in both the United States and the Confederate States. Then, in September 1862, Lincoln gave advance notice of the Emancipation Proclamation. Doing so, he warned Confederates of his intention to abolish slavery in states or parts of states that did not return to Union control before the proclamation's effective date. Tennessee and a portion of Virginia became exempt. On January 1, 1863, however, the proclamation in theory took effect elsewhere in the Confederacy.

By this one dramatic act, Lincoln in principle freed the slaves in noncompliant areas and radically changed the *status quo ante*. Suddenly, reconstruction became much more difficult to imagine as either a set of restorative policies and actions or a modest recalibration, clarification, and revision of antebellum conditions and governance. Confederate outrage grew. On February 27, 1865, a "mass meeting held for Augusta County[, Virginia,] citizens," in a formerly Unionist area, resolved "that we regard reconstruction as but another name for submission to tyranny, and 'we pledge our lives, our fortunes and our sacred honor never to entertain even the idea of it, but to resist it in the future as we have done in the past, to the utmost extremity.[']"14

The December 1865 adoption of the Thirteenth Amendment, freeing all slaves, extended this revolution of norms and expectations to the Border States that had stayed in the Union. Many white Southerners there resisted with the same vehemence as those Augusta County, Virginia, citizens earlier in the year. Former Confederates among them had hoped for an old-fashioned restorative reconstruction of the reunited country. Their willful failure to recognize the consequences of their loss fueled the Republicans' ratification of the Fourteenth Amendment in July 1868 and then, nineteen months later, the Fifteenth Amendment. These amendments gave freedmen citizenship and voting rights, respectively. Reconstruction had become something not encompassed by the term before. It now indicated an outright overturning of past government and prior political and social relations. This rupture took place not only between the federal government and ten of the eleven Confederate states (Tennessee had been readmitted to the Union in July 1866), but also between Southern African Americans (most previously enslaved) and whites.

The use of federal forces to implement Reconstruction also appeared in former Confederates' eyes as a continuation of warfare rather than as a peaceful return to normalcy. That the U.S. troops stayed on in Georgia after the state became the last, in 1870, to ratify the Reconstruction amendments seemed to make the point. The arming of former enslaved men and their organization into militia companies heightened the revolutionary disruption. The recruitment of African Americans into the Republican Party pressed the point home. The freedmen joined not only Northerners, but also Unionist and other anti-Confederate white Southerners in political structures that looked familiar but had radically changed. Across the defeated Confederacy, these Republicans won legislative, judicial, and executive power at local and state levels. They also sent men to Congress as formerly seceded states ratified the Fourteenth Amendment—however reluctantly—and thereby reentered the Union as full-fledged members.

Such developments appalled the elders who had promoted secession and then the Confederacy. Many found themselves at first in denial. Thereafter, they had to deal with cognitive dissonance: words did not mean what they once had; nei-ther did relations. Whites no longer could assume deference to them by African Americans. Simms went to court to defend his former enslaved carriage driver, Isaac Nimmons, against the charge of having set fire to Simms's plantation home. Early in 1865, the house burned as U.S. Major General William Tecumseh Sherman's army crossed the Edisto River nearby on the way to Columbia, South Carolina. The aging writer and planter left the trial unsure of both his judgment in the case and the strength of the bonds that he had long assumed existed between Nimmons and himself.

Nevertheless, the Simms family later maintained the legend that Nimmons had done all he could to save the family's Woodlands home during the fire. Nimmons's family, however, celebrated a different story: that the former coachman had set the place ablaze. The Simmses also claimed that they had paternalistically supported their former slaves in the war's aftermath, even giving some land. The correspon-dence and land records tell a different story. Freedmen on the plantation raised a cotton crop and food, and their leader offered to share a portion with their former master and his family, for whom he said he felt sorry. Subsequently, members of some of these African American families bought land rather than being given it.[15]

Finding himself in this topsy-turvy world, Simms wrote to a New York friend in February 1867: "Every thing is dreary here. No money, the people utterly broken down, & the planters broken up." He added days later: "We are dreadfully anx-ious about our future[,] not about the political but the physical condition of the country. Nobody but our politicians cares a straw about reconstruction. The terror before our people is physical misery, privation, want, hunger, starvation." The next month, Simms recovered some of his combativeness. "Southerners had to submit to the 'despots in Congress,' because they were 'a conquered people,'" he wrote. "But that did not mean that they would 'embrace the knees of the Conquerors.' Rather Southerners only would 'loathe [the victors] the more, and feel . . . at all times free of all obligations.'"[16] In other words, no forced commitment need be honored.

Yet what could such defiance accomplish? Simms feared it meant that "the whole South [was] doomed to be the Ireland of the Union[,] a perpetual incubus." He added to this apocalyptic vision in an April 1867 letter to his young protégé and friend Paul Hamilton Hayne, the Charleston poet and editor: "We are passing through that ordeal of anarchy which prefaces despotism." A year later he was anticipating a race war. He advised the Virginia novelist, poet, and historian John Esten Cooke, twenty-four years his junior, that "seven millions of whites will not rest long under the rule of 3 millions of Negroes. . . . Brood over it; organize promptly in every precinct; get good weapons."[17] Resistance to Reconstruction had become not just Simms's but other former Confederates' determined policy.

Reconstructing Confederate Combatants

The Ku Klux Klan (KKK) had come to the same conclusion. Founded as a social organization by a handful of young elite Confederate veterans in Pulaski, Tennessee, on Christmas Eve 1865, it grew quickly. The minstrelsy of its early public performances mutated into terrorism later. Fueling this development, Northern newspapers read the Klan's mummery and mystery as fostering, while masking, racial and political violence. By 1867, the Klan had found a practical political purpose to direct its activity: it would do everything needful to curb Southern Blacks and Republicans.[18]

The redoubtable Nathan Bedford Forrest, formidable Confederate cavalry commander and former planter and slave trader, joined the campaign. He may initially have shared the Klan's hope of convincing freedmen to return voluntarily to slavery, ostensibly for their own good, as well as for protection from white paramilitary forces. The unsurprising failure of that effort accelerated the Klan's program of intimidation and violence. Forrest told a Cincinnati newspaper in 1868 that more than 550,000 men made up the "protective military organization." The Klansmen marshalled for "midnight parades; 'ghost' masquerades; and 'whipping' and even 'killing Negro voters and white Republicans.'"[19]

In Tennessee, Forrest claimed forty thousand Klan members. As the putative Grand Wizard, with a natural habit of command, he reputedly played a leading and forceful, if sometimes shadowy, role. In early 1869, the Grand Wizard issued KKK General Order Number One. It followed the Tennessee Republican governor's declaration of martial law against Klan violence in particular counties. Asserting that the Klan had largely accomplished its mission, the order disbanded the organization and decreed that the KKK's "masks and costumes . . . be entirely abolished and destroyed." The two prior years had seen thousands of people, mostly African Americans but also white Republicans, killed at the hands of the Klan and similar groups. Many more deaths would follow.[20]

The joint congressional select committee investigating Klan violence in 1871 questioned fifty-five highly placed former Confederates, as well as African American leaders and Northern schoolteachers. In all, it amassed twelve volumes of testimony on which it based its report. That summary and judgment concluded that the almost fifty-year-old "General Forrest and other men of influence . . . , by the exercise of their moral power, induced [the Klansmen] to disband." Three years later, the general offered to help Tennessee's governor "exterminate the white marauders who disgrace their race by . . . [the] cowardly murder of Negroes." The next year, he spoke by invitation to an African American audience in Memphis.[21]

Urging interracial peace nine years after the Memphis race riots of 1866, Forrest insisted: "We have but one flag, one country; let us stand together. We may differ in color, but not in sentiment. Use your best judgment in selecting men for office and vote as you think right." This attitude ran counter to the views of most former Klansmen, who remained willing to go to almost any lengths to reassert or maintain white power. Democratic newspapers in the region reviled Forrest, as well, for having kissed on the cheek the young, biracial woman who presented him with a bouquet when he spoke. Rather than take the action as a sign of racial reconciliation, most white commentators regarded it as a deep transgression of racial and gender mores.[22]

Another Confederate lieutenant-general and reputed Klan leader, John Brown Gordon, fit much better the expectations of the great majority of surviving Confederate soldiers. Although he said that he supported Black education and peaceful relations between the races, he warned his African American auditors in a speech in Charleston, South Carolina, in September 1868, "If you attempt to inaugurate a war of races, you will be exterminated. The Saxon race was never created by the Almighty God to be ruled by the African." As reportedly Georgia's Klan head or Grand Dragon, Gordon continued strenuously to resist Reconstruction, both advocating and pursuing intimidation and restriction of freedoms of African Americans. Committed, as he and other Klansmen were, to the organization's secrecy, he denied knowledge of or involvement with the Klan when testifying before Congress's Joint Select Committee to Inquire into the Condition of Affairs in the Late Insurrectionary States. He did aver, however—much as did Forrest in his testimony—the perceived necessity for whites to counteract the activity of freedmen.[23]

The perception stemmed, Gordon claimed, from multiple causes. For instance, "The negroes would desert the plantations . . . and go off at night in large numbers" to musters and meetings of the Union League. These clubs, he contended, recruited for Republican Party and quasi-military operations against white Southern Democrats. Then, too, Northern "carpetbaggers," who had no local knowledge, connections, or commitments, "were organizing the colored people." Thus marshaled, Blacks claimed "their right to hold . . . property for their own benefit" after driving off plantation overseers and expropriating land. In the aftermath of these developments and the attendant growing lawlessness, including reported incidents of rape, Gordon observed that "apprehension took possession of the entire [white] public mind of the State" of Georgia.[24]

Former Confederates concluded that "this general organization of the black race on the one hand . . . and an entire disorganization of the white race on the other hand" required concerted white action. The general and his fellow Bourbons, or conservative Democrats, helped engineer what they called Redemption—a religiously freighted term—in the December 1870 election in Georgia. As a result, the legislative session in fall 1871 saw Democrats back in power. Gordon subsequently became a U.S. senator, governor, and advocate of the New South industrial movement.

From 1890 to his death in 1914, he also served as the first commander-in-chief of the United Confederate Veterans Association and continued promoting the convict leasing system that benefited his railroad.[25]

Gordon's career notwithstanding, General Forrest did not act alone in his final embrace of Reconstruction. Other former Confederates, including several general officers, also concluded over time that the South needed to accommodate to the realities, or even the ideals, of the new regime and Black enfranchisement. The same age as Forrest, Georgian Lieutenant-General James Longstreet quickly accepted Republican rule. In 1868, he not only regained the U.S. citizenship rights that President Andrew Johnson had blocked; he did so with the support of General Ulysses S. Grant, then supported Grant in his run for the presidency. The next year, Longstreet attended the presidential inauguration on March 4. Soon after, he received a series of federal and state government appointments. The Republican governor of Louisiana even made him adjutant-general of that state's militia.[26]

Edward A. Pollard, a young wartime editor of the *Richmond Examiner,* the principal Confederate newspaper early in the Civil War and later a chief critic of the government, went at least part of the way in the same direction as Longstreet and some other former Confederate military leaders. Before that, however, Pollard, like many, refought the conflict, albeit with his pen, not a sword. Having advocated the reopening of the slave trade on the war's eve, he concluded in his book *The Lost Cause* (1866) that the conflict had pitted against each other two different and increasingly antagonistic cultures. Slavery, he explained, had "established in the South a peculiar and noble type of civilization." Its destruction, through emancipation of the enslaved, ranked, he insisted, as the North's ultimate war crime. The title of his work came to encapsulate the Confederacy's fate in the eyes of many white Southerners and their descendants. The year after the book's publication, Pollard still hoped for the resumption of Confederate arms.[27]

Yet in his revised argument, *The Lost Cause Regained* (1868), Pollard shifted his ground. He still felt that white supremacy was essential. He now contended, however, that the war had not developed as a contest between civilizations. Rather, it had pitted the Union, on the one hand, against the U.S. Constitution, on the other. That analysis stoked his anger against the failures of Confederate leaders. Nevertheless, he concluded that the short-lived nation had not lost just because of ignorance and incompetence, pride and inflexibility. Its way of life helped doom it. The way forward, therefore, meant that Southern whites should "embrace the Union and join the Northern Democrats to support Presidential Reconstruction. No longer fighting the Civil War," Brook Thomas has observed, "Pollard was fighting Radical Reconstruction." He did not, however, stop there. Responding to changing circumstances despite his segregationist views, he expanded his newfound support of limited civil rights legislation and Black suffrage.[28]

A young, slight cavalryman and clerk under General Forrest's command at the end of the war, George Washington Cable, went further. Yet contrary to what many claimed later, the background and war service of this controversial and influential author did not make him an obvious proponent of civil rights—one of the most radical among whites in the postbellum South. Despite his parents' Northern, anti-slavery connections, he had grown up in New Orleans in a household that included up to eight enslaved people. Cable left the federally occupied city with his family and enrolled in the Fourth Mississippi Cavalry in 1863, at nineteen. He did so after his widowed mother refused to pledge allegiance to the United States. Wounded in February 1864, the young cavalryman recovered in time to fight again in mid-July, when General Forrest's forces suffered a rare defeat at Tupelo. In April of the next year, weeks before the surrender of the Confederate Department of Alabama, Mississippi, and East Louisiana, Forrest ordered Cable to write out manumission papers for enslaved teamsters with the department's forces.[29]

Over the next five years, the young man came gradually to regret the cause for which he had fought, ultimately identifying it with the slavery that he concluded had undergirded it. He did so despite his initial racist judgments, early stereo-typed fictional presentations of African Americans, and repeated, positive evocations of Confederate General Robert E. Lee. Starting in 1868, a bout of malaria laid him low for two years. Having taught himself French and Spanish, Cable immersed himself in the area's historical records. As he did, he saw the violence and hope of Reconstruction unfolding around him.[30]

Raised in the Presbyterian Church under the watchful eye of a deeply religious mother, Cable continued the Bible reading and spiritual self-examination that he had pursued since boyhood. Eventually, he led his New Orleans church's Sunday school for African American children.[31] Cable's powers of empathy and social analysis, as well as his sense of logic and equity and his reading of the Bible, helped propel his profound change in perspective on slavery and race as he wrote his way to new understandings. So, also, did his participation in discussions of history and other subjects in an elite local debating society. His sketches, columns, and stories began appearing regularly in the *New Orleans Picayune* in 1870, the year both Simms and Robert E. Lee died. These pieces evoked and analyzed the complex gradations of race and class identity and their fraught consequences in the Crescent City. Starting in 1873, his stories gained national attention. They appeared often in *Scribner's Monthly*, a leading cultural magazine. By the mid-1880s, when Cable and Mark Twain went on a protracted reading tour together, Cable's reputation rivaled that of Twain, his elder by almost nine years.[32]

In his use of dialect and rendering of local culture, Cable had contemporaries, as well as antecedents, as examples. Bret Harte, Joel Chandler Harris, and Twain gave these literary techniques new popularity in the 1880s and '90s. Half a century earlier, humorous writers of the Old Southwest already frequently used "eye-dialect." Simms began writing in dialect-inflected voices even before his Young America days. He did so especially with lower-class and Black characters, to the discomfiture of many conventional and conservative readers who were also disturbed by the graphic violence of his stories.[33]

Unlike the mature Cable, however, but like many Southwestern humorists, Simms did not believe in racial equality. He subscribed instead to stadialism, the eighteenth-century Scottish School understanding that cultures and peoples develop by stages over time, evolving from savagery to civilization. He insisted, therefore, that the Jeffersonian ideal that "all men are created equal" had proved demonstrably false: some peoples, as well as individuals, inevitably demonstrate more advanced characteristics than do others. He justified slavery accordingly. African Americans, even more than Native Americans, he contended, lagged far behind European Americans in their collective historical, social, and psychological development. Individuals from these racial communities might display noble human qualities, such as honor and loyalty—indeed, some do so in Simms's fiction—but they nonetheless shared their peoples' subordinate cultural and historical positions vis-à-vis whites.[34]

Cable came to see history's consequences differently as he wrote about his native New Orleans's past and people. He campaigned with increasing vigor for equal rights and integrated schools for African Americans and people of mixed race. He did so while continuing to fight against political corruption after the end of federal Reconstruction. Then, as many Republicans fled from office and for their lives, the self-identified Redeemers swept into power where they had not already taken over. The former Klan's project to marginalize Black and white Republicans politically and eventually curtail or suppress African American presence in the public sphere became a central commitment of these Redeemer regimes. The sometimes paternalistic-sounding attitudes toward African Americans and poor whites professed by some Bourbons did not forestall General Gordon and other radical conservatives from using violence to maintain racial control. The paternalistic expressions did, however, help deflect continuing Northern concern about African Americans in the South. The language also suggested that Simms's stadialism, not Cable's post-Reconstruction commitment to the equality of all before the law and God, had become in effect the national ruling principle.

As Cable grew more explicit in his depictions and critiques of racism and classism in his native New Orleans and across the region, fellow white Southern writers reacted vehemently. Many attacked him. Paul Hamilton Hayne dismissed Cable as a "mongrel cur" and "miserable little ci-devant clerk and parvenu," as well as a renegade. The Louisiana historian, novelist, and judge Charles Gayarré, another Simms friend, considered Cable's first novel—*The Grandissimes* (serialized in *Scribner's*

Monthly and then issued in book form in 1880)—a "monstrous absurdity." He railed both against the novel's portrayal of social and sexual intermingling by whites and people of color and against the book's rendering of dialect. People in New Orleans warned Cable to move away. Some hinted that he and his writings reflected mulatto antecedents as well as sympathies.[35]

Isoline Rodd Kendall, wife of the literary editor of the *New Orleans Picayune,* observed in 1909 that "a feeling was slowly rising that . . . [Cable] was yielding to Northern Influence. . . . Many of his old friends considered him a traitor to the cause for which he had fought." Kendall went on to observe, however, that "as the years have passed . . . the old feeling against Mr. Cable has died out, and even in the South there are not lacking to-day warm admirers." By then, segregation ruled. Therefore, Cable's remonstrances no longer mattered so much to Southern whites. Since, literary historians have come to regard *The Grandissimes* as one of the first and most important modern, realist fictions of the postbellum South, a precursor of William Faulkner's works. Set in the aftermath of the Louisiana Purchase of 1803 that made French America part of the United States, the novel derived its post-Reconstruction resonances by its presentation both of a fundamental change in ruling regimes and of race as a complicated social and historical construct. The sixty-seven intervening years had augmented rather than diminished the comparisons.[36]

Much to Gayarré's distress, Cable's fiction gleaned positive, national attention. So, too, did his other work, in part undertaken to establish that he did not write as a fabulist but with historical knowledge. His *The Creoles of Louisiana* (1884), commissioned by the U.S. Census Bureau, and his related article on New Orleans for the *Encyclopedia Britannica* (ninth edition), incensed Gayarré, as well. He attacked Cable in newspaper reviews and articles and then in an 1885 lecture at Tulane University in New Orleans: *The Creoles of History and the Creoles of Romance.* Noting that the Creoles by definition were native-born whites of French or Spanish descent, he insisted that they had estimable antecedents. Historically, he continued, they of course had not engaged in interracial alliances or produced mixed race offspring. The claim that they had at once distorted the past and slandered their noble families was cheap romantic invention. It also contradicted what their descendants knew. A quarter-century later, however, Mrs. Kendall candidly admitted that people acknowledged the living evidence of mixed-race people everywhere in New Orleans.[37]

The attacks, "called forth by [Cable's] stories of creole or quadroon types," paled in comparison to the bitter invectives against Cable's lectures and essays. These genres occupied an increasing portion of the writer's time, especially after he left New Orleans. He was still living in the Crescent City, however, when he denounced "The Convict Lease System in the Southern States" at the September 1883 meeting of the National Conference of Charities.[38] The move with his family almost fifteen hundred miles, to Simsbury, Connecticut, came the next summer. Cable explained that his wife's fragile health necessitated it. People assumed, however, that his growing social ostracization and the threats directed at him also played a role. Even after moving again a year later to Northampton, Massachusetts, he ended up much closer to his friend Twain, his publishers, and his lecture audiences.

The outpouring against Cable reached a crescendo in the spring and summer of 1885. Fueling it, Cable gave a September 1884 address to the annual meeting of the American Social Science Association. In its published form, "The Freedman's Case in Equity" appeared the next January in *Century Magazine,* the influential successor to *Scribner's.* There Cable called for civil rights and education for African Americans and reintegration of public transportation and venues. The article came out in the middle of the ironically named "The Twins of Genius" tour—103 performances in some eighty cities over several months. Cable and Twain started in November 1884, reading respectively from, among other things, their new novels—*Dr. Sevier* and the as yet unpublished *Huckleberry Finn.*[39] The tour made it clear that Cable's standing in the North differed radically from his reputation in the white South. Northern enthusiasm, of course, did not drown out Southern outrage. Cable's national literary stature had little relevance to his regional critics by the time he (in)famously visited in the home of an African American lawyer in Nashville in 1889. So stymied, Cable took another five years of intermittent work to complete his coming-of-age Reconstruction novel, *John March, Southerner* in 1894.[40]

Reconstructing Confederate Sons

The young writers increasingly shaping white Southerners' views of Reconstruction and race had different agendas, sensibilities, and beliefs than did Cable. He had begun publishing, after all, when they were still in school and Reconstruction remained in force in parts of the South. The men who grew up after the Confederacy's fall did not always agree with one another, but they did share elements of orthodoxy about white supremacy, Black inferiority, segregation, and the social and political place of African Americans. While the eighty-year-old Gayarré, representing the Old South, sputtered his indignation over Cable to a local audience in New Orleans, the thirty-four-year-old newspaperman Henry W. Grady of Atlanta, representing the New South, led the charge in the national media.

The editors at *Century Magazine* invited Grady to do so. Noting that "no essay on the subject of the freedmen published for many years has attracted wider attention than Mr. Cable's 'The Freedman's Case in Equity,'" the editors decided to select "a single representative essay of some length" to reflect an opposing Southern point of view. They deliberately chose that form of response instead of publishing a variety of "more or less dissenting essays and 'Open Letters.'" They regretted, however, that this decision prevented them from sharing "some amusing reminders of the good old-fashioned bowie-knife and fire-eating days." This tongue-in-cheek lament aside, Grady seemed an obvious candidate to reply to Cable. He was becoming known as "Spokesman of the New South." By 1889, the weekly edition of the *Atlanta Constitution,* the newspaper that he edited, would claim the largest circulation and widest influence of any paper of its type in the nation.[41]

The "son of Confederate Major William S. Grady, who . . . died from wounds suffered at Petersburg, Virginia in the fall of 1864[,] . . . Henry famously launched his campaign on behalf of southern industrialization in a March 14, 1874 editorial." Unlike Lost Cause writers of his generation, Grady did not lament the "South of slavery and secession," noting "that South is dead." He did continue to insist, however, that "the supremacy of the white race of the South must be maintained forever." He made that point the core of his response to Cable, who, Grady claimed, was not a true Southerner and could not speak for the region's white population. Yes, he had been born in New Orleans and fought for the Confederacy, but his parents had come to the Crescent City from the North, where he felt himself culturally at home despite his Southern upbringing.[42]

For Grady, Cable's views reflected a lack of native sympathy and understanding. They struck the Georgian as at once sentimental and unrealistic. Racial prejudice remained fundamental, not something to fix by erasing racial boundaries. Neither Blacks nor whites would ever accept the elimination of those social and cultural divisions. Besides, by ending federal Reconstruction the North had returned solution of "the Negro Question" to white Southerners. The issue properly needed local, not national address. "As a matter of course," Grady concluded, "this implies the clear and unmistakable domination of the white race of the South."

Across the region, attitudes on race continued to harden. Grady acknowledged the legitimacy of Black enfranchisement and limited Black jury service. Yet most of his white Southern contemporaries soon rejected both and sought increasingly to disenfranchise Blacks. White on Black lynching dramatically increased, as well, beginning in the mid-1880s. As Cable made clear, the practice had antebellum and Reconstruction roots. Its new virulence became amplified by public enactments, newspaper accounts, and widely shared photographs. Grady's *Atlanta Constitution* participated, and his state became an epicenter of the murderousness.[43]

After Grady's late-1889 death, the most important Southern political journalist became Tom Watson, another Georgian and the Populist, or Peoples', Party leader. He ultimately would reach an even wider audience. Despite having allied opportunistically with many African Americans against the Bourbons, Watson increasingly excluded Blacks from his campaign on behalf of the little men—farmers and workers. He and his supporters identified themselves as citizens of a restored white agrarian republic with roots in Thomas Jefferson's America. They also claimed honor as (sometimes putative) scions of Confederates. Grady and other Bourbons did as well in the face of all their disagreements with Watson's party. They differed on class issues, but by the time the U.S. Supreme Court decided *Plessy v. Ferguson* in 1896 and the blizzard of Jim Crow laws and customs arose, hardly any white dissent on race appeared in the South. Whiteness ruled, bolstered by segregation and suppression of the Black vote.[44]

Members of these men's generation understood this political reality even when they deprecated the Old South, as did William Peterfield Trent, literary biographer of William Gilmore Simms. A Progressive, like Woodrow Wilson, Trent descended from one of the First Families of Virginia. Born in Richmond in 1862—too late to "recollect ever seeing a slave"—he attended the University of Virginia with Wilson and then Johns Hopkins University, where Wilson had done graduate work and was teaching. Trent in his turn taught and wrote books on American history and literature and English literature, first at the University of the South and then at Columbia University. He founded the *Sewanee Review* in 1892 and contributed to *Century Magazine* and other periodicals. Before becoming the lead editor of *The Cambridge History of American Literature* on the eve of the United States' entry into World War I, he wrote three volumes that treated Southerners—the life of Simms in 1892, the *Southern Statesmen of the Old Regime: Washington, Jefferson, Randolph, Calhoun, Stephens, Toombs, and Jefferson Davis* in 1897 (dedicated to Theodore Roosevelt), and a brief life of Robert E. Lee in 1899. He also edited an anthology of Southern writers in 1905 for use in schools and libraries across the region. Noting the historical significance of earlier figures included, he gave scant attention to much of the then contemporary fiction and verse from the region, which he derogated. He did, however, single out for literary attention Edgar Allan Poe, Sidney Lanier, George Washington Cable, and other authors with a modernist appeal.[45]

Trent subsequently devoted continuing scholarship to such figures. He wrote "with the full consciousness that unless [he] reached certain conclusions it would be unacceptable to a majority of the people . . . to whom [he was] united by ties of friendship" or blood. Yet he "disdained to pander to a provincial sentimentalism that shivers at honest and fair criticism of any man or cause that may have become a shibboleth." While he welcomed correction, he was "certainly not to be turned from [his opinions] by unstinted personal abuse" coming from "hypersensitive portions of the southern people." After the publication of his unflattering *William Gilmore Simms,* the abuse proved intense, despite Northern critics' appreciation. His *Robert E. Lee,* written with "a steadfast determination to see him as he is, . . . a supremely great and good man," got a much friendlier reception in the Southern press. More readers might have bridled had they followed the logic of Trent's conclusion that Lee's "fame should not be limited by the characteristic conceptions of patriotism": his character ennobled him, not his devotion to Virginia.[46]

Trent gave high marks for character and courage to his Southern statesmen, too, but that did not stop him from criticizing them in his University of Wisconsin lectures. He held that Davis emerged as "a failure not so much through his own lack of ability to govern as through the inherent weakness of the cause he represented." Trent concluded that "the Southern Confederacy was bound to fail, because it had been founded precisely as Alexander H. Stephens had claimed, upon slavery as its cornerstone." Southern politicians betrayed the planter, luring him on rather than telling him "that it was slavery that kept his roads bad, that gave him wretched 'Oldfield' schools, that prevented his cities from growing, that kept immigrants from public lands." What distinguished Jefferson and Washington from those who later propounded slavery as a positive good was that they "perceived that the slave basis of [Southern] society . . . was rotten to the core." After these Revolutionaries' era, the South's course became a "constant downward slope." Southerners failed to keep "abreast of the thought of the world" and so did not understand that "the relation of master and slave," based on the premise that "might makes right," had become "abhorrent to civilization and progress."[47]

In Trent's view, slavery had hobbled Southern culture, as well. *William Gilmore Simms*, the first substantive, scholarly study, damned the romancer with faint praise. Impatient with the lingering influence of the overturned order of the Old South, Trent argued that Simms had proved unable to rise to his literary potential in the environment of antebellum Charleston. Giving color to the judgment, Simms himself often had said as much. Moreover, Trent, with his modernist sensibility, was scathing about both the romance tradition and what he judged to be Simms's failure in it. Henry F. May summarized this cultural critique by Trent and others almost seventy years later: "The South, unable to look clearly at slavery in the midst of a Christian and democratic tradition, had developed an inveterate taste for shallow fantasy."

As Trent explained, "On feudality and slavery had been erected an aristocracy which had naturally developed the chief traits of this form of government,—bravery, pride, and conservatism." Yet, happily, "out of the ashes of the Old South, a new and better South [had] arisen." Southerners were adding "to their inherited virtues and powers" new ones as they moved "forward with civilization." Although abhorring the commitment to slavery by antebellum Southern political leaders, urgent for progressive change, and admiring of Cable's stories about the complexities of Creole New Orleans, Trent did not share at all Cable's sense of legal and moral equality across class and color lines. In a piece published in 1901, he wrote: "It is true that in the South there is a socio-political question concerning the suffrage, but this, we trust, is being settled." Guiding his thinking, fellow Columbia University Professor James Hyslop's *Democracy* advocated "differentiating the franchise" between the general population, possessing "personal rights," and those with "political rights."[48]

Tom Watson and Trent, the populist and the progressive, did not agree on much—certainly not on the South's future and reform—but they eventually did on issues of race. From Thomson, Georgia, Watson saw virtues in the past that the present no longer had. At first blush, it might seem that he still could agree with Trent at least about Jefferson. Trent's appreciation glowed: "Manhood suffrage, the rule of the majority, perfect freedom of thought and action, peace rather than war, and devotion to science and the useful arts,—these are the leading ideas that Jefferson inculcated, and they are the leading ideas that guide the American citizen to-day." Trent continued, however: "We no longer have Jefferson's fear of tyranny before our eyes, and we have outgrown his prejudice against manufactures, but we are still in the main his disciples."[49] The first sentence explains how progressives, including Woodrow Wilson, could consider themselves Jeffersonians. The second makes clear that they had different views from Watson and the populists.

Far from having outgrown Jefferson's prejudice and fear, Watson saw in Jefferson a bulwark against capitalism and tyranny. As the masthead of the weekly *People's Party Paper* proclaimed in 1894, the newspaper, edited by Watson, stood as "a fearless advocate of the Jeffersonian Theory of Popular Government" and therefore opposed "to the bitter end the Hamiltonian Doctrines of Class Rule, Moneyed Aristocracy, National Banks, High Tariffs, Standing Armies and for-midable Navies—all of which go together as a system of oppressing the people." Agrarianism inoculated Watson against these interests, he claimed, identifying it with Jefferson and his own antebellum boyhood. As C. Vann Woodward explained in 1938, "Throughout the triumphant rise of the New South, in which [Watson] was to fight his battles, his face remained fixed upon his vision of agrarian bliss." The vision echoed Simms and evoked "that old Southern homestead," which "was a little kingdom, a complete social and industrial organism, almost wholly sufficient unto itself."[50] Watson wanted to recover, or reconstruct and preserve, that world.

Sharecropping, tenant farming, industrialization, and urbanization all un-dermined the idyll. Indeed, they were swallowing the older Southern economy. What the Civil War had not destroyed, money and its rapacious pursuit were accomplishing—thus, Watson's class war against the Bourbons. His beloved South had failed in its bid for independence. In his rearguard action, however, he would not surrender in his pursuit of independence and equality on behalf of those who adhered to the agrarian ethic and populist program. So far, he appeared to agree with Cable, but in the end he included only whites, not Blacks. In his South, African

Americans did not have the status that whites did. On that point, he ultimately concurred with his late political enemy, Henry W. Grady: "The supremacy of the white race must be maintained forever."[51]

Reconstruction's End

Cable tried to complicate racial vision and understanding and undercut its primacy. A few other Confederates, such as Forrest, Longstreet, and Pollard, who also participated as adults in the Civil War and Reconstruction, went at least partway down that path. Some children of the war briefly sought political alliances across the color line, as well. Most, like Grady and Trent, accepted the end of slavery. Yet many, like Watson and so-called Lost Cause writers (as well as those from the elder antebellum generation, such as Simms and Gayarré), regretted the Old South's passing. Despite such differences, Redemption meant not only the end of Reconstruction, conventionally conceived, but also, for most former Confederates, the privileging of racial over other identities. Reconstruction may have held promise as a revolution, but political calculation undermined it. Once the politics of Reconstruction no longer claimed primacy, social justice and the promise of the amended Constitution withered. For all the talk of radical or revolutionary Reconstruction, only a retooled restoration resulted: the defeated Confederates had won after all.

The equation of Reconstruction with militarily protected racial liberalism had condemned the project, its agents, and its sympathizers. In its aftermath, many—not only Southern whites—dismissed it as a misbegotten sociopolitical experiment imposed by outsiders. It lost its potential as a principled effort to rebuild, while transforming, the society, economy, and politics of a war-devastated part of the United States. It took a long time for white Southerners to begin thinking of Reconstruction in more than racial terms. The battle over that legacy has continued even as the word "reconstruction" has regained other meanings and gained many new daily uses.[52]

In the process, civil rights advocates and later scholars have increasingly cast the 1950s–1970s as the second Reconstruction. They have meant that this era saw laws, programs, and activities developed to protect and advance minority rights, as also happened during the first Reconstruction. Most considerations of reconstructions today, however, reference instead medical, anthropological, business, and forensic procedures. People read and talk about reconstructive surgeries; reconstructed crime scenes, DNA, fossils, and artifacts; and legally supervised and directed reconstruction of bankrupt businesses and Federal Emergency Management Administration (or United Nations) recovery efforts after large-scale natural catastrophes.[53]

At the same time, historians argue increasingly that one should not limit consideration of the first Reconstruction to the politics, period, and areas directly shaped by the Reconstruction Acts. Policies, attitudes, and relationships influenced by the federal approach to Reconstruction then reverberated across the nation and in international developments. Native Americans, for instance, progressively came under U.S. military-policed federal supervision. After the Spanish American War, so did Puerto Ricans, Filipinos, and their governments. Federal intervention and investment in transportation accelerated in the Civil War's wake and led to transcontinental railroads, then the Panama Canal. Looking beyond such developments, Steven A. Hahn recently insisted that critical "reconstructions" also occurred between 1890 and 1920. He pointed to "efforts by social, labor, political, and corporate reformers to reconfigure the authority of the state, the proper relations of industrial ownership and investment, the organization of work, the universe of political participation, the nature of social responsibility, and the reach of the nation's imperial arms." Other countries saw such reworkings of prior social, economic, and political habits and relations. In addition, national statist unification movements elsewhere adopted coercive elements, seen in federal Reconstruction, to reduce the centrifugal pull of regional, ethnic or racial, and class loyalties. Consequently, increasing numbers of scholars now contend that the changes attendant on the Civil War and Reconstruction began earlier, lasted longer, and reached farther than conventionally understood.[54]

Notes

1. Antoine Louis Claude Destutt, Comte de Tracy, *A Commentary and Review of Montesquieu's Spirit of Laws,* trans. Thomas Jefferson (Philadelphia: William Duane, 1811), 113. The concept of reconstruction became increasingly polysemic before the American Civil War, as David Prior argues in "Reconstruction from Transatlantic Polyseme to Historiographical Quandary," in *Reconstruction in a Globalizing World,* ed. David Prior (New York: Fordham University Press, 2018), 172–208.
2. Case-sensitive and case-insensitive Ngram analyses of the term "reconstruction" for the years 1500 to 2000 conducted July 16, 2019, at books.google.com/ngrams. Histories of the term's continuing, changing, and expanding meanings and uses in English and French are summarized, illustrated, and added to in successive editions of the *Le Littré* and the *Grand Larousse,* as well as the *Oxford English Dictionary* (*OED*), all envisioned in the mid-nineteenth century and completed, in the case of the *OED,* the last finished, in 1928. *Littré* repeatedly cited the French original of the quote given here in the Jefferson translation. The thesaurus at www.Merriam-Webster.com divides the synonyms between terms having to do with "overhaul, redesign" and those implying some form of "re-creation." Multiple other online synonym listings appeared in searches for "reconstruction synonyms." As of February 7, 2021, some included more than eight hundred terms.

3. See, e.g., Stephen V. Ash, *When the Yankees Came: Conflict and Chaos in the Occupied South, 1861–1865* (Chapel Hill: University of North Carolina Press, 1995); Gregory P. Downs, *After Appomattox: Military Occupation and the Ends of War* (Cambridge, MA: Harvard University Press, 2015); Willie Lee Rose, *Rehearsal for Reconstruction: The Port Royal Experiment* (Indianapolis: Bobbs-Merrill, 1964); David Silkenat, *Raising the White Flag: How Surrender Defined the American Civil War* (Chapel Hill: University of North Carolina Press, 2019).

4. In recent essays and articles, I have joined in analyzing aspects of these changes. See, e.g., David Moltke-Hansen, "When History Failed: William Gilmore Simms's Artistic Negotiation of the Civil War's Consequences," in *William Gilmore Simms's Unfinished Civil War: Consequences for a Southern Man of Letters,* ed. David Moltke-Hansen (Columbia: University of South Carolina Press, 2013), 3–31; David Moltke-Hansen, "Urban Processes in the Confederacy's Development, Experience, and Consequences," in *Confederate Cities: The Urban South during the Civil War Era,* ed. Andrew L. Slap and Frank Towers (Chicago: University of Chicago Press, 2015), 46–73; David Moltke-Hansen, "Honoring Confederate Defeat the Georgia Way," *Georgia Historical Quarterly* 101, no. 1 (March 2017): 1–23; David Moltke-Hansen, "'Consider the Ancient Generations': Share-Cropping's Strange Compulsion," *Let Us Now Praise Famous Men at 75: Anniversary Essays,* ed. Michael A. Lofaro (Knoxville: University of Tennessee Press, 2017), 17–39.

5. Douglas R. Egerton, *The Wars of Reconstruction: The Brief, Violent History of America's Most Progressive Era* (New York: Bloomsbury, 2014); Carole Emberton, *Race, Violence, and the American South after the Civil War* (Chicago: University of Chicago Press, 2013); Equal Justice Initiative, "Lynching in America: Confronting the Legacy of Racial Terror," report, 3rd ed., 2017, https://lynchinginamerica.eji.org/report; Henry Louis Gates Jr., *Stony the Road: Reconstruction, White Supremacy, and the Rise of Jim Crow* (New York: Penguin, 2019); George C. Rable, *But There Was No Peace: The Role of Violence in the Politics of Reconstruction* (Athens: University of Georgia Press, 1984).

6. Bruce E. Baker, *What Reconstruction Meant: Historical Memory in the American South* (Charlottesville: University of Virginia Press, 2007), 13–80; Nicholas Lemann, *Redemption: The Last Battle of the Civil War* (New York: Farrar, Straus and Giroux, 2006); Prior, "Reconstruction from Transatlantic Polyseme to Historiographical Quandary," 179–83; John David Smith and J. Vincent Lowry, eds., *The Dunning School: Historians, Race, and the Meaning of Reconstruction* (Lexington: University Press of Kentucky, 2013); Brook Thomas, "The Unfinished Task of Grounding Reconstruction's Promise," *Journal of the Civil War Era* 7, no. 1 (2017): 16–38, https://www.jstor.org/stable/26070488.

7. Orville Vernon Burton, *The Age of Lincoln* (New York: Farrar, Straus and Giroux, 2008); Seymour Drescher, *Abolition: A History of Slavery and Anti-slavery* (New York: Cambridge University Press, 2009); T. Gregor Garvey, *Creating the Culture of Reform in Antebellum America* (Athens: University of Georgia Press, 2005); Prior, "Reconstruction from Transatlantic Polyseme to Historiographical Quandary," 174; John W. Quist, *Restless Visionaries: The Social Roots of Antebellum Reform in Alabama and Michigan* (Baton Rouge: Louisiana State University Press, 1998); Manisha Sinha, *The Slave's Cause: A History of Abolition* (New Haven, CT: Yale University Press, 2016); Kyle G. Volk, *Moral Minorities and the Making of American Democracy* (New York: Oxford University Press, 2014).

8. Roseann Bacha-Garza, Christopher L. Miller, and Russell K. Skowronek, eds., *The Civil War on the Rio Grande, 1846–1876* (College Station: Texas A&M University Press, 2019); Steven A. Hahn, *A Nation Without Borders: The United States and Its World in an Age of Civil Wars, 1830–1910* (New York: Viking, 2016); Michael A. Lofaro, *Boone, Black Hawk, and Crocket in 1833: Unsettling the Mythic West* (Knoxville: University of Tennessee Press, 2019); Heather

Cox Richardson, *West from Appomattox: The Reconstruction of America after the Civil War* (New Haven, CT: Yale University Press, 2008);.

9. Edward E. Baptist, *The Half Has Never Been Told: Slavery and the Making of American Capitalism* (New York: Basic, 2014); Walter Johnson, *River of Dark Dreams: Slavery and Empire in the Cotton Kingdom* (Cambridge, MA: Harvard University Press, 2013); Moltke-Hansen, "Urban Processes in the Confederacy's Development, Experience, and Consequences."

10. William W. Freehling, *Prelude to Civil War: The Nullification Crisis in South Carolina, 1816–1836* (New York: Harper and Row, 1966), 297. Like his brothers, Smith changed his name to Rhett in 1837 in honor of a distinguished South Carolina ancestor: see William C. Davis, *Rhett: The Turbulent Life and Times of a Fire-eater* (Columbia: University of South Carolina Press, 2001), 74–75.

11. Ian Binnington, *Confederate Visions: Nationalism, Symbolism, and the Imagined South in the Civil War* (Charlottesville: University Press of Virginia, 2013), 44–69; Alfred L. Brophy, *University, Court, and Slave: Pro-slavery Thought in Southern Colleges and Courts and the Coming of the Civil War* (New York: Oxford University Press, 2016), 4–11; Robert J. Brugger, *Beverly Tucker: Heart over Head in the Old South* (Baltimore: Johns Hopkins University Press, 1978), 122–38; John L. Hare, *Will the Circle Be Unbroken? Family and Sectionalism in the Virginia Novels of Kennedy, Caruthers, and Tucker, 1830–1845* (New York: Routledge, 2002), 107–26.

12. David Moltke-Hansen, "Southern Literary Horizons in Young America: Imaginative Development of a Regional Geography," *Studies in the Literary Imagination* 42, no. 1 (2009): 17; William Gilmore Simms, *The Sources of American Independence: An Oration, on the Sixty-Ninth Anniversary of American Independence, Delivered at Aiken, South-Carolina, before the Town Council and Citizens Thereof* (Aiken, SC: Published by the Council, 1844), 30–31.

13. James Everett Kibler and David Moltke-Hansen, eds., "Introduction," in *William Gilmore Simms's Selected Reviews on Literature and Civilization* (Columbia: University of South Carolina Press, 2014), 9–10; David Moltke-Hansen, "Turn Signals: Shifts in Values in Southern Life Writing," in *Dixie Redux: Essays in Honor of Sheldon Hackney*, ed. Raymond Arsenault and Orville Vernon Burton (Montgomery, AL: NewSouth, 2013), 177–80.

14. *Staunton Vindicator,* March 24, 1865, 1, Valley Project, University of Virginia Library and Virginia Center for Digital History, http://valley.lib.virginia.edu.

15. Ehren Foley, "Isaac Nimmons and the Burning of Woodlands [the Simms plantation]: Power, Paternalism, and the Performance of Manhood in William Gilmore Simms's Civil War South," in Moltke-Hansen, *William Gilmore Simms's Unfinished Civil War,* 89–111.

16. Nicholas G. Meriwether, "Sack and Destruction of the City of Columbia, SC," in *Reading William Gilmore Simms: Essays of Introduction to the Author's Canon,* ed. Todd Hagstette (Columbia: University of South Carolina Press, 2017), 329–46; Nicholas G. Meriwether, "Simms's Civil War: History, Healing, and the *Sack and Destruction of Columbia, S.C.,*" *Studies in the Literary Imagination* 42, no. 1 (2009): 97–120; Moltke-Hansen, "When History Failed," 19–21.

17. Moltke-Hansen, "When History Failed," 21.

18. James J. Broomall, *Private Confederacies: The Emotional Worlds of Southern Men as Citizens and Soldiers* (Chapel Hill: University of North Carolina Press, 2019), 131–52; Elaine Franz Parsons, *Ku-Klux: The Birth of the Klan during Reconstruction* (Chapel Hill: University of North Carolina Press, 2015).

19. Allen W. Trelease, *White Terror: The Ku Klux Klan Conspiracy and Southern Reconstruction* (New York: Harper and Row, 1971), argues for Forrest's centrality to the Klan. Parsons, *Ku-Klux,* 50, 92, 195, finds little direct evidence but acknowledges the widespread assumption.

20. "Ku Klux Klan: Revised and Amended Order . . . ," *American Historical Magazine* 5, no. 1 (January 1900): [3]–26, http://www.jstor.org/stable/42657499; Wyn Craig Wade, *The Fiery*

Cross: The Ku Klux Klan in America (New York: Oxford University Press, 1998), 59; Andrew Ward, *River Run Red: The Fort Pillow Massacre in the American Civil War* (New York: Viking, 2005), 386.

21. Eddy W. Davison, *Nathan Bedford Forrest: In Search of the Enigma* (Gretna, LA: Pelican, 2016), 219, 474–75; *Report of the Joint Select Committee to Inquire into the Condition of Affairs in the Late Insurrectionary States . . . , April 20, 1871–February 19, 1872,* 13 vols. (Washington, DC: Government Printing Office, 1872), 1:14, 463; John Richard Stephens, *Commanding the Storm: Civil War Battles in the Words of the Generals Who Fought Them* (Guilford, CT: Lyons, 2012), 319.

22. *Memphis Daily Appeal,* July 6, 1875, 1; "Ex-Confederate Meeting of Cavalry Survivors' Association," *Augusta* [Georgia] *Chronicle,* July 31, 1875; *Macon Weekly Telegraph,* July 20, 1875.

23. *Columbus Weekly Sun,* September 29, 1868, quoted in Alan Conway, *The Reconstruction of Georgia* (Minneapolis: University of Minnesota Press, 1966), 172. The first and second volumes of the testimony from Georgia are recorded in *Testimony Taken by the Joint Select Committee to Inquire into the Condition of Affair in the Late Insurrectionary States* (Washington, DC: Government Printing Office, 1872), vols. 6–7; Gordon's share appears in *Report No. 22, Pt. 6* of this testimony in the House of Representatives, 42d Cong., 2d sess., 6:304–49.

24. *Testimony by the Joint Select Committee,* 6:308 *et passim,* quoted in Ralph Lowell Eckert, *John Brown Gordon: Soldier, Southerner, American* (Baton Rouge: Louisiana State University Press, 1989), 145–49.

25. *Testimony by the Joint Select Committee,* 6:308; Eckert, *John Brown Gordon,* 224–25, 268–69; Gaines M. Foster, *Ghosts of the Confederacy: Defeat, the Lost Cause, and the Emergence of the New South, 1865–1913* (New York: Oxford University Press, 1987), 104–14.

26. Jeffry D. Wert, *General James Longstreet: The Confederacy's Most Controversial Soldier— A Biography* (New York: Simon and Schuster, 1993), 407–27.

27. Jack P. Maddex Jr., *The Reconstruction of Edward A. Pollard: A Rebel's Conversion to Postbellum Unionism* (Chapel Hill: University of North Carolina Press, 1974); Edward Alfred Pollard, *Black Diamonds Gathered in the Darkey Homes of the South* (New York: Pudney and Russell, 1859); Edward Alfred Pollard, *The Lost Cause: A New Southern History of the War of the Confederates* (New York: E. B. Treat, 1866), 50.

28. Jack P. Maddex Jr., "Pollard's *Lost Cause Regained:* A Mask for Southern Accommodation," *Journal of Southern History* 40, no. 4 (November 1974): 595–612; Edward Alfred Pollard, *Life of Jefferson Davis, with a Secret History of the Southern Confederacy* (Philadelphia: National, [1869]); Edward Alfred Pollard, *The Lost Cause Regained* (New York: G. W. Carleton, 1868); Brook Thomas, "The *Galaxy,* National Literature, and Reconstruction," *Nineteenth-Century Literature* 75, no. 1 (June 2020): 57–58.

29. Arlin Turner, *George W. Cable: A Biography* (Durham, NC: Duke University Press, 1956), 25–34; Lawrence N. Powell, ed., "Introduction," in *The New Orleans of George Washington Cable: The 1887 Census Office Report* (Baton Rouge: Louisiana State University Press, 2008), 1–4; Arlin Turner, ed., "George W. Cable's Recollections of General Forrest," *Journal of Southern History* 21, no. 2 (May 1955): 224–28. George Washington Cable, *The Cavalier* (New York: C. Scribner's Sons, 1901), is a fictionalized account involving a Fourth Mississippi cavalryman and draws on Cable's experience. This section on Cable draws substantially, with permission, from my essay "Rival Reconstructions: The *Century Magazine* Debate between George Washington Cable and Henry W. Grady," *Georgia Historical Quarterly* 104, no. 4 (2020): 244–56.

30. Keith Cartwright, *Reading Africa into American Literature: Epics, Fables, and Gothic Tales* (Lexington: University Press of Kentucky, 2002), 192–202; Rien Fertel, *Imagining the Creole City: The Rise of Literary Culture in Nineteenth-Century New Orleans* (Baton Rouge: Louisiana

State University Press, 2014), 71–87; Sharon D. Kennedy-Nolle, *Writing Reconstruction: Race, Gender, and Citizenship in the Postwar South* (Chapel Hill: University of North Carolina Press, 2015), 178–229, esp. 219; Shirley Elizabeth Thompson, *The Struggle to Become American in Creole New Orleans* (Cambridge, MA: Harvard University Press, 2009), 121; Arlin Turner, "George Washington Cable's Literary Apprenticeship," *Louisiana Historical Quarterly* 24, no. 1 (January 1941): 168–86. *N. W. Ayer and Son American Newspaper Annual and Directory* (Philadelphia: N. W. Ayer and Son, 1884), 151, shows the *Picayune*'s dominance by the mid-1880s; twenty years later, Sunday circulation had increased more than fourfold.

31. George Washington Cable, *The Busy Man's Bible and How to Study and Teach It* (Meadville, PA: Flood and Vincent, 1891); Benjamin W. Farley, "George W. Cable: Presbyterian, Romancer, Reformer, Bible Teacher," *Journal of Presbyterian History* 58, no. 2 (Summer 1980): 166–81; Arlin Turner, "George W. Cable's Beginning as a Reformer," *Journal of Southern History* 17, no. 2 (May 1951): 135–61; Ronald C. White Jr., *Liberty and Justice for All: Racial Reform and the Social Gospel (1877–1925)* (Louisville: Westminster John Knox, 1990), 53–57. See also Mark Twain to William D. Howells, letter, November 4, 1882, in *Mark Twain—Howells Letters: The Correspondence of Samuel L. Clemens and William D. Howells, 1872–1910*, 2 vols., ed. Henry Nash Smith and William M. Gibson (Cambridge, MA: Harvard University Press, 1960), 1:418.

32. Guy Cardwell, *Twins of Genius* (East Lansing: Michigan State University Press, 1953); Arlin Turner, ed., *Mark Twain and G. W. Cable: The Record of a Literary Friendship* (East Lansing: Michigan State University Press, 1960).

33. Eva Mae Burkett, *American English Dialects in Literature* (Metuchen, NJ: Scarecrow, 1978); Keri Holt, "Reading Regionalism across the War: Simms and the Literary Imagination of the Postbellum Literary Magazines," in Moltke-Hansen, *William Gilmore Simms's Unfinished Civil War*, 159–82; David W. Newton, "Voices along the Border: Language and the Southern Frontier in *Guy Rivers: A Tale of Georgia*," in *William Gilmore Simms and the American Frontier*, ed. John Caldwell Guilds and Caroline Collins (Athens: University of Georgia Press, 1997), 118–44; Michael D. Picone, "Literary Dialect and the Linguistic Reconstruction of Nineteenth-Century Louisiana," *American Speech* 89, no. 2 (Summer 2014): 143–69.

34. David Moltke-Hansen, "Library of American Books: *Views and Reviews, First and Second Series* and *The Wigwam and the Cabin*," in Hagstette, *Reading William Gilmore Simms*, 197–99; David Moltke-Hansen, "Southern Literary Horizons," 20–21; David Moltke-Hansen, "*The Yemassee: A Romance of Carolina*," in Hagstette, *Reading William Gilmore Simms*, 469–74.

35. Daniel Aaron, *The Unwritten War: American Writers and the Civil War* (New York: Alfred A. Knopf, 1973), 272–73; Charles Gayarré, *The Creoles of History and the Creoles of Romance* (New Orleans: C. E. Hopkins, [1885]); "Judge Gayarré Replies to Mr. Cable," *New York Times,* February 1, 1885, 498, April 27, 1885, 1; Rayburn S. Moore, *Paul Hamilton Hayne* (New York: Twayne, 1972), 28; John David Smith, *Anti-Black Thought, 1863–1925: The Negro Problem,* 11 vols. (New York: Garland, 1993), esp. vol. 2.

36. Alfred Bendixen, "Cable's *The Grandissimes:* A Literary Pioneer Confronts the Southern Condition," in *The Past Is Not Dead: Essays from the Southern Quarterly,* ed. Douglas B. Chambers and Kenneth Watson (Jackson: University Press of Mississippi, 2012), 113–22; Mary German, *The Free People of Color of New Orleans: An Introduction,* 5th ed. (Marrero, LA: Margaret Media, [1994] 2009); Suzanne Jones, "Foreword," in *The Grandissimes: A Novel,* by George Washington Cable (Athens: University of Georgia Press, 1988), v–xv; Mrs. John S. [Isoline Rodd] Kendall, "George Washington Cable," *Library of Southern Literature,* 17 vols., ed. Lucian Lamar Knight et al. (Atlanta: Martin and Hoyt, 1909–23), 2:619–20; Michael Kreyling,

"Introduction," in *The Grandissimes: A Story of Creole Life,* by George Washington Cable (New York: Penguin, 1988), vii–xx.

37. Gayarré, *The Creoles of History;* Kendall, "George Washington Cable."

38. George Washington Cable, "The Convict Lease System in the Southern States," *Century Magazine,* vol. 27, February 1884, 582–99; Paul M. Pruitt Jr., "The Troubles They Saw: Approaches to the History of the Convict Lease System," *Reviews in American History* 29, no. 3 (September 2001): 395–402.

39. Philip Butcher, *George W. Cable: The Northampton Years* (New York: Columbia University Press, 1959); George Washington Cable, "The Freedman's Case in Equity," *Century Magazine,* vol. 29, January 1885, 409–18; Cardwell, *Twins of Genius;* Fertel, *Imagining the Creole City,* 88–93; Daniel Sutherland, *The Confederate Carpetbaggers* (Baton Rouge: Louisiana State University Press, 1988), 326–27.

40. Edward L. Ayers, *The Promise of the New South: Life after Reconstruction* (New York: Oxford University Press, 1992), 347–48; Kennedy-Nolle, *Writing Reconstruction,* 224; Ralph E. Luker, *The Social Gospel in Black and White, 1885–1912* (Chapel Hill: University of North Carolina Press, 1991), 69–71; Open Letter Club [Facsimile] Records, 1886–1967, Tennessee State Library and Archives, Nashville; Brook Thomas, *The Literature of Reconstruction: Not in Plain Black and White* (Baltimore: Johns Hopkins University Press, 2017), 261, 269–71.

41. Paul M. Gaston, *The New South Creed: A Study in Southern Mythmaking* (New York: Alfred A. Knopf, 1970), 48, 140; Henry W. Grady, "In Plain Black and White," *Century Magazine,* vol. 29, April 1885, 909–17; Raymond B. Nixon, *Henry W. Grady: Spokesman of the New South* (New York: Alfred A. Knopf, 1943), 214, 223; Jeremy Wells, *Romances of the White Man's Burden: Race, Empire, and the Plantation in American Literature, 1880–1936* (Nashville: Vanderbilt University Press, 2011), 73–110; Ronald C. White Jr., *Liberty and Justice for All: Racial Reform and the Social Gospel (1877–1925)* (Louisville: Westminster John Knox, 1990), 51–54.

42. Harold E. Davis, *Henry Grady's New South: Atlanta, A Brave and Beautiful City* (Tuscaloosa: University of Alabama Press, 1990), 21–54, 164–90; Grady, "In Plain Black and White"; Joel Chandler Harris, ed., *Life of Henry W. Grady, Including His Writings and Speeches* (New York: Cassell, [1890]), 85–87; Moltke-Hansen, "Honoring Confederate Defeat the Georgia Way," 12–14.

43. Henry W. Grady, "The South and Her Problems," in *The Complete Writings and Speeches of Henry W. Grady,* ed. Edwin Du Bois Shurter (New York: Hinds, Noble, and Eldridge, 1910), 33; Donald G. Mathews, *At the Alter of Lynching: Burning Sam Hose in the American South* (New York: Cambridge University Press, 2018), 48–53 *et passim;* Smith, *Anti-Black Thought,* esp. vol. 9.

44. Moltke-Hansen, "Honoring Confederate Defeat," 2–23. Edward J. Blum, *Reforging the White Republic: Race, Religion, and American Nationalism, 1865–1898* (Baton Rouge: Louisiana State University Press, 2005); Grace Elizabeth Hale, *Making Whiteness: The Culture of Segregation in the South* (New York: Pantheon, 1998), 48 *et passim;* Stephen Middleton, David R. Roediger, and Donald M. Shaffer, eds., *The Construction of Whiteness: An Interdisciplinary Analysis of Race Formation and the Meaning of White Identity* (Jackson: University Press of Mississippi, 2016), 134, 137, 147.

45. Moltke-Hansen, "Turn Signals," 183–85; Wendell H. Stephenson, "William P. Trent as a Historian of the South," *Journal of Southern History* 15, no. 2 (1949): 152–77; Thomas, "The Galaxy, National Literature, and Reconstruction," 75–76.

46. Moltke-Hansen, "Turn Signals," 184–86. The discussion draws on this essay with the publisher's permission, but see Stephenson, "William P. Trent." See also Orville Vernon Burton,

"The South as the 'Other,' the Southerner as 'Stranger,'" *Journal of Southern History* 79, no. 1 (February 2013), 7–50, esp. 27–42.

47. William P. Trent, *Robert E. Lee* (Boston: Small, Maynard, 1899), x, 10–11.

48. William P. Trent, *Southern Statesmen of the Old Regime: Washington, Jefferson, Randolph, Calhoun, Stephens, Toombs, and Jefferson Davis* (New York: Thomas Y. Crowell, 1897), ix–x, 176, 183, 262, 271; James H. Hyslop, *Democracy: A Study of Government* (New York: Charles Scribner's Sons, 1899).

49. Trent, *Southern Statesmen*, ix–x, 176–77, 182, 257, 262.

50. Ibid., 176, 181.

51. C. Vann Woodward, *Tom Watson: Agrarian Rebel* (New York: Macmillan, 1938), 6.

52. Jacquelyn Dowd Hall, "The Long Civil Rights Movement and the Political Uses of the Past," *Journal of American History* 91, no. 4 (March 2005): 1233–63; Melissa Milewski, *Litigation across the Color Line: Civil Cases between Black and White Southerners from the End of Slavery to Civil Rights* (New York: Oxford University Press, 2018); Jennifer Rittenhouse, *Growing Up Jim Crow: How Black and White Southern Children Learned Race* (Chapel Hill: University of North Carolina Press, 2006).

53. Richard Thompson Ford, "Rethinking Rights after the Second Reconstruction," *Yale Law Journal* 123, no. 8 (2014): 2942–62; Kevin. K. Gaines, "The End of the Second Reconstruction," *Modern American History* 1, no. 1 (March 2018): 113–19; Robert V. Ward Jr., "The Second Reconstruction Is Over," *Berkeley Journal of African-American Law and Policy* 16, no. 2 (2015): 75–84.

54. See, e.g., Bruce E. Baker and Elaine S. Frantz, "Against Synthesis: Diverse Approaches to the History of Reconstruction," in *Reinterpreting Southern Histories: Essays in Historiography*, ed. Craig Thompson Friend and Lorri Glover (Baton Rouge: Louisiana University Press, 2020), 218–44; Thomas J. Brown, ed., *Reconstructions: New Perspectives on the Postbellum United States* (New York: Oxford University Press, 2006); Jim Downs, *Sick from Freedom: African-American Illness and Suffering during the Civil War and Reconstruction* (New York: Cambridge University Press, 2012); Hahn, *A Nation without Borders*, 7, 448–500; William A. Link, ed., *United States Reconstruction across the Americas* (Gainesville: University Press of Florida, 2019); David Prior, *Between Freedom and Progress: The Lost World of Reconstruction Politics* (Baton Rouge: Louisiana State University Press, 2019); Richardson, *West from Appomattox*.

Reconstruction at the Centennial Exhibition of 1876

Krista Kinslow

O N MAY 10, 1876, THE bells rang out in Philadelphia as the Centennial Exhibition began. The first major world's fair held in the United States came during a time rife with political and economic strife. Occurring only eleven years after the Civil War, the Centennial Exhibition became a political battleground in the continuing struggles of Reconstruction. In fact, the planners hoped that the event would bring the country back together again—that the sections could reunite on the basis of their shared connection to the American Revolution. But in the midst of Reconstruction, Americans held different ideas about what the Centennial meant to them. The exhibition often exacerbated sectional conflict rather than easing it. The ways in which the Centennial became a contested space for Reconstruction could be seen in how the congressional debates about the fair revolved around ideas of loyalty, citizenship, and the place of African Americans in the nation. Even as states were being called on to fund the fair, white Southerners proclaimed that the exhibition was just another Northern scheme to humiliate them. But they also attempted to create their own narrative that privileged their Southern sensibilities. Meanwhile, African Americans worked out how the advancement of their race could best be showcased, and Union veterans made clear the connection of the nation, Reconstruction, and the Centennial.

The Centennial did not just exhibit sectional strife. There were also clear elements of reunion at work, particularly when reconciliation could be linked to the Revolution. The planners were right: Americans could look to the past to help forge reunion. Racist depictions of African Americans visiting the fair came into play, as well. The Centennial also exemplified how Reconstruction can be seen as a cultural and national process—not just political and Southern. The world's fair in 1876 made clearly visible Reconstruction's twin goals of protecting African American rights and reuniting the nation. In the goals of the planners and Union veterans who sought reunion on Northern terms, the resistance by white Southerners who asserted the doctrines of the Lost Cause, and the attempts by Black citizens to make the fair show their own gains only thirteen years after emancipation, one can see how the conflicts of Reconstruction played out at the Centennial.

Planned by the U.S. Centennial Commission (USCC), which Congress created in 1871, the fair promoted the economic health of the country by marketing American industrial and agricultural goods. In addition to such unabashed boosterism, the planners also hoped the fair would reunite the country after the Civil War. At the first meeting of the USCC in March 1872, commissioners stated their goals for the fair. Joseph Hawley, the commission's president, reflected extensively about the purpose of the exhibition. Throughout his speech, he expressed hope that the Centennial would be a national affair that would reunite the country and clearly indicated that the commissioners were assembled for a national purpose.[1] William P. Blake, another commissioner, continued the theme of reconciliation. "Who could not be impressed," he asked, when they saw "in the banquet hall of our hosts of the Union League, Virginia shaking hands with Connecticut, and pledging united and harmonious action, hand to hand and heart to heart, in the great work of peace, good-will, and civilization confided to our care."[2] Such grandiose rhetoric lacked specificity about how friendship would be restored between the North and South but marked a key theme in the planning of the Centennial.

Fundraising became a critical issue, and the commission worked with the Women's Centennial Committee to collect money.[3] In addition, Congress created a Board of Finance to sell bonds for the fair. The hope was that Americans throughout the country would buy these certificates, and the fair would be privately funded and truly national. After these plans were made, an economic crisis gripped the nation in the wake of the Panic of 1873. Raising money for a fair during a depression proved difficult. Because private fundraising efforts came up short, Hawley, himself a representative from Connecticut, was compelled to go before Congress to beg for money in 1874. Unsurprisingly, the debate surrounding the Centennial became fierce when money was involved. Furthermore, the political context had changed, as Democrats, including white Southerners, gained power in the election of 1872. The nation found itself wavering on the issues of Reconstruction.[4] By mid-1874, with political resistance combining with economic distress, there were real doubts about whether the Centennial should be held at all. Hoping to save the fair, Hawley appealed to Congress for money. He invoked many reasons that the government should pay for the Centennial, including national honor, patriotism, and economic benefits.

But Hawley closed his speech with a ringing endorsement for reconciliation and a true end to the Civil War. Here was the real reason that the government needed to support the fair. It was a matter of national healing. He dared to tread into two fiercely debated political issues: civil rights for Blacks and amnesty for former Confederates. He declared that in 1876, "We of these States will meet under one flag and one name," affirming the Unionist triumph in the war. He called on Congress to "pass our amnesty bills, secure the civil rights of all, clear the ground, and shake hands."[5] By making room for citizenship for both former rebels and African Americans, the Centennial could bring the North and South back together again. But to heal the nation, Congress needed to appropriate the money. Thus, Hawley offered a complex message of reunion that walked the fine line between the warring sides in Reconstruction. In his request for funds, Hawley offered a political compromise that pointed toward making the nation's birthday a true reunion.

Other members of Congress concurred with Hawley, including two of the African Americans in the House of Representatives. Richard Cain of South Carolina thought that the Centennial would "have an influence in healing the wounds caused by the war." When Northerners and Southerners gathered together and saw "the results of the genius and the arts of all of them, they will realize as never before our common brotherhood." He would "heal every wound caused by the war" and "raise up that people with whom I am identified," he said, and ensure they enjoyed "all the privileges and blessings which any citizens of this great nation enjoy." By 1876, Cain believed that Congress would pass both the civil rights and amnesty bills that made up Hawley's compromise. If they did, the Philadelphia Exhibition would be a grand place of celebration where "the North and South, the East and West, can shake hands together . . . and shall there be united as never before—the men of all races on this continent. And then shall be brought to pass the realization of the sentiment that all men are equal and entitled to enjoy the same rights and immunities." The Centennial, Cain concluded, would cause Americans to "realize how great we are and how wonderful has been our progress."[6] Josiah T. Walls of Florida argued that the Fourth of July in 1876 would be the day of "definitive and emphatic termination of all feelings of harshness and bitterness arising from our recent contentions." If the world's fair would "unite more closely together the now somewhat discordant and jarring interests of the North and the South; if it will tend to discourage and extinguish all feelings of sectionalism," how could Congress not fund it?[7]

Of course, not everyone agreed. Many congressmen pointed to the economic condition of the country in arguing against funding the fair. Granville Barrere, a Republican from Illinois, supported the idea of the Centennial, but there was no way the country could afford it. John Coburn, an Indiana Republican, agreed that the government could not afford the appropriation and did not think $3 million would be enough. Besides, he argued, "This is our family gathering; this is our own season 'for exultation, for gratitude, and joy' over the birth of our liberties, and not a mere exposition of our resources," and a World's Fair ultimately cheapened it.[8] A Tennessee Republican also pointed to the economic situation but made sure that he was not grouped with white Southern sympathizers. The region was impoverished because the Confederates caused the war. He also stressed that Southern Democrats voted against freedmen's rights and educational support. Nevertheless, he could not vote for the "Big Show" when there were people "drowning and starving" in his state.[9]

James T. Rapier, another Black congressman, opposed the funding plan because of civil rights. How could he support the Centennial, he asked, "with my own galling chains of slavery hanging about me?" He could not celebrate when he still felt the weight of racial oppression and "could no more rejoice on that occasion in my present condition than the Jews could sing in their wonted style as they sat as captives beside the Babylonish streams." But, he said, he looked "forward to the day when I shall be in the full enjoyment of the rights of a freeman, with the same hope they indulged that they would again return to their native land. I can no more forget my manhood, than they could forget Jerusalem."[10] Clearly, not everyone shared Hawley's rosy vision of a reunited nation.

And some took a Lost Cause position in opposing the scheme to fund the fair. Phillip Cook of Georgia offered the ex-Confederate view of the matter when he denounced the Centennial. Focusing on slavery and Reconstruction, he argued that it was New England's fault that his region was burdened by slavery. Georgia did not want the institution. But once New Englanders had "filled their coffers" with their participation in the slave trade, they were ready to get rid of it. He discussed the onerous taxes on cotton, saying that his state had taxation but no representation, failing to mention that Confederates had started the war that led to Georgia's losing its place in the government. He lamented that his constituents were now being taxed $1.5 million for something they did not want. Those supporting the Centennial "wandered through the Constitution from one provision to another, like a New England tramp or a carpet-bagger." Using such provocative, sectional language cast the debate in the bitter terms of Reconstruction. Looking toward the so-called Redemption of the South by white Democrats, Cook mentioned that the Radical Republicans supported allowing only former Union soldiers to serve in Congress while disenfranchising Confederate veterans. He also jabbed at the Freedmen's Bureau, arguing that it was Republicans who were trying to drum up bitterness and division. He was careful to offer no defense of slavery, instead stressing government overreach and the Constitution while blaming the North for the peculiar institution.[11]

Such arguments against funding the Centennial failed to convince Martin Townsend of New York, however. The nation had just spent $5 billion to secure its survival, so why not demonstrate and celebrate with a world's fair? Just as Mary spent her precious perfume anointing Jesus's feet rather than selling it to feed the poor, the federal government should bestow its resources on securing the exhibition's success. Comparing a world's fair to Jesus Christ surely raised some eyebrows, but nationalism was already a civil religion. Townsend likewise denounced constitutional arguments against the Centennial. "Pretty much the entire confederate phalanx" voted for paper currency, and where was the constitutionality of that? He mistakenly assumed that only former Confederates cared about the constitutionality of the issue and argued that they merely wanted an excuse to not support the bill. He rebuked those Northerners who agreed with the Southerners: "We sat here when he [a Confederate senator] was gone and tried to save this country so that there should be a centennial." Finally, he reminded his colleagues of the history of slavery. "We muzzled the ox," he said. Now it was time for the freedmen to be paid. Justice demanded that "he that does the work" get some of the proceeds. Southerners might complain that the exhibition was a celebration of Northern victory, but Townsend thought that it should be just that. After all, to the victors went the spoils.[12]

In the end, all of the stirring appeals to patriotism and denunciations of the rebels were not enough. The vote failed. Western and Southern representatives especially opposed it. The economic crisis proved too much to overcome, as congressmen were reluctant to support what appeared to be so frivolous during a depression. Without government money, the USCC was left trying to piece together funding from private investors and whatever appropriations various states might contribute.[13]

By the time 1876 arrived, there were very real doubts about whether or not the Centennial Exhibition would actually be open. The money needed never fully materialized and the fair seemed doomed. Desperate to save face, the commissioners returned to Congress, and another funding bill came forward. The commission asked for much less this time—$1.5 million rather than $3 million. Supporters of the bill pointed out that invitations had been sent to dignitaries around the world. Countries in Europe and Asia were preparing for their own representation at the fair. If the exhibition had to be canceled, it would reflect poorly on the United States. Indiana Senator Oliver P. Morton proclaimed, "We cannot turn back now without being disgraced." Others still hoped for reunion, with a Kansas congressmen arguing that "those who lately sought to destroy the Union know they have made a mistake." In Philadelphia, all Americans could "swear eternal fealty" on "the altar of Union and freedom." For this reason, only a few months before the doors would open to the public, the federal government signed off on a loan for the purposes of making the fair a reality. National honor and hopes for national healing required money, and the government finally decided to help the Centennial, but only if such support would be repaid.[14]

In addition to money woes, the Centennial faced opposition from Southerners who had no intention of supporting the exhibition. While the Centennial planners hoped to involve every state and territory in the Union during the planning process and wanted each to have a pavilion at the fair, most of the Southern states refused to participate. Only Arkansas and Mississippi funded the exhibition, but individuals from Virginia and Tennessee saw to it that their two states were represented in an unofficial capacity. Economics partly explained Southern reticence, as some of the states could not afford to participate. But the politics of Reconstruction mattered even more. Many Southern newspapers linked the Centennial to the continuation of Radical Reconstruction, Black civil rights, the expansion of the federal government, and the subjugation of the Southern states. Closely tied to these political issues were cultural considerations. Some Southerners did not want to promote reconciliation or the Unionist victory in the Civil War. Money was only an excuse, as one Republican newspaper pointed out. Though Virginia could not afford to appropriate funds for the Centennial, it felt "wealthy and willing enough to erect a statue to commemorate the insurgent services of Robert E. Lee."[15] Southerners somehow managed to raise money for the Lost Cause even as they claimed to be too broke to pay for the Centennial.

Southern newspapers often suggested alternative ways to celebrate the Centennial. One Louisiana editor recommended celebrating the nation's birthday by creating a new Constitution "from which will be excluded all traces of these silly efforts to force negroes to an elevation their present condition does not justify." He called for a constitutional convention that would ensure that "State rights and Home rule [will] be again in the ascendant." In other words, the unreconstructed rebel wanted to celebrate the Centennial by overturning the Union victory and reinstating the Confederacy. It was little wonder, then, that a Unionist celebration failed to interest most white Southerners. Bitter about their defeat and the policies of Reconstruction, most former rebels thought the fair would be a display of Northern triumphalism. The Louisiana newspaperman said that it was "too much to hope that the Yankees can be diverted just now from the splendid opportunity of gratifying their cupidity, while under the guise of patriotism they are preparing Philadelphia for their characteristic huckstering."[16] The fair was a perfect target for white Southerners who resisted Reconstruction, and they used it to vent their frustrations.

Southern cynicism about the fair seemed to be correctly placed when the exhibition opened on May 10, 1876. After all, President Ulysses S. Grant was a Union hero, and he was joined on the platform for the opening ceremonies by other men who stood as symbols of the Northern victory, such as General Philip Sheridan and General William Tecumseh Sherman. To make matters worse for the rebels, notable Radical Republicans also sat on the stage that day, including Senator Morton and his colleagues from New York and Maine, Roscoe Conkling and James G. Blaine. All three of these leading Republicans hoped to win their party's presidential nomination, and they had all supported the Reconstruction policies that so many white Southerners hated. To add insult to injury, Grant invited Frederick Douglass to sit on the stage with him in Philadelphia, and the famed African American orator accepted. When Douglass tried to make his way up to the platform, however, the guards tried to keep him from joining the dignitaries seated there. Douglass, rather than entering with the other invited guests, apparently worked his way through the crowd and approached the stage from the wrong direction. The guard, thinking he was just another man in the throng of thousands, kept him from going up to the stage. Conkling, however, aided Douglass by vouching for his identity, and when Douglass finally made it to the stage, the crowd gave him "a most hearty congratulatory round of applause."[17] To Southern rebels, having this Black abolitionist prominently taking part in the opening ceremonies alongside Union generals and Radical Republicans confirmed their worst fears about the Centennial being a celebration of Northern victory.

White Southerners rushed to say that they had predicted what the fair was really about. A Georgia columnist reported, "As usual, it will be seen the inevitable African appears on the programme."[18] An Alabama editorialist also opined about the individuals gathered together on the stage that opening day: Blaine, "a human hyena"; Grant, "a corrupt and dishonest president"; Sheridan, "the man who murdered a camp of helpless Indians because they were afflicted with smallpox, and wanted the Southern people of Louisiana declared banditti that he might murder them"; and Douglass, simply "a nigger." A third account noted that Sheridan and Douglass "seemed to be the only lions that elicited cheers," and to make them the

FIGURE 1. "The American Volunteer," granite statue exhibited at the 1876 Centennial Exposition by the New England Granite Company, stereoscopic view by Centennial Photographic Company. (Author's collection)

"only objects of their enthusiasm was in bad taste." In short, he declared, "The proceedings read to Southern people rather more like a Northern jubilee than a national celebration."[19] The author went on to note that, while the foreign visitors at the Centennial were not acquainted with the "pedigree in crime" of the individuals gathered together, white Southerners were. Visitors from that region would be "subjected to many insults of a similar character before the thing is over." The newspaper concluded with the advice: "Better to stay home."[20] The presence of so many living symbols of Northern victory and Radical Reconstruction offended the delicate sensibilities of the bitter rebels.

White Southerners who did attend the exhibition found plenty of other examples of Reconstruction politics on display. The fair housed many art exhibits dealing with the Civil War and slavery. They appeared even though the art selection committee aimed to keep out anything that would offend Southerners by depicting scenes of the "rebellion." Many of the exhibitions on the fairgrounds promoted an explicitly Unionist message, showcasing Northern triumph and the might of the federal government. This was literally the case with the *American Volunteer* or *American Soldier* statue, an imposing twenty-one-foot figure that stood outside Memorial Hall until the end of the exhibition, when it was moved to Antietam National Cemetery to commemorate the Northern victory purchased with soldiers' blood. One critic noted that the statue "is a sentinel not to be trifled with, as he leans with both hands clasped around his gun-barrel."[21]

The towering statue of a Union soldier created by the New England Granite Company served as a reminder of Northern victory and Southern defeat. His placement also indicated the business of memorializing the Civil War as Americans came to terms with what the conflict had meant and what it had cost. Statues of solitary soldiers would come to decorate the landscape of Civil War battlefields.[22] Busts

FIGURE 2. "The Battle of Gettysburg," by P. F. Rothermel, 1870; engraving by John Sartain, 1872. (Library of Congress)

and portraits of Northern war heroes and politicians were spread throughout the exhibition, but not a single Confederate appeared on the walls. Southerners recognized this disparity and complained about it. So while planners spoke of promoting reconciliation, they did not mean that both sides were equal. The Centennial promoted the Union. It made no space for rebels and traitors. Other works of art displayed in Memorial Hall depicted the Civil War and brought dramatic reactions in newspapers that indicated deep disagreements about the conflict's meaning.

One such controversy involved Peter Rothermel's depiction of Pickett's Charge. The *Battle of Gettysburg* was one of the most famous paintings displayed at the Centennial and was reviewed in newspapers, artistic criticism, and visitors' diaries. All remarked on the huge size of the painting that was hung in a prominent place in the American section of the vast art gallery. Southerners, seeing it as an insult, complained that it reminded them of their defeat. Some Northerners agreed that it insulted the South, and one Philadelphia paper said that "its offensiveness" should have been reason enough to ban it: "Its presence . . . is an insult to our Southern guests, because it is a reminder to them of defeat and humiliation, and because it represents all those who fought on the losing side as men of the most brutal and ruffianly type, and all those on the winning side as the noblest and most heroic."[23]

However, a correspondent in the *Christian Recorder,* an African American paper, reported it as being "original and life-like . . . a grand success," criticizing those

BEFORE THE GREAT PICTURE OF THE BATTLE OF GETTYSBURG.—FIGHTING THE BATTLE OVER AGAIN.

FIGURE 3. "Before the Great Picture of the Battle of Gettysburg," from Bricktop's *Going to the Centennial, and A Guy to the Great Exhibition* (New York: Collin and Small, 1876), 32. (Author's collection)

who judged it harshly and reporting that "Generals Meade, and Sherman and other military men, express their satisfaction with it, leading it in the highest terms. So the criticism of the envious is not of much value."[24] Other Northerners defended the painting, and one editor criticized "sentimental sticklers" who were so easily offended. He noted the irony of Southerners being insulted but also insisting that they be allowed to publicly promote their own view of the Civil War. For example, Southerners called for placing a wreath on Stonewall Jackson's grave, and many monuments to the Lost Cause were already being built across the South. "If the statues of rebel generals may be set up in a public place," the Northern editor argued, "and a picture of Union triumph must not be hung for a few months in an art gallery, we are puzzled as to the outcome of that war for the Union." He concluded by asking, "Were we righteously vanquished?"[25] Certainly, the painting offended those who had suffered defeat. One Southern writer critiqued the painting at length, seeing it as an "exhibition of ferocious and bloody antagonism." He found the "representations of Northerners bayoneting Southerners . . . cruel" and thought the painting a disgrace.[26]

One New York writer satirized these reactions—depicting an old Union and Confederate veteran battling in front of the painting. He described the scene: "Two one legged relics of the late war . . . stood before it, wrangling and almost fighting it over again."[27] The image might have been humorous to some, but most Americans found it deadly serious in the midst of Reconstruction. Remembering the war and fighting over its meaning was not just the pastime of old, crippled veterans. Instead, such arguments remained central to the politics of the time, and the meaning of the image spoke volumes to those who gazed on the giant painting.[28]

Thomas Bryant Kingsbury published *The International Exhibition Guide for the Southern States: The Only Guide Book Specially Suited to the Southern Visitor,* a Centennial guidebook specifically designed for those white Southerners who chose to attend the fair. He began with a question: "Shall we go to the Centennial?" He reflected that such a question was probably asked "in the South a thousand times a day." To such a question, he answered, "By all means, whether or not your state has contributed money and material, let all go who can afford to do so, for it is *our* Centennial as well as the Centennial of the Northern people. We are a part of the Union. This country is our country." He continued by stressing the country's shared history, noting that the fair should "awaken the patriotic ardor" of all sections in the country and asked whether "it is not altogether fitting that we should show to the world what has been accomplished." If Southerners did not go to the Centennial, the rest of the world would be "in utter ignorance of our people."[29] Kingsbury clearly recognized that Southern visitors might not attend the Centennial because of continued sectional prejudice. He preached a message of national and sectional greatness, appealing to both sentiments to entice Southerners to make their way north.

However, the majority of Southern states elected not to officially participate. While most Northern, Midwestern, and even several Western states appropriated funds to erect buildings, Mississippi and Arkansas were the only Southern states to officially pay for exhibits. Some governors, such as Virginia's James Kemper, claimed their state was too impoverished to contribute. Other governors never appeared to go on the record at all regarding the fair. Some governors faced a complicated situation because they were Republicans elected to office during Radical Reconstruction. The most prominent example of such a Republican was Adelbert Ames of Mississippi, who pushed for an appropriation for the Centennial. The Democrats in the state opposed the $5,000 appropriation even as they also worked to impeach Ames, but they were ultimately unsuccessful at both.[30] Eventually, Ames resigned his office in 1876, another victim of the abandonment of Reconstruction by Northerners. The former Union general saw that his defeat was inevitable when the Democratic Redeemers swept back into power, so he stepped down. But his efforts meant that the state participated in the Centennial. Mississippi built a log cabin to serve as its state house at the fair, even as one paper lamented that this funding was just a "trap to take in . . . the South" and "a stupendous Yankee invention for the cleaning out of the pockets of the Southern people when the money thus needlessly wasted is needed at home for the purchase of bread."[31]

Yet Southerners, too, took it upon themselves to present an image of their former glory. A group of Southerners put on a jousting tournament at the fair that spoke to a romanticized memory of the past. Centennial officials dedicated a day to the states of Virginia, Delaware, and Maryland to commemorate Washington's victory at Yorktown. Despite Governor Kemper's claims that they could not afford it, others from Virginia wanted a show at the exhibition. On October 19, Virginia Day, fifteen knights, representing the original thirteen states, the Union, and the Centennial, participated in a tournament to capture golden rings.

Individuals mainly from Virginia and Maryland put on this tournament that was both well attended and, apparently, confusing, as some Northern onlookers seemed unacquainted with the meanings of medieval tournaments.[32] However, Southerners steeped in a culture of honor understood it well. As Elizabeth Fox-Genovese and Eugene Genovese have noted, elite Southerners during antebellum years enjoyed tournaments, especially because they promoted the ideology of the master class about the importance of hierarchy rather than liberalism. In this view, Southerners idealized the Middle Ages because of the precapitalist structure in which everyone knew his or her place in society. The imagery also evoked a sense of protecting white womanhood, which would take on its own special meaning in the years after the war, as white Southerners proclaimed their women imperiled by Black men.[33] The tournament, while fun and games, was also a way to assert Southern masculinity, especially when juxtaposed to those fair maidens who made up the court. The second illustration definitely evoked such an image, as the white knight crowned the queen of the Centennial. Whatever way they actually understood their attachment to the romanticized past, Southerners continued their interest in chivalry and feudalism during Reconstruction.[34] The tournament showed that Southerners staunchly held to a vision of society that Northerners could not understand.

One example of cultural sectionalism involved food. Edward Mercer, a businessman from Georgia, opened his Restaurant of the South. This dining spot and hotel also featured a "band of old-time plantation 'darkies' who will sing their quaint melodies and strum the banjo before the visitors of every clime."[35] Following on this theme, the state house representing Mississippi also featured an African American musician. These two instances portrayed a romanticized and mythologized South in which Blacks were not political agents but, rather, entertainers. This conformed to a Lost Cause interpretation, where African Americans and whites coexisted peacefully, at least before the end of slavery. Indeed, one Mississippi newspaper that opposed the Centennial also defended racial relations in the state. The editor pointed out that the Democrat in charge of the state's log cabin "takes with him a Mississippi negro and places him in charge, as custodian, of such valuable packages as Mississippi visitors may desire to deposit," commenting that they doubted any state house representing the North would entrust such responsibility to African Americans. "And we call the attention of Morton and Blaine to the fact," jabbing at the two Radical senators by claiming that Northerners were hypocrites regarding race relations. Thus, the author insinuated that Southerners could handle race relations if the Yankees would just leave them alone. Reconstruction was a waste of time, and those Radical Republicans, such as Oliver Morton, would do well to focus on the racial issues of their own regions and leave the South alone.[36]

But white people did not speak for African Americans at the Centennial. Black Americans were more than willing to speak for themselves and used the fair as a place to promote their own interests. From the beginning of the planning process, African Americans wondered what they should do. In response to an article in a Black newspaper about organizing the event, a reader wrote in to ask and answer the question: "What shall be the action of the colored people when this country shall exhibit the history and progress of American industries, her inventions and discoveries in art and science, her contributions to the progress of civilization?" He alluded to the history of slavery but did not dwell on it: Blacks had "contributed not only unpaid toil," but had also been instrumental in the "mechanic and manufacturing arts," and it was those latter contributions that men and women should put on display at the Centennial. He admonished his fellow African Americans, "Don't let us forget in the heat of battle, in the pursuit of political advantages, that we must also be spiritually elevated, that the soul (in us) must make its power felt and seen in other walks of life, by which so many comforts and conveniences in civilized life are produced." He expressed concern that Blacks had become too focused on electoral politics and had ignored other ways to show the gains of their race to the rest of the country.[37] Participating in the Centennial Exhibition, then, took on a broader significance, as it showed racial advancement to both the nation and the world.

The best example of African American agency and grassroots involvement originated with a publication of the African Methodist Episcopal (AME) church, the *Christian Recorder,* and its influential editor, Benjamin Tanner. In 1874, the editor called for Blacks to contribute to the Centennial Exhibition. In early 1874, Tanner asked his readers, "Why can't we do it? Why can't we, *as a church,* have a hand in the great Centennial?" Expressing both the ecumenical tenor and anti-Catholic sentiments of the time, Tanner noted that other churches were participating, including the "alien Romanists, who are not, and cannot be truly American," who built a fountain dedicated to their faith (and to temperance). But, Tanner went on, "We have too much at stake. . . . Not to be present there will tend mightily to prove the words of an enemy, true: The negro race never supplied one atom to the materials which compromise the civilization of the world," including "religion." The AME church, then, needed to erect a statue to "Religious Liberty," with the denomination's founder, Richard Allen, as the face of freedom. A statue to Allen would be a testament not only to their faith, but to the accomplishments of the race. Religion and race were not separate but were both key components of identity.[38]

A few months later, the *Recorder* reminded its readers about the idea for a statue of Allen, saying it would be the "grandest thing the Negro ever did," but their appeal seemed to fall on deaf ears until November.[39] At that time, the Arkansas AME annual conference issued a resolution calling for donations to support the statue. Their statement told a story of Black improvement and progress: "The Negro race has figured so conspicuously in the history of the United States, and has been the cause of much legislation, war, and blood shed, and has steadily advanced in religion, refinement, culture, wealth and statesmanship since 1863." It also emphasized a need to remember the past, as "we feel that the history of our race, and slanders of our enemies demand that we be represented in the celebration." Participating in the Centennial Exhibition would show the country the gains that had been made only eleven years after the war, and it would prove to their "enemies" that African American success was real and not just some Radical Republican conspiracy.[40]

Throughout the next two years, readers wrote in to the *Recorder,* voicing their support of the statue. Andrew Chambers, who had been appointed the treasurer of the Allen monument fund, also submitted letters. He published a circular in the

Recorder, calling for the churches to contribute: "It is for you to say whether four millions of wronged and outraged sons of freedom shall mingle their shouts of patriotism, liberty, and equality with the conglomerate nationalities who shall feel the warm blood swelling in their veins when old 'Liberty Bell' peels out 'our first hundred!'" he told his readers. "It is for you to decide, my Brother, whether the glorious progeny which has sprung forth with transcendent beauty from the fumes of the blacksmith shop, shall take her stand by the side of the mighty and progressive. A mite from each member of your congregation will be amply sufficient. Shall it be given? . . . Will you enlist all your energies in this grand cause? Say not that we are too poor, when millions are annually squandered by us for 'rum,' and the 'filthy weed.'"[41]

Churches, particularly in the South, helped the efforts to support the statue.[42] "We are coming," proclaimed Amos Williams, part of the AME executive committee in Arkansas. The Centennial, Richard Allen, and freedom were all linked in his letter.: "When the booming cannon shall announce that a century of the nation's independence has rolled away with its slavery and many of its prejudices, and the nation has commenced its new era of Christian education with liberty, justice and equality to all of its citizens," he declared, "let the comely statue of *Allen* be unveiled that the shouts of his followers be heard throughout the broad land. We are coming." He continued, "The heavy wheels of time roll on, crushing beneath their weight the mighty forces of slavery, prejudice and every thing that oppose us," seeing an optimistic future. He wanted Christians to "let the cross of Christ stand preeminent before us and the glory of his religion sink deep within our hearts and we are bound to succeed. A monument to *Allen* would give African Methodism an upward, forward, progressive character in the right direction. Come brethren, agitate its subject. We expect every African Methodist to do his whole duty."[43]

But the statue kept being delayed. The original plan was to debut the statue on July 4; however, the sculptor had not yet finished it. The statue was to be unveiled in September on the anniversary of the preliminary emancipation proclamation. The *Recorder* announced the triumph of the completion of the statue, which would recognize "our Emancipation, enfranchisement, manhood, and representation at the New World's Fair."[44] But the train that was carrying the bust derailed, destroying much of the monument and necessitating more delays.

In the end, two celebrations occurred on the fairgrounds—the first in July for the base, and the second in November, when the monument was finally put up. Examining the speeches at these two ceremonies presents two very different views. The first was a condemnation of the federal government and a reminder that it was not at all peaceful in the South. The second message provided a more optimistic view about what had been accomplished in the recent past.

One man who used the Centennial as a way to point out the violence in the South was the AME Pastor John T. Jenifer, from Arkansas. While ostensibly dedicating a bust of Allen, Jenifer spoke at length about the current problems of Reconstruction, worsening racial relations in the South, and the memory of the Civil War. "The Southern question is an important question," he said, and "made important because the destiny of a struggling race is involved in it. It is the problem of the nation." After noting acts of violence against Blacks in the South, which "are the death struggles of the Lost Cause," he called for better schools and protection against these acts of violence—and noted it was the national government that was responsible. Government action would "maintain peace" in the South, he said, and "make certain the acts of reconstruction and . . . perpetuate the Union," thus fulfill-ing the purpose of the Civil War. Blacks, and the nation in general, should not be discouraged at the seeming slowness of progress—recalling the history of slavery: "The work of centuries cannot be undone in a decade."[45]

That was in July, but the bust itself was not erected until the last week of the fair. A local African American paper covered the proceedings, describing the size, with its nine-foot pedestal and three-foot bust of Allen. While hardly the most imposing statue on the fairgrounds, at twelve feet tall it was enough to attract attention and not be lost in the crowd. There were hundreds of Blacks in attendance that day, but the paper also mentioned others in the audience, indicating that it was a mixed-race crowd. A professor of religious history, John M. Brown of Howard University, like-wise delivered an inclusive dedication speech. He discussed how the AME churches had managed to raise the funds necessary to create the statue, with $3,000 coming from a congressional appropriation—a government donation that made Allen the "first and only colored man thus honored." The first money given for the project had been $50 by the white governor of Arkansas. The largest individual donation, of $100, came from a Black Southerner. Brown also noted that even the poorest Blacks had given what they could. His remarks were surely made to note the unifying na-ture of the Allen statue: it brought the races and classes together. He argued that "prejudice [is] not invincible" and reminded his listeners of the greatness of African Americans such as Allen. While many did not remember such historical figures, he said, "The mistake is in us—we demand this recognition."[46] African Americans were now taking their place in the nation, Brown showed, especially by publicizing key Black figures.

However, the statue of Allen was not the only contribution by African Americans. While dismissed or forgotten by historians, one man displayed technical and entre-preneurial success: Alexander Ashbourne patented a process for refining coconut oil and keeping it from going rancid. He established a factory in California and later went abroad, taking his product to an international market. He came back to the

United States for the Centennial, however, spending $7,000 to bring his product to the fair. His products included "the desiccated coconut for pies, puddings, etc., pomade for the skin matting from the fiber of the husk, vinegar white and pure from the milk, perfumed soap, tooth-powder from their shells, hair-oil, lithographers and other inks, etc."[47] At the fair, he marketed his product, showcasing that the centennial was also a trade show for businessmen, including Black entrepreneurs. Another notable contribution was by Benjamin Montgomery of Mississippi, who had been the property of Joseph Davis of Davis Bend. Joseph Davis, of course, was the brother of the president of the Confederacy, Jefferson Davis. Montgomery became the manager of the Davis Plantation in the antebellum years, and after the Civil War he bought the place for himself. The former slave won first place for his superior commercial cotton at the exposition. It was with this example that one really sees the changes that Reconstruction brought to the South, even if they did not last.[48]

Finally, the presence of Civil War soldiers, rather than promoting reunion, played a much more complicated role at the world's fair. The Army of the Potomac decided to hold its 1876 reunion in Philadelphia specifically because of the Centennial. On July 3, about five thousand marched through the Centennial fairgrounds, with men carrying "the tattered and worn battle flags . . . [of] the late war."[49] One of the speakers was John Dix, a former Union general now serving as governor of New York. He placed the meeting in the context of the centennial anniversary, noting that one hundred years earlier the colonies had stressed a right for representative government and an individual's political voice. The century ended, however, in "the assertion and application . . . of the great principle of universal emancipation." Both free government and free people were the reason to celebrate the centennial. He devoted nine of the remaining twelve pages of his speech to explaining the country's history of slavery and the eventual abolition of that system. Abolition made the Civil War the second greatest political event in the country, second only to the Declaration of Independence. The conflict itself, without abolition, "will only be remembered as one of those unsuccessful attempts to overthrow a government," but emancipation "and their elevation to the rank of freemen by a single act of executive authority, stands alone in the annals of our race." Thus, the New Yorker insisted that slavery and abolition were central to the war.[50]

But Dix did not view slavery as a sectional issue; rather, he said, "It belongs to the history of the country," condemning the North as well as the South, making slavery a national sin. Dix was perhaps too optimistic when he said that slavery should be "discussed without passion or prejudice." To illustrate his point, he referred to an earlier draft of the Declaration of Independence in which Jefferson criticized the king for forcing slavery on America. After covering the ban of slavery in the Northwest Ordinance, he moved on to the constitutional convention, where he celebrated the ban of the slave trade. He then tipped his hat to Virginia, which would "at a future day regard with satisfaction and pride the part her revolutionary sages bore in this triumph of freedom and humanity." Of course, that could not occur yet, he acknowledged, because "there are wounds to be healed." Dix elected to not discuss the Missouri Compromise or the "angry" congressional debates, but moved on to praise Abraham Lincoln, who "held sacred" every right and who led the fight for the Union and to end slavery. Cutting off criticisms of Lincoln operating outside the bounds of law, Dix defended the martyred president for not emancipating slaves sooner. Although Lincoln personally hated slavery, he had taken an oath that required him to save the Union, and he could not emancipate the slaves in the rebel states "while there was hope that they would return to their allegiance." But the president did free the slaves and by doing so "introduced a new element into the conflict." He told his audience: "You were no longer fighting for the preservation of the Union alone: you were fighting also for the vindication of the principles of universal freedom." Loss would have meant both the dissolution of the Union and the reestablishment of slavery.[51]

Dix then shared a private letter he had received from the president while serving as a general. Lincoln asked him whether "colored troops" should be used to guard two forts, "leaving the white forces . . . to be employed elsewhere." One fort was perhaps too strategic to leave in the hands of new recruits, but at the other "there was no place where they could be used with less objection." To underscore the point that African Americans were worthy of respect and that they had served well in the army, Dix went on to recount the story of the assault on Fort Wagner, which proved Black soldiers' "courage and constancy." While he gave much of the credit to Robert Shaw in his leadership, calling him a martyr, he acknowledged the Black troops' own fighting ability. Shaw and the 54th Massachusetts regiment provided the nation "an additional fund of patriotism" and bravery to draw from "the four millions raised by Mr. Lincoln to the rank of freemen." Thus, Black soldiers helped to secure their own freedom, as well as to preserve the Union.[52]

Dix closed with an appeal to "re-establish the amicable relations which existed before the war," but admitted that there were those in the North who wanted revenge and those in the South who "persevere in fomenting the ancient bitterness, and insist that their prosperity depends on the restoration of a social order on which the hand of Providence has set the seal of fate." Nevertheless, he called for restoring the spirit of 1776, "promoting our common prosperity" and expressing thanks for the deliverance "from the dangers we have passed." He stressed the technological progress of the previous one hundred years and argued that the United States was now an equal to countries of Europe. Indeed, the exhibition was proof of that.[53]

William Tecumseh Sherman also spoke at the meeting. The famous Union general pointed toward forgiveness but at the same time turned it into something of a joke. He connected his speech to Dix's but also suggested that if any of them had been born in the South, they, too, might have embraced slavery, so "let us therefore forgive and forget—provided they do the same." This element of reciprocity occurred again: "If the people of the south will accept the garland wreath and wear it gracefully and kindly, let us thank God and be pleased. . . . We cherish only feelings of charity, of kindness, of forgiveness toward the people of the south." But he did not stop there. If Southerners were not willing to accept the outcome of the war and set aside old differences, Sherman said, "These are the things" and pointed toward the cannon on the stage. The audience responded with "great applause." He told them, "I see that you understand your business," while they shouted, "You showed it to us once." Sherman's joke was also a threat, coming as it did from the man who had led the March to the Sea, and the audience appreciated it. Many Northerners saw the problem with being so caught up in sentimentality about reconciliation: it ignored what Southerners were doing and saying. With that in mind, Sherman counteracted the tendency to promote forgiveness at all costs, and his Northern audience agreed with him.[54]

Black soldiers also had their place at the fairgrounds. While previous historians have painted an image of racial exclusion at the Centennial, several incidents reveal the complexities of race relations and the conflicting legacies of the Civil War.[55] There were at least two encampments of African American soldiers—on the opening day and on Connecticut Day in August. Other sources hint at further visits by Black militias.[56] Even more significant: on that opening day in May, Black regiments marched during the proceedings. One paper reported that the USCC "was severely criticized by the followers after Democratic idols" for allowing Black soldiers to parade on the fairgrounds, indicating just how radical this march truly was. Every band that encamped had to have written permission from the governor, as well.[57] The context of race relations that summer made the Black soldiers at the Centennial all the more controversial. When white Southerners became angry about a Black militia assembling in South Carolina in July 1876, the result was a race riot called the Hamburg Massacre. Six Black soldiers and one white man were killed and a number of others were wounded by the mob.

Another significant event occurred for African Americans military men that speaks to the very real changes that occurred during Reconstruction. In 1873, West Point admitted one of the academy's first African Americans, Henry Ossian Flipper, into officer training. Flipper graduated after four years and entered the U.S. Army, but he was still cadet in 1876 when his class was ordered to encamp for ten days at the Centennial. Three hundred cadets made their way to Philadelphia that summer, but none attracted more attention than Flipper. In his autobiography, he remembered that some were surprised to see him there, including one person who commented: "You are quite an exhibition yourself. No one was expecting to see a colored cadet."[58]

A Philadelphia paper commented on Flipper's presence, noting that his fellow cadets had nothing to do with him. When asked whether he was intelligent, a cadet replied that he was, that he saw no reason why he would not graduate, and that "in color he is rather light." An African American paper picked up on this news item, lamenting, "It is a pity your whole race did not have less to do with the negro, and then this young colored cadet . . . would not have been in color so light." While calling to mind the sexual coercion that coexisted with slavery, the quote also hints at anger about interracial relationships' having become more common after the war.[59] The West Point cadets also marched in the July 4 celebration, so it is likely Flipper was with them. Being Black and a military man was incredibly significant as white Southerners especially saw this expression of masculinity as a threat to their stability and power. Naturally, a slave would not have become a cadet; thus, Flipper became a living symbol of both the Civil War and Reconstruction. Both his admittance to West Point and his acceptance at the Centennial indicated the tremendous progress won by the abolition of slavery. However, Flipper did discuss in his autobiography that being a Black cadet was not easy. Writing about the event in later years, he did not shy away from recounting instances of casual racism and outright hostility he faced, which suggests that he also would have explained harsh treatment at the fair. Instead, the trip to the Centennial proved to be an exciting diversion for him.

Certainly, many visitors shared Flipper's experience and came to the Centennial to have fun. But they also brought with them individual understandings of the context of the day. Thus, debates about the meaning of Reconstruction played out both during the planning and at the Philadelphia Centennial Exhibition itself. Organizers intended to bring the country back together again, but in the end the bitter politics and deep cultural differences proved to be too much. At all stages, the issues of Reconstruction came into play, and the fair focused more on current political events than on the American Revolution it was supposed to celebrate. Former rebels, African Americans, and Union veterans all went to the Centennial fair and made the nation's birthday party reflect their own image.

Notes

1. U.S. Centennial Commission, *Journal of the Proceedings of the United States Centennial Commission at Philadelphia, 1872* (Philadelphia: E.C. Markley and Son, 1872), 42.
2. Ibid., 65–66.

3. On the women's centennial committee, see Mary Frances Cortado, "Toward a New Century: Women and the Philadelphia Centennial Exhibition, 1876," *Pennsylvania Magazine of History and Biography* 107, no. 1 (1983): 113–35.

4. For more on national economic debates during Reconstruction, see Terry L. Seip, *The South Returns to Congress: Men, Economic Measures, and Intersectional Relationships, 1868–1879* (Baton Rouge: Louisiana State University Press, 1983).

5. Joseph R. Hawley, *The Centennial Celebration and International Exhibition of 1876—Their Advantages, Duties, and Honors. Speech of Hon. Joseph R. Hawley, of Connecticut, in the House of Representatives, May 7, 1874* (Washington, DC: Government Printing Office, 1874), 24.

6. *Congressional Record,* 43rd Cong., 1st sess., 3675–76.

7. Ibid., appendix, 252.

8. Ibid., 270.

9. Ibid., 249.

10. Ibid., 4782

11. Ibid., 44th Cong., 1st sess., 527–28.

12. Ibid., 522.

13. S. Edgar Trout, *The Story of the Centennial of 1876: Golden Anniversary* (Lancaster, PA: N.p., 1929), 25–26.

14. *Congressional Record,* 44th Cong., 1st sess., 968, 501.

15. *National Republican,* January 21, 1876.

16. *Louisiana Democrat,* June 17, 1874.

17. *Philadelphia Inquirer,* May 11, 1876; Dee Brown, *The Year of the Century: 1876* (New York: Charles Scribner's Sons, 1966), 120. The historians who reference this encounter have all agreed that racism caused the guard to prevent Douglass's ascension, but newspaper accounts provide the impression that confusion reigned on opening day and that the crowds and noise were oppressive. African American newspapers did not reference this event, and Douglass apparently never mentioned it, either, which indicates that the guard intended no malice. Douglass returned to the fair in June, which likewise indicates that he did not hold any grudges about the earlier incident. *Rutland Daily Globe,* June 6, 1876. For an alternative interpretation, see Philip S. Foner, "Black Participation in the Centennial of 1876," *Phylon* 39, no. 4 (1978): 283–96.

18. *Macon Weekly Telegraph,* May 16, 1876.

19. *Bristol News,* May 16, 1876.

20. *Tuscaloosa Gazette,* quoted in *National Republican,* June 2, 1876.

21. Edward Strahan, *Illustrated Catalogue: The Masterpieces of the International Exhibition, 1876, the Art Gallery* (Philadelphia: Gebbie and Barrie, 1876), 63.

22. Kirk Savage explains how this specific type of statue gained prominence in the years after the Civil War. For his interpretation of how the citizen soldier homogenized the racial landscape and helped reconcile nationalism and individualism, see Kirk Savage, *Standing Soldiers, Kneeling Slaves: Race, War, and Monument in Nineteenth Century America* (Princeton, NJ: Princeton University Press, 1997), 162–208. Originally, the Maryland government decreed that the Antietam Cemetery would inter both Union and Confederate dead. But the park managers went around this law, and only national soldiers would be buried there. For the debate over admitting Confederate veterans to Antietam Cemetery and the refusal of this plan, see John R. Neff, *Honoring the Civil War Dead: Commemoration and the Problem of Reconciliation* (Lawrence: University Press of Kansas, 2005), 116–24.

23. *Philadelphia Inquirer,* May 17, 1876. The Pennsylvania state legislature commissioned the painting, granting $30,000 for its creation: *Frank Leslie's Illustrated Newspaper,* March 9, 1867.

24. "The Centennial Exhibition," *Christian Recorder*, September 28, 1876

25. *Trenton State Gazette*, June 1, 1876

26. *Times-Picayune*, September 3, 1876.

27. Bricktop, *Going to the Centennial, and A Guy to the Great Exhibition*, Laughing Series 7 (New York: Collin and Small, 1876), 32.

28. Susanna Gold discusses this illustration in "'Fighting It over Again': *The Battle of Gettysburg at the 1876 Centennial Exhibition*," *Civil War History* 54, no. 3 (2008): 277–310. Brian Craig Miller also includes the illustration, arguing that it highlights the real battle that soldiers, particularly in the South, faced in the 1870s—dealing with their lost limbs in *Empty Sleeves: Amputation in the Civil War South* (Athens: University of Georgia Press: 2015), 141

29. Theodore Bryant Kingsbury, *The International Exhibition Guide for the Southern States: The Only Guide Book Specially Suited to the Southern Visitor* (Raleigh, NC: R. T. Fulghum, 1876), 5–6.

30. *Hinds County Gazette*, February 23, 1876.

31. Ibid., May 17, 1876.

32. James D. McCabe, *The Illustrated History of the Centennial Exhibition, Held in Commemoration of the One Hundredth Anniversary of American Independence* (Philadelphia: National, 1876), 766.

33. For the illustrations, see Frank Leslie, *Frank Leslie's Historical Register of the Centennial Exhibition, 1876* (New York: Frank Leslie's Publishing House, 1877), 204–5.

34. Elizabeth Fox-Genovese and Eugene Genovese, *The Mind of the Master Class: History and Faith in the Southern Slaveholders' Worldview* (Cambridge: Cambridge University Press, 2005), 353–58. For a classic alternative analysis of how chivalry was part of the ethic of honor, see Bertram Wyatt-Brown, *Southern Honor: Ethics and Behavior in the Old South* (New York: Oxford University Press, [1982] 2007).

35. *Hand-book to the Centennial Grounds and Fairmount Park: Where to Go and What to See* (Philadelphia: John E. Potter, 1876), 16.

36. *Vicksburg Tribune*, reprinted in *Hinds County Gazette*, May 17, 1876.

37. "The Centennial Celebration," *New National Era*, February 22, 1872.

38. "Why Can't We Do It," *Christian Recorder*, March 5, 1874.

39. "That Statue to Allen," *Christian Recorder*, August 13, 1876.

40. "Allen Monument," *Christian Recorder*, November 5, 1874.

41. "Allen Monument Circular," *Christian Recorder*, November 26, 1874.

42. "Allen Statue," *Christian Recorder*, January 27, 1876.

43. "We Are Coming," *Christian Recorder*, February 3, 1876.

44. "The Allen Monument a Success!" *Christian Recorder*, September 7, 1876.

45. "Extract from an Address by Rev. J. T. Jenifer in Laying the Base of the Allen Monument in the Centennial Grounds," *People's Advocate*, July 8, 1876

46. "Bishop Allen Monument," *Christian Recorder*, November 9, 1876.

47. "Walks through the Centennial Exposition," *Christian Recorder*, February 8, 1877.

48. For more on the story of Montgomery, see Janet Sharp Hermann, *The Pursuit of a Dream* (Oxford: University of Mississippi Press, 1999).

49. *San Francisco Bulletin*, July 5, 1876.

50. *Society of the Army of the Potomac, Record of Proceedings at the Seventh Annual Re-union, Held in Philadelphia, PA, June 6, 1876* (New York: American Church Press, 1877), 10–11.

51. Ibid., 14, 17. His speech fits well with Gary Gallagher's interpretation: see Gary Gallagher, *The Union War* (Cambridge, MA: Harvard University Press, 2011).

52. *Society of the Army of the Potomac*, 18–19.

53. Ibid., 20.
54. Ibid., 29.
55. For views arguing that the fair shut out African Americans, see William A. Blair, *Cities of the Dead: Contesting the Memory of the Civil War in the South, 1865–1914* (Chapel Hill: University of North Carolina Press, 2004), 139; Kathleen Clark, *Defining Moments: African American Commemoration and Political Culture in the South, 1863–1913* (Chapel Hill: University of North Carolina Press, 2005), 123; Foner, "Black Participation in the Centennial of 1876"; Robert Rydell, *All the World's a Fair: Visions of Empire at American International Expositions, 1876–1916* (Chicago: University of Chicago Press, 1984), 27–29. While less overt, Gary Nash likewise paints an image of racial exclusion even while noting that Black men assembled and drilled on the fairgrounds: Gary Nash, *First City: Philadelphia and the Forging of Historical Memory* (Philadelphia: University of Pennsylvania Press, 2002), 270–71. Bruno Gilberti, in an aside, calls for a "more nuanced understanding of the exhibition as a social phenomenon" after sharing a quote detailing racial intermingling: Bruno Gilberti, *Designing the Centennial: A History of the 1876 International Exhibition in Philadelphia* (Lexington: University Press of Kentucky, 2002), 96. Ultimately, Foner's article has proved to be the most influential, and many have taken his word as the defining interpretation of the fair.
56. In reporting that Virginia failed to appropriate funds, the *People's Advocate* also noted that the Attucks and Carney Guards of Richmond were expected to attend: *People's Advocate,* April 29, 1876. In a report on the opening day's festivities, the *New York Herald* noted that two different Black regiments marched: *New York Herald,* May 11, 1876.
57. *Daily Inter Ocean,* May 27, 1876.
58. Henry Ossian Flipper, *The Colored Cadet at West Point: Autobiography of Lieut. Henry Ossian Flipper, U.S.A., First Graduate of Color from the U.S. Military Academy* (New York: Homer Lee, 1878), 119.
59. *Savannah Tribune,* July 22, 1876.

Mark Twain and the Failure
of Radical Reconstruction

J. Mills Thornton

P ERHAPS NO SIGNIFICANT AMERICAN writer of his generation was more
deeply conflicted about the events of the Civil War and Reconstruction than
Mark Twain. Twain grew up surrounded by slavery. The Census of 1840,
when young Sam was four years old, records his father, the attorney John Marshall Clemens, as owning a young Black woman between ten and twenty-three.
An attorney, and eventually a judge, Clemens may have acquired additional slaves
before his death in 1847, though by 1850 the family no longer owned any.[1] By that
time, however, their cousin Jeremiah Clemens, of whom they were quite proud,
was a U.S. senator from Alabama and was spouting Southern rights doctrines in
the debates over the Compromise of 1850.[2] With the secession of states of the
lower South, Sam, now twenty-five, answered the summons of Missouri's Southern rights Governor Claiborne Jackson and joined his Hannibal friends in forming
a militia company to repel the Union forces dispatched to St. Louis by President
Lincoln. Sam was elected the company's second lieutenant. After several weeks
of marching around the Missouri countryside, the young men received word that
a Union detachment under Ulysses S. Grant was on its way to engage them. Sam
promptly deserted and took half the company with him. Later that summer, he
accompanied his older brother Orion to the Nevada Territory, where he waited out
the war, after the passage of the Conscription Act, effectively as a draft dodger.
During this period, his enemies at least had no hesitation in classifying him as
a Copperhead.[3]

Twain's courtship of Olivia Langdon during 1868 and 1869, and their marriage
in February 1870, introduced him to many Burned-Over District abolitionists who
were Langdon family friends, and these new acquaintances led him to an increasingly clear understanding of the immorality of slavery. After 1873, Harriet Beecher
Stowe and her husband were the Clemenses' next-door neighbors in Hartford,
Connecticut. Twain eventually came to believe that the emancipation of the slaves

had not only freed them but, in a sense, had freed Southern whites, as well, from the bondage of an institution that had prevented their region from fully embracing American democratic ideals. Nevertheless, Twain's deep affection for the antebellum world of his youth and early manhood remained. It is apparent in his reminiscences *Life on the Mississippi*, published in 1883, the same year that the U.S. Supreme Court declared unconstitutional the Civil Rights Act of 1875. It is even clearer in *Tom Sawyer*, the loving and profoundly nostalgic portrait of antebellum Southern boyhood that he published in 1876, in the very midst of the bitterly contested presidential election that would bring the federal government's efforts to reconstruct the South to their final, disastrous conclusion.

The conflict between Twain's affectionate memories of his childhood and his clarified understanding of the injustice that had given form to his world dominates *Tom Sawyer*'s sequel, *Huckleberry Finn*, which appeared in 1885. In *Huckleberry Finn*, the warmly humorous surface is at every moment prepared to crack to reveal a dark and violent substrate of callous cruelty, vicious exploitation, and ignorance. But for all its ability to bring this conflict vividly to life, *Huckleberry Finn* offers no solutions to it. We are left, as Twain was also, to recognize and accept the coexistence of both levels of reality as Huck has experienced them. And that inevitably led Twain—who had just lived through the failure of Reconstruction—to muse on the possibility of transforming such a society. The result was *A Connecticut Yankee in King Arthur's Court*. Twain began work on this novel in 1885, just as *Huckleberry Finn* was appearing, and wrote much of it in 1887. It was published in 1889. Though set in a heavily mythologized sixth century, it is a novel about the capacity of the modernizing democratic faith of a Connecticut Yankee to reform the recalcitrant reality of a world with very different assumptions and ideals. It is, in other words, an allegory about the possibility of Reconstruction.[4]

Twain's own doubts about Reconstruction are unmistakable. His novel *The Gilded Age*, coauthored with his close friend Charles Dudley Warner, would christen the entire period with its mordantly satirical name. Published in 1873, the book gave powerful expression to the hostility of the Liberal Republicans in the preceding year's presidential election to the corruption of the Reconstruction Congress, which they regarded as ruled by special interests and posturing hypocrites. One of the latter is the character Senator Dilworthy, a Stalwart Republican scoundrel who pretends to be a friend of the freedmen to line his own pockets. Despite his commitment to the Liberal Republican perspective, however, Twain was fully aware that there was much in the South that needed reformation; *Huckleberry Finn* rests squarely on this recognition. It is just that, thanks to his Southern upbringing, Twain also recognized that the region retained cultural strengths not readily apparent to Northern Republicans, whether Liberal or Stalwart. It was the existence of these two, warring realities with which Twain sets out to confront the Connecticut Yankee in his new novel.

The Yankee, whose name we learn late in the novel is Hank Morgan, is a foreman at the Colt Arms factory in Hartford, who as a result of a blow sustained in 1879 in a fight with one of the workmen, regains consciousness in Arthurian England, in 528, and is promptly taken prisoner by one of the Knights of the Round Table, Sir Kay. The Yankee is, he tells us at the outset, "a Yankee of the Yankees—and practical; yes, and nearly barren of sentiment, I suppose—or poetry, in other words."[5] And so, "being a practical Connecticut man," he almost at once concludes, "I would boss the whole country inside of three months; for I judged I would have the start of the best educated man in the kingdom by a matter of thirteen hundred years and upwards" (63). Indeed, playing on the ignorance and superstition of the court, he has, within two days, used his knowledge of an impending solar eclipse to compel King Arthur to declare him Boss, and the rest of the novel is given over to his efforts to use this power to bring modernity and democracy to the Dark Ages.

From the beginning, the Yankee understands his opponents in this enterprise to be the aristocracy and the established church. He takes the aristocracy to be the source of the hierarchical society, imposed by force on the subordinate classes. And he takes the church to be the institution that keeps the lower classes from recognizing their oppression. The masses

> were nothing but rabbits. It was pitiful for a person born in a wholesome free atmosphere to listen to their humble and hearty outpourings of loyalty toward their king and Church and nobility; as if they had any more occasion to love and honor king and Church and noble than a slave has to love and honor the lash, or a dog has to love and honor the stranger that kicks him! . . . The most of King Arthur's British nation were slaves, pure and simple, and bore that name, and wore the iron collar on their necks; and the rest were slaves in fact, but without the name; they imagined themselves men and freemen, and called themselves so. The truth was, the nation as a body was in the world for one object, and one only: to grovel before king and Church and noble; to slave for them, sweat blood for them, starve that they might be fed, work that they might play, drink misery to the dregs that they might be happy. . . . There you see the hand of that awful power, the Roman Catholic Church. In two or three little centuries it had converted a nation of men to a nation of worms. Before the day of the Church's supremacy in the world, men were men, and held their heads up, and had a man's pride and spirit and independence; and what of greatness and position a person got, he got mainly by achievement, not by birth. But then the Church came to the front, with an axe to grind; . . . she preached (to the commoner) humility,

obedience to superiors, the beauty of self-sacrifice; she preached (to the commoner) meekness under insult; preached (still to the commoner, always to the commoner,) patience, meanness of spirit, non-resistance under oppression; and she introduced heritable ranks and aristocracies, and taught all Christian populations of the earth to bow down to them and worship them. (109–13)

The Yankee's hostility to Roman Catholicism knows no bounds—accurately reflecting in fact the influence of Know-Nothingism in the Yankee's New England. But to maintain it, he has almost willfully to blind himself to the sources of the church's strength. When a group of priests at one point informs him of the oppression of a castle functionary, they "were generously hot to have him punished. Something of this disagreeable sort was turning up every now and then. I mean, episodes that showed that not all priests were frauds and self-seekers, but that many, even the great majority, of these that were down on the ground among the common people, were sincere and right-hearted, and devoted to the alleviation of human troubles and sufferings. Well, it was a thing which could not be helped, so I seldom fretted about it . . . But I did not like it, for it was just the sort of thing to keep people reconciled to an Established Church." (206–7) Despite such evidence, the Yankee presses on with his scheme "to overthrow the Catholic Church and set up the Protestant faith on its ruins—not as an Established Church, but as a go-as-you-please one" (444); he intends to have the church "cut up into forty free sects, so that they will police each other, as had been the case in the United States in my time" (207). His republic is to have freedom of religion, just as long as everyone is a Protestant.

The same blindness characterizes the Yankee's understanding of the aristocracy. Even at the outset he notes that "the speech and behavior of these people were gracious and courtly" (66), but he is repulsed by their gratuitous and casual brutality: "Many a time I had seen a couple of boys, strangers, meet by chance, and say simultaneously, 'I can lick you,' and go at it on the spot; but I had always imagined until now that that sort of thing belonged to children only, and was a sign and mark of childhood; but here were these big boobies sticking to it and taking pride in it clear up into full age and beyond." Yet he is forced to concede that

there was something very engaging about these great simple-hearted creatures, something attractive and lovable. There did not seem to be brains enough in the entire nursery, so to speak, to bait a fish-hook with; but you didn't seem to mind that, after a little, because you soon saw that brains were not needed in a society like that, and indeed, would have marred it, hindered it, spoiled its symmetry—perhaps rendered its existence impossible. There was a fine manliness observable in almost every face; and in some a certain loftiness and sweetness that rebuked your belittling criticisms and stilled them. (68–69)

Throughout the novel, the clarity of the Yankee's ideological analysis of the social situation keeps being confounded by the complexity of the social reality. In fact, he is himself increasingly altered by it. He is deeply hostile to the church's manipulation of popular superstition and ignorance, but he entirely depends on that superstition and ignorance to maintain his power. In the Valley of Holiness, when he discovers that the Holy Fountain has ceased flowing not because of divine retribution but because it is actually a well that has sprung a leak, he does not simply repair it but, rather, arranges an elaborate fireworks display to awe the thousands who have gathered to watch as he commands the flow to resume. Then he actually teaches the monks who tend the fountain to operate the pump he has installed behind a screen so they can continue satisfying—and exploiting—the many pilgrims who visit the shrine (262–70). Similarly, it had been exactly the cheekiness and lack of deference of the young page Clarence that had originally commended him to the Yankee. Under the Yankee's tutelage, Clarence grows up to be his right-hand man and administrator of the Yankee's many enterprises. The Yankee therefore puts Clarence in charge of bringing out the first newspaper, the *Camelot Weekly Hosannah and Literary Volcano*. But when the initial issue appears, the Yankee is put off precisely because it displays Clarence's characteristic impudence. "It was good Arkansas journalism," the Yankee concedes, "but this was not Arkansas. . . . [T]here was too lightsome a tone of flippancy all through the paper. It was plain I had undergone a considerable change without noticing it. I found myself unpleasantly affected by pert little irreverencies which would have seemed but proper and airy graces of speech at an earlier period of my life" (304).

These changes are reflected in the Yankee's growing appreciation of the virtues of the aristocracy, particularly because of his increasingly warm friendship with King Arthur and Sir Launcelot. His new understanding matures during his travels with King Arthur incognito to observe the condition of the kingdom. When they come upon a hut where the family is dying of smallpox, the Yankee wants to flee the infection. King Arthur tells him, "Ye mean well, and ye speak not unwisely. But it were shame that a king should know fear, and shame that belted knight should withhold his hand where be such as need succor." The king goes into the loft of the hut to bring down a dying girl:

> There was a slight noise from the direction of the dim corner where the ladder was. It was the king, descending. I could see that he was bearing something in one arm, and assisting himself with the other. He came forward into the light; upon his breast lay a slender girl of fifteen. She was but half-conscious; she was dying of small-pox. Here was heroism at its last and loftiest possibility, its utmost summit; this was challenging death in the open field unarmed, with all the odds

against the challenger, no reward set upon the contest, and no admiring world in silks and cloth of gold to gaze and applaud; and yet the king's bearing was as serenely brave as it had always been in those cheaper contests where knight meets knight in equal fight and clothed in protecting steel. He was great now; sublimely great. The rude statues of his ancestors in his palace should have an addition—I would see to that; and it would not be a mailed king killing a giant or a dragon, like the rest; it would be a king in commoner's garb bearing death in his arms that a peasant mother might look her last upon her child and be comforted. (329–32)

The Yankee's emerging recognition that the aristocracy were not merely the exploitative parasites he had thought them to be, together with his grudging appreciation of the sincerity of the common clergy, might have permitted him to develop a more nuanced comprehension of the social structure that surrounded him, had they not almost immediately been overwhelmed by his own devastating experience of slavery.

Twain almost certainly has sent his Yankee to the sixth century exactly so that he can force a readership saturated with racism to contemplate slavery practiced on white people. And he now leads us to confront all its horrors. The enslavement of the Yankee and the king results from a series of incidents growing out of a heated quarrel that the Yankee has with a village miller over protective tariffs, an allusion, of course, to antebellum American political conflict (368–79). And we are very quickly carried into a consideration of the contrast between American civil liberties and the operation of the Fugitive Slave Act of 1850. As the Yankee and the king are being sold, "by hideous contrast a redundant orator was making a speech to another gathering not thirty steps away in fulsome laudation of 'our glorious British liberties,'" something exceedingly unlikely in sixth-century England but commonplace in antebellum America. The protestations of the Yankee and king that they are freemen attract the orator's attention. "'If indeed ye are freemen,'" he tells them, "'ye have nought to fear—the God-given liberties of Britain are about ye for your shield and shelter! (Applause) Ye shall soon see. Bring forth your proofs.'" "'Thou'rt insane, man,'" the king storms. "'It were better, and more in reason, that this thief and scoundrel here prove that we are *not* freemen.'" But as the Yankee knows, "This same infernal law had existed in our own South in my own time, more than thirteen hundred years later, and under it hundreds of freemen who could not prove that they were freemen had been sold into life-long slavery without the circumstance making any particular impression upon me; but the minute law and auction block came into my personal experience, a thing which had been merely improper before became suddenly hellish" (391–92). From this point the Yankee's personal experience extends to include a brutal slave trader, a wretched coffle marched from town to town, heartrending sales of wives from husbands and mothers from children, savage floggings and inhuman burnings at the stake, all of which Twain describes in bitter detail. When the Yankee and the king are just on the point of being hanged for the death of the slave trader in a struggle, the Knights of the Round Table, led by Sir Launcelot, arrive on bicycles to rescue them. If the knights had come on horses, they would have been too late, but Clarence has taught them to ride bicycles, and this bit of modern technology saves the day. After having lived through the abominations of slavery and having been rescued by modernity, the Yankee puts away all of what had been his growing consciousness of the society's complexity and presses on without further hesitation toward its total transformation, and to ultimate disaster.

The core of the Yankee's failure lies not in his misdiagnoses of the social roles of the aristocracy and the church, though they are profound. It lies in his misunderstanding of the attitudes and beliefs of the commoners. Despite all of the evidence of their deference and religious devotion all around him, and that he himself often notes, he remains convinced that they actually long for equality and democracy. And his conviction derives in substantial part from his beliefs about the antebellum South. When many peasants in one neighborhood join in the lynching of others suspected in the burning of a baron's castle, the Yankee comments, "The painful thing observable about all this business was, the alacrity with which this oppressed community had turned their cruel hands against their own class in the interest of the common oppressor. . . . This was depressing—to a man with the dream of a republic in his head. It reminded me of a time thirteen centuries away, when the 'poor whites' of our South who were always despised and frequently insulted by the slave-lords around them, and who owed their base condition simply to the presence of slavery in their midst, were yet pusillanimously ready to side with the slave-lords in all political moves for the upholding and perpetuating of slavery, and did also finally shoulder their muskets and pour out their lives in an effort to prevent the destruction of that very institution which degraded them." But the Yankee then continues, "And there was only one redeeming feature connected with that pitiful piece of history; and that was, that secretly the 'poor white' did detest the slave-lord; and did feel his own shame. That feeling was not brought to the surface, but the fact that it was there and could have been brought out, under favoring circumstances, was something—in fact it was enough; for it showed that a man is at bottom a man, after all, even if it doesn't show on the outside." And a bit later, when under questioning of the Yankee one of the peasants reveals his secret sympathy with the arsonists, the Yankee exults, "There it was, you see. A man *is* a man, at bottom. Whole ages of abuse and oppression cannot crush the manhood clear out of him. Whoever thinks it a mistake, is himself mistaken. Yes, there is plenty good enough material for a republic in the most degraded people that ever existed—even the Russians" (343, 346).

In the grip of this conviction, the Yankee spends his first years in power scouring the countryside for people who express some discontent with the existing order, whom he then sends to secret reeducation centers, which he calls "manfactories," to be taught the tenets of democracy and various technological skills. The aristocracy, he is convinced, is nothing more than a group of Southern large slaveholders: "The blunting effects of slavery upon the slaveholder's moral perceptions are known and conceded, the world over; and a privileged class, an aristocracy, is but a band of slaveholders under another name. . . . One needs but to hear an aristocrat speak of the classes that are below him to recognize—and in but indifferently modified measure—the very air and tone of the actual slaveholder; and behind these are the slaveholder's spirit, the slaveholder's blunted feeling. They are the result of the same cause in both cases: the possessor's old and inbred custom of regarding himself as a superior being" (285). If he can convince King Arthur to abolish slavery, the Yankee then expects his corps of reeducated commoners to become the shock troops of republicanism. The king resists abolition until he and the Yankee are themselves enslaved. After this experience, the king embraces the reform. The Yankee then overawes the aristocracy by killing a number of them at a joust with a brace of pistols. With that, he makes public his man-factories, and economic and social transformation—railroads, telephones, schools and colleges—spreads rapidly across the land. But though the Yankee has successfully transformed the English political economy, he has reckoned without the English heart.

The Yankee has turned the Round Table into a stock exchange. But when Sir Launcelot manipulates the stock of a railroad being built from London to Dover, the aggrieved knights on the losing end of the deal take vengeance by revealing to Arthur Launcelot's illicit affair with Queen Guinevere. The result is a civil war in which Arthur, Launcelot, and much of the aristocracy are killed. The Yankee seizes this moment to attempt to establish his republic. He issues a proclamation filled with American assumption:

> The monarchy has lapsed, it no longer exists. By consequence, all political power has reverted to its original source, the people of the nation. With the monarchy, its several adjuncts died also; wherefore there is no longer a nobility, no longer a privileged class, no longer an Established Church: all men are become exactly equal, they are upon one common level, and religion is free. A Republic is hereby proclaimed, as being the natural estate of a nation when authority has ceased. It is the duty of the British people to meet together immediately, and by their votes elect representatives and deliver into their hands the government. (469)

However, the church seizes on the same moment to bring to a head its long death struggle with the Yankee, now deprived of his royal protector. The papacy places all of Britain under an interdict, to continue as long as the Yankee is alive. The British masses must therefore choose between the Yankee and the established church; only one of them can survive. The Yankee, Clarence, and fifty-two teenage boys from the man-factories soon find themselves alone in a cave, besieged by the entire British nation. Even the newly emancipated slaves join against them. (In terms of the analogy with the South, Twain seems here, in common with other Liberal Republican Mugwumps and Northern Democratic supporters of Grover Cleveland—both of which Twain was, by turns—to be taking Southern election returns during the Redemption period literally rather than heeding the carpetbaggers' desperate and all too authentic warnings of Southern Democratic intimidation and fraud.)

Clarence, playing the role of the scalawag Republican to the Yankee's carpetbagger, has sought to explain to the Yankee that he is pressing his reforms too far. He pleads with the Yankee at least to proclaim only a constitutional monarchy, rather than a republic, and he tells him, of the civil war, that "'if there hadn't been any Queen Guenever, it wouldn't have come so early; but it would have come, anyway. It would have come on your account by and by; by luck, it happened to come on the queen's'" (458). The Yankee had expected the masses to rally to his cause, but at a minimum he had thought that the people educated in his man-factories would remain true to him. "'Did you think you had educated the superstition out of those people?'" Clarence asks him in exasperation. "'I certainly did think it,'" the Yankee replies. "'Well, then, you may unthink it,'" Clarence tells him (464). He says that only the fifty-two teenagers who had grown up in the protected man-factories and had known no other world could be trusted and explains that "'all the others were born in an atmosphere of superstition and reared in it. It is in their blood and bones. We imagined we had educated it out of them; they thought so, too; the Interdict woke them up like a thunderclap! It revealed them to themselves, and it revealed them to me, too.'" Only the boys "'have had no acquaintance with the Church's terrors'" (465–66).

In a sense, the entire novel is about the power of myth to create perception, as with Cervantes's Don Quixote. Early in the novel, the Yankee is induced by the maiden Alisande, whom the Yankee calls Sandy and who will become his adored wife, to undertake a quest to free a group of princesses who are being held captive by three ogres. When they arrive at the ogres' castle, the Yankee discovers that the castle is a pigsty; the princesses, a herd of hogs; and the ogres, three swineherds. Sandy is astounded that the Yankee sees pigs and not princesses (230). Just as the hogs are princesses to Sandy, longing to be freed, so the brutalized and deferential masses of Arthurian England are potential republicans to the Yankee, yearning for democracy and equality. He remains blinded by this myth to the bitter end, when it destroys both him and his dream.

What, then, is the implication of Twain's allegory for the failure of Reconstruction? The Reconstruction South had no "belted knights" or Established Church, of course. The novel is explicit, however, in equating the medieval aristocracy with large slaveholders. And in the superstition that the Yankee believes sustains the Established Church, which the Yankee calls an "established slave-pen" (185–86), Twain certainly sees the ignorance and prejudice that the nineteenth-century South had in full measure. Just as the church is able to call on fear and superstition to bind all of Britain together across its social divisions to oppose the Yankee's reforms, so the Southern Democratic Party leadership was able to call on comparable racial prejudice and fear to bind all whites together across class lines to defeat the reforms of the Radical Republicans. Does Twain have an alternative path toward which he wants to direct us?

In 1887, while he was in the midst of writing *Connecticut Yankee,* Twain commented to his devoted friend William Dean Howells that if he had lived at the time of the French Revolution, he would have been a sansculotte and a follower of Jean-Paul Marat. The novel contains numerous hints of these sentiments. The Yankee from time to time launches into a paean to "the ever-memorable and blessed [French] Revolution, which swept a thousand years of such villainy away in one swift tidal-wave of blood" (157), and he comments on "the ungetaroundable fact that, all gentle cant and philosophizing to the contrary notwithstanding, no people in this world ever did achieve their freedom by goody-goody talk and moral suasion: it being immutable law that all revolutions that will succeed, must begin in blood, whatever may answer afterward. If history teaches anything, it teaches that. What this folk needed, then, was a Reign of Terror and a guillotine." But he then immediately adds, "I was the wrong man for them" (229). As he says at another point, he often longed to resign his royal position "and get up an insurrection and turn it into a revolution; but I knew that the Jack Cade or the Wat Tyler who tried such a thing without first educating his materials up to revolution-grade is almost certain to get left" (160). And so the Yankee focused instead on his reeducation establishments.

Nevertheless, despite all the Yankee's efforts to effect a peaceful revolution, his reforms do end in the "swift tidal-wave of blood" that he had thought so purifying for the French. The civil war between Arthur and Launcelot has killed off much of the aristocracy so that, according to the Yankee's estimate, there are only some 25,000 of them left. These 25,000 lead the assault on the cave in which the Yankee, Clarence, and their fifty-two teenagers are besieged. But the Yankee and Clarence have prepared dynamite traps and successive lines of electrified fences for them—as much symbols of the achievements of modernity as are schools and railroads, of course. And particularly because the aristocrats are all encased in suits of armor, these electrified fortifications prove sufficient to kill all 25,000. Their bodies lie piled in great waves against the cave's mouth. The Yankee is initially convinced that, having eliminated the aristocratic leadership, he has won the war. He soon discovers, however, that—like the Southern Republicans late in Reconstruction, effectively unable to venture out from the towns garrisoned by Union troops—he and his boys cannot leave the cave without being murdered by the commoners united against them, because of the interdict. And if they remain in the cave, the putrefaction of the decaying aristocrats condemns them inescapably to slow death by disease. Clearly, then, the execution of the aristocracy is not to be seen as the path to a successful Reconstruction. And indeed, as a historical fact, the Reign of Terror in France led not to revolutionary triumph, but to Napoleon. Perhaps, therefore, as the Yankee himself had thought, the only real path to a successful Reconstruction lay through the gradual evolutionary process of education—a process that, on the example of the Yankee's teenage supporters, would take at least a generation.

This situation prepares the way for the final intervention of the Yankee's great rival, Merlin. The Yankee has nothing but contempt for Merlin—"that cheap old humbug, that maundering old ass," playing on "childish, idiotic, chuckle-headed, chicken-livered superstitions" (84)—and we have been led throughout the novel to see him in the same light, as the Yankee repeatedly exposes and humiliates him. Merlin is "the champion of the frivolous black arts," while the Yankee, as he sees himself, is "the champion of hard unsentimental common-sense and reason" (430). But Merlin now sneaks into the cave and casts a spell on the Yankee—a genuine, successful spell—that causes him to sleep until he awakes back in the nineteenth century. Clarence catches Merlin in the process of casting the spell, but too late. "'Ye were conquerors; ye are conquered,'" Merlin cackles. "'These others are perishing—you also. Ye shall all die in this place—every one—except *him*. He sleepeth now—and shall sleep thirteen centuries'" (489). Merlin then trips on one of the live wires and is electrocuted. He dies, however, with the contented smile of victory on his face.

The preface and postscript of the novel make clear why Merlin had wanted the Yankee to live to return to the nineteenth century rather than have him die with Clarence and the boys. When the Yankee awakes in the 1880s, he does not embrace the modernity that he has now recovered. Rather, he spends his final years, a man out of time, wandering around the remaining monuments of the Middle Ages. Twain first meets the Yankee as the Yankee is tagging along at the rear of a group touring a collection of medieval armor in Warwick Castle (47). At the end of the novel, when Twain has completed reading the Yankee's memoir and goes to his hotel room to return it, he finds the Yankee dying and, in his delirium, convinced that the nineteenth century in which he has been living has been a nightmare and that he is about to awake into the arms of his beloved wife, Sandy. Thinking that he is speaking to her, he says that in his nightmare he "'was set down, a stranger and forlorn in that strange England, with an abyss of thirteen centuries yawning between me and you! between me and my home and my friends! between me and all that is dear to me, all that could make life worth living! It was awful—awfuler than you can ever imagine, Sandy.'" As he dies, he says, "'Death is nothing, let it come, but not with those dreams, not with the torture of those hideous dreams—I cannot endure *that* again'" (493).

Obviously, we are meant to understand that Merlin had known all along that this would be the Yankee's response if, once having experienced the Arthurian world, he was then forced to reenter the reality of the modernity that he had blindly sought to force on the sixth century. It is that knowledge that is the source of Merlin's final smile of triumph. And so, if we return to the question of Twain's prescription for a successful Reconstruction, it would seem that education is not much more likely to have vanquished the forces of reaction than is a Reign of Terror. Not only did the Yankee's efforts at reeducation fail before the church's interdict, but even the Yankee's own commitment to modernity fails when, returned to it, he finds himself deprived of all the things about the Arthurian age that he had gradually and insensibly come to love and value. Twain had lived in both antebellum and postbellum eras, and he wants us to recognize that the antebellum order rested on both the violence and racial prejudice that he explored in *Huckleberry Finn* and the more benign experiences of *Tom Sawyer* and *Life on the Mississippi*. These disparate elements combined to make it highly unlikely that any Reconstruction that relied on the power of democracy—that is, on the sentiments and prejudices of voters—to transform society would ever succeed.

The transformative power of democracy, its capacity to redeem the evils of the very voters who are its constituent elements, is a distinctively American faith. Despite its failure in Reconstruction, we have since pressed on to attempt to make it work in societies around the world—something to which Twain, a leader of the American Anti-Imperialist League, became increasingly sensitive in his later years, as he sought in his own maturing experience to apply the lessons of Reconstruction to the emerging atrocities of colonialism. *A Connecticut Yankee in King Arthur's Court* is intended to be a response to this American faith. It wishes us to grapple with the question of the extent to which democratic institutions and economic modernization can successfully remedy what we perceive to be the injustices in another society.[6] "'Did you think you had educated the superstition out of those people?'" Clarence asks the Yankee. "'I certainly did think it,'" he replies. "'Well, then, you may unthink it,'" Clarence says (464).

Notes

1. In his reminiscence "The Private History of a Campaign That Failed," Twain says, "My father owned slaves," though he adds, "I had heard my father say, some years before he died, that slavery was a great wrong, and that he would free the solitary negro he then owned if he could think it right to give away the property of the family when he was so straitened in means": Mark Twain, "The Private History of a Campaign that Failed," *Century Magazine,* vol. 31, no. 2, 1882, 193.

2. On Jeremiah Clemens (1814–65), see Johanna Nicol Shields, *Freedom in a Slave Society: Stories from the Antebellum South* (New York: Cambridge University Press, 2012), 115–28, 276–86. In his autobiography, Twain makes special note of his kinship with Senator Clemens; see Mark Twain, *The Autobiography of Mark Twain,* ed. Harriet Elinor Smith, vol.1, 205, 349, 527. Like Twain, Senator Clemens became a unionist in response to the war.

3. See Joe B. Fulton, *The Reconstruction of Mark Twain: How a Confederate Bushwhacker Became the Lincoln of Our Literature* (Baton Rouge: Louisiana State University Press, 2010); on the themes of this essay, see esp. 40–49, 166–77.

4. Despite the essential role of slavery in the novel's plot and the numerous references in the text to Southerners and the South, earlier accounts have persistently understood the novel as an attempt to contrast American or democratic ideals and institutions with European or hierarchical ones. See, e.g., Darryl Baskin, "Boss Morgan: Mark Twain and American Political Culture," *Mark Twain Journal* 51 (2013): 67–85; Everett Carter, "The Meaning of A Connecticut Yankee," *American Literature* 50 (1978): 418–440; Chadwick Hansen, "The Once and Future Boss: Mark Twain's Yankee," *Nineteenth Century Fiction* 28 (1973): 62–73; Amy Kaplan, "Realism against Itself: The Urban Fictions of Twain, Howells, Dreiser and Dos Passos" (Ph.D. diss., Johns Hopkins University, Baltimore, 1982), 1–73; Stefan Kehlenbach, "'I Am an American': The Political Consequences of Hank Morgan's Lack of Identity," *Mark Twain Journal* 52 (2014): 92–111; Jerome Loving, *Confederate Bushwhacker: Mark Twain in the Shadow of the Civil War* (Lebanon, NH: University Press of New England, 2013), 197–218; Henry Nash Smith, *Mark Twain's Fable of Progress: Political and Economic Ideas in A Connecticut Yankee* (New Brunswick, NJ: Rutgers University Press, 1964). Erich Nunn, "A Connecticut Yankee in Dixie: Mark Twain's Reconstruction," *Mark Twain Annual* 9 (2011): 20–30, recognizes the centrality of Reconstruction to the meaning of the novel, but my reading of it differs from Nunn's in important respects. On the general intellectual context in which Twain wrote, see Brook Thomas, *The Literature of Reconstruction: Not in Plain Black and White* (Baltimore: Johns Hopkins University Press, 2017). On Twain's own politics, see Brook Thomas, *Civic Myths: A Law-and-Literature Approach to Citizenship* (Chapel Hill: University of North Carolina Press, 2007), 125–76.

5. Mark Twain, *A Connecticut Yankee in King Arthur's Court,* ed. Bernard L. Stein (Berkeley: University of California Press, 1979), 50. Hereafter, page numbers cited in parentheses refer to the text of the novel in this volume.

6. Joel A. Johnson makes a comparable point in "A Connecticut Yankee in Saddam's Court: Mark Twain on Benevolent Imperialism," *Perspectives on Politics* 5 (2007): 49–61. See also Kaplan, "Realism against Itself," 67.

Teaching Du Bois's *Black Reconstruction*

Garry Bertholf and Marina Bilbija

D URING FRUSTRATING PERIODS OF writer's block or lesson-planning crises, the two of us have found ourselves returning again and again to W. E. B. Du Bois's *Black Reconstruction in America* (1935). We take as our inspiration Du Bois's monumental work because its lessons extend far beyond the historiography of the Civil War and Reconstruction, illuminating the relationship among whiteness, truth claims, and storytelling that produced a racialized (read *racist*) "common sense" of American history and culture. In this essay, we make a case for the uses of *Black Reconstruction* in an English literature (or interdisciplinary) classroom and share strategies for teaching it in a variety of courses.

Even though one of us has taught primarily in the South and the other in the North, we find that our students collectively have very little to say about the period of Reconstruction, regardless of where they are from and in spite of how much they might know about the Civil War or Jim Crow. Students are typically receptive to *Black Reconstruction,* mostly because they are captivated by the beauty of its prose, but they have hardly any knowledge of the discourse in which Du Bois is intervening, given how little they were previously taught about the history of Reconstruction. In our experience, this is true of students taking English literature and Africana studies courses, majors and non-majors alike, at elite institutions across New England and down South as far as the Carolinas.

We call our readers' attention to this lacuna in our students' knowledge of American history to reveal the divide between the significance that many of us accord to the period of Reconstruction and the glaring omission of this period in our students' historical imaginations. In this context, how would the stakes of teaching *Black Reconstruction* change? For students whose first foray into Reconstruction is Du Bois, what new thoughts and ideas does *Black Reconstruction* make possible? And as we cherish the opportunity to transform this lacuna into a potentiality, we must also remain vigilant about the grip of racist historiographies from this period and how they continue to subtend national teleologies of progress and rights. More than anything else, however, we wish to seize the opportunity to re-enchant the history of Reconstruction with its radical potential, especially since this might be the very first time students ever read about the decades between the Civil War and Jim Crow. The essay that follows aims to show how positioning *Black Reconstruction* at the front and center of English literature and Africana studies syllabi has helped us teach about the relationship between literary and political representation, about structures of forgetting and revisionism in knowledge production, and about the political and intellectual stakes of citational practices. As literary scholars, we cannot speak to the specific experiences of historians teaching *Black Reconstruction,* but we hope that our discussion of its uses in English literature and Africana studies classrooms might inspire new, interdisciplinary conversations about both the study and teaching of Reconstruction.

While we both teach *The Souls of Black Folk* (1903), *Darkwater* (1920), and *Dark Princess* (1928), texts from Du Bois's oeuvre more commonly found in English literature syllabi, it is to *Black Reconstruction*—or, rather, excerpts from it—that we turn to at the beginning of our courses when we wish to set the terms and parameters of the kind of knowledge production we wish to embark on with our students. *Black Reconstruction* is one of our go-to texts when we open up discussions with our students about the relationship between institutional racism and university curricula: why we read what we read and how syllabi get constructed and replicated. For this purpose, we excerpt Du Bois's introduction (titled "To the Reader") and final chapter ("The Propaganda of History"). Indeed, the latter begins with the question "What are American children taught today about Reconstruction?"[1] Here Du Bois is worth quoting at length:

> The treatment of the period of Reconstruction reflects small credit upon American historians as scientists. We have too often a deliberate attempt so to change the facts of history that the story will make pleasant reading for Americans. . . . If history is going to be scientific, if the record of human action is going to be set down with that accuracy and faithfulness of detail which will allow its use as a measuring rod and guidepost for the future of nations, there must be set some standards of ethics in research and interpretation. . . . If, on the other hand, we are going to use history for pleasure and amusement, for inflating our national ego, and giving us a false but pleasurable sense of accomplishment, then we must give up the idea of history either as a science or as an art using the results of science, and admit frankly that we are using a version of historic fact in order to influence and educate the new generation along the way we wish. . . . It is propaganda like this that has led men in the past to insist that history is "lies agreed upon."[2]

At first glance, this passage may seem out of place in an English literature classroom because it addresses the institutional history of History rather than the discipline of English literature. Upon closer examination, however, students grasp Du Bois's critique of "the massed hirelings of Religion, Science, Education, Law, and brute force," as he puts it, or institutional racism.[3]

Of course, *Black Reconstruction* is not the only history book to be taught in English literature departments. Thomas Carlyle's histories, for example, are as central to surveys of Victorian belles lettres as Chronicles and Annals are to specialized courses in medieval and premodern English literature. Together we bring an Africana-literary approach to *Black Reconstruction* and examine its uses in academic classrooms outside the field of history while at the same time engaging with Du Bois's critique of the "Propaganda of History." Our leveraging of *Black Reconstruction*'s argument here is not merely to highlight the institutional racism of the field of history in the late nineteenth century and early to mid-twentieth century. Rather, we extend this critique to knowledge production in U.S. academia writ large, as Du Bois himself did, and, perhaps more important, we turn this critique inward to bear on our own fields. Despite the fact that it was written almost a century ago, Du Bois's magnum opus has proved to be one of our most reliable and teachable resources for relaying how race and anti-Black racism in the New World have historically informed not just the basic principles of knowledge production within and outside of the U.S. academy, but also the foundational conventions of American literary and historical narratives. These important issues extend well beyond the purview of Africana studies—again, to include history, English literature, and other related fields.

The Politics of Citation

We are happy to report that, as instructors, despite having very different racialized and gendered experiences from each other, and despite having taught in different regions of the United States, neither of us has ever had a student show up to defend the Dunning School; nor have any of our students showed up with a critique pathologizing African Americans for the so-called failure of Reconstruction. This is not to suggest that such a defense or critique is everywhere defunct. We are simply pointing out that these have not been our experiences in the classroom. One explanation for this phenomenon could be the self-selecting algorithm of course enrollments; another would be students' seemingly increasing interest in social justice and antiracism (in its varying iterations)—that is, despite all signs that the world's political center of gravity seems to be shifting rightward. Or perhaps our students are simply taught less about Reconstruction than they are about slavery or, for that matter, Jim Crow. While most of them seem barely to know what or when Reconstruction was, some of them are already reading bestsellers from the "new" historiography of slavery and capitalism. In our courses, we seek to draw the genealogical line sharply between *Black Reconstruction* and some of the more recent publications mentioned later. We do so to double down on Du Bois's important lesson in "The Propaganda of History": beware of racist citational practices.

In "The Racist Dawn of Capitalism" (2016), Peter James Hudson placed pressure on the discourses of the "new" in the popular reception of the new economic history of capitalism and slavery. Here he was referring to discussions of a body of scholarly texts published shortly after Nicholas Draper's *The Price of Emancipation: Slave-Ownership, Compensation and British Society at the End of Slavery* (2010), including Walter Johnson's *River of Dark Dreams: Slavery and Empire in the Cotton Kingdom* (2013), Edward Baptist's *The Half Has Never Been Told: Slavery and the Making of American Capitalism* (2014), and Sven Beckert's *Empire of Cotton: A Global History* (2014).[4] Like Hudson, we call this economic history "new" not because of its recent publication, but because of its indebtedness (it is more indebted, despite what some of these historians may realize or claim) to what the late Cedric Robinson has called "the Black Radical Tradition."[5] According to Hudson, Baptist and Beckert do not acknowledge their debts to this previous tradition as generously as they should, while Draper and Johnson, we are told, "approach it head on."[6] Among those from the previous generation to which we need to pay heed are Du Bois, C. L. R. James, Eric Williams, and Walter Rodney, to name a few. Indeed, seminal texts such as *Black Reconstruction in America* (1935), *The Black Jacobins* (1938), *Capitalism and Slavery* (1944), and *How Europe Underdeveloped Africa* (1972) all come to mind. In the context of specific works, Beckert's *Empire of Cotton* could have made room for mention of Du Bois's *The World and Africa* (1947), particularly Du Bois's theorization of the "cotton kingdom."[7] "Since the rise of the sugar empire and the resultant cotton kingdom," writes Du Bois, "there has been consistent effort to rationalize Negro slavery by omitting Africa from world history, so that today it is almost universally assumed that history can be truly written without reference to Negroid [*sic*] peoples. I believe this to be scientifically unsound and also dangerous for logical social conclusions."[8] To be sure, *Black Reconstruction* is another text that is frequently glossed over.

As Hudson explains, "Today, eighty years after publication, [*Black Reconstruction*] is invoked but not read, cited but not mined, and noted but not engaged. . . . [Du Bois] and other radical scholars are selectively cited, completely ignored, or borrowed without acknowledgment of either the authors or the political-economic contexts in which they were produced and to which they responded."[9] Likewise, the first edition of James's *The Black Jacobins* makes perfunctory appearances in historical and literary scholarship. As Christopher Taylor reminds us, "Great books do not always have great effects, at least not immediately," concluding that "sometimes the non-citations of James' book approach the absurd."[10] Absurd, indeed, but perhaps citation, important though it may be, is not the worst. In "Rewriting History: The Publication of W. E. B. Du Bois's *Black Reconstruction in America* (1935)" (2009), Claire Parfait reveals some of the difficulty of academic publishing:

> As for publication in white scholarly journals, such as *The Journal of American History* or *The American Historical Review,* Du Bois was again an exception: his article on Reconstruction ("Reconstruction and Its Benefits"), published in 1910 in the *American Historical Review,* was the first and only essay by an African American to appear in this journal for nearly seventy years.[11]

We treat this lacuna in contemporary scholarship as an invaluable teaching opportunity. To start, we usually spend an entire period reading and thinking about selected excerpts from *Black Reconstruction,* while the following class meeting is typically dedicated to a research and writing workshop. Between this class meeting and the following one, then, students are assigned excerpts from new economic histories of slavery and capitalism (Beckert, Baptist, and others); essays from periodicals such as the *New Yorker, The Atlantic,* and, most infamously, *The Economist,* as well as book reviews from academic journals. The first quarter of the class is devoted to summarizing the arguments of the assigned historiographical readings; the second is spent studying the different genres of writing, paying particular attention to methods and audience (general versus "scholarly"); in the third quarter, we divide students into groups, present them with hard copies of endnotes and bibliographies from some of the "new" economic histories mentioned earlier, and ask them to keep track of the number of times Du Bois is cited; and last, as a class, we discuss all of the (non?)citations—what Hudson calls the "disavowal of radical scholarship" and use this specific "aha!" moment of the class to form broader conclusions about the politics of citation and institutional knowledge production.[12] Proving Hudson's argument in the classroom alerts students to the persistence of the problems Du Bois raises in "The Propaganda of History." When students make the connection between Du Bois and Hudson, therefore, it offers them a powerful glimpse into the dynamics of institutional minoritizing processes—that is, it reveals to students examples of how well-meaning white scholars (with antiracist agendas) can end up reproducing the very systems of knowledge they believe themselves to be challenging. They do so, once again, through their citational apparatuses.

Moving forward in the semester, we extend the discussion from the reproduction of footnotes and citations to the reproduction of "core texts" in syllabi and curricula, arriving at a pyramid scheme of the marginalization of Black knowledge production. Even though this particular exercise is focused on knowledge production in the field of history, much of the discussion about "core texts" also extends to the discipline of English literature, which (as we know) commits similar acts of epistemic violence through its own citational negligence of Black writing. However dead-ended, following footnote trails allows students to gain new insight into the meaning of the *MLA Style Guide* and *Chicago Manual of Style* that we force them to know, without always remembering to explain the point of citation beyond protecting oneself from charges of plagiarism. The drudgery of properly format-ting citations suddenly has political meaning for them. It is our experience that once students learn about the ideological framework of citation, they become more thoughtful when selecting and documenting their sources.

As soon as our students become comfortable with or even adept at thinking about the politics of citation, we begin to pivot around *Black Reconstruction,* intro-ducing them to other works by Du Bois about the racism of knowledge production and canon formation. In courses that focus on modernist literature, we encourage pairing "The Propaganda of History" with a transcription of Du Bois's "Criteria of Negro Art" (1926), a speech that examines propaganda in more specifically artis-tic and literary directions. Reading these two texts in tandem helps capture the interdisciplinary reach of institutional racism, allowing students to understand why, exactly, Du Bois intervened in so many different fields, including sociology, history, and literature. Attending to Du Bois's cross-disciplinary interventions necessarily involves reading across a wide variety of archival materials—materials that make frequent appearances as epigraphs or intertexts. Teaching some of these outside materials (e.g., popular abolitionist songs, classical libretti, Romantic po-etry, and slave narratives) underscores Du Bois's preoccupying concern with con-ventional modes of representation.[13] We ask our students to compare the following two passages:

> The only chance [white authors] had to tell the truth of pitiful human degrada-tion was to tell it of colored people. I should not be surprised if Octavius [sic] Roy Cohen had approached the *Saturday Evening Post* and asked permission to write about a different kind of colored folk than the monstrosities he has created; but if he has, the *Post* has replied, "No. You are getting paid to write about the kind of colored people you are writing about." . . . In other words, the white public today demands from its artists, literary and pictorial, racial pre-judgment which deliberately distorts Truth and Justice, as far as colored races are concerned, and it will pay for no other.[14]

> Negroes have done some excellent work on their own history and defense. It suf-fers of course from natural partisanship and a desire to prove a case in the face of a chorus of unfair attacks. Its best work also suffers from the fact that Negroes with difficulty reach an audience. . . . It is most unfortunate that while many

young white Southerners can get funds to attack and ridicule the Negro and his friends, it is almost impossible for first-class Negro students to get a chance for research or to get finished work in print.[15]

Together these passages foreground some of the problems concerning racist representations of Blackness, their publication and circulation; these passages also highlight, once again, the racial segregation of academic publishing and the inaccessibility of segregated archives. Here and elsewhere, Du Bois notes the exclusion of African Americans from various cultural arenas—not just art schools and exhibitions, but also elite academic institutions and scholarly journals. Much like the unit on the politics of citation, this exercise attunes readers to the relationship between representation and power.

Our aim in teaching Du Bois's theses in "The Propaganda of History" and what we might call "The Propaganda of Art" is to get our students to a place in their thinking where they understand why and how to interrogate the categories of objectivity and propaganda.[16] In many ways, this is a lesson in cultural hegemony and knowledge production, routed not through excerpts from Antonio Gramsci's *Prison Notebooks* (1929–35) or Louis Althusser's essay "Ideology and Ideological State Apparatuses" (1970), but through the theoretical work of a single Black writer. Thinking about the specific ideological and material conditions that have enabled the very possibility of reading a text such as *Black Reconstruction,* for example—right now, in this semester, at this institution, inside this classroom, with this instructor and these peers—the question "How did this book get here?" is a way to get students to think about the relationship between something beautiful and seemingly immaterial such as storytelling and something seemingly disconnected from questions of storytelling and aesthetics, such as political struggles on the basis of race, class, gender, sex, sexuality, and ability.

The Question of Representation

Suppose the only Negro who survived some centuries hence was the Negro painted by white Americans in the novels and essays they have written. What would people in a hundred years say of black Americans?

—W. E. B. Du Bois, "Criteria of Negro Art"[17]

Assuming, therefore, as axiomatic the endless inferiority of the Negro race, these newer historians, mostly Southerners, some Northerners who deeply sympathized with the South, misinterpreted, distorted, even deliberately ignored any fact that challenged or contradicted this assumption. If the

Negro was admittedly sub-human, what need to waste time delving into his Reconstruction history? Consequently historians of Reconstruction with a few exceptions ignore the Negro as completely as possible, leaving the reader wondering why an element apparently so insignificant filled the whole Southern picture at the time. . . . But in propaganda against the Negro since emancipation in this land, we face one of the most stupendous efforts the world ever saw to discredit human beings, an effort involving universities, history, science, social life and religion.
                    —W. E. B. Du Bois, *Black Reconstruction in America*[18]

For literary scholars, the construction of narrative and the question of character are the key objects of analysis. From these epigraphs we see that these are the central objects of Du Bois's writings, too. This concern animates the introduction (titled "To the Reader") and several chapters of *Black Reconstruction,* including, but not limited to (in order), "The Black Worker," "The White Worker," "The Coming of the Lord," and "The Propaganda of History." In fact, these are the chapters we assign in units on race and representation. They ask the reader to consider the events of the American Civil War and Reconstruction from the perspective of African Americans—and from their perspective not just as human agents, but also as the most important historical actors in this period, rather than as the collateral damage of white tragedy and national crisis (which is, of course, how their role was often conceived in the so-called Dunning School).

Confronted with Du Bois's critique of the gatekeeping mechanisms in academic publishing (namely, in history and literature), students are alerted to the ways in which race and difference determine *what* and *who* get to enter academic spaces in the first place.[19] In his prefatory note "To the Reader," Du Bois acknowledges that an entire stratum of the educated reading public will have made up their minds about his topic and will be unwilling to engage his arguments and explanations:

It would be only fair to the reader to say frankly in advance that the attitude of any person toward this story will be distinctly influenced by his theories of the Negro race. If he believes that the Negro in America and in general is an average and ordinary human being, who under given environment develops like other human beings, then he will read this story and judge it by the facts adduced. If, however, he regards the Negro as a distinctly inferior creation, who can never successfully take part in modern civilization and whose emancipation and enfranchisement were gestures against nature, then he will need something more than the sorts of facts that I have set down.[20]

Out of all the passages that we teach, this is perhaps the most startling one to our students, apparently because of its boldness. They often ask what the reaction of his contemporaries was to this introduction. Some argue that its rhetorical "payoff" is to anticipate racist opposition and dismiss it a priori. Other students contend that this boldness has an alienating effect and would have ruffled the feathers of white historians, who would have then immediately dismissed Du Bois as a propagandist without even reading the rest of the book. Either way, the passage sparks a lot of conversation about how to address a reader; it can also function as a segue into practical writing workshops before final papers, where students discuss the pitfalls and gains of bold "opening hooks."

Together with "The Propaganda of History" chapter, Du Bois's note "To the Reader" introduces students not just to the historiography of the American Civil War and Reconstruction, but also to the narrative-based disciplines of the humanities in general. Race, Du Bois argues, is, again, a key factor in determining who gets to tell stories and which historical actors get to play leading roles in those stories. Du Bois begins his own story this way: "The story of transplanting millions of Africans to the new world, and of their bondage for four centuries, is a fascinating one."[21] This opening sentence thus establishes slavery as a central theme of the book. When read alongside the book's title, which grounds the discussion of Reconstruction in Blackness (or *Black* Reconstruction), this opening sentence also suggests that the seemingly well-known story of slavery will have a different focus—the experience and actions of slaves.

English majors are used to discussing perspective and the problem of narrative unreliability, a key example of which is William Faulkner's *The Sound and the Fury* (1929). But our students are less accustomed to dealing with the question of unreliability vis-à-vis nonfiction. Indeed, students often recite variations on the "history-is-written-by-the-victors" platitude—no matter how ideologically "good" or "bad" the history may seem. Du Bois, by contrast, pictures another kind of historiographical subjectivity—what Paul Gilroy has called Du Bois's "historicality."[22] In "The Propaganda of History," already quoted at length, Du Bois, once again, discerns between "the idea of history either as a science or as an art using the results of science."[23] In similar fashion, C. L. R. James, who was a fan of Du Bois, takes up the very same distinction between history *qua* art and history *qua* science:[24]

> The traditionally famous historians have been more artist than scientist: they wrote so well because they saw so little. . . . Great men make history, but only such history as it is possible for them to make. Their freedom of achievement is limited by the necessities of their environment. To portray the limits of those necessities and the realisation [*sic*], complete or partial, of all possibilities, that is the true business of the historian. . . . The analysis is the science and the demonstration the art which is history.[25]

In *Black Reconstruction,* Du Bois may call history a science, but he is well aware that historiography is a type of storytelling. By placing Black slaves at the heart of his narrative, Du Bois effectively arrives at a *new* story. By paying attention to questions of story, plot, and characters in Du Bois's narrative, students are able to make astute observations about the relationship between "objective" historical writing and "imaginative" literary writing. Even better, they are able to see how the reading practices that they use in the literature classroom, and the objects of their study—storytelling, character analysis, and narrative unreliability—are applicable to critical inquiries outside of their major. This unit teaches them to think critically about the different kinds of sources they encounter and to question the disciplinary canons and determinants on which most traditional academic fields rest. Students also learn that the narratives we construct about the past, today, will necessarily continue to shape our future.

The Universality of *Black Reconstruction*

We all need histories that no history book can tell, but they are not in the classroom—not the history classrooms, anyway. . . . How does one write a history of the impossible?

— Michel-Rolph Trouillot, *Silencing the Past*[26]

While it is clear that *Black Reconstruction* is a historically specific—and historiographically specifiable—work about a particular historical context, in our classrooms it enjoys the same kind of hermeneutic attention and serious consideration as the "Great Books" at the heart of the literary canon. This means that we attribute to Du Bois's study of a seemingly national phenomenon a universality typically granted only to works about white labor movements. Teaching Du Bois's book as a narratological experiment has transformed the way we think about historical agency and about the global reach of national "plots." Indeed, long after its initial publication, *Black Reconstruction* continues to resonate with international liberation movements. As Ferruccio Gambino explains, "Du Bois's book was a milestone of historiography for all those whose history had been denied or stolen."[27] If Gambino could apply the lessons he learned from *Black Reconstruction* to the anticolonial struggles and "worldwide movement" in the 1960s, it was only because Du Bois had already mapped it out for him.[28] "Black labor," writes Du Bois in the very first chapter of *Black Reconstruction,* "became the foundation stone not only of the Southern social structure, but of Northern manufacture and commerce, of the English factory system, of European commerce, of buying and selling on a world-wide scale; new cities were built on the results of black labor, and a new labor problem, involving all white labor, arose both in Europe and America."[29] The Black worker, Du Bois argues, is the universal figure of labor—only through him (gender advised) can we understand local, national, regional, and global models of exploitation. As literary scholar-teachers, then, we like to add that only through them can we tell the *stories* of local, national, regional, and global models of exploitation.

Because *Black Reconstruction* is a counternarrative, the demand on our students necessarily rises to discern "between what [*really*] happened and that which is said to have happened."[30] Their lack of discernment here will most probably have more than a little to do with the fact that Reconstruction is a period about which many of our students seem to know very little (if, indeed, they have any prior knowledge at all). In our view, "that which is said to have happened" should not be taken for granted in the classroom, since, for many students, the history of Reconstruction will, again, most probably be, quite literally, unthinkable. In *Silencing the Past: Power and the Production of History* (1995), Michel-Rolph Trouillot famously theorized the "unthinkability" of the Haitian Revolution, while Du Bois continues to teach us about the unthinkability of a *Black* Reconstruction.[31] And just to give our readers a better sense of the problem, most of our English literature and Africana studies students are usually able to sketch something of an African American history, even though their version is circumscribed by two distinct teleologies: *from* slavery *to* emancipation, on the one hand, and *from* Jim Crow *to* civil rights, on the other. Still, having taught *Black Reconstruction* to a variety of undergraduate audiences at public and private research universities and liberal arts colleges, we have found many ways to use Du Bois's revisionism to best advantage.

What an odd feeling it was to be teaching a chapter originally titled "The Dictatorship of the Black Proletariat in South Carolina" at a predominantly white institution in South Carolina, the former plantation of John C. Calhoun; at a public university whose foundations were literally laid by the hands of slaves, sharecroppers, and convict laborers; in campus buildings named after white supremacists such as Benjamin "Pitchfork" Tillman and Strom Thurmond; in English literature classrooms that were overwhelmingly white, to students whose political center of gravity was fundamentally evangelical or neoliberal and at a time and in a place defined by the murder of Walter Scott, the massacre at Emanuel AME Church, the removal of the Confederate flag from statehouse grounds, and the onset of Donald Trump's 2016 presidential campaign. In this unique context, the effect of *Black Reconstruction* might seem inevitably didactic, even vindicationist. But *Black Reconstruction* is not a morality play; nor is it a cultural history, despite what its title may claim or suggest. Indeed, Du Bois's radical Marxist-historical approach is laid bare in *Black Reconstruction,* which is a history of global reach across the *longue durée,* as it were, and across the "color-line," so to speak.[32] Of course, all of us are implicated in this kind of history—the history of what Du Bois calls "the world's greatest experiment in democracy."[33]

To be sure, Du Bois focuses his hermeneutics on the Southern states: Virginia, North Carolina, South Carolina, Georgia, Florida, Alabama, Louisiana, and Mississippi are central to his analysis (see, e.g., chapters 10–13 in *Black Reconstruction*). At the same time, however, he also calls our attention to the historical significance of the Northern states, the so-called Border States, and the southwestern frontier. Du Bois's chapter "The General Strike" offers a good point of entry for thinking about geography as a pedagogical strategy. One of the most striking passages in "The General Strike" concerns the (false?) North-South dichotomy:

> The North was not Abolitionist. It was overwhelmingly in favor of Negro slavery, so long as this did not interfere with Northern moneymaking. But, on the other hand, there was a minority of the North who hated slavery with a perfect hatred; who wanted no union of slaveholders; who fought for freedom and treated Negroes as men.[34]

This passage, let it be said clearly, is not meant to vindicate "good" white people from the South; nor is it meant to implicate white students from the North. By situating the North within the Global South (as Du Bois begins to do), instructors can begin to unsettle romantic presumptions about the so-called North (or "the North"), legitimate Du Bois's historical perspective, and establish our own critical impartiality. (Craig Wilder's *Ebony and Ivy: Race, Slavery, and the Troubled History of America's Universities* [2013], for example, might work well here as a supplementary reading concerning the political economy of the Global South.)

Another dichotomy to which Du Bois attends thoughtfully is the Black-white divide. Indeed, Black and white students are often surprised to encounter chapters titled "The White Worker" and "The White Proletariat" in a history titled *Black Reconstruction*. Central to Du Bois's history, we remind our students, is a critique of America's failure to realize a "dictatorship of the proletariat"—the failure to move from a "general strike" against slavery to a *global* struggle against capital.[35] At the same time as he focuses on the precarious fate of "four million black slaves," Du Bois calls our attention to the fraught position of "five million non-slaveholding poor white farmers and laborers."[36] *Black Reconstruction,* in this regard, is labor history—and a history that might help to energize interracial class solidarities and political struggles against capitalist inequality, despite recent debates about the affordances, privileges, and so-called wages of whiteness.[37] Consider this passage:

> The political success of the doctrine of racial separation, which overthrew Reconstruction by uniting the planter and the poor white, was far exceeded by

its astonishing economic results. The theory of laboring class unity rests upon the assumption that laborers, despite internal jealousies, will unite because of their opposition to exploitation by the capitalists. According to this, even after a part of the poor white laboring class became identified with the planters, and eventually displaced them, their interests would be diametrically opposed to those of the mass of white labor, and of course to those of the black laborers. This would throw white and black labor into one class, and precipitate a united fight for higher wage and better working conditions. Most persons do not realize how far this failed to work in the South, and it failed to work because the theory of race was supplemented by a carefully planned and slowly evolved method, which drove such a wedge between the white and black workers that there probably are not today in the world two groups of workers with practically identical interests who hate and fear each other so deeply and persistently and who are kept so far apart that neither sees anything of common interest.[38]

This passage opens the door to considerations of identity politics, its limitations, and more. More important, it forces students to think more closely about the importance of building working-class solidarities across the color line. (In a course spanning the late nineteenth and early twentieth centuries, instructors might consider coupling Du Bois's *Black Reconstruction* with Robin Kelley's *Hammer and Hoe: Alabama Communists during the Great Depression* [1990], even though Kelley's history is a different affair altogether.) Beginning with the North-South and Black-white dichotomies, then, seems to prepare students for many of the revisionist alternatives that follow, not least Du Bois's critique of Abraham Lincoln.

Against the grip of hagiography, Du Bois casts a different light on the popular "Lincoln freed the slaves" narrative. Like the Haitian Revolution, the abolition of slavery in America was largely "unthinkable." According to Du Bois, Lincoln could scarcely fathom the idea, even though, as he explains time and again, thousands of slaves were already free. Compare the following two passages:

What the Negro did was to wait, look, and listen and try to see where his interest lay. . . . As soon . . . as it became clear . . . the slave entered upon a general strike against slavery by the same methods that he had used during the period of the fugitive slave. . . . The slave, despite every effort, was becoming the center of war. Lincoln, with his uncanny insight, began to see it. He began to talk about compensation for emancipated slaves, and Congress, following almost too quickly, passed the Confiscation Act in August 1861, freeing slaves which were actually used in war by the enemy. Lincoln then suggested that provision be made for colonization of such slaves. He simply could not envisage free Negroes in the United States. What would become of them? What would they do? Meantime, the slave kept looming . . . , and if Lincoln could hold the country together and keep slavery, he would do it. But he could not, and he had no sooner said this than he began to realize that he could not. In June, 1862, slavery was abolished in the territories. Compensation with possible colonization was planned for the District of Columbia. . . . In August, Lincoln faced the truth, front forward; and that truth was not simply that Negroes ought to be free; it was that thousands of them were already free, and either the power which slaves put into the hands of the South was to be taken from it, or the North could not win the war. Either the Negro was to be allowed to fight, or the draft itself would not bring enough white men into the army to keep up the war. . . . In August, 1862, Lincoln discussed Emancipation as a military measure.[39]

In the ears of the world, Abraham Lincoln on the first of January, 1863, declared four million slaves "thenceforward and forever free." The truth was less than this. . . . Hundreds of thousands of such slaves were already free *by their own action.*[40]

There is so much here in just the first passage that would take an entire lecture to unpack, so much in Du Bois's rich history of Reconstruction, that we still fail to appreciate or do not well comprehend it.

Perhaps we cannot hope to speak of *Black Reconstruction* with any final authority, but there are specific moments in Du Bois's text with which all students ought to come to grips. Du Bois's deconstruction of the North-South and Black-white dichotomies are, in this way, obligatory reading. Teaching them together, then, forces students to think about the political limitations of identitarianism—that "Blackness" and "whiteness," even "Southernness" and "Northernness" are effortful, ideologically informed social constructions. These and other epiphanies students have while reading *Black Reconstruction* are due in large part to the heuristic experience Du Bois creates for the reader. It is evident from the very first page that he knows quite well what will and will not "curtail [his] audience."[41] In a sense, teaching Du Bois may simply mean bringing students into his world.

Teaching "The Coming of the Lord" Chapter

Thus, when Emancipation finally came, it seemed to the freedman a literal Coming of the Lord. His fervid imagination was stirred as never before, by the tramp of armies, the blood and dust of battle, and the wail and whirl of social upheaval. He stood dumb and motionless before the whirlwind: what had he to do with it? Was it not the Lord's doing, and

marvellous [sic] in his eyes? Joyed and bewildered with what came, he
stood awaiting new wonders till the inevitable Age of Reaction swept
over the nation and brought the crisis of today.

—W. E. B. Du Bois, "Of the Faith of the Fathers," in *The Souls of Black Folk*[42]

The [Emancipation] Proclamation made four and a half million laborers willing almost in mass to sacrifice their last drop of blood for their
new-found country. It sent them into transports of joy and sacrifice. It
changed all their pessimism and despair into boundless faith. It was the
Coming of the Lord.

—W. E. B. Du Bois, "The Coming of the Lord," in *Black Reconstruction in America*[43]

Du Bois's critique of Lincoln in "The General Strike" continues and culminates in
one of the most difficult chapters in *Black Reconstruction*—the fifth chapter, "The
Coming of the Lord," in which Du Bois problematizes the allegorical epistemology
of the newly freed slaves (i.e., their teleological understanding of emancipation
as a kind of divine intervention). Here Du Bois understands Black religion as a
distraction from what he calls "the truer deeper facts of Reconstruction."[44] "Yet
we are blind and led by the blind," writes Du Bois. "We discern in [the history of
slavery] no part of our labor movement . . . no part of our religious experience."[45] As
Du Bois's summarizes his own plot: "The slave went free; stood a brief moment in
the sun; then moved back again toward slavery."[46] It is important here, however, to
note that, in stark contrast to Du Bois, Black intellectuals such as Zora Neale
Hurston, Hortense Powdermaker, and Arthur Fauset understood very well the po-
tentiating effects of Black religion on "real" politics.[47] Still, Du Bois remains deeply
skeptical about the coupling of religion and politics, a perceived dichotomy that
animates much of his published work. Indeed, there is so much here that points
back to *The Souls of Black Folk* that we often teach Du Bois's "The Coming of Lord"
together with "Of the Faith of the Fathers," chapter 10 of *The Souls of Black Folk*.
The epigraphs are meant to underscore Du Bois's preoccupying concern with the
allegorical imagination of the newly freed slave. Students are often taken aback by
Du Bois's condescending language. We ask our students to compare the following
two passages:

Suppose on some gray day, as you plod down Wall Street, you should see God
sitting on the Treasury steps, in His Glory, with the thunders curved about
him? Suppose on Michigan Avenue, between the lakes and hills of stone, and in
the midst of hastening automobiles and jostling crowds, suddenly you see living and walking toward you, the Christ, with sorrow and sunshine in his face?
. . . Foolish talk, all of this, you say, of course; and that is because no American

now believes in his religion. Its facts are mere symbolism; its revelation vague
generalities; its ethics a matter of carefully balanced gain. But to most of the
four million black folk emancipated by civil war, God was real. They knew Him.
They had met Him personally in many a wild orgy of religious frenzy, or in the
black stillness of the night. His plan for them was clear; they were to suffer and
be degraded, and then afterwards by Divine edict, raised to manhood and power;
and so on January 1, 1863, He made them free. . . . It was all foolish, bizarre, and
tawdry. Gangs of dirty Negroes howling and dancing; poverty-stricken ignorant
laborers mistaking war, destruction and revolution for the mystery of the free
human soul; and yet to these black folk it was the Apocalypse.[48]

A sort of suppressed terror hung in the air and seemed to seize us,—a pythian
madness, a demoniac possession . . . a scene of human passion such as I had
never conceived before. . . . Those who have not thus witnessed the frenzy of a
Negro revival in the untouched backwoods of the South can but dimly realize
the religious feeling of the slave; as described, such scenes appear grotesque and
funny, but as seen they are awful. . . . the mad abandon of physical fervor,—the
stamping, shrieking, and shouting, the rushing to and fro and wild waving of
arms, the weeping and laughing, the vision and the trance. . . . And so firm a
hold did it have on the Negro, that many generations firmly believed that without this visible manifestation of the God there could be no true communion
with the Invisible.[49]

Taken aback, indeed: Du Bois's religious skepticism notwithstanding, students are usually confused, even floored, by his characterization of Black people
as "dumb," "wild," "dirty," "poor," "foolish," "bizarre," "tawdry," "ignorant," "mad,"
"demoniac," "grotesque," "funny," "awful," and so on. Perhaps no explanation here
would suffice—in fact, here we often find ourselves empathizing with our students,
even though we use this moment as an occasion also to revisit the end of "Of the
Training of Black Men," chapter 6 of *The Souls of Black Folk,* in which Du Bois lik-
ens himself, curiously, to figures such as William Shakespeare, Honoré de Balzac,
Alexandre Dumas, Aristotle, and Marcus Aurelius.[50] The analogy is, of course, beside the point. We turn to this passage to think about what Du Bois says next: "I
dwell *above* the Veil."[51] Of course, this seems like an odd thing for Du Bois to say,
since he begins his narrative with authentic pretensions: "I who speak here am
bone of the bone and flesh of the flesh of them that live within the Veil."[52] It is
our experience that these and other ideological blind spots in Du Bois are rarely
broached in undergraduate and graduate classrooms.[53] In courses that also take
up African American literary criticism, we highly recommend Hazel Carby's *Race
Men* (1998). Indeed, after reading Carby students are less likely to accept Du Bois's

language simply as a matter of his Victorian leanings. In her first chapter, "The Souls of Black Men," Carby levels accusations of intellectual elitism against Du Bois and his protectors.[54]

While many of our students are at first perturbed by Du Bois's peculiar characterization here of Black people, some of them are drawn to other seemingly problematic aspects of the quoted passages. However presentist, one can imagine religious students taking issue with Du Bois's axiom that "no American now believes in his religion."[55] The demands here, of course, rise for those of us teaching at religiously affiliated institutions or, say, at institutions in the so-called Bible Belt. Teaching "The Coming of the Lord" in these contexts raises new questions about narrative unreliability. It is hard to imagine, for example, that many religious students will appreciate Du Bois's patronizing description of "a wild orgy of religious frenzy."[56] As instructors, then, what do we do when the defamiliarizing shock of the truth claim of a text threatens to foreclose the reliability of the narrator? To start, we might begin with a discussion of what anthropologists call "critical distance"—indeed, the same kind of critical distance that Du Bois himself seems here to be modeling.[57]

Instead of just reflecting on Du Bois's condescending language, we find it much more productive to comment on his ambivalence. Getting students to accept a text's ambivalence—that is, without adjudicating between its opposing points of view—is one of the most challenging, but also rewarding, tasks of teaching literature. After all, this is the point to which we want to lead our students: where they can sit with ambivalence and ambiguity, and even discuss their effect, rather than falling back on the Lincoln-Douglas style of debate to which so many of them have become accustomed. This is key to understanding literary texts writ large—and especially texts about race. How else can students learn to discuss the warring impulses of a sentimental text, which, as Lauren Berlant has shown, needs to produce affect to engage the reader, even though it falls into the trap of substituting affect for political action. Yet, as Berlant cautions, we cannot altogether do without this affective element, since it is key to awakening the reader to the worldview of others.[58]

Whatever Du Bois's language here might mean, it is important to note that it was these Black folk who saw God, not the slave masters or the pious female abolitionists such as Harriet Beecher Stowe. In locating this experience of the Divine in the lowest and poorest sector of society, Du Bois is, strangely enough, following the very logic of the religion from which he wishes to distance himself. Even as he attempts to write himself out of this tableau, he inscribes the reader into it, inviting us to see the world and to see Christ through the eyes of the slaves. Taking a closer look at the quoted passage reveals that it is "you" (the interpellated reader) that is "[plodding] down Wall Street . . . [or] Michigan Avenue . . . [when] suddenly you see living and walking toward *you,* the Christ, with sorrow and sunshine in his face."[59] In this moment, your vision is the same as that of the "tawdry" Black masses—or, rather, it is mediated through their primary access. Yours is secondary to theirs. This is a useful teaching moment insofar as it showcases the difficulties of representing and preserving affective moments in historical texts. Moreover, it indexes the problem of unreliability in historical narratives by highlighting the different epistemologies of both the people represented and the historians representing them. In *Black Reconstruction,* Du Bois toggles between a ventriloquized voice of the formerly enslaved—which, by its definition, must play their perspective straight—and the "scientific" voice of the academic historian. We use this particular passage, finally, to attune our students to the possibilities and limitations of different writing genres.

In the end, then, it is worth remembering that Du Bois's prefatory note, "To the Reader," is addressed not just to his fellow historians but also, more broadly, to an interpretive community of "students of human culture," to students interested in the story of "the sudden freeing of these black folk in the Nineteenth Century and the attempt, through them, to reconstruct the basis of American democracy from 1860–1880."[60] And to whom else here could Du Bois possibly be referring other than our very own humanities students? As humanities scholars committed to interdisciplinary inquiry and collaboration, we have found that *Black Reconstruction* as a whole—and specifically Du Bois's mode of address—is one of the strongest arguments for interdisciplinarity. Despite his lengthy discussion of the major tenets of historiography, his dismissal of the Dunning School as "romance," and his insistence on a more "scientific" approach to Reconstruction, Du Bois issues a clarion call to historians to decolonize History with a capital "H" as well as capital "H" Historiography.[61] In *Black Reconstruction,* Du Bois sheds light on the interdisciplinary life of racism—the coordinated efforts of "the massed hirelings of Religion, Science, Education, Law, and brute force," as he puts it, or "field[s] devastated by passion and belief."[62] It is our hope that this essay points not just to the richness of Du Bois's magnum opus but also to the many different forms of radical pedagogy his work inspires.

Notes

1. W. E. B. Du Bois, *Black Reconstruction in America, 1860–1880* (New York: Free Press, 1998), 711.
2. Ibid., 713–14.
3. Ibid., 708.
4. Peter James Hudson, "The Racist Dawn of Capitalism," *Boston Review,* March, 14, 2016, https://www.bostonreview.net/articles/peter-james-hudson-slavery-capitalism.

5. Cedric J. Robinson, *Black Marxism: The Making of the Black Radical Tradition* (Chapel Hill: University of North Carolina Press, 2000).

6. Hudson, "The Racist Dawn of Capitalism."

7. See, e.g., W. E. B. Du Bois, *The World and Africa: An Inquiry into the Part Which Africa Has Played in World History*, ed. Henry Louis Gates Jr. (New York: Oxford University Press, 2007), xxxi, 38–46, 64, 144, 168, 215–18.

8. Ibid., xxxi.

9. Ibid.

10. Christopher Taylor, "*The Black Jacobins:* From Great Book to Classic?" *Age of Revolutions* (blog), May 2, 2016. https://ageofrevolutions.com/2016/05/02/the-black-jacobins-from -great-book-to-classic.

11. Claire Parfait, "Rewriting History: The Publication of W. E. B. Du Bois's *Black Reconstruction in America* (1935)," *Book History* 12 (2009): 269.

12. Hudson, "The Racist Dawn of Capitalism."

13. For studies of Du Bois's use of music in *Black Reconstruction,* see Garry Bertholf, "Listening to Du Bois's *Black Reconstruction:* After James," *South* (formerly *Southern Literary Journal*) 48, no. 1 (2015): 78–91; Marina Bilbija, "Democracy's New Song: *Black Reconstruction in America, 1860–1880* and the Melodramatic Imagination," *Annals of the American Academy of Political and Social Science* 637 (2011): 64–77.

14. W. E. B. Du Bois, "Criteria of Negro Art," in *The New Negro: Readings on Race, Representation, and African American Culture, 1892–1938,* ed. Henry Louis Gates Jr. and Gene Andrew Jarrett (Princeton, NJ: Princeton University Press, 2008), 290–97.

15. Du Bois, *Black Reconstruction in America,* 724–25.

16. "Thus all Art is propaganda and ever must be, despite the wailing of the purists. I stand in utter shamelessness and say that whatever art I have for writing has been used always for propaganda for gaining the right of black folk to love and enjoy. I do not care a damn for any art that is not used for propaganda. But I do care when propaganda is confined to one side while the other is stripped and silent": Du Bois, "Criteria of Negro Art," 290–97.

17. Ibid., 258.

18. Du Bois, *Black Reconstruction in America,* 727.

19. W. E. B. Du Bois, *The Souls of Black Folk,* ed. Henry Louis Gates Jr. (New York: Oxford University Press, [1903] 2007).

20. Du Bois, *Black Reconstruction in America,* xix.

21. Ibid.

22. For more on the ideological foundations of Du Bois's "historicality (*Geschichtlichkeit*)," see Paul Gilroy, "'Cheer the Weary Traveller': W. E. B. Du Bois, Germany, and the Politics of (Dis)placement," in *The Black Atlantic: Modernity and Double Consciousness,* by Paul Gilroy (Cambridge, MA: Harvard University Press, 1993), 111–45.

23. Du Bois, *Black Reconstruction in America,* 714.

24. "Du Bois had opened out the historical perspective in a manner I didn't know. He had been at it for many years. He was a very profound and learned historian. . . . Did you ever think that the attempt of the black people in the Civil War to attempt democracy was the finest effort to achieve democracy that the world had ever seen? . . . You have to grapple with that. . . . Du Bois knew about it, and he said the tragedy of these millions from Africa was a tragedy that 'beggared the Greek.' . . . Du Bois taught me to think in those terms. . . . That was a tremendous thing for Du Bois to say!": C. L. R. James, "*The Black Jacobins* and *Black*

    Reconstruction: A Comparative Analysis (15 June 1971)," in "Lectures on *The Black Jacobins*," ed. David Scott, *Small Axe* 4, no. 2 (2000): 85–86.

25. C. L. R. James, "Preface to the First Edition," in *The Black Jacobins: Toussaint L'Ouverture and the San Domingo Revolution*, by C. L. R. James (New York: Vintage, 1989), x–xi.

26. Michel-Rolph Trouillot, "An Unthinkable History: The Haitian Revolution as a Non-event," in *Silencing the Past: Power and the Production of History*, by Michel-Rolph Trouillot (Boston: Beacon, 1995), 71–72.

27. Ferruccio Gambino, "Reading Black Reconstruction on the Eve of 1968," *South Atlantic Quarterly* 112, no. 3 (2013): 532.

28. Ibid., 530.

29. Du Bois, *Black Reconstruction in America*, 5.

30. Trouillot, "An Unthinkable History," 106.

31. Ibid., 70–107.

32. For more on the *"longue durée,"* see Fernand Braudel, *On History*, trans. Sarah Matthews (Chicago: University of Chicago Press, 1980), 75. In *The Souls of Black Folk*, Du Bois defines the "color-line" as "the relation of the darker to the lighter races of men in Asia and Africa, in America and islands of the sea": Du Bois, *The Souls of Black Folk*, 8.

33. Du Bois, *Black Reconstruction in America*, 715.

34. Ibid., 83.

35. Ibid., 345.

36. Ibid., 29.

37. Adolph Reed Jr., "Du Bois and the 'Wages of Whiteness': What He Meant, What He Didn't, and, Besides, It Shouldn't Matter for Our Politics Anyway," *Nonsite.org*, June 29, 2017, https://nonsite.org/editorial/du-bois-and-the-wages-of-whiteness.

38. Du Bois, *Black Reconstruction in America*, 700.

39. Ibid., 57–82.

40. Ibid., 84, emphasis added.

41. Ibid., xix.

42. Du Bois, *The Souls of Black Folk*, 136.

43. Du Bois, *Black Reconstruction in America*, 87.

44. Ibid., 728.

45. Ibid., 74.

46. Ibid., 30.

47. Barbara Savage, "Illusions of Black Religion," in *Your Spirits Walk beside Us: The Politics of Black Religion* (Cambridge, MA: Harvard University Press, 2008), 68–120.

48. Du Bois, *Black Reconstruction in America*, 123–24.

49. Du Bois, *The Souls of Black Folk*, 128–29.

50. Ibid., 76.

51. Ibid., emphasis added.

52. Ibid., 4.

53. Du Bois's polemics against Marcus Garvey are especially telling in this regard: see Colin Grant, "Not to Mention His Colour" and "Behold the Demagogue or Misunderstood Messiah," in *Negro with a Hat: The Rise and Fall of Marcus Garvey and His Dream of Mother Africa*, by Colin Grant (New York: Oxford University Press, 2008), 298–317, 318–48.

54. Hazel Carby, "The Souls of Black Men," in *Race Men*, by Hazel Carby (Cambridge, MA: Harvard University Press, 1998), 9–41.

55. W. E. B. Du Bois, *Black Reconstruction in America*, 124.

56. Ibid.

57. For more on "the epistemic importance of critical distance," see Jean Comaroff and John L. Comaroff, "Millennial Capitalism: First Thoughts on a Second Coming," in *Millennial Capitalism and the Culture of Neoliberalism,* ed. Jean Comaroff and John L. Comaroff (Durham, NC: Duke University Press, 2001), 45.

58. See Lauren Berlant, "Poor Eliza," *American Literature* 70, no. 3 (1998): 635–68.

59. W. E. B. Du Bois, *Black Reconstruction in America,* 123–24, emphasis added.

60. Ibid., xix.

61. Ibid., 723.

62. Ibid., 708, 725.

Three Historians and a Theologian

HOWARD THURMAN AND THE WRITING
OF AFRICAN AMERICAN HISTORY

Peter Eisenstadt

O N FEBRUARY 21, 1936, Howard Thurman (1899–1981), dean of chapel at Howard University; his wife, Sue Bailey Thurman; and Edward Carroll became the first African Americans to meet with Mohandas K. "Mahatma" Gandhi, the world-famous leader of the Indian independence movement. They were three of the four members of the "Negro Delegation" sent by the American Student Christian Federation on a "Pilgrimage of Friendship" to their Indian counterparts. (One person was indisposed.) By February 21, the delegation had been on an extended speaking tour of British colonies in South Asia for four months, participating in some two hundred speaking engagements. Gandhi was almost as excited by the meeting as were the Thurmans and Carroll, and when they arrived, he bounded out of his bungalow tent and started peppering them with questions about Blacks in the United States. Thurman gave Gandhi a short lesson in African American history, telling him that in the words of Gandhi's secretary, Mahadev Desai, that W. E. B. Du Bois was "offering a challenging intellectual solution to the Negro problem through his latest book—*Black Reconstruction.*"[1] Drawing from its pages, once again in the words of Desai: "He explained how the situation in the Southern States was still difficult, as the flower of the aristocratic Whites were all killed in the War of 1861–84 [*sic*] and as soon as the armies moved to the North the economic structure was paralyzed, leaving the whole in the hands of the poor Whites who smarted under the economic competition of the Negro." Thurman extended this analysis to the 1930s, expanding it to the entire country: "Among the masses of workers there is a great deal of tension, which is quite natural when the White thinks the Negroes very existence is a threat to his own."[2]

Thurman's touting of Du Bois's radical vision in *Black Reconstruction in America* to Gandhi is one indication of his lifelong interest in the study of African American history. It is an aspect of Thurman's thought that has received little attention. In general, Thurman has received less attention by scholars than his importance warrants. He was born and raised in Florida at the height of the Jim Crow era. Despite coming from an impoverished background, he graduated from Morehouse College and Rochester Theological Seminary with honors; taught at his alma mater and Spelman College; and subsequently taught at Howard University, where he was both a professor of religion and dean of chapel. In 1944, he became co-pastor (later sole pastor) of the Church for the Fellowship of All Peoples in San Francisco, one of the first churches in the United States organized on a consciously interracial and interdenominational basis. In 1953, he became dean of chapel at Boston University, retiring in 1965. One of the preeminent religious thinkers in mid-twentieth century America, a mystic, and a mentor to the Civil Rights Movement, Thurman was the author of more than twenty books and many articles. For more than half a century he was a tireless deliverer of lectures and sermons to colleges, churches, synagogues, and organizations of all kinds, and he was much in demand among both Black and white audiences.[3]

Among the interests of Howard and Sue Bailey Thurman was the promotion of African American history. One cause, over the decades, was the restoration of Harriet Tubman's derelict home in Auburn, New York. Sue Bailey Thurman and her daughter, Anne, wrote books and tour guides and created maps on Black history; they were also instrumental in establishing an African American history museum in Boston in the early 1960s.[4] In March 1962, Thurman wrote to his old friend and classmate James M. Nabritt Jr., then the president of Howard University, suggesting that Nabritt establish an African American history museum in Washington, DC, and help raise the general awareness of Black history: "One of the needful things, as our young people storm the gates on the Frontiers of Freedom, is some sense of history that will enable them to share responsibly in laying out the new city." In Thurman's last years, at the helm of the Howard Thurman Education Trust, the promotion of Black history projects was one of his chief interests.[5]

Thurman's interest in history formed an important part of his religious thinking. For both individuals and peoples, perhaps the most important task—for Thurman, it was always a religious task—was the search for self-knowledge. For individuals, this involved rigorous self-examination and "centering down" into one's truest and deepest self to find the "bit of God" within.[6] No one can presume to define or control anyone else's inner life. Thurman saw a somewhat similar process at work for nations and peoples. African Americans, he thought, were a people that had been robbed and stripped of their history by the slave trade and its aftermath, and had been invidiously defined by white America, usually as a collection of pathologies and inherited inferiorities.[7] For Thurman, Africans enslaved in America, with their past obliterated and forced to live as human property, had little besides the potential to make their own history. The Negro spirituals for Thurman were a prime example of a people creating their own history through the struggle for individual and collective self-knowledge. The spirituals were fashioned from whatever raw materials were at hand: remembered scraps of African rhythm and religion, shards of their master's Christianity, suitably recast into a basically new religion in which they, and all people, enjoyed the infinite equality of being children of the same God. Thurman wrote about spirituals extensively from the 1920s on. Most who wrote on spirituals at the time, Black and white, emphasized their African qualities, such as some supposedly innate inherited talent for music, for spirituality, or for suffering. For Thurman, impatient with the deterministic aura of innate qualities—he was always what contemporary scholars call an antiessentialist—the spirituals were the product of African peoples interacting historically with their new American realities.[8] This was how the nameless and voiceless, in the most trying circumstances possible, became historical actors. As one of Thurman's historical disciples, Nathan Huggins, wrote, Thurman's work "brought slave religion into discussion for the first time as a truly historical phenomenon." Thurman's analyses, Huggins lamented in 1982, "are now so commonly accepted, so commonplace, that we too often forget to honor [their] source."[9] Thurman wrote that the challenge for oppressed people seeking to create their own history was to take "responsibility for how . . . I must react to the forces that impinge upon my life, forces that are not responsive to my will, my desire, my ambition, my dream, my hope—forces that don't know that I'm here."[10]

Thurman's key work in which this process is explored was *Jesus and the Disinherited* (1949).[11] It is, perhaps, a work of Black historicity rather than Black history as such. It is certainly a work of history without many names, dates, or locations. For Thurman, this was to place the reader into the minds and choices of its protagonists, which are made universal because of the lack of specificity. It is a short book with an epic story: the story of Black people overcoming the three hounds of hell—fear, deception, and hate—then moving forward on the hard-won path toward true self-knowledge, discovering a capacious love of all life that must include one's enemies. This is a journey that must be undertaken by the oppressed themselves. Perhaps the most radical aspect of *Jesus and the Disinherited* is that it is not directed at white Americans at all (although Thurman definitely wanted whites to read the book). It is addressed exclusively to those "with their backs against the wall."[12] It was an invitation for oppressed people to shape their own history and thereby create a way for them to coexist as equals with their former oppressors.

Thurman, a master analysist and taxonomist of white racism, Black rage, and the tangled complexities of racial interaction, was a thoroughgoing integrationist.[13] He was not happy with the turn to Black nationalism and separatism in the late 1960s and 1970s. In 1965, he decried "black chauvinism," calling it a "great betrayal of the future."[14] The following year, he attacked the vogue for Black Power as this year's "current unreflective slogan."[15] The same year he left the advisory board of the Congress of Racial Equality (CORE), which he had been on since its founding in 1942, for its adoption of a Black Power ideology.[16] Thurman, in 1971, in *The Search for Common Ground,* with an angry outspokenness and sarcasm quite unusual for him, lamented that those uncomfortable with the new cult of Blackness were now often "regarded as Uncle Toms" and that "vulgarity" had become the trademark of many who had "freed themselves of the contamination of white society."[17] Speaking of the book, he said that it was "an expression of his concern about the way in which so many blacks were reacting to the King assassination by 'separating themselves behind self-imposed walls.'"[18] "The Black Experience," Thurman wrote the same year, "cannot be separated from the totality of experience and the sense of being cut off or isolated, despite the intensity of the reality, has no ultimate significance and justification."[19]

And yet, despite Thurman's adamant opposition to separatism and Black nationalism, this did not prevent him from being admired by some of the era's most prominent Black Power advocates. Jesse Jackson (b. 1941) was one of the main inheritors of the mantle of Martin Luther King Jr., but unlike King he became a sharp critic of integration, saying, for instance, in 1970 that integration was a "systematic plan to destroy blacks."[20] But Jesse Jackson idolized Thurman, and when they were together he was said to have "literally sat at the master's feet."[21] He has claimed that his most famous catchphrase, "I am somebody," came from reading *Jesus and the Disinherited.* Thurman was, for Jackson, "a teacher of teachers, a leader of leaders, a preacher of preachers."[22] In 1981, Jackson delivered the main eulogy at Thurman's funeral.[23]

Derrick Bell (1932–2011) was a controversial legal theorist, the first tenured African American professor at Harvard Law School. He is widely seen as the primary founder of critical race theory, and his views on integration, the possibility of racial progress, and racial reconciliation were caustically negative.[24] Bell wrote in 1992 that "black people will never gain full equality in this country. Even those herculean efforts we hail as successful will produce no more than temporary 'peaks of progress,' short-lived victories that slide into irrelevance as racial patterns adapt in ways that maintain white dominance."[25] He is remembered for arguing that the U.S. Supreme Court should have modified the *Plessy v. Ferguson* precedent in 1954 rather than overturning it, because, he felt, *Brown* merely weakened Black institutions without providing for Black educational equality.[26]

Bell loved Thurman and was deeply influenced by his teachings. In 1978, after watching a recent full-length interview with Thurman that was broadcast on PBS, Bell wrote to him, telling him that he wanted to be "among the multitudes who deluge your office with favorable comments. . . . Our whole family enjoyed it immensely." He thought that one interview was not enough, and Bell wrote to PBS suggesting that the broadcaster sponsor "a whole series of shows that would give a long-term forum" to present his philosophy.[27] In 1982, Bell, invited to the wedding of a former student, could not attend but sent a present: a copy of Thurman's autobiography, *With Head and Heart*. "As wedding gifts go, we hope you will consider this a combination toaster-oven, silver platter, crystal goblet for your soul," he wrote. "Howard Thurman was a great man whose greatness grew out of life experiences that with his abiding faith in God, he translated into sermons and writings that offered insight and provided uplift to all who came into contact with him."[28]

Bell suggested that the essence of critical race theory and the spirituals were "quite similar." Both "communicate understanding and reassurance to needy souls trapped in a hostile world."[29] Bell often quoted Thurman on the spirituals and Black religion.[30] For Bell, as for Thurman, the spirituals were the first and most enduring example of how people of African descent in American captivity, during and after legal slavery, were able to "make something out of nothing," carving out "a humanity for themselves with absolutely nothing to help—save imagination, will, and unbelievable strength and courage."[31] Bell appreciated Thurman's emphasis on Black spiritual survival, a self-generated connection to God that could not be taken from them and did not depend on legal or citizenship status. I was told that when Bell was dying, he asked that Thurman's *The Negro Spiritual Speaks of Life and Death* be read to him. In its final passage, it states that enslaved people discovered that God "was not, nor could he be exhausted by, any single experience or any series of experiences. To know Him was to live a life worthy of the loftiest meaning of life. Men in all ages and climes, slave or free, trained or untutored, who have sensed the same values, are their fellow-pilgrims who journey together with them."[32]

This vision of Black historicity helped shape the work of the three historians who are the subject of the remainder of this chapter: Lerone Bennett Jr. (1928–2018), Vincent Harding (1931–2014), and Nathan I. Huggins (1927–89). They are three of the most prominent historians of Black America during the civil rights era. They were African American, and all knew Thurman well; they looked to him as a spiritual mentor, and his imprint on their work as historians was profound. The differences among them were as significant as what they had in common. Bennett was a journalist by training, writing for a nonacademic audience, a master of the genre of popular history. Harding was an academically trained historian but spent much of his career teaching at religious seminaries and wrote extensively on the confluences between religious belief and history. Huggins was an academic historian who occupied some of the loftiest positions in the profession.

It is easy to make a strong case for Thurman's influence on these historians. A more challenging issue is to explain how this influence persisted across what appears to be a considerable ideological divide between Thurman and two of the historians, Bennett and Harding, who were among the most influential supporters of Black Power during the civil rights era.

Sorting African American political and social thought into neat pigeonholes—integrationist, assimilationist, nationalist, separatist—belies its complexity. If Thurman's public statements on racial reconciliation were usually hopeful and unfailingly irenic, in the right mood, and to the right Black audience, he could be as outspoken in condemning white racism as any 1960s radical. In 1937, he wrote to a friend about the limitations of the "stupid white mind." He no doubt spoke even more frankly with his closest Black peers—or when writing only for himself.[33] In 1970, while traveling overseas, he recorded in a journal his "sense of shame to be classified with American white society and regarded in the same way. Sometimes I have wanted to shout, I am with them by necessity but I am not one of them."[34]

Thurman and his younger admirers strenuously tried to bridge the generational gap. If they listened with great attention to Thurman, Vincent Harding recalled "how carefully and sympathetically he questioned me about the Black Power/Black Identity movement. What are the young people doing, what are they thinking, where do you think they are going? Critical, compassionate, hopeful, and eager to understand—he was all of those things as we talked into the night."[35] Thurman, from before his time in India, had been a vehement opponent of Western imperialism. He appreciated that the Black nationalist turn in the United States was part of a worldwide rejection of white authority. When asked in 1967 about whether the "new black is back movement" was "a racial craze or cure," Thurman told a reporter that he was uncertain but that the nationalist turn had a "much broader base" than its predecessors, such as the movement of Marcus Garvey: "It's part of a worldwide wave that is just now lapping at our shores."[36] Thurman memorably described his complex reaction to Black radicalism in *The Search for Common Ground*: "We are angered by their anger, even though secretly we marvel at the courage of their anger. . . . [W]e are shocked by their failure to respond to our values, even as we are humiliated by our own sense of failure and inadequacy. It is from the life of our youth that we discover that we have lost our way. . . . [T]hey turn and rend us because we have sought to nourish them with the sense of our failure."[37]

Lerone Bennett, a native of Mississippi, was born in 1928. Like Thurman, he was a Morehouse Man, class of 1949, and through the Morehouse connection knew Thurman.[38] Bennett was a journalist and by the mid-1950s was living in Chicago, working for Johnson Publishing Company, the publisher of *Ebony*, where, in various capacities, he would remain for the rest of his long career.[39] Bennett's politics from the early 1950s on have been described as "militant."[40] In 1962, he published the first of many editions of *Before the Mayflower: A History of the Negro in America, 1619–1962*. It would be the most widely read African American history of its generation, only one of a number of historical and political works he would publish.[41]

As much as anyone, Bennett popularized the term "Black Power." His first *Ebony* article on Reconstruction, "Black Power in Dixie," appeared in July 1962, and he started a longer series about Reconstruction, under the heading "Black Power," beginning in November 1965, some eight months before Stokely Carmichael's famous "Black Power" speech in Greenwood, Mississippi, on July 28, 1966, which is usually credited with popularizing the phrase. In 1967, Bennett's essays on Reconstruction were reprinted under the title *Black Power U.S.A.: The Human Side of Reconstruction, 1867–1877*.[42]

Bennett's history writing has been described by its most careful student as "offering a black nationalist infused historical vision which celebrated the 'power of blackness' across time and space."[43] In a 1967 article in *Jet* (another Johnson Publishing Company magazine) on the revival of Garveyism during the Black Power era, Bennett is quoted in direct refutation of Thurman:

> According to famed Negro theologian-educator-philosopher Dr. Howard Thurman, Garvey's movement failed because it contained "one fatal flaw; alienation." Most Negroes, Dr. Thurman points out, feel that this is their land, too, and want to make their stand here for equality.
>
> Historian Bennett grapples with the alienation view by declaring: "Just our roots are here. We helped build this country. But black people are de facto aliens, no matter what anyone else says."[44]

Like many activists in the late 1960s, Bennett took up the cudgels for what he called, in a memorable address in 1969, "the challenge of blackness."[45] Many of his writings during this period strongly and aggressively promoted a revolutionary Black agenda, decrying the internal colonialism present in the inner cities and speculating on schemes for autonomous Black governance, either within or outside existing American constitutional structures.[46] At that time, for several years he was closely associated with the Atlanta-based Institute of the Black World, led by Vincent Harding. Throughout, he remained close to Thurman, and in 1971, when Thurman was annoyed by what he thought was a preponderance of "white camp followers" of Martin Luther King Jr. writing histories of the Civil Rights Movement, he thought it would be a "a vast catastrophe" if this story was not also told from a Black perspective and wanted Bennett to remedy the omission.[47]

To say that Bennett admired Thurman is a great understatement. In 1978, Bennett published a lengthy profile in *Ebony*, "Howard Thurman: 20th Century Holy Man."[48] Probably no article about Thurman published in his lifetime reached a larger African American audience. The article described Thurman as a "shy, retiring,

God-intoxicated theologian," stating that some of his admirers, in whose ranks Bennett certainly included himself, say that he "is a saint or, at the least, the nearest thing to a saint we are likely to see in the 20th century." After Thurman's death, Bennett wrote about Thurman that "it was an honor to live in the same world with this man." If his contemporaries had failed to take his full measure, future generations would recognize him as one of "the great souls of the 20th century."[49]

Vincent Harding was born in New York City in 1931, of Barbadian parents, and received his doctorate in American religious history from the University of Chicago in 1965. But by then had already thrown himself into the civil rights struggle and became a close aide of Martin Luther King Jr. He was the primary drafter of the famous address on April 4, 1967, at Riverside Church in Manhattan in which King decisively broke with the Johnson administration over the war in Vietnam.[50] After King's assassination, Harding became the first director of the King Center and affiliated Institute of the Black World (IBW), an African American think tank. Harding remained with the IBW when its radicalism and nationalism led to a severing of ties with the King Center. The IBW was never able to find a firm financial footing, and he left in the mid-1970s.[51] He thereafter taught both history and religious studies, and from 1981 until his retirement he taught at the Iliff School of Theology in Denver.

While Bennett has a claim to be the popularizer of the term "Black Power," Harding is a candidate for the first promoter of the idea of Black theology, as the term has come to be understood. By 1967, while still personally close to King, he was writing that Black people were ready to move beyond the time when "nonviolence was our watchword and integration our heavenly city," with its combination of "smugness and self-sacrifice," linking arms while singing "our song."[52] In 1968, he wrote that the necessary radical social movement towards Black liberation would not take place without the acute suffering and shedding of blood that has long been predicted by the Black radicals. If Black people must kill, let them not murder children in Vietnam, but "the fat, pious white Christians who guard their lawns and their daughters while engineering slow death for us."[53] That same year, he wrote about King's "Pollyanna voice" and that "King's God often seems no less dead than anyone else's."[54]

In 1970, the IBW published a short pamphlet by Harding titled, *Beyond Chaos: Black History and the Search for the New Land*. In it, Harding drew a distinction between "Negro history" and "Black history." Negro history was a history that "did not intend to threaten the established heroes or basic values of America" and believed that Negroes could be incorporated into "an American society which would not be basically changed by their presence." Black history, instead, insists that "the Black past cannot be remade and clearly known without America's larger past being shaken at its foundations," an America that is "counter-life, counter-joy, in league with ultimate nothingness and death." Who, he asks, "wants to integrate with cancer?"[55]

Harding's major historical opus was *There Is a River: The Black Struggle for Freedom in America* (1981).[56] *There Is a River* is a study of antebellum Black resistance to slavery, the narrative ending in 1865. It is uncompromising. In it, Harding largely dismisses the entire white abolitionist tradition and Black abolitionists he thought were beholden to it, such as Frederick Douglass, as a "burden" to Black people for thinking that a peaceful solution to the problem of slavery was possible.[57] Even John Brown was faulted for just wanting to free the slaves and failing to recognize that "black freedom could not be obtained without revolutionary transformation of the entire society."[58]

Howard and Sue Bailey Thurman had few greater admirers than Harding and his wife, Rosemary Freeney Harding. In 1974, they wrote a testimonial to Thurman, read at a public tribute: "In more ways than we can say, you have been a deep river for us, and our entire beings are richer and stronger for the recurrent baptisms in your presence."[59] The phrase "deep river" was not chosen at random. It was the title of Thurman's best-known book on Negro spirituals, to which Harding pays tribute in the title of *There Is a River.*[60] Harding's book was published a few months after Thurman died, in April 1981. Thurman had helped him find a publisher.[61] Its dedication page opens with this tribute:

> To the memory of Howard Thurman,
> Father in the faith,
> Companion in the way,
> Dauntless and peaceable warrior
> For a world of love, justice, and truth.[62]

Harding remained committed to preserving Thurman's legacy, helping to edit the first anthology of his writings, and was the author of several important essays about his teachings, including a luminous foreword to a 1996 reissue of *Jesus and the Disinherited.*[63]

Nathan Irvin Huggins was born in Chicago in 1927, son of a Black father and an Ashkenazi Jewish mother. His father deserted his family when Nathan was twelve. His mother moved the family to San Francisco, but she died two years later. In the mid-1940s, the teenage Huggins moved into the ambit of the Thurmans, and he and his younger sister, Kathryn, in all but name became members of the Thurman family.[64] Thurman and Huggins would refer to their relation as that of father and son.[65] In the acknowledgments to his first book, Huggins wrote about his intimate friendship with Thurman and their "casual Sunday talks" while "watching televised morality plays in the guise of professional football, unraveled theological knots.

In those struggles between Good and Evil, Evil, true to life, triumphed more often than not."[66] Sue Bailey Thurman was the dedicatee of his second book: "My debt to the one this book is dedicated to goes beyond explanation. Her belief in me, when there was little to rest it on, was a profound influence on my spiritual and intellectual development. She reared me from the subjunctive to the declarative mood."[67] His 1989 obituary in the *New York Times*—he died much too soon—lists his survivors as his wife and "his adoptive mother, Sue Bailey Thurman of San Francisco."[68] While this was a spiritual and not a legal adoption, it was just as binding and enduring. Of the three historians studied here, Huggins was the closest personally and intellectually to Thurman.

With the guidance and support of the Thurmans, Huggins, who had dropped out of high school to support his sister and himself, entered the University of California, Berkeley, then went to Harvard, where he obtained his doctorate in history, studying with Oscar Handlin. Huggins wrote a pathbreaking study of the Harlem Renaissance in 1971 and, among other works, published *Black Odyssey: The Afro-American Ordeal in Slavery* in 1977.[69] In his many articles and essays, in the words of David Blight, Huggins was a "a kind of epistemologist of African American history," someone who addressed and "loved the big questions."[70]

No issue was bigger for Huggins, or for academic historians in the 1980s in general, than the quest for new "master narratives" an endeavor that, to quote Blight again, became "a preoccupation, indeed a virtual genre among American historians" demanding a "return to 'narrative' and synthesis."[71] This was certainly a preoccupation of Huggins, in large part because he felt the new African American and social history had punctured the prevailing paradigms and scholars of Black history had a crucial role to play in putting American history back together again. This demanded unblinking honesty from both white and Black scholars. "We have come to expect direct, straightforward, honest, self-critical, socially critical, and proud black self-expression," he wrote in 1971.[72] History was one thing; "moralistic hero worship" was another.[73] He rejected the notion that in response to the standard historical narratives that marginalized Blacks, "Negroes should create their own myths, call them history, and thus serve their own emotional needs and self-concept."[74] Huggins called for a vibrant African American history, but not "historical emotionalism" or history "obliterated by strong feelings of black rage and white guilt."[75] (These he compared to "biting on an aching tooth, sucking pleasure from the pain of it."[76])

At the same time, Huggins thought that a new historical synthesis had to do much more than blandly add African Americans and other neglected groups to the existing "master narratives" in some sort of mechanical or perfunctory fashion. A new synthesis had to place African Americans at its center and emphasize "what is remarkable about much that is called black culture is its Americanness;

and conversely, much of what is considered most uniquely American is essentially Afro-American."[77] It was Huggins's deepest belief that "there can be no white history or black history, nor can there be an integrated history that does not begin to comprehend that slavery and freedom, white and black, are joined at the hip."[78] As he wrote in the concluding words of his final essay, written as he knew he was dying: "Our times seem to call for new myths and a revised master narrative that better inspire and reflect upon our new condition. Such a new narrative would find inspiration, for instance, in an oppressed people who defied social death as slaves and freedmen, insisting on their humanity and creating a culture despite a social consensus that they were 'a brutish sort of people.'"[79] In 1993, Harding wrote about his departed friend: "The relentless quest for a new 'master narrative' of our nation's history was the magnificent obsession of our late colleague, Nathan Irvin Huggins."[80]

Huggins's "magnificent obsession" was one that Harding himself and Bennett also sought, in their own ways. It was Thurman's obsession, as well. A key but understated message of *Jesus and the Disinherited* was that African Americans in the mid-twentieth century needed to think of themselves as did Jews in first century CE Palestine, as possessors of a universal message of freedom. What makes an oppressed people unique is also what makes their story universal. Oppression cannot—or, at least, should not—be hoarded. To lift the burden, its meaning has to be shared. This was a crucial aspect of America's "search for a soul," which Thurman could speak of in rapt Hegelian-providential terms.[81] The three historians, in their work, in different ways, responded to the challenge of Thurman's demand for a new Black universalism.

After Thurman's death, Bennett said of him that he was "a *black* man—a black man totally, passionately, creatively engaged in a quest for a common ground beyond race, beyond creed, beyond labels. I knew him, in short, as a world soul, but the world soul I knew was a black man rooted in the universality of his own idiom . . . who came out of the black religious tradition with a message of hope and wholeness for all men, all woman, all people."[82] In his article about Thurman in *Ebony,* Bennett recorded the following conservation:

> "You see, I feel that all life is one. . . . I don't remember when I didn't think it. And this is the thing that created the emotional crisis in my life when dealing with white people. It's—he paused, searching for the right word—it's the most *basic* concept I have about life and its meaning that all life is one. And that—he slapped his thigh—has to include White people." He paused, and added with a whoop of a laugh, "And some Negroes I know."[83]

Bennett argued that Blacks "are the most historical of" peoples "because we were created by history and because that history never lets us go."[84] When he argued that "history is life" and "history is everything, it is everywhere," he was to some extent substituting "history" for what Thurman saw as the oneness of "life."[85] Like Thurman, Bennett insisted on the universal message of Black history: "African Americans were forced by their circumstances to struggle for a deeper meaning of freedom in America."[86] Bennett was a Black nationalist who had great admiration for white abolitionists such as Thaddeus Stevens, who he thought responded genuinely and creatively to the Black freedom struggle. An impetus for Bennett's lifelong crusade against what he believed was the inflated historical reputation of Abraham Lincoln was his feeling that undue homage to Lincoln obscured the importance of both white and Black radicals. A quarter of the twenty persons and heroes of the Black freedom cause profiled in the volume *Pioneers in Protest* (1969) were white.[87]

For Huggins, Thurman's message was a liberation from "the narrow provincialism" of self, race, and sect.[88] But for Huggins the new Black history was also a way for Black scholars such as himself to find themselves amid an academic "sea of Eurocentric whiteness" and liberate themselves from white mentors or colleagues who "were inclined to regard what they did not know about [Black history] of being of little or no importance" and from the crushing assumption that Black scholars "could not be objective about their history."[89] Huggins understood the need for and potency of new Black myths but felt they required Black historians to tell the right sort of stories to Black audiences—stories that would inspire without distorting the past or making false promises about the future. His study of the Harlem Renaissance was less a conventional history than an extended analysis of what it meant to be part of that "intriguing moment when a people decide that they are the instruments of history-making and race-building."[90] But for Huggins, most of the major Renaissance figures expended too much time trying to construct a flattering counter-myth rather than seriously grappling with Black history and Black reality. They were too engaged in rejecting Black servility to realize that Blacks had never been servile, too intent on creating High Negro Art to acknowledge the extraordinary Black creativity all around them. They had no "clear sense of the past"; for them "it was a general and abstract thing."[91] They failed to seriously grapple with the phenomenon of slavery, which embarrassed them. Africa, too, was just a symbol, another way to distance themselves from their own American histories. They tried too hard to justify Black lives to a white audience, rather than just describe it. In this, Huggins was echoing Thurman's long-held disdain for performative Blackness, which for Thurman meant defining oneself in terms of one's relation to white America, even if this involved its bitter condemnation. Huggins and Thurman were not advocates of Black Power. But they both strongly believed in the need for African Americans to come to know themselves as a people, and if this had to be done, for want of an alternative, within a racist white America, it could be accomplished only by Black people themselves.

Black Odyssey was Huggins's most extended effort at trying to understand the historical processes of Black self-knowledge and, at the same time, lay the foundations for a better African American mythology. It is one reason that it is a very unusual work of history and strains at the conventions of history writing. It is a history of African American slavery written with few dates or place names, with few quotations from slave narratives or references to the contemporary historiography on slavery (a historiography that Huggins knew backward and forward). It was a history that, as Huggins wrote, attempted to provide "a model, an archetype" of the experience of slavery. He wanted to capture "wherever possible the emotional and spiritual essence of [enslaved people's] experience"; he felt he had to "cho[o]se a style, often evocative and impressionistic, which departs from the conventional descriptive and analytic exposition of standard histories" to get closer to the "hearts and minds" of people whose lives "are outside our experience to know."[92] It was a book in which "the strokes are broad, antithesis muted or denied."[93] Some readers did not know what to make of it, and some did not think it was a real work of history.[94]

"We blacks writing Afro-American history," Huggins wrote in 1986, "no matter how much distance we like to maintain, are drawn to 'tell the story of our people' on epic scale."[95] In addition to *Black Odyssey,* he mentioned only one other example of epic Black history: Harding's *There Is a River.* After acknowledging that the two books had many differences in "scale, vision, in sense of history," he claimed that they had much in common. They shared a "literary character, the use of literary devices to insinuate oneself and one's ideas into the experience of both the subject." Both were books that "attempt to include the reader into the *we* of the history. These are not *they* and *me* books. *We* and *our* are the dominant (though often implied) pronouns; we as reader, we as writer, we as Africans, we as Afro-Americans, we as slaves."[96]

This could be a description, as well, of *Jesus and the Disinherited,* and both books by Huggins and Harding reflect the thought world and literary style of Thurman. This is most apparent for *Black Odyssey,* though an unfamiliarity with Thurman's work has led even its most astute readers to overlook this.[97] In a central passage, Huggins paraphrases the main argument of *Jesus and the Disinherited* that fear, deception, and hatred are the "three hounds of hell that track 'the trail of the disinherited.'"[98] Huggins writes that enslaved people, "as oppressed people, their souls' great challenges were three: that they might fall victim to fear of their oppressor, that they might compromise their integrity by deception, and that they might give their souls to hatred—natural enough tendencies given the circumstances. Some succumbed to them; but the remarkable thing is that most did not."[99]

The influence of Thurman on *There Is a River* is perhaps less obvious. In a review, August Meier asked how Harding could square the sometimes fierce Black nationalist sentiments in the book with his admiration for Thurman, who, said Meier, "was acutely aware of the tension involved in remaining true to the black tradition while contending for justice in America's multiracial society."[100] It was a good question. In *There Is a River,* Harding was trying to work toward an answer. There is in the book a distancing from his hard nationalism of a decade earlier, as when he writes in the introduction: "When King first came among us speaking of the need to carry on a struggle for justice and truth that would 'redeem the soul of America,' many of us tended to smile patronizingly or turn away in annoyed disbelief at such naiveté. It appears to me now that we rather than him might have been the innocents."[101]

Harding's turn to a version of Thurman's Black universalism would become more apparent in his later work. *There Is a River* was intended as the first volume of a two- or three-volume set. Harding never got around to writing the other volumes, probably because he decided that its scope was too limited. As early as 1983, he criticized his book for its failure to treat women's history in any depth and called for seeing America "through a variety of eyes, blacks, women, poor people, native Americans, Chicanos, Asian Americans, immigrants old and new."[102] In the same interview, asked for the influences on his historical writing, he went out of his way to praise Thurman. For Harding, he "was one of those older Black men who constantly lived ahead of their time. . . . [He] cannot easily be labeled. He was theologian, mystic, visionary, pastor, and concerned citizen-creator of a new, multiracial American reality."[103] Thurman told a friend, late in life, that he believed "the outcome of every sectarian religion or point of view is inclusive rather than exclusive," but "one cannot be everywhere if one doesn't start from somewhere." He gave an example: "Black revolutionaries are no longer considering separatism."[104] Perhaps he was thinking of Harding.

In his later works, Harding was a pioneer of multicultural history. In a review published in 1994, he praised Ronald Takaki's *A Different Mirror: A History of Multicultural America,* one of the first widely read multicultural histories, as showing that if we are satisfied only with "the story of our own group's life and times," it "will likely leave us in the state of fragmentation, confusion, and isolation."[105] In a 1997 interview, Harding was asked about the movement in his scholarly writings "from a focus on African American history" to "a more all-encompassing way of talking about issues of democracy." He answered that he had not changed so much as that he now emphasized the inherent potential for all peoples to benefit from the Black struggle for freedom: "Black people were in a sense breathing in the fragrance of what democratic development could do for us and the nation."[106] But if he found a limitation in Takaki's work, it was his relative neglect of religion, which "deprives us of one of the crucial elements in the struggle for common ground."[107]

Creating this new America, against the insuperable odds it faced, was for all three historians a religious task, as Thurman understood it, and as they understood Thurman, as a refusal to give way to despair. Huggins described African American history since Reconstruction as what happens when "with each achievement a new corner would seem to have been turned . . . , yet each turning seemed to lead back to the same place."[108] The final words of *Black Odyssey* are the closing words of F. Scott Fitzgerald's masterpiece, *The Great Gatsby*: "So we beat on, boats against the current, borne ceaselessly into the past."[109] Bennett's, Huggins's, Harding's, and Thurman's deep rivers all flow in the same directions, toward a lost and misunderstood past and toward a future in which America, in all of its fissiparous divisions, is truly made whole.

In *The Search for Common Ground*, Thurman wrote, "As long as I can remember . . . [I have had] a tendency—even more, an inner demand—for 'whole-making,' a feel for a completion in and of things, for inclusive consummation."[110] Wholes could be found in nature, in community, in life, or in God or they could be created by historians from the hard world of recalcitrant and adamantine facts. To synthesize, to make complex wholes out of seemingly disparate parts, was to touch the divine. In his final essay, his testament, Huggins, probably the least religious of the historians profiled here, wrote, "Whenever we write history, we do so with a sense of transcendent meaning," for it was "God's presence if you will—that shapes our work ideologically and morally, as well as scientifically."[111]

In the 1920s, Thurman rejected the advice of his main adviser at Rochester Theological Seminary, George Cross, that he should choose between "transitory social problems" and his gift for elucidating the "timeless issues of the human spirit." Cross, he thought, just did not understand that "a man and his black skin must face the 'timeless issues of the human spirit' together."[112] Thurman's common ground was a meeting place of Black particularity and human universality. During his final illness in early 1981, after one near-death experience, going in and out of consciousness, he awoke he told his wife, Sue, that he had finally solved the problem of duality that had haunted him since his childhood. He "had encountered the 'particular' man and the 'universal' man within himself and wrestled them to earth, until he won the consent of both—to Life, to Death, and back to Life."[113] Thurman took the secret of this final reconciliation with him, and that is probably fitting. These final words from Thurman were about many things—life and death, the individual and the collective, male and female, Black and white, the universe and God. But if it was not only about overcoming the contradictions of the particularities and universalities of African American history, it was surely part of it.

Notes

1. W. E. B. Du Bois, *Black Reconstruction in America, 1860–1880* (New York: Atheneum, [1935] 1992).

2. Mahadev Desai, "With Our Negro Guests," in *The Papers of Howard Washington Thurman*, 5 vols. ed. Walter Earl Fluker (Columbia: University of South Carolina Press, 2009–19) (hereafter, *PHWT*), 1:333–34. On the India trip, see Quinton Dixie and Peter Eisenstadt, *Visions of a Better World: Howard Thurman's Pilgrimage to India and the Origins of African American Nonviolence* (Boston: Beacon, 2011).

3. See Peter Eisenstadt, *Against the Hounds of Hell: A Life of Howard Thurman* (Charlottesville: University of Virginia Press, 2021).

4. For Thurman on Tubman, see Eisenstadt, *Against the Hounds of Hell*, 479–80n27. For Sue Bailey Thurman's historical interests, see *PHWT*, 4:325n1, 326n3; *PHWT*, 5:171n1.

5. Howard Thurman to James M. Nabritt, letter, March 6, 1962, in *PHWT*, 4:320–22. On the interest of the Howard Thurman Educational Trust in African American history, see *PHWT*, 5:xix–xx.

6. As in the description in James Farmer, *Lay Bare the Heart: An Autobiography of the Civil Rights Movement* (New York: Plume, 1985), 136.

7. Thurman wrote in 1939 that "slavery stripped the African to the literal substance of himself, depriving him of those props on which men commonly depend—language, custom, and social solidarity. In addition to all of this he was a slave; without freedom of movement or of person": Howard Thurman, "Religious Ideas in Negro Spirituals," *Christendom* 4 (Autumn 1939): 515.

8. See "The Message of the Spirituals" (October 1928), in *PHWT*, 1:126–38; Howard Thurman, *Deep River and the Negro Spiritual Speaks of Life and Death* (New York: Harper and Brothers, 1955); Eisenstadt, *Against the Hounds of Hell*, 123–126.

9. Nathan Irvin Huggins, *Black Odyssey: The Afro-American Ordeal in Slavery* (New York: Vintage, 1977), 250 (reprinted in 1990 as *Black Odyssey: The African American Ordeal in Slavery*); Nathan Huggins, Memorial Tribute, in "Simmering on the Calm Presence and Profound Wisdom of Howard Thurman," special issue of *Debate and Understanding*, ed. Ricardo A. Millet and Conley H. Hughes (Spring 1982): 82.

10. Howard Thurman, "America in Search of a Soul" (1976), in *A Strange Freedom: The Best of Howard Thurman on Religious Experience and Public Life*, ed. Walter Earl Fluker and Catherine Tumber (Boston: Beacon, 1998), 272.

11. Howard Thurman, *Jesus and the Disinherited* (New York: Abingdon-Cokesbury, 1949).

12. Ibid., 11.

13. For other works by Thurman defending integration, see "A 'Native Son' Speaks" (June 1940) and "The Will to Segregation" (August 1943), in *PHWT*, 2:246–52, 337–42; "Desegregation, Integration, and the Beloved Community" (September 1966), in *PHWT*, 5:147–59.

14. Howard Thurman, *The Luminous Darkness: A Personal Interpretation of the Anatomy of Segregation and the Ground for Hope* (New York: Harper and Row, 1965), 58–59.

15. *PHWT*, 5:151.

16. See ibid., 5:140–44.

17. Howard Thurman, *The Search for Common Ground* (New York: Harper and Row, 1971), 96–97.

18. George K. Makechnie, "Remembering Dr. Howard Thurman," *New Crisis* 106 (November–December 1999): 26–28.

19. Howard Thurman, "Review: Liberation and Reconciliation: A Black Theology," Howard Thurman Papers, Howard Gotlieb Archival Research Center, Boston University (hereafter,

Thurman Papers), box 7, folder 56. This is a review of J. Deotis Roberts, *Liberation and Reconciliation* (Philadelphia: Westminster, 1971).

20. "Jackson Sees Plot in Integration Guise," *Baltimore Afro-American,* September 19, 1970.

21. Walter Earl Fluker, *Ethical Leadership: The Quest for Character, Civility, and Community* (Minneapolis: Fortress, 2009), 17.

22. George K. Makechnie, *Howard Thurman: His Enduring Dream* (Boston: Howard Thurman Center, Boston University, 1988), 81.

23. For Thurman's friendship with Jesse Jackson, see *PHWT,* 5:234–36; Eisenstadt, *Against the Hounds of Hell,* 369–70, 373, 393.

24. Bell was critical race theory's "intellectual father figure." Richard Delgado and Jean Stefancic, "Introduction," in *Critical Race Theory: An Introduction,* by Richard Delgado and Jean Stefancic (New York: New York University Press, 2001), 5. See also Jelani Cobb, "The Man behind Critical Race Theory," *New Yorker,* September 13, 2021.

25. Derrick Bell, "Racial Realism" (1992), in *The Derrick Bell Reader,* ed. Richard Delgado and Jean Stefancic (New York: New York University Press, 2005), 74.

26. For Bell on the *Brown* decision, see Derrick Bell, *Silent Covenants: Brown v. Board of Education and the Unfulfilled Hopes for Racial Reform* (New York: Oxford University Press, 2004.) See also Derrick Bell, "Serving Two Masters: Integration Ideals and Client Interest in School Desegregation Litigation" and "*Brown v. Board of Education* and the Interest Convergence Dilemma," in *Critical Race Theory: The Key Writings That Formed the Movement,* ed. Kimberlé Crenshaw, Neil Gotanda, Gary Peller, and Thomas Kendall (New York: New Press, 1995), 5–19, 20–28.

27. Derrick Bell to Howard Thurman, letter, February 27, 1978, in *PHWT,* 5:286–90. In the letter, Bell praises Lerone Bennett's article "Howard Thurman: 20th Century Holy Man" (*Ebony,* vol. 33, no. 4, February 1978, 68–70, 72, 76, 84–85) as a "spiritual oasis." Bell wrote a letter to Thurman on May 15, 1978, regretting a missed opportunity for a meeting. In response, Thurman wrote to Bell that he looked "forward to a time when it will be possible for you and me to have a long visit about many things relevant to our journey. I am sure you know that your life and career are a source of authentic inspiration to me": Thurman Papers, box 48, folder 22. Bell was the author of the unpublished paper "Howard Thurman and the Christians as Racist Paradox" (see *PHWT,* 5:289n8), a copy of which I have been unable to obtain. See also Eisenstadt, *Against the Hounds of Hell,* 370.

28. Derrick and Jewel Bell to Cleo[phus] and Carla, July 1982, letter in the author's possession. I thank Cleophus Thomas Jr. for sharing this letter with me and allowing me to quote it for publication: Howard Thurman, *With Head and Heart: The Autobiography of Howard Thurman* (New York: Harcourt Brace Jovanovich, 1979).

29. Derrick Bell, "Who's Afraid of Critical Race Theory?" (1995) in Delgado and Stefancic, *The Derrick Bell Reader,* 81–83.

30. Derrick Bell, *And We Are Not Saved: The Elusive Quest for Racial Justice* (New York: Basic, 1987), 215–17, quoting in full Thurman's "On Viewing the Coast of Africa," his meditation on African bodies in slave ships. Thurman's meditation was reprinted in several various places, including in *With Head and Heart,* 193–94. Bell quotes Thurman's book of meditations *Deep Is the Hunger* (New York: Harper and Brothers, 1951), in *Ethical Ambition: Living a Life of Meaning and Worth* (New York: Bloomsbury, 2002), 61–62.

31. Bell, *Ethical Ambition,* 172–73.

32. Rev. Dr. Paul Smith, in "Tributes in Memory of Professor Derrick Bell," *Derrick Bell Official Site,* October 14, 2011, accessed April 25, 2016, http://professorderrickbell.com/tributes/rev-paul-smith; Paul Smith, interview by the author, February 29, 2016. Howard Thurman, *The*

Negro Spiritual Speaks of Life and Death (1947; repr. *Deep River and the Negro Spiritual Speaks of Life and Death* [New York: Harper and Brothers, 1955]), 56. (In separate pagination after *Deep River*.)

33. Howard Thurman to (Miss) Joe E. Brown, letter, January 15, 1937, Thurman Papers, box 24, folder 14.

34. Howard Thurman, "Pacific Journal," in *PHWT*, 5:209–10.

35. Vincent Harding, "Introduction," in *For the Inward Journey: The Writings of Howard Thurman*, ed. Anne Spencer Thurman (New York: Harcourt Brace Jovanovich, 1984), xiii.

36. Chester Higgins, "What's Ahead for Blacks in U.S.?" *Jet*, August 10, 1967, 18.

37. Thurman, *The Search for Common Ground*, 93.

38. Lerone Bennett and W. E. Cross to Howard Thurman, June 6, 1956, Thurman Papers, box 35, folder 6.

39. For Bennett's biography, see James E. West, "*Ebony* Magazine, Lerone Bennett, Jr., and the Making of Modern Black History, 1943–1957" (Ph.D. thesis, University of Manchester, 2015), 37–40.

40. Ibid., 38. See also James E. West, *Ebony Magazine and Lerone Bennett Jr.: Popular Black History in Postwar America* (Urbana: University of Illinois Press, 2020).

41. Lerone Bennett Jr., *Before the Mayflower: A History of the Negro in America, 1619–1962* (Chicago: Johnson, 1962). Beginning in 1964, *Before the Mayflower* was published in paperback by Penguin, and after 1969, with an ever later end date, with the subtitle *A History of Black America*.

42. Lerone Bennett Jr., *Black Power U.S.A.: The Human Side of Reconstruction, 1865–1877* (Chicago: Johnson, 1967).

43. West, "*Ebony* Magazine, Lerone Bennett, Jr., and the Making of Modern Black History," 27.

44. Higgins, "What's Ahead for Blacks in U.S.?" 14–15.

45. Lerone Bennett, Jr, "The Challenge of Blackness," in *The Challenge of Blackness*, by Lerone Bennett Jr. (Chicago: Johnson, 1972), 33–44.

46. Ibid.

47. Cited in Eisenstadt, *Against the Hounds of Hell*, 373. See also *PHWT*, 5:199–201.

48. Bennett, "Howard Thurman." Thurman and his great friend Benjamin Mays were the co-dedicatees of Bennett's *The Shaping of Black America* (Chicago: Johnson, 1975).

49. Lerone Bennett, Memorial Tribute, in *Debate and Understanding*, 71–72.

50. For King's speech on Vietnam, see James M. Washington, ed., *A Testament of Hope: The Essential Writings and Speeches of Martin Luther King, Jr.* (New York: HarperCollins, 1986), 231–44.

51. See Derrick E. White, *The Challenge of Blackness: The Institute of the Black World and Political Activism in the 1970s* (Gainesville: University Press of Florida, 2011).

52. Vincent Harding, "Black Power and the American Christ" (January 1967), in *Black Theology: A Documentary History, 1966–1979*, ed. Gayraud S. Wilmore and James H. Cone (Maryknoll, NY: Orbis Books, 1979), 35–42.

53. Ibid.

54. Vincent Harding, "The Religion of Black Power," in *The Religious Situation: 1968*, ed. Donald R. Cutler (Boston: Beacon, 1968), 34. This was likely written before King's assassination. See also the interview in A. N. Said, "Dr. King Was 'Too Good' to Start Revolution," *Baltimore Afro-American*, August 30, 1969.

55. Vincent Harding, *Beyond Chaos: Black History and the Search for the New Land* (Atlanta: Institute of the Black World, 1970). Harding would later argue that this distinction was

overdrawn, done to sharpen debate: Henry Abelove, Betsy Blackmar, Peter Dimock, and Jonathan Schneer, eds., *Visions of History* (New York: Pantheon, 1983), 229.

56. Vincent Harding, *There Is a River: The Black Struggle for Freedom in America* (New York: Harcourt Brace Jovanovich, 1981).

57. Ibid., 128.

58. Ibid., 206. Harding also credits Bennett as an intellectual and personal influence, stating that he was a "peer, teacher, inspiration, and friend" and adding that, like many others, he found some of his earliest exposures to serious Black history in the pages of *Ebony*. "Here is somebody, almost totally outside the academy, who has taught me some very important lessons": Harding, quoted in Abelove et al., *Visions of History,* 234. The two men also contributed essays to a famous castigation of William Styron's *The Confessions of Nat Turner:* see Lerone Bennett Jr., "Nat's Last White Man," and Vincent Harding, "You've Gone and Taken My Nat," in *William Styron's Nat Turner: Ten Black Writers Respond,* ed. John Henrik Clarke (Boston: Beacon, 1968), 3–16, 23–33.

59. Vincent Harding to Howard Thurman, "For Howard Thurman: Brother, Father, Comrade," November 5, 1974, Thurman Papers, box 46, folder 23.

60. Thurman, *Deep River and the Negro Spiritual Speaks of Life and Death.*

61. On Thurman's friendship with Harding and his efforts to help him find a publisher, see *PHWT*, 5:249–54.

62. In the acknowledgments section of *There Is a River,* Harding calls Thurman his "surrogate father and spiritual guide," and one "who must still be recognized and thanked, even in the most imperfect and inadequate of ways": Harding, *There Is a River,* 334.

63. Harding, "Introduction," xiii; Vincent Harding, "Foreword," in Thurman, *Jesus and the Disinherited,* i–xii.

64. On Huggins, see David W. Blight, "In Retrospect: Nathan Irvin Huggins, the Art of History, and the Irony of the American Dream," in *Beyond the Battlefield: Race, Memory and the American Civil War,* by David W. Blight, (Amherst: University of Massachusetts Press, 2002), 258–77; Lawrence W. Levine, "The Historical Odyssey of Nathan Irvin Huggins," and Leon W. Litwack, "Nathan Huggins: A Personal Memoir," in *Revelations: American History, American Myths,* by Nathan Irvin Huggins, ed. Brenda Smith Huggins (New York: Oxford University Press, 1995), 3–20, 284–88. (Levine and Litwack were classmates of Huggins at Berkeley.)

65. For Thurman's relation to Huggins, see *PHWT*, 5:169–73.

66. Nathan Irvin Huggins, *Protestants against Poverty: Boston's Charities, 1870–1900* (Westport, CT: Greenwood, 1971), xiv.

67. Nathan Irvin Huggins, *Harlem Renaissance* (New York: Oxford University Press, 1971), xiv.

68. Alfonzo A. Narvaez, "Nathan I. Huggins, Educator, 62; Leader in Afro-American Studies," *New York Times,* December 7, 1989.

69. Huggins, *Harlem Renaissance;* Huggins, *Black Odyssey.*

70. Blight, "In Retrospect," 260.

71. Ibid., 263–64.

72. Nathan Irvin Huggins, "Review: The Quality of Hurt: The Autobiography of Chester Himes," *New York Times Book Review,* March 12, 1971.

73. Nathan I. Huggins, "Afro-American History: Myths, Heroes, Reality," in *Key Issues in the Afro-American Experience,* ed. Nathan I. Huggins, Martin Kilson, and Daniel M. Fox (New York: Harcourt Brace Jovanovich, 1971), 12.

74. Ibid., 10.

75. Ibid., 14.

76. Ibid., 14.

77. Ibid., 17.
78. Huggins, *Black Odyssey*, xiv.
79. Huggins, *Revelations*, 283.
80. Vincent Harding, "Healing at the Razor's Edge: Reflections on the History of Multicultural America," *Journal of American History* 81, no. 2 (September 1994): 571–72.
81. Thurman, "America in Search of a Soul," 264–72.
82. Bennett, Memorial Tribute, in *Debate and Understanding*, 71–72.
83. Bennett, "Howard Thurman."
84. Bennett, *The Challenge of Blackness*, 198.
85. Ibid., 194; Lerone Bennett Jr., "Listen to the Blood," *Ebony*, November 1985, 185–94.
86. Bennett, *The Challenge of Blackness*, 200; Bennett, "Listen to the Blood."
87. Lerone Bennett Jr., *Pioneers in Protest* (Chicago; Johnson, 1969). Wendell Phillips, William Lloyd Garrison, John Brown, Charles Sumner, and Thaddeus Stevens were profiled. For the culmination of Bennett's lifelong campaign against what he thought was Lincoln's inflated and undeserved reputation, see the six hundred-plus pages of *Forced into Glory: Abraham Lincoln's White Dream* (Chicago: Johnson, 2000). Thurman was an admirer of Lincoln.
88. Huggins, Memorial Tribute, in *Debate and Understanding*, 82.
89. Nathan I. Huggins, *Afro-American Studies: A Report to the Ford Foundation* (New York: Ford Foundation, 1985), 35–36. Both Huggins and Harding wrote their doctoral theses (which, in Huggins's case, became his first book) on non–African American subjects at the urging of their dissertation advisers.
90. Huggins, *Harlem Renaissance*, 3.
91. Ibid., 138.
92. Huggins, *Black Odyssey*, 2.
93. Nathan I. Huggins, "Integrating Afro-American History into American History," in *The State of Afro-American History: Past, Present, and Future*, ed. Darlene Clark Hine (Baton Rouge: Louisiana State University Press, 1986), 164–65.
94. Carl N. Degler, "Experiencing Slavery," *Reviews in American History* 6, no. 3 (September 1978): 277–82. For other reviews, most somewhat negative, see the citations in Blight, *Beyond the Battlefield*, 265. Blight relates that at the Organization of American Historians meeting in 1989, Huggins related to him that he felt that *Black Odyssey* "had never been fully understood or appreciated": ibid., 275n12.
95. Huggins, "Integrating Afro-American History into American History," 164–65.
96. Ibid.
97. Suggestions for Huggins's models include Huggins's dissertation adviser Oscar Handlin's *The Uprooted: The Epic Story of the Great Migration That Made the American People* (Boston: Little, Brown, 1951) and W. E. B. Du Bois's *The Souls of Black Folk* (Chicago: A. C. McClurg, 1903): see Blight, "In Retrospect," 261, 265–66, 268. Both are likely influences, but neither is mentioned by Huggins, who closes the book's bibliographic essay—there are no footnotes—with a tribute to Thurman: Huggins, *Black Odyssey*, 250.
98. Thurman, *Jesus and the Disinherited*, 35.
99. Huggins, *Black Odyssey*, 80–81.
100. August Meier, "Whither the Black Perspective in Afro-American Historiography," *Journal of American History* 70, no. 1 (June 1983): 101–5.
101. Harding, *There Is a River*, xxiii. Harding would later write extensively on King, emphasizing his radical politics and spirituality: see Vincent Harding, *Martin Luther King: The Inconvenient Hero* (Maryknoll, NY: Orbis Books, 2008).
102. Abelove et al., *Visions of History*, 238.

103. Ibid., 234.
104. Jean Burden, "Meditation on Howard Thurman on the Occasion of his Memorial Services April 10, 1981" (1982), Thurman Papers.
105. Harding, "Healing at the Razor's Edge," 580.
106. Rachel E. Harding and Vincent Harding, "Biography, Democracy and Spirit: An Interview with Vincent Harding," *Callaloo* 20, no. 3 (Summer 1997), 693–95.
107. Harding, "Healing at the Razor's Edge."
108. Huggins, *Black Odyssey,* 245.
109. Ibid., 247.
110. Thurman, *The Search for Common Ground,* 76.
111. Huggins, *Revelations,* 283.
112. Thurman, *With Head and Heart,* 60.
113. Sue Bailey Thurman, Memorial Tribute, in *Debate and Understanding,* 91.

Killing Calvin Crozier

HONOR, MYTH, AND MILITARY OCCUPATION AFTER APPOMATTOX

Lawrence T. McDonnell

WHITE LIES MATTER. ONE hundred fifty years after Reconstruction, that vanquished revolution for democratic rights, economic opportunity, and racial equality remains understudied in its local complexities and mired in myth and recrimination in the public memory. Since the 1960s, research has transformed scholarly understandings of this era. Yet Americans still mostly see the years after Appomattox through the images the filmmaker D. W. Griffith presented a century ago in *The Birth of a Nation:* corrupt, do-nothing lawmakers; duplicitous demagogues; ungovernable, overreaching Blacks; harassed, humiliated whites.[1] Polity, economy, community all teetered on the edge of ruin, in this view, until admirable, honorable Southern whites redeemed traditional values, conservative government, and racial order. A new nation was birthed thereby, rooted in white supremacy, economic inequality, and political disfranchisement. Ultimately, we are told, this arrangement best served—serves best—the needs of all.[2] Confederates lost the "War between the States" but won the peace and saved the nation by their steadfast labors, conservative patience, and personal sacrifice. Refined and transmuted across time, these deceitful claims have passed down racist poison as a "heritage" to succeeding generations. Almost since Appomattox, America's history remains ensnared in a web of vicious white lies.[3]

The reasons for the failure of a revolutionary history of Reconstruction to take hold in the public mind are consonant with the causes of the failure of Reconstruction itself. Liberal revisionist and radical scholarship has achieved much by a mostly top-down approach, focusing on national, state, and regional policy initiatives; the passage of constitutional amendments; the growth of schools and churches; changing systems of land tenure; and the reformation of gender, culture, and community.[4] Such histories have ruled the academy for decades now, yet they have failed altogether to counter what W. E. B. Du Bois called "The Propaganda of History." Across the South and far beyond, the white lay public has refused to surrender flawed and false narratives about their ancestors and their communities on which they base claims of personal and social identity, along with demands for special status and political power.[5]

From the beginning, at the local level, adulation of the Lost Cause grounded a political strategy of racial subjugation and class control. The monuments to Confederate military service that mark hundreds of communities across the South both honor white victimhood, resilience, and triumph and reinforce local imaginings of this contested era in a public way on a daily basis.[6] Against such highly specific, rich remembrances rooted in kinship, soil, and faith, scholarly analyses of a distant, abstract Reconstruction have stood no chance. Local readings of a cherished past may be tendentious, self-serving, and uninquisitive, imposing current prejudices and hatreds on faded and complex events, but history-as-alibi works precisely because it is grounded in the power of place. As during Reconstruction, forces urging revolutionary change too often turn out to be too far away to be much committed to going toe to toe over any particular scrap of ground.[7] Neo-Confederates prevail today in the war for the memory and meaning of Reconstruction for the same reason ex-Confederates won out in the 1870s: they are dug in and prepared to defend each of ten thousand tiny battlegrounds with a knowledge of terrain and a will to win that progressive scholars have utterly failed to match.[8]

To their credit, Southern conservatives make their point plain: in their histories of Reconstruction and beyond, white lives matter.[9] Revisionist and radical scholars have been more mealymouthed, yet they ironically reinforce the same claim. After 1865, they sigh, America was not ready for, not worthy of emancipation's bright promise. Reconstruction's revolution remained unfinished more than a century after Appomattox—alas! Yet there was little prospect that any more could have been gained any sooner. The emancipation of Black lives depended, regretfully, on the transformation of white hearts. It just took time—generations of lamentation and legislation—to topple racial barriers.[10]

But that liberal view roots pessimism in thin soil. It ignores how badly class struggle misfired in the Reconstruction era, downplays the decline of Republican dominance into self-seeking misrule, forgets how racial friction usually appeared first as class division.[11] By 1877, we are told, Reconstruction had run its necessarily limited course and perished of causes, if not quite natural, then certainly intrinsic to its operations. Surely, it had not been murdered in its prime. Nor should we fault freedpeople, their white allies, or the nation-state for failing to dish out the sort of violence required to defend radical goals that its enemies would eventually employ so ruthlessly to hoist themselves back into the saddle. That would have been, somehow, *too much*.[12] Long-standing white prejudice and fears of "negroes with guns" still warps scholarly analysis of the revolutionary potential of the Reconstruction era.[13]

Likewise, local fictions—white lies—doom any comprehensive reassessment of Reconstruction to death by a thousand cuts. Unless radical scholars take up conservatives' method of close combat over the past, it will be impossible to seize and hold any point on the intellectual battlefield, change minds, or influence public policy. Smashing monuments may feel cathartic, but it is a rejection of the power of historical analysis, and poor politics besides.[14] This essay advocates iconoclasm of a different sort. By focusing on the stories partisans of Confederate "heritage" love to tell, examining them closely, and retelling them more fully and accurately, we can beat the Rebs at their own game. The deeper we dig, I contend, the more radical—and altogether new—Reconstruction begins to look.

Here let us focus on a single public site of historical interpretation: a roadside marker in rural Newberry County, South Carolina, erected to commemorate a story of white honor, Black savagery, and Yankee perfidy supposedly enacted in the aftermath of Appomattox. Calibrating local claims handed down across the generations against a close reading of the documentary record provides the best strategy for transforming popular understanding of Reconstruction in years to come.[15] Examining afresh why one ex-Confederate came to face a Black firing squad in the autumn of 1865 shows how we have misjudged the parameters and dynamics of military occupation in the Civil War era. Even more, that killing may point to the secret of why Reconstruction failed, suggesting implications for our own time. At the least, we may set one small fable of Reconstruction a little straighter, in the spirit of benediction.

That is a lot to hang on the brutal demise of one man in a small town in 1865. Still, I am not the first to seek big meanings from this little incident. More than a hundred years ago, Newberrians proudly say, Governor "Pitchfork" Ben Tillman recounted the story of Calvin Crozier's killing to a North Carolina visitor. Thomas Dixon made that tale a key plot point in his best-selling novel of 1905, *The Clansman*.[16] A decade later, that book became *The Birth of a Nation*, "history written with lightning"—and deep prejudice.[17]

Today, an official-looking marker set up at the side of State Highway 395 recites the tale to passersby as they slow to cross railroad tracks near the southern edge of town. Hard by a pleasant garden center and a thriving heating and cooling business, it declares this to be the "Calvin Crozier Murder Site":

Colonel Charles Trowbridge of the 33rd U.S. Colored Troops ordered the execution of Calvin Crozier, former private 3rd Kentucky Cavalry, on Sept. 8, 1865. Crozier, while en route to his Texas home, cut a troop member on the back of the neck during a quarrel concerning two ladies traveling with Crozier. Soldiers of the 33rd arrested an innocent man for the assault, but Crozier identified himself as the assailant. He was taken to 33rd headquarters, shot, and buried in a shallow grave about 100 yards south. The same day residents of Newberry exhumed the body, placed it in a coffin, and reburied it. In 1891 citizens moved Crozier's remains to Rosemont Cemetery about 1.4 miles west and erected a monument to his memory. The army court-martialed Trowbridge for Crozier's execution.[18]

The matter with the marker is that its words lay out a narrative that hardly seems to justify notice. Military executions—and wrongful ones, too—were not rare in the Civil War era.[19] Crozier's death was a miscarriage of military justice, we learn. But the deeper wrong of this summary killing was greater than a failure of due process. There is no sign of racism, strictly construed, in the marker's wording, no hint of inaccuracy. Yet insinuation and silence shape the story it tells, culminating in the inflammatory charge of "murder": here an unoffending Southern white man, dutifully defending honor's principles, was slain by Northern-led Blacks. On its face, this was a racial killing inflicted as retribution by vengeful Blacks on a brave Confederate veteran who aimed only to go home in peace.

Crozier's "quarrel," in some way, concerned "two ladies"—decent white women, we suppose. Just how the quarrel erupted or what matter it turned on readers must imagine for themselves. Certainly, there are familiar templates of gendered disputation between Southern Blacks and whites, accumulated across the decades of lynching and segregation, from which to draw.[20] The creators of this marker—a local branch of the Sons of Confederate Veterans—reconstruct this rebel as hero and victim both, a fitting symbol of the Lost Cause. The local community rescued his broken body, restoring it to a resting place of admiration and respect. Here is the Crucifixion, á la Jim Crow. In honoring Crozier, white Newberry esteems its ancestors and itself, too.

Such tropes fuel neo-Confederate sympathies across the region and abiding animosity toward those unable to recognize Reconstruction as a tragic crime inflicted on a depleted white citizenry. The problem is that white witnesses in Newberry, their descendants, and supporters from New York to Texas have skewed and embellished the Crozier story far beyond the documentary record. The tale they told grew fuller across the decades, more lurid, more satisfying to local tastes—and quite unlike what surviving evidence reveals today. Making sense of the power and attraction of myth—and dispelling it—requires excavating its complex genesis, layer by layer. Let us listen, then, to the discordant voices of the white Southern chorus who created the tale of Calvin Crozier's fate, then return to the Newberry train yard on the night of September 7, 1865, to untangle fiction from fact.

The first report of Crozier's execution appeared in South Carolina newspapers a week after his death. "Horrible Murder," announced the Columbia Daily Phoenix: a letter from "a gentleman of the first character" confirmed rumors that had circulated for days.[21] Late in the afternoon of September 7, the writer declared, a train carrying the 33rd U.S. Colored Troops (USCT) arrived in Newberry, and the regiment disembarked. Although the soldiers made camp outside the town, some slipped back to a Black "rendezvous" near the depot and "made night hideous by their profanity and loud talking—the result of drink, we take it for granted." Shortly after 11 PM, "one of the negroes" entered a car on a different train "in which some ladies were spending the night." There was no hotel room available in town, the paper explained, and the white women were "under the protection of" Mr. Calvin Crozier, of Galveston, Texas, "in bearing and appearance a perfect gentleman." When Crozier warned the Black man off, that "insolent" soldier threw "offensive language" toward him, and "a fight ensued." As others joined in, Crozier "used a knife on one of the negroes" by way of self-defense. How Black intruders shifted so suddenly from the singular to the plural or what happened next, the white writer did not say, but "shortly afterward," a sergeant and six men of the 33rd arrested Crozier, held him until daybreak, and "deliberately" executed him "by musketry." The white ladies—now "in a most painful agony of mind"—informed local authorities of the night's events, and Newberrians soon found Crozier's body tumbled "head foremost" into a shallow grave, "only partly buried." The coroner convened an inquest and saw the deceased decently interred. The "regrets of the entire community" poured forth. What else could "be expected," the *Phoenix* lamented, "from the employment of negro troops throughout the State," except "cold-blooded tragedy" such as this?

But that tale was swiftly disputed. Three days later, the paper printed an indignant response from Sergeant-Major Louden S. Langley of the 33rd. Crozier died because he had "essayed to kill, and did *horribly* cut" one of his comrades, the Black soldier explained. The white gentleman who wrote to the *Phoenix* got important details wrong, Langley insisted. First, the testimony of all arriving on the scene immediately after the "fight" agreed that the fellow Crozier stabbed was "*alone* and *unassisted*." Even Crozier's post-arrest statement affirmed that point. Also, the unnamed sergeant directing the execution had not fired a pistol into Crozier's head as a coup de grâce—it was a private who shot without orders after the official volley. Beyond this, Langley asked, what sort of "perfect gentleman" was Crozier imagined to be? Having committed a "bloody crime," he "attempted to escape, and was arrested a distance from the place" of the stabbing. If whites wanted an inquest, they should go ahead, the soldier warned. "The *facts* court investigation."[22]

That taunt was a red flag to South Carolina's newly installed bull of a provisional governor.[23] Benjamin Perry demanded that Federal authorities launch an inquiry, and in the spring of 1866, a court-martial acquitted Lieutenant-Colonel Charles T. Trowbridge, commander of the 33rd, "of all blame." When General Charles Devens ordered a review of the verdict, "the court persisted in its former opinion."[24] By that time, Trowbridge's troops had mustered out and dispersed to their homes. Though Crozier's killing was widely reported, it dropped quickly out of public view. "The case exerted much interest at the time," one editor explained in May 1866, "but in the midst of innumerable scenes of wanton bloodshed and unprovoked outrages, the people have almost allowed the circumstances to be blotted from memory."[25]

Time's passage did not lessen the impact of Crozier's story as white Southerners told and retold it across the decades. The same article that announced the matter nearly blotted out introduced a host of new claims and embellishments. "Just before" the train carrying Crozier and the ladies reached Newberry, it said, "some negroes" belonging to the 33rd USCT, "who had got aboard at a wood station," entered their car and began "insulting the passengers." A Black soldier named Mills put "his arm around the waist of one of the ladies, attempting to kiss her." A scuffle ensued "of course"; Mills was stabbed; and "a furious mob of negroes" surrounded the train (now, apparently, arrived at its destination). Crozier was arrested and—"although there was no evidence" of his guilt—he was shot "within twenty minutes thereafter" on Trowbridge's command, "without any trial whatever." Elaboration here only piled up ambiguity and uncertainty about just how events transpired. Nonetheless, it was a travesty of justice that the "bloodthirsty scoundrel" Trowbridge should have incited "black ruffians" to kill a good man in a manner "so foul and disgraceful." Nothing more could be hoped, declared the New York News, in this hour of "military occupation and the suspension of Habeas Corpus."[26] Once, civilized men had feared punishment and dishonor for a killing like this, the New Orleans Crescent mourned. Now times had grown dark and villains jeered in triumph:

> We, better bred, and than our sires more wise,
> Such paltry narrowness of soul despise;
> To virtue every mean pretence disclaim,
> Lay bare our crimes and glory in our shame.[27]

Across the South in these months, white newspapers detailed endless incidents of "black devils" in blue committing "hellish enormities" against defenseless vanquished whites. At summer's end, the tale of Crozier's death had blended into the frenzied recital of Black "atrocities"—imagined, embellished, and anticipated—bubbled briefly, and disappeared from view.[28]

More than twenty years passed before a local history revived the story of the stabbing and the execution, polishing its details and lessons in service to segregationist ethical and political purposes. Publication of John Chapman's completion of Judge John Belton O'Neall's Annals of Newberry provoked a minor sensation across South Carolina's upcountry in 1892. For three years, Chapman had promoted his manuscript in a series of advertisements and speeches, showcasing the Crozier story as an example of heroism and "ennobled Christian character." At an open-air meeting at the county courthouse on a warm Sunday in 1889, he praised the Confederate's "Christ-like spirit" and dutiful "self-sacrifice."[29] In the aftermath of this address—complete with scripture reading—locals proposed a monument honoring the brave Rebel who "died that another might live."[30] By this telling, Crozier came to symbolize all that was best of white Southern manhood.

According to Chapman, Crozier and the ladies arrived in Newberry entirely un-molested, and, "it being a beautiful moonlight night, they walked out to enjoy the quiet and the beauty of the night." If there were drunken Black troops carous-ing nearby, as earlier versions of the story said, their profane uproar here became magically muted. Upon returning to the train, however, Crozier's party discovered a Black soldier "prowling about the coach." Whatever such "prowling" entailed, when the Confederate "spoke to him about the impropriety of his being there," the in-truder set to cursing. Crozier urged him "to remember that ladies were present," to no avail. After a scuffle, the offending Black was "cut," and Chapman's scene ends abruptly. "In a little while," however, an "infuriated crowd" of Black soldiers ar-rived, mistakenly seizing a local railroad official, Jacob Bowers, as the perpetrator. Just why Bowers was out so late, where Crozier sited himself after the stabbing, or how he passed the crucial minutes of Bowers's misapprehension went unexplored in this telling. But once it appeared that an innocent man might be lynched in his stead, out Crozier strode. The hero "ordered" the mob to release its prey, "de-claring that he had defended the ladies." He even flashed his knife as proof. From there, the arrest, the "mock trial," and the execution followed like clockwork. A Black sergeant, Prince Rivers (later a prominent Republican state legislator), of-fered to save Crozier's skin if only he would deny his honorable deed. Still the proud veteran stood firm. "Unbind these hands," Crozier warned, "and I'll show you what I'll do." The melodramatic contrast between white courage and Black cowardice swelled even after the fatal shots. In haste to "double-quick" from the scene of their crime, Black "merciless wretches" jumped on Crozier's corpse to cram it into the inadequate grave they had dug. Soon after, worthy white Newberrians retrieved his broken body and washed and reburied it reverently, honoring his "estimable," "brave and generous" soul. Transmuted from man to hero to victim to angel, Crozier would find a central place in the culture of a community he barely glimpsed.[31]

Polished up as a chapter in *The Annals of Newberry,* this version of Crozier's de-mise gained broad regional notice. Now Crozier's train came to halt in the town for reasons unknown; the passenger coach was transformed to a crude box car, and the action took place after "some colored soldiers" intruded and "made their pres-ence very unpleasant to the ladies." Otherwise, the narrative was familiar. Once again, a Black offender was "slightly wounded." From there, events played out until the "soldier mob . . . danced upon the shallow grave."[32] In Newberry's Rosemont Cemetery, the monument raised to Crozier's honor in 1892 summarizes the same claims. Released from a Federal prison after Appomattox, it declares, Crozier had been on his way home to Texas when he was "called upon" at Newberry "to protect a young white woman temporarily under his charge from gross insults offered by a Negro Federal soldier of the garrison stationed there." A "slight cut" caused "infuriated soldiers" to seek "savage revenge" upon the wrong man. Crozier "promptly came forward and avowed his own responsibility" and was "hurried" to his doom: shot at sunrise "without even the form of trial" and "his body mutilated."[33]

The cult of Calvin Crozier reached its zenith in the following two decades as regional newspapers and novelists spread his story, and Griffith's film broadcast its moral to tearful, outraged audiences across the country. Texan readers learned that before Crozier arrived in "Newbury," the town had already "been plundered and her citizens subjected to all the indignities that a drunken negro mob could offer." As soon as the train reached the station, it "was immediately surrounded by a drunken, howling crowd of negro soldiers." As armed Blacks "swarmed through the cars like a set of demons set free from the infernal regions," Southern "white soldiers on board were helpless and at their mercy." Only Crozier, "a determined follower of the lost cause," resisted the onslaught. "Tall and stately, with piercing black eyes," and a "massive head of hair" that "well became his brawny face," the hero rallied to the despairing plea of a young Southern lady caught in a "loathsome embrace." "I will protect you if I die for it!" cried Crozier, striding down the aisle and burying "the keen blade of a knife . . . to its hilt in the breast of the black ruffian." That snippet captures well the flavor and politics of the overwrought piece. History disappears further under racist didactics as the dauntless Southron saves the innocent railroad man, digs his own grave, and stands "erect and stretching out his arms." Like Christ crucified, in this version Crozier meets his end stoically, "amid the deafening shouts of the multitude." He is more than a man: indeed, unnamed throughout the tale, Crozier stands as symbol, "the grandest tribute to southern chivalry—that no other land under the sun rears men who give their lives to protect the honor of unknown women."[34] "Does history record any nobler sacrifice?" asked Bill Arp, the *Atlanta Constitution*'s popular columnist. Visiting Crozier's grave in 1897, he retold the tale in more restrained terms than the Texan account, in aid of the same moral. Again, "lawless negro soldiers" had "grossly insulted" ladies in Crozier's charge. The Rebel takes his stand, and a "melee" ensues. The Black soldier is stabbed; the white railroader is seized and saved. Crozier dies nobly. "The negro soldiers danced with fiendish delight upon and around his shallow grave," Arp imagined, contrasting their savagery with the reverent action of "the good people of Newberry," who laid him to rest and honored his sacrifice.[35]

Across the twentieth century, the importance of the story of the "Humble Hero's" defense of Southern values seemed obvious to all, fueling pro-Confederate, segregationist, and white supremacist initiatives. In 1961, South Carolina's Confederate

War Centennial Commission funded an "official float," constructed by penitentiary inmates, that depicted Crozier digging his grave as one of six images representative of the state's Civil War heritage. Beachgoers and tourists, visitors to the state fair, schoolchildren and Southern partisans watched its perambulations from town to town.[36] More locally, Newberry's "Improved Order of Heptasophs" named their "conclave" in his honor in 1901, and similar tributes sprouted across the South in subsequent decades.[37] In Texas, the United Daughters of the Confederacy (UDC) memorialized Crozier in their Confederate Museum collection (privatized in 2012). A "Calvin Crozier" UDC chapter flourished for decades in Newberry, sponsoring named scholarships at the local college and a statewide essay competition for female collegians, awarding a Crozier Medal. In 1913, the chapter dedicated a square stone marker for the spot where "Calvin Crozier was murdered . . . by the 33d U. S. Regt of Negro Federal Soldiers." Likewise, Sons of Confederate Veterans chapters honoring Crozier have risen and fallen across the region, and unaffiliated tributes laud the "Texas Martyr" and his "devotion to the Cause" online—sometimes on the most racist and hate-driven websites.[38] Available on YouTube and Amazon, "The Ballad of Calvin Crozier" has become a popular "heritage" song, and a brief novel about the "murder" appears on both Google Books and Amazon. Yet for all the labor and creativity bestowed on it, the fiction of *Crozier: Four Days in September, 1865* cannot stand as history, much less a full and fair analysis of the documentary record.[39]

From the first newspaper report of Crozier's execution to the present day, imagination, prejudice, and conservative political agendas have shaped the public narrative and its academic interpretation. Even Scott Poole's recent analysis of white intransigence in the Reconstruction Era summons Crozier's killing only to claim that ex-Confederates had cause to fear a violent backlash by freedpeople and their allies.[40] That is an incurious reading of events, at best. "The *facts* court investigation," announced the only African American voice in the whole controversy, barely a week after the execution. But nothing like a full and careful study of the evidence has yet been offered. Not even all the witness testimony has been considered. Crozier's version of events has been overlaid with erroneous motive and circumstance from the first telling. And nobody so far has thought to ask after the account of the other central participant, Private Gloster Mills of the 33rd USCT. Let us retrace our steps.

Newberry in September 1865 was still reeling from the Confederacy's collapse. The town had escaped comparatively undamaged by contending Rebel and Union forces. Both sides used the local college as a military hospital and nearby structures for command and supply functions. Still, troops garrisoned there or simply passing through had appropriated anything that looked edible or valuable and smashed a good bit that did not.[41] Although harvest season beckoned, there was not much of a cotton crop likely to come to market and less hard currency to buy it with. Adjudication of debts, transfer of property, and dispersal of estates remained largely ad hoc.[42] Forty-five miles away, amid Columbia's charred ruins, a state convention was scheduled to meet on September 13, charged with abolishing slavery and establishing new rules to govern changed relations of race and class. Instead, two weeks later, that conservative gathering brought forth a new constitution that put white racism and Rebel intransigence on full display. Crozier's killing and its aftermath catalyzed that disastrous defiance.[43]

As the month began, white Federal troops crowded Newberry—the 56th New York, preparing for transshipment north and a speedy muster out; the 1st Maine Infantry Battalion, shifting from Florence to the troubled upcountry.[44] Late in the afternoon of September 7, the most famous Southern-raised Black regiment, the 33rd USCT, completed an eighty-mile journey from Anderson County, high in the northwestern corner of the state, detraining in search of supper and sleep. Originally raised by General David Hunter and General Rufus Saxton from self-emancipated and impressed slaves of the coastal Sea Islands as the 1st South Carolina Volunteers, the unit stood among the most politically radical formations in the Union Army.[45] Commanded into the spring of 1864 by the abolitionist firebrand Thomas Wentworth Higginson, the regiment had refused to accept lower wages than white soldiers received; maintained "a steady, conscientious devotion to duty"; and won its demands. Though its soldiers saw only small-scale combat during the war along the South Carolina coast, in the summer and fall of 1865 they performed dangerous duty as troops of occupation shuttling across the piedmont to quell recalcitrant Rebels. Renumbered the 33rd USCT in the autumn of 1864, the unit attracted new recruits in the months after Appomattox, thanks to steady pay, good rations, and humane treatment. Most veterans, though, were ready to go home. "I mean to fight de war through," one private promised, "an' die a good sojer wid de last kick."[46] But did peace not bring that bargain to a close? "The Biggest Majority of our mens never had a Home Science this late wor Commence," one soldier explained; "jest Run away from they Rebels master . . . & come Right in under the Bondage of Soldiers life." Though the war was over, "We hadent nothing atoll & our wifes & mother most all of them is aperishing." While other freedpeople flourished, "we will have a Hard struggle to get along," the veteran believed, "& then all the Southern white Peoples will have us for alaughin & game after for our Braverist that we did to Run away from them & come asoldiers."[47]

The wonder is that these ex-slaves, having risked all to run toward military service, and having served with "ropes around our necks," had they fallen into Rebel hands, did not walk away after Appomattox in the face of such hardships. White troops, North and South, by the tens of thousands had calculated self-interest and political loyalty more cynically, and ultimately it was Rebel desertion that sealed the Confederacy's fate.[48] Soldier and civilian alike testified to the superb discipline and deep sense of purpose in the ranks of the 33rd, searching for its sources. "Now we sogers are men—men de first time in our lives," explained Sergeant Prince Rivers. "Now we can look our old masters in de face"—and "run the bayonet through them," too, if the chance presented itself. Black men and women both felt elevated by their connection to the Union cause. "I taught a great many of the comrades . . . to read and write," recalled Susie King Taylor, a regimental laundress and nurse. "I gave my services willingly for four years and three months without receiving a dollar." Louden Langley hinted at the source of sustaining motivation in the story he told of visiting the Columbia convention of September 1865. Uniformed as a Federal sergeant, the Black man strode confidently into the hall where former Confederates debated South Carolina's future, wordlessly demonstrating authority. "Great God! brudder, see whar dat man are goin'," exclaimed one elderly freedman. "He goin' right in dar." The bottom rail was on top, sure enough. And that was precisely the point: showing perfect martial bearing, meeting every order without complaint, the soldiers of the 33rd commanded acknowledgment as men and demanded respect for their service. The "general aim and probable consequences" of the war were "better understood" by the men of the 33rd USCT, Colonel Higginson avowed, "than in any white regiment" in the Union army. Guided by a passionate "love of liberty," he explained, "there was no trouble to come from the men, and none ever came."[49]

Trouble came instead as the regiment performed provost duty for the Freedmen's Bureau in South Carolina's rugged "dark corner." Traveling by rail from Charleston to the outskirts of Augusta in July 1865, Lieutenant-Colonel Trowbridge marched the 33rd ninety miles north to Anderson, assuming command of a military subdistrict comprising three seething white-majority counties. Tasked with negotiating agricultural contracts between freedpeople and whites who "most thoroughly hated" them, and with pacifying an area rife with Confederate intransigence, Trowbridge soon came to loathe the place and its people. At Anderson, local citizens "implored" him "not to bring them niggers into their town." At Walhalla, a company detailed to defend the rule of law saw its popular white lieutenant "assassinated"— beguiled into conversation by "a tall, villainous-looking ex-Confederate," shot in the back, and finished off with two bullets to the brain. Trowbridge sped to the rescue, threatening to burn the village unless locals surrendered the killer. The townspeople called his bluff. Some were unified; others, terrified. All feigned ignorance. The reckless "desperado," Manse Jolly, taunted Trowbridge and rode rings around his troops for weeks to come, threatening to "kill every man" in the regiment before they left the county. For the soldiers of the 33rd, dispersed by companies in iso-lated communities across many miles, that threat had teeth. Surely they longed to strike back.[50]

Worse news from Augusta compounded that anger. Newly discharged from Company C, Captain Andrew Heasly had been convalescing there. But an ailing Yankee officer was a tempting target to Rebel intransigents in the summer of 1865, especially a "damn niggerly son of a Bitch" who was supposed to have "shoved" a young lady "off the side walk and told her he would kick her damned ass off the side walk" for blocking his path. Four ex-Confederates lay in wait to "beat him to death" one night in July, but they missed their man, who "should have died long ago," by their reckoning. It was another trio of vengeful Georgians who "assassi-nated" Heasly a few days later and fled to Savannah. By summer's end, the men of the 33rd knew neither whether their white captain's killers would be punished nor who among them would be struck down next.[51]

At the beginning of September, as Trowbridge prepared to redeploy his troops by rail outside Charleston, warning came of impending disaster. No less a figure than Governor-elect James L. Orr sent word that his "entire regiment would be annihilated" as soon as it left Anderson. Right on cue, when their train crossed a high trestle on the night of September 6, someone pulled a coupling pin. The locomotive sped off, abandoning Trowbridge's men in closed boxcars atop the nar-row bridge. Hidden assailants fired into the marooned train as others worked to burn the bridge beneath them. Only the swift action of a military detail guard-ing the train crew averted catastrophe. Placing a pistol to the engineer's temple, a Black soldier ordered him to back up the locomotive and rescue the stranded sol-diers. That ruthlessness saved the regiment, for all anyone knew. By the time they reached Newberry the next evening, the men of the 33rd were hungry, tired, wary, and "highly exasperated" about their treatment by treacherous civilians. Colonel Trowbridge's problem was to cool tempers and prepare his men for the next day's long march toward the coast. He posted a platoon under Sergeant Rivers to guard the depot and took the rest of his soldiers to bed down in a grove of trees a quarter-mile away.[52]

Who could have known that, four hours later, a westbound train carrying paroled ex-Confederates would jump the track right beside Trowbridge's cars? Probably, to police the rail yard, Rivers's sentries had placed the obstacle that stopped it. Shaken up and annoyed by the crash, the white passengers of the derailed train were equally distressed by their proximity to USCT troops—now (by their account) joined by Black women of the neighborhood. Not only was the "most obscene conversation" inflicted on their ears, whites later complained. The "insulting and taunting manner of the negroes" seemed calculated to "create a disturbance." Would a wrong word set off a riot? Some former Rebels decided not to find out, decamping for town "to try and find a place to stay as the negro soldiers were so insulting they were afraid to remain there."[53]

If that is an accurate version of how events unfolded, it demonstrates a remarkable breakdown of regimental discipline, quite unlike any moment in the unit's history up to that point. That such a lapse would have occurred under the supervision of Prince Rivers is still more unbelievable. Color Sergeant Rivers was the commanding presence of the 33rd, "as superb as a panther," tall, brave, and "distinguished." No one had "more absolute authority over the men," Higginson remembered. "They do not love him, but his mere presence has controlling power over them." That was why all provost duties had focused on him for more than two years. Can it be that the detailed platoon now disregarded their "natural king"?[54] We cannot say, but perhaps it is more likely that local Black civilians, drawn to the depot by the arrival of the USCT regiment and emboldened by the derailment of the second train, took advantage of the moment to mock the stranded, worried whites.

Either way, the jeering did not last long. Dr. James Pillsbury, contract surgeon to the Federal troops, demanded that rollicking Blacks watch their language, as there were "white ladies" on the other train. They "stopped it" promptly.[55] The night was warm; no one was looking for a fight, and for civilians, the pleasures of convivial drink and roistering lay not far off. That combination of factors should have brought the evening to a close around the train yard. Station Agent Jacob Bowers was already on the scene with a work crew, striving to get the westbound cars back on the tracks. But Calvin Crozier seems to have been far from satisfied by the sight of Black soldiers in blue performing guard duty. His subsequent actions made plain that he had scores to settle.

We know little of Crozier. Although just twenty-five years old in 1865, he had witnessed the Civil War in various theaters and phases and come out worse for wear. Born to a minor slaveholding family, he enlisted in the 1st Texas Artillery shortly after Fort Sumter; transferred to Richard Gano's 7th Kentucky Cavalry the following year; and was captured near Syracuse, Ohio, during Morgan's Raid in July 1863. For almost two years, Crozier languished at Camp Douglas, the Federal prison near Chicago, before being exchanged in Maryland in March 1865. Journeying south to North Carolina, he fell ill for a time, traveling on only at summer's end. Certainly, there was a lot of war stored up in the man when his train pulled into the Newberry depot on the evening of September 7.[56]

Dressed from head to toe in Confederate gray and carrying a Bowie knife just out of sight, Crozier was not the sort of fellow to back down from a fight. Even before entraining at Orangeburg that afternoon, he had "engaged in badinage" with a Union sergeant "so warm" that the Yankee Dr. Pillsbury had "stopped it, and reprimanded Crozier for his language." What accounts for that hot talk? Was

Crozier looking to get up a brawl with a former foe, or simply showing off for the young women he was now, by some arrangement, escorting? Either way, when the doctor upbraided Crozier, he made the proper signs of submission and held his tongue. Later that evening, when the same Union officer demanded quiet from rowdy Blacks, Crozier cannot but have felt overmastered. This was the second time that day the Southern soldier had been bested by his Northern counterpart in matters of honor. That may help to explain why Crozier and the ladies did not follow his compatriots in search of a hotel bed away from the train. Certainly, he was stewing from the day's events and much more.[57]

What happened next is muddled. Most agree that Crozier left the ladies' side just after Pillsbury silenced the Black catcallers, alighting from the cars "on private business." While he smoked or urinated nearby, a Black soldier is supposed to have appeared aboard the train. At a coroner's inquest the next day, James Brown, a white railroad worker, asserted that the phantom soldier "insulted the ladies grossly" and Crozier, returning, had ordered him out. But Brown was standing on the platform near the rear of the cars and could have seen nothing of this exchange—if anything like it took place at all. Dr. Pillsbury said that the insults had come earlier, from the taunting Blacks outside the train, and that he had quelled them quickly.[58]

Captain George Fickett of the 1st Maine told this part of the story more melodramatically. The Black soldier's insult here consisted simply of taking "a seat near the young ladies" and refusing Crozier's demand to leave. "The Negro replied that he would be d——d if he would, that he was going to sleep there." Enraged, Crozier attacked the dozing back talker with his knife, stabbing him below the right eye and—oddly—in the back of his neck. Again, however, Fickett was nowhere near the scene of the supposed confrontation. According to Brown, Crozier drew no blade and made no attack. Instead, he went off to complain to "a Captain"—Pillsbury—"about the treatment he had received from a negro soldier." By this account, it was Crozier's honor that had been infringed on, not the virtue of the women in his care. In Fickett's telling, there was no hint of imminent sexual assault. Proximity was the sum of the physical danger the sleepy soldier offered. And, indeed, in every version of the encounter from 1865 to the present day, the supposedly endangered women disappear from the story at just this point. Who were they? Where were they from? Where were they going? Few accounts add any details at all. How these damsels in distress escaped their peril, or what became of them as Crozier was marched off to his doom, no one bothered to ask. Nameless and forgotten, they serve as props to trigger the fateful scuffle and as alibi for Crozier's violence.[59]

The only person who claimed to have witnessed what put Crozier in trouble was Jacob Bowers, the white railroad worker who was trying to get the derailed cars back on the tracks. Standing at the rear of the train, he saw a scene very different from the one his coworker Brown described: "two men engaged in a fight" *outside* the cars and nowhere near where the white women were seated. "After a while one of them ran past me," Bowers recounted, "and the other went in a contrary direction, calling out that he was cut." That second man was Private Gloster Mills of the 33rd, bleeding profusely from two big gashes on his face, plus a four-inch stab wound inflicted to the back of his neck, "severing muscles and parts." Mills was headed toward the locomotive, the depot, and medical aid. The surgeon who treated him said he was sure to die.[60]

If Bowers remembered rightly, Crozier must have run away from the train, and the women, into the darkness. Dr. Pillsbury was the next person to see Crozier, who ran up minutes later "asking him to save his life." A month after the execution, Pillsbury offered an elaborate account of the fight on the train. In this version, other Black troops rushed "to the spot" of the stabbing "and as they were overpowering [Crozier], he broke away, and ran to us for assistance." But Pillsbury never claimed to be aboard the train at any point in his narrative. Nor did he explain how Crozier managed to stab Mills, fight off a crowd of armed soldiers, jump down from the cars, and outrun his pursuers. Nor does this tale explicate what led the soldiers to seize Bowers, thinking that he had done the stabbing. Bowers, after all, was far away from where the scuffle was supposed to have occurred—at the tail end of the train. Ultimately, too, Pillsbury's story matches up poorly with what Crozier had to say when he finally faced Lieutenant-Colonel's Trowbridge's interrogation.[61]

If the heroic story of Crozier's defense of white female virtue begins to wilt under close examination, the account of how he boldly declared his deed and saved Bowers's life fares no better. Within minutes of the stabbing, USCT soldiers had grabbed Bowers at one end of the train, and Pillsbury had secured Crozier near the other end. All contemporary evidence shows that Pillsbury turned Crozier over to Provost Sergeant Rivers, insisting that he be taken to headquarters unharmed. Rivers did just that, shielding Bowers from summary justice at the hands of his detail, angry and embittered by the second instance of bushwhacking they had endured in the course of a single day. Crozier was stoic here, not saintly. "I have hurt one," he declared. "If the others attempt to impose on me I will hurt as many as I can."[62]

But just how had Crozier "hurt one"? White testimony on the stabbing seems fragmented and garbled. Yet scholars have taken no steps at all to recover Black testimony on the assault. Published in 1902, Susie King Taylor's narrative of her experience with the 33rd USCT contains a host of details that may shed light here. Taylor remembered the assassination of Lieutenant Jerome Furman, shot by "South Carolina bushwhackers at Wall Hollow [Walhalla]." She recalled how ex-Rebels "hid in the bushes and would shoot the Union boys every chance they got"—referring to their ordeal atop the trestle bridge. More elaborately, she described how white Southern killers "would conceal themselves in the cars":

And when our boys, worn out and tired, would fall asleep, these men would come out from their hiding places and cut their throats. Several of our men were killed in this way, but it could not be found out who was committing these murders until one night one of the rebels was caught in the act, trying to cut the throat of a sleeping soldier. He was put under guard, court-martialed, and shot at Wall Hollow.[63]

Nothing like this took place while the regiment sojourned at Walhalla. A day later, though, the sequence of events Taylor recounts—stabbing, arrest, court-martial, and execution—unfolded at Newberry. There is no comparable incident in the regimental records of the 33rd USCT, or in Taylor's narrative. It is Crozier's assault and death she is describing. But can we believe her explanation of this midnight assault? Instead of defending imperiled white women from marauding Black Yankees, had the Southern would-be hero simply aimed "to cut the throat of a sleeping soldier"?

Aspects of white testimony offered to the Newberry coroner's inquest and at Lieutenant-Colonel Trowbridge's trial support this interpretation. Recall that James Brown said that the assault happened outside the cars. Captain Fickett placed Crozier's victim on the train but lying down, about to go to sleep, when the assault occurred. Neither put Crozier in the coach struggling with Private Mills to save white women from sexual assault. As for Mills himself, he stayed behind at the hospital after the 33rd left Newberry the next day but was not deposed at the coroner's inquest. Months later, at Trowbridge's trial, Mills's recovery from his wounds was noted and discussed, but again no one bothered to ask for his version of events.

It was not until 1881, when thirty-four-year-old Gloss Mills applied for a military pension, that anyone wanted to know how he had been wounded. Over the next several years, the veteran and his former comrades laid out their version of the confusing night in Newberry that left the teenager—one of the youngest, smallest, greenest men in the regiment—struggling for life. To win his claim, lawyers, surgeons, and bureaucrats dressed up his story in various ways. But the facts as the men of the 33rd remembered them were simple. Private Gloster Mills had been asleep on picket duty when Crozier struck.[64]

To be sure, Mills was still as much a field hand as a soldier that September night, standing sentry at "Post No. 5." He had come down from the Augusta area to Savannah and signed up only three months before the march to Anderson, and like any illiterate, rural ex-slave, he still had much to learn about military discipline. Sleeping on post was a shooting offense in wartime and a disqualifying condition for anyone seeking a government pension. That was why the official documents and certificates in Mills's claim speak absurdly of a "skirmish" with "an element of Wheeler's Cavalry," when all knew that the "ugly gash" as "deep as the bone" Mills suffered came by "no fault" of his own. Captain Levi Metcalf well remembered "the Boy who had his throat cut by a Reb"—except that "he cut in the dark and cut the Back instead of the front side of your neck." Metcalf heard that Mills had been "lying asleep in one of the freight cars" on the regiment's train—not Crozier's train at all—and that the assault was caused by "pure cus[s]edness on the part of Mr. *Rebel*." Whether Mills was at his post, as he attested—out in the darkness a short distance from the trains—or had snuck back to an empty boxcar for a quiet snooze, we cannot say. Either way, he was dead to the world when Crozier stabbed, and survived only by chance. The rebel's slash "severed all the muscles & ligaments" on one side of his neck, leaving Mills's head "drawn forward and to one side" ever after. "I did not see the wound inflicted," Metcalf admitted. "Neither did anyone as I know." But the blow Crozier struck threw the regiment into a fury. Had the Rebel not blurted out a confession as soon as he stumbled into Pillsbury, the lust for vengeance might have exploded across the town.[65]

There was no explosion. Instead, Prince Rivers's men hustled Crozier back to camp and presented their prisoner for examination. Confronted shortly after midnight with the news of yet another casualty and the "desperado" who caused it, Charles Trowbridge faced a crisis. "I asked him what he stabbed that man for, he replied that, 'I did not intend to kill the damn nigger, I gauged my knife with my thumb and finger when I stick it into him.'" Such sass hardly helped Crozier's case, and claims of premeditation—though not borne out by medical evidence—marked him as a sneak and a bushwhacker. "From his air and manner I inferred that he was a desperate character," Trowbridge later testified. Doctors and soldiers told him that Private Mills had been attacked while sleeping on guard duty. All believed that his wound was mortal. How would the colonel respond?[66]

Prince Rivers's comrades had demanded that Crozier be killed outright, insisting that, unless he was hanged, "they would put a bullet through [their own] sergeant" for missing his chance. Trowbridge believed that "the best thing" would have been "to shoot the man right off." He warned his superiors that unless immediate action was taken, "the town of Newberry would be burned" by his angry men. What to do with the "would-be assassin"? The order came back: "Shoot him."[67]

Shortly before dawn on September 8, as Trowbridge formed his regiment in column, six men under the command of Lieutenant Henry Wood executed Crozier with a volley, burying his body in a shallow grave dug on short notice. Crozier's final statement wanted to claim that he died "for his country," but a Yankee wrote instead that he admitted forfeiting his life "for stabbing a U. S. Soldier." The 33rd USCT marched five miles south of Newberry to pick up their train that morning, for fear that they might yet break ranks and fire the town.[68] Ahead of them lay a difficult march: supplies were short, the terrain was swampy, the rail line torn up. At Orangeburg, they found soldiers of the 54th New York near mutiny. Danger lurked on all sides. By the time they reached Charleston, fear and anger seethed. In Gloster Mills's company, soldiers fought with their superiors, cursed them openly, and threatened murder. Yet for all that, "turbulent" men such as Private John Smith insisted that his character had always been that of "a good soldier." Morale cracked only because men feared they had been betrayed.[69]

In the weeks that followed, inquests, inquiries, and a general court-martial weighed the evidence of what had happened after Calvin Crozier's train—and fate—derailed. At every level, Colonel Trowbridge's actions were vindicated, though clearly Crozier's execution had served "to satisfy and allay the excitement among the enlisted men of the 33rd USCT, certainly a very poor reflection upon its discipline." When Trowbridge spoke of his career with the regiment in after years, Crozier's story went studiously unmentioned.[70]

In Newberry, though, and more sporadically around the region, white Southerners never stopped talking about Calvin Crozier, piling exaggeration, conjecture, and racism into a monument of lies. As shown here, the circumstances leading up to that moonlit September night have been entirely neglected in the popular record, the documentary evidence surrounding the affray and execution employed haphazardly and mingled with melodramatic local lore. The killing of Calvin Crozier has been slanted and distorted to win neo-Confederates the sort of tragic tale of loss and victimization on which they so thrive.

Revising the record here not only redresses the political balance. It links a half-forgotten killing of apparently minor significance to some of the biggest questions facing Southern and military historians today: Who decides when a war is over, and how? What is the difference between a civilian assault on a soldier and a terrorist act? When an occupied population resists military government, is there a viable option beyond violence? Did Reconstruction in the American South fail because of incidents such as this execution—or precisely because there were too few such firing squads? What good is a dead Rebel, no longer clad in myths of honor and gallantry, eight generations after he was shot at sunrise? What are the real purposes, present and future, of a roadside marker, erected on a nowhere road a century and a quarter after a picayune incident of flawed military justice, so obviously seeking to skew the past? White lies and dark truths can address big questions if we will read the record clear.

Notes

Members of the Society of Military Historians discussed a version of this essay in April 2016 at their annual meeting in Ottawa, Canada. My thanks to all who offered criticism and suggestions. Steve Berry, Vernon Burton, William McKee Evans, Kathleen M. Hilliard, Cynthia Lyerly, John Lynn, and the late Eugene Genovese shaped the ideas presented here, sometimes in ways they might well reject.

1. Cf. Adam Domby, *The False Cause: Fraud, Fabrication, and White Supremacy in Confederate Memory* (Charlottesville: University of Virginia Press, 2020). For recent assessments of Reconstruction, see David W. Blight and Jim Downs, eds., *Beyond Freedom: Disrupting the History of Emancipation* (Athens: University of Georgia Press, 2017); Thomas J. Brown, ed., *Reconstructions: New Perspectives on the Postbellum United States* (New York: Oxford University Press, 2006); Carole Emberton and Bruce Baker, eds., *Remembering Reconstruction: Struggles over the Meaning of America's Most Turbulent Era* (Baton Rouge: Louisiana State University Press, 2017). On the unfulfilled revolutionary potential of Reconstruction, see Orville Vernon Burton, *In My Father's House Are Many Mansions: Family and Community in Edgefield, South Carolina* (Chapel Hill: University of North Carolina Press, 1985); W. E. B. Du Bois, *Black Reconstruction in America: An Essay Toward a History of the Part Which Black Folk Played in the Attempt to Reconstruct Democracy in America, 1860–1880* (New York: Harcourt Brace, 1935); Eric Foner, *Nothing but Freedom: Emancipation and Its Legacy* (Baton Rouge: Louisiana State University Press, 1983); Willie Lee Rose, *Rehearsal for Reconstruction: The Port Royal Experiment* (Indianapolis: Bobbs-Merrill, 1964); Joel Williamson, *After Slavery: The Negro in South Carolina during Reconstruction, 1861–1867* (Chapel Hill: University of North Carolina Press, 1965); and the volumes published as *Freedom: A Documentary History of Emancipation, 1861–1867* (New York: Cambridge University Press and Chapel Hill: University of North Carolina Press, 1982–), under the editorship of Ira Berlin and colleagues. On Griffiths and the source of his vision of this era, see Anthony Slide, *American Racist: The Life and Films of Thomas Dixon* (Lexington: University Press of Kentucky, 2004); Melvyn Stokes, *D. W. Griffiths' 'The Birth of a Nation': A History of "The Most Controversial Motion Picture of All Time"* (New York: Oxford University Press, 2007).

2. This interpretation derives from the work of William Dunning, his students, and acolytes: see, e. g., William A. Dunning, *Reconstruction, Political and Economic, 1863–1877* (New York: Harper and Brothers, 1907); Walter L. Fleming, ed., *Documentary History of Reconstruction, Political, Military, Social, Religious, Educational, and Industrial, 1865 to the Present Time*, 2 vols. (Cleveland: A. H. Clark, 1906–1907).

3. Cf. Henry L. Gates Jr., *Stony the Road: Reconstruction, White Supremacy, and the Rise of Jim Crow* (New York: Penguin, 2020); Heather C. Richardson, *How the South Won the Civil War: Oligarchy, Democracy, and the Continuing Fight for the Soul of America* (New York: Oxford University Press, 2020); Dylan Rodriguez, *White Reconstruction: Domestic Warfare and the Logic of Genocide* (New York: Fordham University Press, 2020).

4. See, e. g., Laura Edwards, *Gendered Strife and Confusion: The Political Culture of Reconstruction* (Urbana: University of Illinois Press, 1997); Thavolia Glymph, *Out of the House of Bondage: The Transformation of the Plantation Household* (New York: Cambridge University Press, 2008); Tera Hunter, *To 'Joy My Freedom: Southern Black Women's Lives and Labors after the Civil War* (Cambridge, MA: Harvard University Press, 1998); Gerald D. Jaynes, *Branches without Roots: Genesis of the Black Working Class in the American South, 1862–1882* (New York: Oxford University Press, 1989); Steven Hahn, *A Nation under Our Feet: Black Political Struggles in the Rural South from Slavery to the Great Migration* (Cambridge, MA: Harvard University Press, 2003); Chandra Manning, *Troubled Refuge: Struggling for Freedom in the Civil War* (New York: Alfred A. Knopf, 2016); Michael Perman, *Reunion without Compromise: The South and Reconstruction, 1865–1868* (New York: Cambridge University Press, 1973); Heather C. Richardson, *The Death of Reconstruction: Race, Labor, and Politics in the Post–Civil War North, 1865–1901* (Cambridge, MA: Harvard University Press, 2001); Leslie Schwalm, *A Hard Fight for We: Women's Transition from Slavery to Freedom in South Carolina* (Urbana: University of Illinois

Press, 1997); Harold D. Woodman, *New South, New Law: The Legal Foundations of Credit and Labor Relations in the Postbellum Agricultural South* (Baton Rouge: Louisiana State University Press, 1995).

5. Du Bois, *Black Reconstruction in America*, 711–29.

6. David Blight, *Race and Reunion: The Civil War in American Memory* (Cambridge, MA: Harvard University Press, 2002); Gaines M. Foster, *Ghosts of the Confederacy: Defeat, the Lost Cause, and the Emergence of the New South, 1865–1913* (New York: Oxford University Press, 1987); Ethan J. Kytle and Blain Roberts, *Denmark Vesey's Garden: Slavery and Memory in the Cradle of the Confederacy* (New York: New Press, 2018); Anne Marshall, *Creating a Confederate Kentucky: The Lost Cause and Civil War Memory in a Border State* (Chapel Hill: University of North Carolina Press, 2010).

7. Yi-fu Tuan, *Space and Place: The Perspective of Experience* (Minneapolis: University of Minnesota Press, 1977).

8. William A. Blair, *Cities of the Dead: Contesting the Memory of the Civil War in the South, 1865–1914* (Chapel Hill: University of North Carolina Press, 2004); Karen L. Cox, *Dixie's Daughters: The United Daughters of the Confederacy and the Preservation of Confederate Culture* (Gainesville: University Press of Florida, 2003); Tony Horwitz, *Confederates in the Attic: Dispatches from the Unfinished Civil War* (New York: Vintage, 1998).

9. E. Merton Coulter, *The South during Reconstruction, 1865–1877* (Baton Rouge: Louisiana State University Press, 1947); J. G. de Roulhac Hamilton, *Reconstruction in North Carolina* (New York: Columbia University Press, 1914); Twelve Southerners, *I'll Take My Stand: The South and the Agrarian Tradition* (Baton Rouge: Louisiana State University Press, [1930] 2006); J. D. Vance, *Hillbilly Elegy: A Memoir of a Family and Culture in Crisis* (New York: Harper, 2016); Jerry L. West, *The Reconstruction Ku Klux Klan in York County, South Carolina, 1865–1877* (Jefferson, NC: McFarland, 2002).

10. Gregory P. Downs, *After Appomattox: Military Occupation and the Ends of War* (Cambridge, MA: Harvard University Press, 2015); Andrew F. Lang, *In the Wake of War: Military Occupation, Emancipation, and Civil War America* (Baton Rouge: Louisiana State University Press, 2017). For South Carolina, the achievements and weaknesses of this argument are on full display in Martin Abbott, *The Freedman's Bureau in South Carolina, 1865–1872* (Chapel Hill: University of North Carolina Press, 1967); Alrutheus A. Taylor, *The Negro in South Carolina during the Reconstruction* (Washington, DC: Association for the Study of Negro Life and History, 1924); Richard Zuczek, *State of Rebellion: Reconstruction in South Carolina* (Columbia: University of South Carolina Press, 1996).

11. Cf. Steven H. Hahn, *The Roots of Southern Populism: Yeoman Farmers and the Transformation of the Georgia Upcountry, 1850–1890* (New York: Oxford University Press, 1983); Thomas C. Holt, *Black over White: Negro Political Leadership in South Carolina during Reconstruction* (Urbana: University of Illinois Press, 1979); David R. Roediger, *The Wages of Whiteness: Race and Making of the American Working Class* (New York: Verso, 1991).

12. Stephen Budiansky, *The Bloody Shirt: Terror after Appomattox* (New York: Penguin, 2008); Douglas Egerton, *The Wars of Reconstruction: The Brief, Violent History of America's Most Progressive Era* (New York: Bloomsbury, 2014); Charles Lane, *The Day Freedom Died: The Colfax Massacre, the Supreme Court, and the Betrayal of Reconstruction* (New York: Holt, 2008); George C. Rable, *But There Was No Peace: The Role of Violence in the Politics of Reconstruction* (Athens: University of Georgia Press, 1984).

13. Cf. Charles E. Cobb Jr., *This Nonviolent Stuff'll Get You Killed: How Guns Made the Civil Rights Movement Possible* (Durham, NC: Duke University Press, 2015); Akinyele O. Umoja, *We Will*

Shoot Back: Armed Resistance in the Mississippi Freedom Movement (New York: New York University Press, 2014); Robert F. Williams, *Negroes with Guns* (New York: Marzani and Munsell, 1962).

14. What to do with Confederate monuments is a hot topic in academia inasmuch as they have been identified recently as symbols of racism. That is a rather jejune analysis of this sad statuary, abandoning considerations of class and gender altogether. The Confederacy dedicated itself to the preservation of slavery as a labor regime, after all, and a system of social organization, not as a scheme of racial oppression for its own sake. The Rebel South was, moreover, decisively defeated in its awful endeavor. Any effort to contextualize such symbols must be rooted in particularities of time and place. More than this, though, it must recognize the Confederate soldier as a military worker, not simply a nameless poor white guy with a gun. Imagine if we started the conversation there? Cf. Thomas J. Brown, *Civil War Canon: Sites of Confederate Memory in South Carolina* (Chapel Hill: University of North Carolina Press, 2015); Catherine Clinton et al., *Confederate Statues and Memorialization* (Athens: University of Georgia Press, 2019); Karen L. Cox, *No Common Ground: Confederate Monuments and the Ongoing Fight for Racial Justice* (Chapel Hill: University of North Carolina Press, 2021); Roger C. Hartley, *Monumental Harm: Reckoning with Jim Crow Era Confederate Monuments* (Columbia: University of South Carolina Press, 2021); Ty Seidule, *Robert E. Lee and Me: A Southerner's Reckoning with the Myth of the Lost Cause* (New York: St. Martin's, 2021).

15. Note the excellent examples of Thavolia Glymph, "Rose's War and the Gendered Politics of Slave Insurgency in the Civil War," *Journal of the Civil War Era* 3 (2013): 501–32; James K. Hogue, *Uncivil War: Five New Orleans Street Battles and the Rise and Fall of Radical Reconstruction* (Baton Rouge: Louisiana State University Press, 2006); Mark M. Smith "'All Is Not Quiet in Our Hellish County': Facts, Fiction, Politics, and Race: The Ellenton Riot of 1876," *South Carolina Historical Magazine* 95 (1994): 142–55.

16. Thomas Dixon, *The Clansman: A Historical Romance of the Ku Klux Klan* (New York: A. Wessels, 1905); Cynthia L. Lyerly, "The 'Murder' of Calvin Crozier," http://werehistory.org/calvin-crozier; *Herald and News* (Newberry, SC), February 3, 1905; *Bamberg Herald* (Bamberg, SC), February 9, 1905.

17. Cf. Matthew C. Hulbert and John C. Inscoe, eds., *Writing History with Lightning: Cinematic Representations of Nineteenth-Century America* (Baton Rouge: Louisiana State University Press, 2019).

18. "Calvin Crozier Murder Site," Newberry County, South Carolina, Historical Marker Database, https://www.hmdb.org/marker.asp?marker=13305. Cf. George L. Sumner, *Newberry County, South Carolina: Historical and Genealogical Annals* (Newberry, SC: N.p., 1950), 24.

19. See, e.g., Barton A. Myers, *Executing Daniel Bright: Race, Loyalty, and Guerrilla Violence in a Coastal Carolina Community, 1861–1865* (Baton Rouge: Louisiana State University Press, 2011); Phillip S. Paludan, *Victims: A True Story of the Civil War* (Knoxville: University of Tennessee Press, 1981).

20. R. G. Crozier to Andrew Johnson, letter, November 4, 1865, Letters Received, Record Group 94 (RG 94): Records of the Adjutant General's Office, National Archives, Washington, DC (hereafter, NA); Martha Hodes, "The Sexualization of Reconstruction Politics: White Women and Black Men in the South after the Civil War," in *American Sexual Politics: Sex, Gender, and Race since the Civil War,* ed. John Fout and Maura Tantillo (Chicago: University of Chicago Press, 1993); Edwards, *Gendered Strife and Confusion;* Kate Côté Gillin, *Shrill Hurrahs: Women, Gender, and Racial Violence in South Carolina, 1865–1900* (Columbia: University of South Carolina Press, 2013).

21. *Columbia Daily Phoenix,* September 12, 1865.

22. Ibid., September 15, 1865. On Langley, see Elise A. Guyette, *Discovering Black Vermont: African American Farmers in Hinesburgh, 1790–1890* (Barre: Vermont Historical Society, 2010).

23. Lillian A. Kibler, *Benjamin F. Perry, South Carolina Unionist* (Durham, NC: Duke University Press, 1946).

24. *Baltimore Sun*, May 9, 1866.

25. *Anderson Intelligencer* (Anderson, SC), May 24, 1866.

26. *Galveston Daily News*, July 1, 1866.

27. *New Orleans Crescent*, May 29, 1866.

28. *Keowee Courier* (Pickens, SC), June 2, 1866.

29. *Newberry Herald and News*, June 27, 1889.

30. Ibid., September 11, 25, 1890.

31. Ibid., June 27, 1889.

32. John Belton O'Neall and John A. Chapman, *The Annals of Newberry* (Newberry, SC: Aull and Houseal, 1892), 762–63.

33. Inscription on Calvin Crozier monument, Rosemont Cemetery, Newberry, South Carolina, Find a Grave website, https://www.findagrave.com/memorial/17935122/calvin-crozier /photo. A full description of the monument appears in *Lancaster News* (Lancaster, SC), May 27, 1899; Robert S. Seigler, *A Guide to Confederate Monuments in South Carolina: "Passing the Silent Cup"* (Columbia: South Carolina Department of Archives and History, 1997), 422–23.

34. *Galveston Daily News*, July 12, 1891.

35. *Watchman and Southron* (Sumter, SC), May 17, 1897; David B. Parker, *Alias Bill Arp: Charles Henry Smith and the South's Goodly Heritage* (Athens: University of Georgia Press, 2009).

36. *Augusta Chronicle*, July 5, 1903; *The State* (Columbia, SC), October 22, 1961.

37. *Newberry Herald and News*, June 4, 1901; South Carolina Genealogical Society, "I Salute You, Calvin Crozier," *Carolina Herald and Newsletter*, vol. 6, no. 1, 1978, 3.

38. "Division Notes," *Confederate Veteran* 30 (1922): 394; Bud Kennedy, "Dallas Saw Too Much Rebel in Texas Civil War Museum," *Star-Telegram* (Dallas), April 24, 2018, https://www .star-telegram.com/opinion/opn-columns-blogs/bud-kennedy/article209722614.html; Seigler, *Guide to Confederate Monuments in South Carolina*, 424–25; John Weaver, "Calvin Crozier, Texan Martyr," video, posted March 7, 2010, https://www.youtube.com/watch?v= T5vgwdkaTiI.

39. Charles Hanson, *Crozier: Four Days in September, 1865* (N.p., 2005).

40. W. Scott Poole, *Never Surrender: Confederate Memory and Conservatism in the South Carolina Upcountry* (Athens: University of Georgia Press, 2004), 98–99. The account given here is not substantially different from the racist scholarship of John P. Hollis, *The Early Period of Reconstruction in South Carolina* (Baltimore: Johns Hopkins University Press, 1905), 46; John S. Reynolds, *Reconstruction in South Carolina, 1865–1877* (Columbia: State Company, 1905), 6.

41. Jacqueline G. Campbell, *When Sherman Marched North from the Sea: Resistance on the Confederate Home Front* (Chapel Hill: University of North Carolina Press, 2003), 54–57; W. Scott Poole, *South Carolina's Civil War: A Narrative History* (Macon: Mercer University Press, 2005).

42. Reflected in the disordered records for 1865 in Conveyance Books, Register of Mesne Conveyance; Civil Journals, Records of the Court of Common Pleas; Equity Report Books, Court of Equity; Will Books, Probate Court, all in Newberry County Records, South Carolina Department of Archives and History, Columbia, SC.

43. *Journal of the Convention of the People of South Carolina, Held in Columbia, S.C., September, 1865. Together with the Ordinances, Reports, Resolutions, Etc.* (Columbia, SC: J. A. Selby, 1865);

Francis B. Simkins and Robert H. Woody, *South Carolina during Reconstruction* (Chapel Hill: University of North Carolina Press, 1932), 7–12, 17–28.

44. Frederick H. Dyer, *A Compendium of the War of the Rebellion* (Des Moines: Dyer, 1908).

45. Ira Berlin, Joseph P. Reidy, and Leslie S. Rowland, eds., *Freedom: A Documentary History of Emancipation, 1861–1867, Series 2: The Black Military Experience* (New York: Cambridge University Press, 1982), 54, 59, 524, 527; Ray A. Billington, ed., *The Journal of Charlotte L. Forten* (New York: Dryden, 1953), 154–57; William Wells Brown, *The Negro in the American Rebellion: His Heroism and His Fidelity* (Boston: Lee and Shepard, 1867), 60–73, 159–62; Leon F. Litwack, *Been in the Storm So Long: The Aftermath of Slavery* (New York: Oxford University Press, 1979), 75–77; Rose, *Rehearsal for Reconstruction*, 11–13; Joseph T. Wilson, *The Black Phalanx: A History of the Negro Soldiers of the United States in the War of 1775–1812, 1861–65* (Hartford, CT: American Publishing, 1888), 145–65, 249–85.

46. Susie King Taylor, *Reminiscences of My Life in Camp with the 33rd United States Colored Troops, Late 1st S.C. Volunteers* (Boston: S. K. Taylor, 1902), 15–16; Thomas W. Higginson, *Army Life in a Black Regiment* (Boston: Lee and Shepard, 1869), 25, 48.

47. Berlin et al., *Freedom*, 777–78. Although the regiment ranked with the most widely noticed Black units of the war during the conflict itself, it left no unit history and has attracted no modern academic analysis: see Higginson, *Army Life in a Black Regiment;* Thomas W. Higginson, *Cheerful Yesterdays* (Boston: Houghton Mifflin, 1898), 246–68; Christopher Looby, ed., *The Complete Civil War Journal and Selected Letters of Thomas Wentworth Higginson* (Chicago: University of Chicago Press, 2000); Bennie J. McRae Jr., Curtis M. Miller, and Cheryl Trowbridge-Miller, *Nineteenth-Century Freedom Fighters: The 1st South Carolina Volunteers* (Charleston, SC: Arcadia, 2007).

48. The literature on desertion on both sides is vast and growing—and mostly misses the central point: that soldiers who abandoned military service were withdrawing their labor deliberately from a cause they did not believe in. On this, see esp. Du Bois, *Black Reconstruction in America*, chap. 2.

49. Berlin et al., *Freedom*, 60; *Burlington Daily Times* (Burlington, VT), October 24, 1865; Higginson, *Army Life in a Black Regiment*, 4; Higginson, *Cheerful Yesterdays*, 266–67; Taylor, *Reminiscences of Camp Life*, 21; Williamson, *After Slavery*, 20; Keith P. Wilson, *Campfires of Freedom: The Camp Life of Black Soldiers during the Civil War* (Kent, OH: Kent State University Pres, 2002), 18–24. This is not to say that individual soldiers did not misbehave. Regimental records document arrests and punishments, but offences were strikingly few, were minor, and almost never involved direct insubordination or desertion: William A. Dobak, *Freedom by the Sword: The U.S. Colored Troops, 1862–1867* (Washington, DC: U.S. Army Center for Military History, 2011), 470. See also Morning Reports, 33rd United States Colored Infantry (USCI), Book Records of Volunteer Union Organizations, RG 94, NA; Company F, Regimental Description Book, 33rd USCI, Book Records, RG 94, NA; Benjamin Papina Compiled Service Record, 33rd USCI, RG 94, NA; Special Orders 79–80, October 13, 17, 1865, Regimental Letter, Order, Endorsement, and Casualty Book (hereafter, Order Book), RG 94, NA.

50. Company K, List of Commissioned Officers, Regimental Description Book, 33rd USCI, Book Records, RG 94, NA; Charles T. Trowbridge, *Six Months in the Freedman's Bureau with a Colored Regiment* (Minneapolis: N.p., 1909), unpaginated typescript at South Carolina Historical Society, Charleston. For more on Jolly, see Rod Andrew Jr., "In Search of Manse Jolly: Mythology and Facts in the Hunt for a Post–Civil War Guerrilla," in *The Civil War Guerrilla: Unfolding the Black Flag in History, Memory, and Myth*, ed. Joseph M. Beilein Jr. and Matthew C. Hulbert (Lexington: University Press of Kentucky, 2015), 175–206; Robert S.

McCully, ed., "Letter from a Reconstruction Renegade," *South Carolina Historical Magazine* 77 (1976): 34–40; Poole, *Never Surrender,* 104–5.

51. Affidavit of Caroline L. Chambers, September 24, 1865, filed with Alexander Heasly Compiled Service Record, 33rd USCI, RG 94, NA; Company C, List of Commissioned Officers, Regimental Description Book, 33rd USCI, Book Records, RG 94, NA; *Baltimore Clipper,* December 23, 1865. Only one of Heasly's killers was convicted, serving fifteen years at Auburn Penitentiary in New York.

52. Trowbridge, *Six Months in the Freedman's Bureau;* Special Orders 66–69, September 1865, Order Book, 33rd USCI, Book Records, RG 94, NA; Morning Reports, September 1865, 33rd USCI, Book Records, RG 94, NA.

53. Charles T. Trowbridge, 33rd USCT, Case MM3193, November 8, 1865, in Court-Martial Case Files, Record Group 153 (RG 153): Records of the Office of the Judge Advocate General, NA.

54. Higginson, *Army Life in a Black Regiment,* 57, 60; Looby, *Complete Civil War Journal and Selected Letters of Thomas Wentworth Higginson,* 114.

55. Trowbridge, Case MM3193.

56. Calvin Crozier, "Carded" Records Showing Military Service, Records of the Adjutant General's Office Relating to the Military and Naval Service of Confederates, Record Group 109: War Department Collection of Confederate Records, NA.

57. Trowbridge, Case MM3193.

58. Affidavit of James B. Brown, October 24, 1865, Calvin Crozier File, Union Provost Marshals' File of Papers Related to Individual Civilians, War Department Collection of Confederate Records, Record Group 109 (RG 109), NA.

59. Richard Morton to James B. Steedman, September 18, 1865; J. J. Bonner to D. J. Crooks, October 9, 1865; Affidavit of James B. Brown, October 24, 1865, all in Calvin Crozier File, Union Citizens File, RG 109, NA.

60. Affidavit of Jacob S. Bowers, October 26, 1865, Calvin Crozier File, Union Citizens File, RG 109, NA.

61. Trowbridge, Case MM3193.

62. Ibid.

63. Taylor, *Reminiscences of My Life,* 44–45.

64. Gloster Mills Pension Application (502493), Company C, 33rd USCI, Civil War Pension Index, Record Group 15: Records of the Veterans Administration, NA.

65. Affidavit of Gloss Mills, May 25, 1884; Affidavit of Samuel Eulins and Joe Blocker, August 4, 1884; Levi W. Metcalf to Gloster Mills, August 20, 1884; H. M. Cleckley, Examining Surgeon's Certificate, February 6, 1884, all in Gloster Mills Military Pension Claim, Certificate 281581, Company C, 33rd USCI, Civil War Pension Records, Record Group 15: Records of the Veterans Administration, NA.

66. Trowbridge, Case MM3193.

67. Ibid.

68. Affidavit of Simon P. Kinard, October, 1865, in Calvin Crozier File, Union Citizens File, RG 109, NA.

69. John Smith, 33rd USCT, Case MM3185, November 7, 1865, in Court Martial Case Files, RG153, NA. On the collapse of morale as a consequence of perceived betrayal of a soldier's mission, see Jonathan Shays, *Achilles in Vietnam: Combat Trauma and the Undoing of Character* (New York: Simon and Schuster, 1995).

70. Trowbridge, Case MM3193; Trowbridge, *Six Months in the Freedman's Bureau with a Colored Regiment.*

CONTRIBUTORS

ORVILLE VERNON BURTON is the Judge Matthew J. Perry Jr. Distinguished Professor of History, Sociology and Anthropology, Pan African Studies, and Computer Science at Clemson University and emeritus University Distinguished Teacher/ Scholar, University Scholar, and Professor of History, African American Studies, and Sociology at the University of Illinois. He is the author or editor of more than twenty books, including (with Armand Derfner) *Justice Deferred: Race and the Supreme Court, Penn Center: A History Preserved, The Age of Lincoln*, and *In My Father's House Are Many Mansions: Family and Community in Edgefield, South Carolina.*

J. BRENT MORRIS is a professor of history at Clemson University. He is the author or editor of several books, including *Oberlin, Hotbed of Abolitionism: College, Community, and the Fight for Freedom and Equality in Antebellum America, Yes, Lord, I Know the Road: A Documentary History of African Americans and South Carolina 1526–2008, A South Carolina Chronology*, and *Dismal Freedom: A History of the Maroons of the Great Dismal Swamp.* He was the 2010 recipient of the South Carolina Historical Society's Malcolm C. Clark Award; the 2016 University of South Carolina Breakthrough Star for Research and Scholarship; and the 2018 Award of the Order of the South.

NICOLAS BARREYRE teaches American history at École des Hautes Études en Sciences Sociales in Paris. He is the author of *Gold and Freedom: The Political Economy of Reconstruction* (University of Virginia Press, 2015) and coeditor of *Historians across Borders: Writing American History in a Global Age* and *A World of Public Debts: A Global History.*

GARRY BERTHOLF is an assistant professor of African American studies at Wesleyan University. His work has appeared or is forthcoming in *Anthurium: A Caribbean Studies Journal, Journal of Popular Music Studies, South* (formerly the *Southern*

Literary Journal), Viewpoint Magazine, Diacritik, The Martyr's Shuffle, Philosophical Quarterly, and the Faulkner and Yoknapatawpha series at the University Press of Mississippi. His current book project is tentatively titled "The Black Charismatic: Demagoguery and the Politics of Affect."

MARINA BILBIJA is an assistant professor of English and affiliated African American studies faculty at Wesleyan University. Her work has appeared in *American Literary History, Annals of the American Academy of Political and Social Science, Atlantic Studies, Modern Fiction Studies, Public Books,* and *South Atlantic Review.* Her current book manuscript is tentatively titled "Print Worlds of Color: Traveling Black Editors and the Making of the Anglophone World."

MARI N. CRABTREE is an associate professor of African American studies and an affiliate of the History Department at the College of Charleston. She is the author of *My Soul Is a Witness: The Traumatic Afterlife of Lynching,* and her next book project is titled "Shuffling like Uncle Tom, Thinking like Nat Turner: Humor, Deception, and Irony in the African American Cultural Tradition."

DON H. DOYLE is a professor emeritus of history at the University of South Carolina. He is the author of *The Cause of All Nations: An International History of America's Civil War, Nations Divided: America, Italy, and the Southern Question,* and *Faulkner's County: The Historical Roots of Yoknapatawpha;* the editor of *Nationalism in the New World, Secession as an International Phenomenon,* and *American Civil Wars: The United States, Latin America, Europe, and the Crisis of the 1860s;* and a coeditor of *The Transnational Significance of the American Civil War.* He is currently at work on a sequel to *The Cause of All Nations.*

PETER EISENSTADT is an independent historian. He was the managing editor of *The Encyclopedia of New York City* and the editor-in-chief of *The Encyclopedia of New York State.* He is the author and editor of numerous books, including the award-winning *Rochdale Village: Robert Moses, 6,000 Families, and New York City's Great Experiment in Integrated Housing,* and *Against the Hounds of Hell: A Life of Howard Thurman.*

MARK ELLIOTT is an associate professor of history at the University of North Carolina, Greensboro. He is the author of the Avery O. Craven Award–winning *Color-Blind Justice: Albion Tourgée and the Quest for Racial Equality from the Civil War to Plessy v. Ferguson* and coeditor (with John David Smith) of *Undaunted Radical: The Selected Writings and Speeches of Albion W. Tourgée.*

ERIC FONER, DeWitt Clinton Professor Emeritus of History at Columbia University, is one of this country's most prominent historians. His *Reconstruction: America's Unfinished Revolution, 1863–1877* won the Bancroft, Parkman, and Los Angeles

Times Book prizes and remains the standard history of the period. In 2006, he received the Presidential Award for Outstanding Teaching at Columbia University. He has served as president of the Organization of American Historians, the American Historical Association, and the Society of American Historians.

A. JAMES FULLER is a professor of history at the University of Indianapolis. Among his many publications are *Chaplain to the Confederacy: Basil Manly and Baptist Life in the Old South, 1798–1868; America, War and Power: Defining the State, 1775–2005* (coedited with Lawrence Sondhaus); and *Soldiers of Christ: Selections from the Writings of Basil Manly, Sr., and Basil Manly, Jr.* (coedited with Michael Haykin and Roger Duke).

KRISTA KINSLOW received her doctorate in U.S. history from Boston University in 2019.

LAWRENCE T. MCDONNELL is an associate professor of history at Iowa State University. He is the author of *Performing Disunion: The Coming of the Civil War in Charleston, South Carolina.*

DAVID MOLTKE-HANSEN is an independent scholar. He is the founding director of the Center for the Study of the American South; past director of the Southern Historical Collection and curator of manuscripts at the University of North Carolina; founding director of the William Gilmore Simms Initiatives at the South Caroliniana Library; and founding codirector of Cambridge University Press's Cambridge Studies on the American South.

ARLISHA NORWOOD is an assistant professor of history at the University of Maryland, Eastern Shore. She received her doctorate from Howard University in 2019. She is currently working on a manuscript titled "To Never Truck with No Man: Single African American Women in Post–Civil War Virginia."

TROY D. SMITH is an associate professor of history at Tennessee Tech University (TTU), where he teaches various American Indian studies courses. He is the director of the Upper Cumberland Humanities and Social Sciences Institute and a co-leader of the National Science Foundation–funded Gadugi project at TTU. He wrote the chapter on Indian Territory in the *Oxford Handbook of American Indian History* and is a novelist, having twice won the Spur Award from Western Writers of America.

J. MILLS THORNTON is a professor emeritus of history at the University of Michigan. He is the author of *Dividing Lines: Municipal Politics and the Struggle for Civil Rights in Montgomery, Birmingham, and Selma,* a winner of the Organization of American Historians' Liberty Legacy Prize, and *Politics and Power in a Slave Society:*

Alabama, 1800–1860, a winner of the American Historical Association's John H. Dunning Prize.

PETER WALLENSTEIN is an award-winning professor of history at Virginia Tech. Among his many publications are *From Slave South to New South: Public Policy in Nineteenth-Century Georgia; Cradle of America: A History of Virginia;* and *Tell the Court I Love My Wife: Race, Marriage, and Law—An American History.*

Recent books in the series

A Nation Divided: Studies in the Civil War Era

Printed in the USA
CPSIA information can be obtained
at www.ICGtesting.com
LVHW041927170823
755573LV00004B/178